DATE DUE			

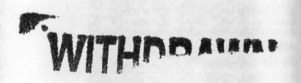

FELLAH AND TOWNSMAN IN THE MIDDLE EAST

FELLAH AND TOWNSMAN IN THE MIDDLE EAST

Studies in Social History

Gabriel Baer

*Institute of Asian and African Studies,
Hebrew University of Jerusalem*

FRANK CASS

First published 1982 in Great Britain by
FRANK CASS AND COMPANY LIMITED
Gainsborough House, Gainsborough Road,
London, E11 1RS, England

and in the United States of America by
FRANK CASS AND COMPANY LIMITED
c/o Biblio Distribution Centre
81 Adams Drive, P.O. Box 327, Totowa, N.J. 07511

British Library Cataloguing in Publication Data

Baer, Gabriel
Fellah and townsman in the Middle East.
1. Near East – Social conditions
I. Title
956 HN656.A8

ISBN 0–7146–3126–4

Typeset by Computacomp (UK) Ltd, Fort William, Scotland
Printed in Great Britain by
A. Wheaton & Co. Ltd., Exeter

CONTENTS

INTRODUCTION

This volume deals with the history of the common people of the Middle East, both villagers and inhabitants of towns and cities. It tries to investigate some of the characteristic traits of the structure and development of urban and rural society in pre-modern and modern Middle Eastern history, in particular of the lower layers of the population. The subjects studied are the division of this population into different groups, the relation between these groups, the relation between the common people and the upper layers of society, the notables, and in particular their relation with the government. One of the principal themes of this complex is the position and function of the intermediaries between the common people and the government, such as shaykhs of villages or guilds, the *ulama*, and notables. Their position has been of crucial significance for the function of the units of the common people and for the social history of the Middle East in general and has therefore been investigated in great detail.

Among the relations between different groups of the population, a central position is occupied by the problem of urban-rural dichotomy. Differences, contacts and conflicts between village and city form the subject of Part One of this volume, but these themes reappear in other parts as well. A second major question dealt with is violent resistance of the urban and rural common people to government or to their overlords. We have tried to find out the background, aims, participation, leadership, organization and results of popular revolt and rebellion in various countries of the Middle East and in various periods.

The period covered by this volume extends from the sixteenth century, when the Arab-speaking population of the Middle East was conquered by the Ottomans and the Ottoman guilds emerged as an important feature of urban life, up to the 1960s. However, not all the essays go through the history of four centuries, and in each case the limitation of the period dealt with has an obvious and, we hope, convincing reason. The different geographical ranges of the different chapters are the result of the fact that some of them were written as case studies or monographs. The area studied comprises present-day Turkey, Egypt, and 'Greater' Syria, including Lebanon and Palestine. It has been one of the principal aims of these studies to elucidate the common traits of this area, its unity, as well as the variety of social features which exist within it, and to explain the reasons for different structures and developments.

Methodically the essays are of three different kinds. They begin with a monograph on a satirical treatise on the Egyptian fellah written by Yūsuf al-Shirbīnī in the seventeenth century and a critical evaluation of its significance. Parts Two and Three are detailed case studies of the village shaykh in Palestine and the Turkish guilds. In addition to the description and analysis of the available material, we have tried to make comparisons with parallel findings on Egypt which we published a few years ago. Finally, the volume includes essays which are analyses of some larger themes based partially on former studies, my own and those of others, and partially on new material. To this category belong the discussions of the relations between village and city, of fellah rebellion, as well as the reassessment of our knowledge about Ottoman guilds.

The study of social history can derive information from a large variety of sources. Among those used in this volume are the following: a work of literature (Shirbīnī's satire on the Egyptian fellah); chronicles, such as those of Shidyāq for Lebanon or Jabartī for Egypt (including his most illuminating earlier *Tārīkh* of the French Occupation of Egypt); manuscripts of local histories of shorter periods, both published (such as those of Niqūlā Turk for Egypt or Abū Shaqrā and 'Aqīqī for Lebanon) and unpublished (such as Aḥmad Çelebi's chronicle); biographies and encyclopedias (such as the works of Muḥibbī and Murādī, and in particular the opus of 'Alī Mubārak); diaries, both published (such as that of Monk Neophytos) and unpublished (such as Hekekyan's Diaries in the British Library); travel accounts (for instance, the books of Sonnini or of Menahem Mendel of Kamenets) and collections of letters, (like those of Lady Duff Gordon).

Important material may be found in various kinds of archives. We have used such archival sources both directly and indirectly – through collections and studies of others. For the study of urban society the most important documents are the records of the Qāḍī's Court, the *sijill*, and our study of the Turkish guilds is based primarily on Osman Nuri's collection of these records. In addition, Egypt's urban and rural history is very well reflected in the consular correspondence and records to be found in the Public Record office in London. Rustum's collections from the Egyptian archives, as well as the studies of some scholars who used Turkish, French and Russian archives, were of great additional value. To the same category belong Refik's collections of firmans concerning life in Istanbul. The files of the Jordanian administration of the West Bank, now kept in the Israel State Archives, served as the basis of our study of the village mukhtār in Palestine.

For the more recent periods, newspapers are of great value, probably even more for social history than for political developments. Finally, we have of course used a great variety of publications and studies which are referred to in the footnotes and need not be enumerated here in detail. We would like, however, to draw attention to the important material found in a number of contributions to the impressive *Description de l'Egypte* of Napoleon's savants concerning one of the main themes of this volume, the relation between town and countryside.

ACKNOWLEDGMENTS

About one-third of the contents of this volume is being published here for the first time. The rest has been published before, and the right to republish it, with some additions and corrections, is duly acknowledged as follows.

Part I, Chapter 1, paragraphs i–iii, were first published in *Asian and African Studies*, Vol. 8, No. 3, 1972; most of paragraph iv is new and has not been published before. Part I, Chapter 2, was originally written as a paper for the Princeton Conference on the Economic History of the Middle East, held in June 1974. The papers have now been published in A. L. Udovitch (ed.), *The Islamic Middle East, 700–1900: Studies in Economic and Social History*, Darwin Press, Princeton. Part I, Chapter 3, was first published in *Asian and African Studies*, Vol. 11, No. 1, 1976.

The chapters in Part II are parts of a longer study called *The Village Mukhtar in Palestine – A History of his Position and his Functions*, published in Hebrew by the Harry S Truman Research Institute of the Hebrew University of Jerusalem. They were originally published in English in Joel S. Migdal (ed.), *Palestinian Society and Politics*, Princeton University Press, 1979, and in G. Ben Dor (ed.), *The Palestinians and the Middle East Conflict*, Ramat Gan, 1978.

In Part III, Chapter 1 was first published in *International Journal of Middle East Studies*, I, 1, January 1970. Chapter 2 was originally published in *Journal of the Economic and Social History of the Orient*, Vol. 13, Part 2, 1970. Chapter 3 was published in the *Proceedings of the Israel Academy of Sciences and Humanities*, IV, 10. Chapter 4 was originally presented as a paper to the First International Congress on the Social and Economic History of Turkey, held at Hacettepe University, Ankara, on 11–13 July 1977.

Chapter 1 of Part IV was originally published in *Der Islam*, Vol. 54, No. 2, 1977. Chapter 2 has not been published before.

Part One

FELLAH AND TOWNSMAN IN EGYPT AND SYRIA

1

SHIRBĪNĪ'S HAZZ AL-QUḤŪF AND ITS SIGNIFICANCE

I. WHO WAS YŪSUF AL-SHIRBĪNĪ?

Yūsuf b. Muḥammad b. ʻAbd al-Jawād b. Khaḍr al-Shirbīnī's book *Hazz al-quḥūf fī sharḥ qaṣīd Abī-Shādūf* was first published in Cairo in the year A. H. 1274/1857–8 C. E.[1] Since then it has been mentioned in many works on Egyptian colloquial Arabic and on the history of modern Arabic literature.[2] However, to the best of our knowledge no systematic study has yet been made of Shirbīnī's book. Such a study cannot be the work of a single scholar, since *Hazz al-quḥūf* is capable of yielding a rich harvest in various fields. Notwithstanding Mehren's and Vollers' beginnings, much linguistic material still awaits analysis.[3] Moreover, no attempt has yet been made to explain this work in the context of literary history, to reveal its antecedents, show its influences on later works and find parallels in the literatures of other languages.[4] *Hazz al-quḥūf* also abounds in invaluable anthropological material, such as information on dress, diet, customs and agricultural work.[5] In addition, the book makes an important contribution to our knowledge of agrarian relations in Ottoman Egypt which have so far been described primarily from external sources, such as the *Description de l'Egypte*, and in any case from sources dating from the end of the eighteenth century. From Shirbīnī we learn of village institutions in the seventeenth century and of the relations between the fellah and the *multazim*, the *ṣarrāf*, the *mushidd* etc.[6] Finally, Shirbīnī touches on many aspects of the relations between the fellah and the city and between urban and rural *ʻulamāʼ*. These relations may well be considered the central theme of his book, and they form the main subject of the following study.

Shirbīnī is not mentioned by any of the biographers of the eleventh/

seventeenth century. Only a few concrete data are given by himself in his book. Yūsuf b. Muḥammad was born in Shirbīn, which he calls *baladī* or *baldatī Shirbīn* (130:27–28, 202:8–9)[7] – a small place on the Damietta branch of the Nile in the north-eastern corner of Gharbiyya province.[8] The only date mentioned by him is that of his *ḥajj*, namely A. H. 1074/1663–4 C. E. (100:2–3).[9] Two more clues for a chronology of Shirbīnī's activity are the deaths of his teacher (*'shaykhunā'*) Aḥmad Shihāb al-Dīn al-Qalyūbī, i.e. the year A. H. 1069/1659 C. E., and the *'ālim* Aḥmad b. 'Alī al-Sandūbī who induced Shirbīnī to write his book, namely the year A. H. 1097/1686 C. E.[10] No further facts of his *curriculum vitae* are stated directly by himself or by the above mentioned authors who dealt with his book.[11]

However, a thorough perusal of *Hazz al-quḥūf* enables us to gather much more information on the life and background of Yūsuf al-Shirbīnī. It is obvious that Shirbīnī was an *'ālim*: he frequently quotes ḥadīth, Qur'ān exegesis, law, theology, Ṣūfī literature and various branches of belles-lettres – a field in which he himself seems to have been active.[12] He exhorts his readers to pray frequently and on specific occasions (147:10–12, 177:2–23), and tells us that on the way to Mecca he used to sit in a *zāwiya*, deliver sermons and give religious instruction (100:3–4). He declares certain practices of *multazims* and *kāshifs* to be *ḥarām* (unlawful) or *ithm* (a sin) (115:18, 23, 116:3–4, 28, 122:24–25). He also complains that fellahs have no respect for the *'ulamā'*: *'al-'ilm 'indahum ḥaqīr'* (5:27) *'wa-laysa fīhim raḥma li-'ālim, lākin li-ahli al-sharr wa'l-maẓālim'* (85:17).

It is less obvious, but most probable, that Yūsuf al-Shirbīnī lived in Cairo, moving there from his native village Shirbīn. Aḥmad al-Sandūbī who induced Shirbīnī to write his book, taught at al-Azhar.[13] He identifies the term *al-madīna* with Cairo (25:12–14, 201:11) and is full of praise for Cairo, its inhabitants, its women, its *'ulamā'* and its rulers *'li'annahā madīnat al-uns wa'l-ṣafā wa'l-surūr wa'l-wafā'* (155:9–11, 201:11–16 and the following poem). Thus Shirbīnī seems to belong to quite a large group of *'ulamā'* born in the Egyptian countryside who moved to Cairo in order to study at al-Azhar (or one of the *madāris*), remained there and became part of Cairo's corps of *'ulamā'*. According to Muḥibbī's biographical dictionary for the eleventh/seventeenth century *Khulāṣat al-athar*, about one quarter of Cairo's *'ulamā'* during that period were born in the Egyptian countryside.[14] Even the first known Shaykh al-Azhar, Muḥammad b. 'Abdallāh al Khirshī, a contemporary of Shirbīnī who died in A. H. 1101/1690 C. E., was born in a village called Abū Khirāsh in Buḥayra province.[15]

Nevertheless, Shirbīnī seems to have maintained close connections with the *rīf* in general and his native village in particular. The clearest indication of these connections are the numerous detailed descriptions of rural customs and institutions to be found in *Hazz al-quḥūf*. These include descriptions of a village wedding, of a *shādūf*, of jewellery and dresses of village women, of various kinds of food in the villages, of pigeon-towers, of the physical setting of villages and much more.[16] In addition, a recurring theme of *Hazz al quḥūf* is the comparison between rural and urban food, dress, customs, institutions, building etc., and in many cases Shirbīnī records fine distinctions which show that he was familiar with both environments.[17] In some cases he even says that he often witnessed the rural custom or object which he describes (6:4, 101:14). He gives details about the agrarian system of his village (144:28–145:2), which he visited, apparently, from time to time (130:27–28). This too was not unusual: for instance, Jabartī tells us about an Azharite shaykh born in a village near Rosetta who visited his village every year.[18] On the basis of the biographies of *'ulamā'* in Mubārak's *Khiṭaṭ*, the following has been observed with regard to the nineteenth century: 'The 'ulamā's links with the rural population were maintained not only through the birth of many 'ulamā' in the village, but also physically . . . There were 'ulamā' who returned to the village after their studies . . . but there were also 'ulamā' whose principal income was from teaching in Cairo yet who frequently visited their birthplace.'[19]

But although he had close connections with his village, the members of Shirbīnī's family were not fellahs. He praises God for having relieved his forefathers from agriculture and its troubles: *'wa-lākin naḥmidu Allāh alladhī arāḥana min al-filāḥa wa-hammihā wa-lam takun li-ābā'ina wa-lā ajdādinā* (147:18–19, 22). What, then, were his connections with the village? Unfortunately, no positive statements about his family's occupation are found in his book. However, circumstantial evidence may help us to elucidate the socio-economic position of Shirbīnī and his family. First, they certainly were in a superior position *vis-à-vis* the fellahs. The kind of complaint Shirbīnī voices is that if you offer the fellahs advice they bear you malice; if you do them a favour, they disavow it; if you are gentle with them they hate you; if they are not oppressed, they oppress others (5:26–29, 6:2).[20] The good fellah obeys the *multazim* and his officials and refrains from causing ruin or mischief, while the bad one is detested by his *multazim*, and is wicked, quarrelsome and mischievous (126:1–24). The presence of the *kāshif* (governor of a province) in a village is of great benefit, *inter alia* because he is able severely to punish fellahs who riot or revolt against their *multazim* or *qā'immaqām*: he may destroy the village and kill all those who deserve to be killed (122:20–23).

Yet Shirbīnī or his family probably were not *multazims* themselves. Shirbīnī frequently condemns oppression by *multazims* or unlawful demands from the villagers (115:18–23, 115:26–116:4), especially all newly introduced additional contributions which were not levied in earlier times (141:17–24). Moreover, the typical *multazim* depicted in Shirbīnī's stories (or *ustādh*, as he is called) is a Mamluk *amīr*, or at least speaks Turkish (e.g., 12:26–27, 19:24–25). In the seventeenth century, *'ulamā'* had not yet become *multazims*, a process which took place in Egypt towards the end of the eighteenth century.[21]

It would seem that Shirbīnī was what he calls a *mu'āmil*, a merchant and money-lender doing business with fellahs, or at least that this was the occupation of the family or social group to which he belonged. This is indicated by the frequent discussion of this subject in *Hazz al-quḥūf*. Shirbīnī says: '. . . Some fellahs borrow money with interest or pledge their produce in advance for a smaller sum than its selling price; or they sell their milking animal or pawn their wives' jewellery and even sell it against (their wives') will in order to pay the tax-collector . . . (The good fellah), when he borrows money from a *mu'āmil* does not spend it on a bad purpose but uses it for his agricultural produce and his animals . . . with the intention of paying it back to the creditor . . . When the *mu'āmil* comes, he settles his debt; when he demands it a second time he pays . . . (The bad fellah) . . . spends without any order . . . and is always in debt. He is unable to pay a debt; a thousand or two thousand are always outstanding . . . he does not pay the *mu'āmil* his due' (125:18–126:21).

The specific position of the *mu'āmil vis-à-vis* the fellah and the *multazim*, and Shirbīnī's own attitude in this conflict, is shown very clearly in the *urjūza* concluding the first half of his book. This portion of the *urjūza* deserves full quotation:

> Don't trust him (the fellah) in business (*mu'āmala*) – you will not get anything from him except the delay of the payment. If you increase (your demand from) him he will immediately quarrel with you; he will say: '(I shall pay you) after I have paid my debt to the *multazim*; if then anything of the produce remains, it is yours.' Take it, otherwise you have no hope at all. If you go on quarrelling with him he will do you harm and hit you; he will draw the mace and the strap and even force you to pay his taxes. He may even say to the *multazim*: 'This man wants to do away with my possessions; (he wants) to use this trick in order to take my produce, and then, O *amīr* of my village, the taxes will remain (unpaid). Thus I will be ruined soon and the land will remain uncultivated by an indebted fellah.' Then the *amīr* will deprive the creditor of his due, and he (the creditor) will become perplexed and disgraced. (83:18–25).[22]

To judge by this passage and those cited above, Shirbīnī, the *'alīm* from a non-fellah family in Shirbīn who lived in Cairo, maintained his connection with the countryside by doing business with the fellahs, *inter alia* by lending them money.[23] In the course of this activity conflicts arose not only with the fellahs but also with the *multazims*, who demanded that the fellah first of all pay his taxes. The reconstruction of this background is important for explaining those aspects of *Hazz al-quḥūf* with which we are going to deal in the following pages.

II. VILLAGE AND TOWN IN SEVENTEENTH CENTURY EGYPT

Shirbīnī's book is divided into two main parts. The second part is written as a commentary on a poem allegedly composed by a fellah called Abū Shādūf in which the poet laments his own bad fortune and the fellah's destiny in general.

The first part serves as a long introduction whose general theme is also the Egyptian village and the fellah. Both parts are full of stories, legends, poems, jokes, suggestive witticisms, and in particular obscenities, and there is no doubt that Shirbīnī's composition greatly amused his contemporaries, especially the urban educated classes. However, the book also includes interesting and illuminating descriptions of the fellah and the countryside in Ottoman Egypt. Among the most prominent aspects of these descriptions are observations on the differences and the relations between village and city and between the fellah and the townsman.

Terms

Before analysing the differences, contacts and conflicts between village and town as they emerge from Shirbīnī's *Hazz al-quḥūf*, a few words on the terms he uses are in order. First, a general and widely used term for a place in which people live is *balad*, pl. *bilād*. This term is used for towns, and thus we have *bilād al-mudun* (112:6, 176:6, 204:25),[24] as well as for villages, and thus we have *bilād al rīf* (6:22) or *bilād al-aryāf* (112:6, 8, 166:2).[25] In some instances the same village is called alternately *balad* and *qarya* (21:10–11, 37:19, 23), which is the case especially with regard to Shirbīn, the author's native village (130:28, 144:29, 185:14, 202:8). Even a small hamlet (*kafr*) may be called *balad* (19:10, 168:1), but on the other hand, it may be considered as something different from a *balad* (*ṭulūʿ al-mushidd aw al-multazim aw al-naṣrānī ilā al-kafr aw al-balad* – 115:1).

A *kafr* is a small village (168:1). Shirbīnī frequently compares *al-kufūr* with *bilād al-baḥr*, the villages on the shore of the Nile. The inhabitants of *bilād al-baḥr* eat more refined food (148:1–3, 8, 14), and their economic facilities are less primitive. Thus the *kufūr* have a common mill where everybody mills his own corn with his own bull, while the inhabitants of *bilād al-baḥr* pay a miller who works his mill with horses (167:27–168:1).

To judge by one of Shirbīnī's stories, the *qarya* also differs from a *kafr* in having a Friday mosque: a native of a *kafr* visits a *qarya* on the shore of the Nile and is perplexed by the Friday prayer, which he describes to his fellow fellahs in extremely funny terms using his own primitive concepts (21:9–22:13). This is confirmed by Aḥmad Jazzār Pasha who wrote the following in his *Nizamname-i Mısır*: 'Behind some of the villages there are small villages without minarets. The people of Egypt call them *kafr*'.[26] The use of the word 'behind' is significant and confirms Shirbīnī's confrontation between the villages on the shore of the Nile and the smaller ones farther away. Generally the *kafr* was an offshoot of the village bearing the same name, but in the course of time these offshoots became independent *qurā*. The term was used in Lower Egypt only, with very few scattered cases in Middle Egypt.[27]

A village is called by Shirbīnī *qarya* but the most frequently used term in Shirbīnī's *Hazz al-quḥūf* is *rīf* or *aryāf*. Villagers are called *'awāmm al-rīf, ahl al-rīf, al-aryāf, al-sākin fi'l-rīf, fallāḥīn al-rīf, quḥūfat al-rīf, ajlāf al-rīf, ahl al-riyāfa*, etc.,[28] and villages *bilād al rīf, qarya min qurā al-rīf, bilād al-aryāf*, etc.[29] It is important to elucidate what exactly Shirbīnī meant by this term. In Egyptian usage *al-rīf* has two meanings, the countryside in general and more especially Lower Egypt.[30] This ambiguity led to a discussion of the meaning of *al-rīf* in the symposium on Middle Eastern urbanism held at Berkeley in October 1966.[31] There can be no doubt that Shirbīnī uses the term *rīf* in the general meaning of countryside. Upper Egypt (al-Ṣa'īd) appears only once in *Hazz al-quḥūf* (149:1–8), but not in contrast with *rīf*. In some cases, especially in connection with different ways of preparing dishes (see below), Shirbīnī divides Egyptian society into three parts: *ahl al-rīf* (which in this context means the inhabitants of the small villages), *bilād al-baḥr* (i.e. the larger villages on the shore of the Nile) and *ahl al-mudun* (see, e.g., 165:1–19, 168:15–169:7). However, in general, the opposite of *rīf* or *ahl al-rīf* is *al-mudun, al-ḥaḍar, al-madīna*, or *bilād al-mudun*,[32] and the relations between these two economic, social and cultural environments are the main theme of Shirbīnī's work and of the following analysis.

Differences

There seems to be general agreement among scholars that a principal difference between town and village was the former's function as the exclusive administrative centre. Shirbīnī's fellahs who come to town are impressed before anything else by the fact that they find soldiers there: *'madīnat Miṣr kulluhā janādī wa-'askar'* (20:10–11, 26:18, also 13:26–28). The *multazim* (*ustādh*) of the village lives in the town and only visits his village from time to time: *'iltazama ba'ḍu al-umarā' bi-qarya min qurā al-rīf fasāfara ilayhā li-yanẓura aḥwālahā kamā huwa 'ādat al-multazimīn'* (12:26–27, also 29:22). His assistants, the *mushidd* (steward) and the *naṣrānī* (the Christian tax collector) do not live in the village either but come to the village only in order to collect the imposts, and then the fellahs must make arrangements for their sustenance (115:1 ff.). Thus the village differed from the town in that nobody belonging to the ruling institution lived there.[33]

There is a further distinction between Egyptian towns and villages. While the urban population in the seventeenth century was organized in professional guilds, no guilds existed in Egyptian villages. If additional confirmation of this difference is necessary, it may be found in the fact that Shirbīnī does not say a word about the existence of guilds in villages although he has something to say about every function or institution of village life. But even more convincing is another document from the seventeenth century, namely the poems from *Li'b al-timsāḥ*, the Crocodile play, published by Kahle about sixty years ago. The cardinal point of these poems, and the Crocodile shadow play in general, is that a fellah tries to exercise a craft, namely fishing, without being a member of the guild. He is severely rebuked and punished for this transgression by being swallowed by the crocodile.[34]

On the other hand, the traditional view that the distinctive feature of town life was the *jāmi'*, the Friday mosque, can no longer be maintained. It has already been pointed out that 'the Friday mosque was a feature of settlement of all sorts, "urban" and "rural" from the geographical point of view, *madīna* and non-*madīna* from the political point of view . . . the introduction of *jāmi'*s in villages goes back at least as far as the tenth century according to the geographers.'[35] As we have seen above, according to Shirbīnī the absence of a Friday mosque characterizes the small *kafr*, not the villages on the shore of the Nile. The village mosque might be neglected, full of dung and mud, and might remind one of an enclosure for cattle; indeed, Shirbīnī claims that it was sometimes used for sheltering calves (32:19–21). Nevertheless, Mubārak's encyclopedia confirms that the overwhelming majority of Egyptian villages had mosques, a considerable proportion of which were Friday mosques (*jāmi'*).

In view of Shirbīnī's writings it would seem that another definition which was suggested at the above-mentioned symposium fits seventeenth century Egypt much better. Professor Grabar observed that 'by the twelfth century a place that merely had a mosque, even with a *minbar*, did not necessarily qualify as a city. What qualified as a city was a place that had the whole range of different kinds of religious buildings – *madrasas*, *ribāṭs* etc.'[36] In particular, institutions of learning were completely absent from the village. Men of learning are advised not to dwell in a village lest they lose their learning: *'lā taskun al-qarya fa-yaḍī' 'ilmuka'* (6:20). According to Mubārak's list of Egyptian villages referring to the nineteenth century, there were only 85 villages out of more than one thousand which had a *maktab* (Qur'ān school) and none with a traditional *madrasa*. Two centuries earlier the situation certainly was not better. *'Ulamā* did not live in the countryside, with very few exceptions which were mentioned expressly.[37]

As a result the fellahs were ignorant even of the basic precepts of Islam and thus differed markedly from the urban population which at least in this respect had the opportunity to acquire some knowledge. Fellahs, says Shirbīnī, are known for 'paucity of religion' (*qillat al-dīn*) and for ignorance.[38] Nobody instructs them in prayer and worship, and therefore they don't care for prayer or religion (5:16, 10:24–25). None of them genuflects or prostrates himself in prayer and they do not know the difference between the customary and the obligatory prayer (*lā ya'rifūna al-sunna min al-farḍ*) (6:17, 5:26). In Shirbīnī's stories one fellah while praying complained in a loud voice of a headache; another asked God in his prayer to preserve his animals, dogs, cats, donkeys and his son, and when a knowledgeable Muslim rebuked him he replied that this was the custom of his father and grandfather; a third did not dress properly for prayer so that he uncovered his genitals; others gave instructions concerning their work while at prayer, or let themselves be diverted by their children; still others included various unprescribed words and Shirbīnī riducules them by making these sayings very funny (at the end, as usual in his book, the stories become more and more obscene). In short, the fellah differs from the townsman by being ignorant of all formal prescriptions for Muslim prayer (30:25–32:10).

In addition, fellahs do not know the difference between ritual cleanliness and impurity (*lā ya'rifu al-ṭahāra min al-najāsa*) (13:21). They do not realize that dung is unclean (61:25–27), they usually do not practise the ritual ablution before prayer, and they do not clean their garments (85:9–10; see also 6:16–17).

The Egyptian village of the seventeenth century further differed sharply from the town by its markedly lower level of material well-being. The fellah's dismal poverty is reflected throughout *Hazz al-quḥūf*; the following story told by Shirbīnī symbolizes it: 'A villager was sitting with his friends when his son entered weeping and said: O father, the cock died. The father said: There is no might and no strength but in God (*lā ḥawla wa-lā quwwa illā bi'llāh*), last year a cock and this year a cock! My son, we are afflicted by misfortune and blows. May God compensate us. Then his friends condoled him as if some of his relatives had died.' (15:16–19). The material level of the village is so low that even the village headman, the *shaykh al-kafr*, is extremely poor. Shirbīnī describes the misery of these *mashāyikh* in a satirical way, by relating how one of them boasts about his possessions which turn out to amount to a house full of straw and chaff, a goat, a red shoe, two chicken, a cock, a magazine full of bones and a long fellah-cap (14:23–25). A little larger, but similarly ridiculous is the list of the belongings of Abū Shādūf's father who was the *shaykh* of his *kafr* (93:21–24).[39]

The different level of material well-being manifested itself most clearly in the contrast between urban and rural building. Town houses were high, used much wood, and their walls were overlaid with plaster and lime. They were built of red brick and cut stone. As against this, village houses were built of *kirs* (dry dung mixed with urine), mud and dung. Only *dār al-shādd*[40] or the *dār al-multazim* were high houses (112:6–11, 166:1–2). The detailed descriptions of Egyptian villages two centuries later by Mubārak confirm this distinction, although by that time some large villages had erected higher houses as a result of the prosperity of the nineteenth century. According to Mubārak, houses in villages generally had one storey only,[41] and in exceptional cases he specially mentions that some of the houses of a certain village were plastered like those of the chief towns of provinces or, in some of the larger villages, that their houses were higher than rural houses in general.[42]

Similarly, there was a palpable difference between the ways villagers and townsmen dressed. According to Shirbīnī the fellahs wore rags or shabby clothes, and their children too were always in rags (*dā'iman fī shalātīt wa-sharāmīṭ*). In fact, says Shirbīnī, they went about almost naked, except for a cover on their privy parts. If they wore robes, they were dirty – even those of the rural religious functionaries – *fuqahā' al-rīf*.[43] All villagers used to go about barefoot, fellahs, *fuqahā' al-rīf*, and even rural notables – *akābiruhum*.[44]

wa-ba'ḍ akābirihim al-mushār ilayhi
wa'l-mu'awwal fi'l-umūr 'alayhi
idhā ṭala'a Miṣr li-muqābalat al-amīr
aw qaḍā' ḥāja min al-wazīr
tarā 'alayhi libs maḥbūb
wa-ma'a dhālika yamshī ḥāfī bi-lā markūb

Instead of wearing their shoes they tied them with a cord to a stick and carried them behind their back.[45] As a result of going barefoot, the skin of their feet was chapped (10:22). Their felt-caps were also ragged (10:20).

The fellah's poverty, compared with the easier life of townspeople, brought about marked differences in food. Fellahs eat meat only once a year, on *'īd al-naḥr* (the feast of the Sacrifice) (198:13–14). They never eat *al-samn* (butter) and *al-ḥarārāt* (stimulating foodstuffs) (198:22–23). Only towndwellers and especially *amīrs*, eat *kunāfa* (pastry of sweet vermicelli) and Shirbīnī relates a story about a fellah who boasts that when in town he had eaten *kunāfa*, which he hadn't, because he did not know what *kunāfa* was (26 : 5–29). As against this, all his life the fellah eats lentils, mashed beans (*baysār*), groats with sour milk (*kishk*), broad beans, and baked beans (*mudammas*), and is not acquainted with the urban refined dishes (15 : 8–9). His culinary imagination is extremely limited and does not go beyond lentils, beans, and maize bread (14 : 28).

Moreover, foodstuffs are prepared in a primitive and coarse manner in villages, especially in the small villages (*kufūr*), while urban dishes are much more delicate – in most cases because they are cooked with meat.[46] Furthermore, the eating habits of the fellah are unrefined and vulgar: he swallows enormous quantities of food (150 : 21–151 : 11), he uses parts of his garments as receptacles for his food (175 : 25–176 : 2), and he wipes his mouth with his sleeve (61 : 8–20).

Many additional examples taken from daily life are adduced by Shirbīnī to show that fellahs are primitive and vulgar, compared with the refined townsmen. For instance, when fellahs celebrate they shout, scream and shriek (6 : 3, also 84 : 7–15) *idhā aqāmū afrāḥ lā takūn illā bi'l-'ayāṭ wa'l-ṣirākh wa'l-ṣiyāḥ*. The excremental and sexual aspects of this difference are also treated by Shirbīnī in detail. Fellahs do not clean themselves after relieving their bowels (85 : 5); there are no lavatories in villages, only in towns.[47] Fellahs do not take care that their privy parts be covered.[48] Fellah women have a bad smell (8 : 29, 9 : 3), and fellah love is low and coarse (pp. 55–57, espcially 57 : 21). Even the sexual intercourse of fellahs is coarse and unrefined compared with the habits of townspeople – which is illustrated by a humorous story about a fellah who had the opportunity of observing his *multazim*'s bedroom at night, and who tried to apply what he had learnt at home – with disastrous results (18 : 27–20 : 9).

Finally, Shirbīnī states that fellahs invariably have a darker complexion than townsmen because their skin is always exposed to the heat. Other observers of life in Ottoman Egypt have recorded this same difference between town and countryside.[49]

Notwithstanding all the exaggeration and prejudice involved in Shirbīnī's stories and dicta, they certainly reflect a substantial difference between the rough and primitive life and habits of villagers and those of the more refined city. However, the question must be asked whether these different ways of life are to be attributed to town and countryside or perhaps to distinct groups of people to be found in both environments.[50] True, in the towns of seventeenth century Egypt there must have been groups of the population with incomes not much higher than those of fellahs, although we do not know much about their material life, let alone their attitudes. It would seem, however, that this alone does not invalidate the structural and functional differences mentioned above, or even a general marked difference in the material level of the two environments. Moreover, was there really at that time enough urbanization to blur these differences? Was the population of the cities and their environment really drawn 'into a single interlocking social body conceived in religious terms'?[51] Let us see what Shirbīnī has to say about the contacts and conflicts between town and countryside in his time.

Contacts and conflicts

Shirbīnī relates instances of fellahs who came to town, i.e. to Cairo. Most of them came in order to sell their produce: eggs (27:1), straw (27:7), or lupine (209:6–8). This they did in order to pay their taxes: in one of Shirbīnī's stories a fellah comes to town to sell a cage full of chicken in order to pay his taxes with the proceeds (22:14–15); another fellah came to sell eggs for the same purpose (200:18–19). In another anecdote a fellah just comes to town in order to deliver the taxes to the *multazim* (18:27–28), or to 'arrange something' with his *multazim* (29:22). If the fellah was unable to pay his taxes his son would have to come to town, namely as a hostage pending settlement of the debt (60:27–28).[52] Some fellahs stayed in town as pages (*ghulām*) of Mamluk *amīrs* (30:4, 7). As against this, rural notables (*akābir al-rīf*) would come to town in order to meet an *amīr* or to arrange things with a *wazīr* (6:9–10).

However, there are no signs in *Hazz al-quḥūf* of a great influx of fellahs into town or of permanent settlement in towns by those who came there occasionally. On the contrary, there are some indications of the opposite. First of all, fellahs apparently did not come to town frequently: some of Shirbīnī's fellahs say that they had never before been in Cairo (13:27, 34:1), and some of them do not know the difference between village and town (13:29–14:1). Secondly, they do not stay for a long time: the hostages go home as soon as the taxes are paid,[53] and the pages are sent home as soon as the *amīrs* don't want them any more (30:6, 17); in general, even if they stay they do so only temporarily (*muddatan*) (6:8–9). Moreover 'immigrants fleeing rural hardship' flee into the hills and later return to their village (84:25–26) or at least do not take refuge in the town (125:23–24).

These indications are of course no proof of lack of urbanization in seventeenth century Egypt, but any evidence to the contrary would have been surprising. Seventeenth century Cairo was far from stable politically or developing economically,[54] and an all-embracing guild system made the influx of labour from outside extremely difficult.[55] The only kind of 'urbanization' for which there is both evidence and plausible explanation was the movement of students from the countryside to Cairo to enlist in a *madrasa* or *al-Azhar*, the result being that many of the *'ulamā'* were of rural origin.

The occasional visits of fellahs to the town were one of the two main sources of conflict between the fellah and the town. Since he was ignorant of urban customs and institutions, he was made to feel uncomfortable, and was frightened, ridiculed, cheated or robbed wherever he went. Shirbīnī illustrates this kind of conflict by various anecdotes and stories. In some cases fellahs who come to town clash with the soldiers (25:28–26:3, 27:1–7). A recurring theme, which Shirbīnī apparently considered extremely funny, was the uneasiness caused to the fellah by the fact that in town he was supposed to use a lavatory, but it was difficult to find one, and when at last he found it it was occupied (19:12–13, 25:5–12). Moreover, a sly Cairene even squeezed the last pennies out of a fellah for showing him the way to a lavatory after shop-owners and other people had repeatedly prevented him from easing himself (25:12–26:5). This, however, is a trifle compared with the exploits of the three Cairene harlots who met a miserable fellah carrying on his head a cage of chicken which he wanted to sell in order to pay his taxes. One of the harlots said: 'What would you say about taking the chicken from this fellah?' Said the second: 'And I undertake to deprive him of his clothes.' Said the third: 'There is nothing clever in all that. She will be clever who sells him as a slave for the galleys or for dredging canals (*al-shaṭāra fi-'llī tbī'u bay' al-'abīd aw al-miqdhāf aw al-jarrāfa*).[56] The rest of the story relates in detail how each of the three harlots carried out her part of the pledge (22:13–25:5).

The second much deeper source of conflict between the fellah and the town was the exploitation and oppression of the fellah by a political, social and economic urban elite. As we have seen, the *multazim* lived in the town and his assistants, the *mushidd* and the *naṣrānī*, did not live in the village either. Moreover, members of this urban ruling establishment spoke Turkish, which alienated them even more from the village population.[57] It was this group of town people to whom the fellahs had to pay their taxes. And if the fellah could not pay, he was frightened, beaten and imprisoned (125:17–18), or his son or brother was taken as a hostage (60:27–28, 125:21–23). Sometimes the fellah would borrow money in order to pay his taxes, and then he would clash sooner or later with another towndweller, namely the money-lender.

In addition to delivering the taxes to the *multazim*, the fellah was compelled to do all the agricultural work on the *ūsiyya* of the *multazim*, i.e. the part of the land which the *multazim* of the village kept as his private demesne. For this work the fellah did not receive any recompense; it was called *al-'awna* or *al-sukhra*.[58] On the order of the *mushidd*, the watchman (*ghafīr*) would go around and shout: *'al-'awna yā fallāḥīn, al-'awna yā baṭṭālīn'*, and every fellah who neglected this duty would be punished or fined by the *mushidd*. Shirbīnī says that this was a great calamity for the fellah (144:14–28).

Moreover, the fellah had to provide for the *multazim*'s upkeep and that of his entourage when they came to the village to levy the tax. This obligation was called *wajba*.[59] It was imposed on the fellah in proportion to his share in the village land. The fellah had to maintain the *multazim*, the *mushidd*, the *naṣrānī* and their animals; if he refused, he would be beaten and imprisoned by the *mushidd*, and if he fled the village, the provision would be squeezed out of his wife, who would have to pawn her jewellery and to deprive her children of their food. Sometimes the fellah would abstain from eating his own chicken, butter, or wheat in order to keep all this for the *wajba*; he would eat coarse food and supply the *multazim* and his entourage with delicatessen (115 : 1–15).[60]

On top of all this, these people who came from the town would punish the fellah severely for one reason or other. The *kāshif* (governor of province) would bring a great calamity and affliction upon him if he did not cultivate the *multazim*'s *ūsiyya* (35 : 21); the *multazim* himself (*ustādh al-kafr*) might send the fellah to the galleys or the *jarrāfa* (26 : 27) and the fellah was always afraid of being taken to his *multazim* and killed by him (33 : 28–34 : 1); and the *mushidd* would imprison the fellah and beat him for not supplying the *wajba* (115 : 7–9).

All these conflicts apparently led from time to time to rural unrest and clashes. Shirbīnī mentions as one of the functions of the *kāshif* the suppression of riots or revolts of fellahs against their *multazim* or the *qā'immaqām* by punishing the fellahs severely and by destroying the village and killing all those who deserve to be killed.[61]

If we try to sum up and evaluate Shirbīnī's observations on the relations between village and town in seventeenth century Egypt the following conclusions seem to be appropriate: First, differences between the two environments at that time were sharp enough to be impressed on the people's consciousness. It may well be that these differences were less pronounced in earlier centuries and weakened in later centuries.[62]

The same is true with regard to contacts between towns and villages. It may well be that in some earlier centuries urbanization and the bonds between towndwellers and the people of their hinterlands were stronger, but in the seventeenth century there cannot have been much urbanization and the differences and conflicts as described by Shirbīnī must have been considerable and very much in people's minds. Modern urbanization began in the nineteenth century and accelerated in the twentieth; it strengthened the contacts and bonds between villager and townsman and created an urban mass of people without definite occupation who differed little in their attitudes and manner of life from villagers. However, conflicts between town and village persisted in the modern period, with ups and downs, according to changing political, social and economic factors.[63] It would seem, therefore, that in the seventeenth century, or in the Ottoman period in general, the urban-rural dichotomy in Egypt reached one of its high-water marks.

III. 'ULAMĀ' AND FELLAHS – ATTITUDES AND PREJUDICES

So far we have dealt with Shirbīnī's *Hazz al-quḥūf* as a source indicating actual differences, contacts and conflicts, between town and countryside. We now propose to study his attitudes to, and prejudices against, various elements of Egypt's rural population.

Shirbīnī has not many words of praise for the Egyptian fellah. To begin with, in his view the fellah is stupid and naïve, like all peasants all over the world in the opinion of towndwellers. Various anecdotes and jokes serve to illustrate the same well known image of the fellah (e.g., p. 30). The most ignorant among the fellahs is the ploughman, for the simple reason that at daytime he is with the bull and at night with women in the *dawār*[64] *'li'annahu fī'l-nahār rafīq al-athwār wa-fī'l-layl rafīq al-nisā' fī'l-dawār fa-lam yakmil lahu 'aql'* (44:6–7).

The incessant contact with animals is not only the cause of his ignorance and simplicity but also an important reason for his other vices:

lā taṣḥab al-fallāḥ law annahu — *nāfija aryāḥuhā ṣā'ida*
thīrānuhum qad akhbarat 'anhum — *bi-annahum min ṭīna wāḥida*
(5:12–13).[65]

A similar important reason for his bad character is his dealing with mud (5:10). This steady immersion in dung and mud makes the fellah contemptible (5:16); his occupation of ploughing and dredging canals is vile, and, in general, agriculture is an affliction (147:22).

The immersion in dung and mud is connected in Shirbīnī's view with a materialistic attitude of the fellah (5:16). Instead of praying or reading the Qur'ān they think about their flocks (6:11–12) *'wa-wirduhum fī'l-asḥār al-tafakkur fī'l-ghanam wa'l-abqār'*. They meet in the mosque in order to do business (6:17), and while praying they occupy themselves with all kinds of profane matters (31, *passim*; 35:25–27).

This materialistic attitude of the fellahs applies to their kinship bonds as well as to religion. They respect the tax-collector more than their own kin: *'indahum qābiḍ al-māl a'azz min al-'amm wa'l-khāl* (5:28, 85:15–16). They even beat their parents (85:7), and their bulls take the place of their children (68:15–16). When they are in love they pay attention to their stomach more than to their beloved (63:27–28). The fellah will not do you a favour gladly, and for every favour he will demand compensation (83:13–14).

Even worse, the fellahs are thieves. In one of Shirbīnī's stories a fellah boasts of the numerous thefts he has committed (15:25ff.). Fellahs steal sheep, chicken and dung, cut other peoples' crops and by night secretly take part of their partners' crops (54:8–10). According to Shirbīnī it is quite usual for fellahs to steal shoes of other fellahs during prayer in the mosque (206:1, 6). He explains in detail that this requires great skill (206:19–25, 207:1–5).

Stealing from each other is only one expression of the mutual hostility existing among the fellahs. They cannot agree about anything, although ostensibly all are Muslims (5:24–25). They do not keep promises and they do not trust each other: in his poem Abū Shādūf says that he was taking refuge from the tax collector with the women, and Shirbīnī explains that he was afraid that his own kin would betray him to the *naṣrānī* (the Christian tax collector) because, says Shirbīnī, the fellahs do not keep *amān* (pledge of security for a person who seeks protection) and no *'ishra* (intimate friendship) to each other, especially among relatives! (130:9–12). Incessant quarrels and mutual distrust and hostility must have been considered by Egyptian townsmen, at least by *'ulamā'*, to be among the most typical traits of the Egyptian fellah. We find the same characterization of the fellah in Jabartī's chronicle: *'mukhāṣamatuhum al-qadīma ma'a ba'ḍihim bi-mūjibāt al-taḥāsud wa'l-karāhiyya al-majbūla wa'l-markūza fī ṭibā'ihim al-khabītha.'* And further on Jabartī speaks about their perfidy and their doing wrong to each other . They even wish, so he says, to have oppressive *multazims* in order to hurt each other *'li-yanālū bi-dhālika aghrāḍahum bi-wuṣūl al-adhā li-ba'ḍihim.'* To emphasize these statements Jabartī quotes from a poem by Ḥasan al-Badrī al-Ḥijāzī, an *'ālim* who lived somewhat later than al-Shirbīnī (he died in A. H. 1131/1718–9), in which the afflictions of the fellah are enumerated. In addition to their black faces, their poverty, their hard work, and their fights with the governors, the tax collectors, the *multazims* and their stewards and the village shaykhs, their internecine wars are mentioned as one of their great misfortunes.[66]

Another expression of the lack of friendly feeling among fellahs is their deficient hospitality. They receive their guests in a ridiculous manner and give them poor food (6:5–8). Moreover, the gifts they present on different occasions are ridiculous. In one of the stories a fellah promises the caliph to present him with a camel load (*ḥiml*) of dung, a pail of milk from his red cow and five eggs.[67] This, however, seems to be connected with still another of the fellah's defects: he does not show appropriate honour to important persons. In one of Shirbīnī's stories, for instance, a fellah sues somebody else in court, and while pleading he compares the *qāḍī* to his bull; his case is of course immediately dismissed.[68]

On the other hand, according to Shirbīnī fellahs respect the oppressor (5:27–28), and if they are not oppressed they oppress others. They are fond of power and tend to exploit others (83:15–17), and have no mercy for the small and the weak (6:16, 18–19).

This does not exhaust the list of the fellah's faults. As we have seen above, ingratitude is another of his shortcomings. He is also importunate and pertinacious (83:13). In addition, he does not escape a kind of vilification which is common in various branches of Arabic literature, namely the accusation of sodomy (with animals) (14:9–13).

All these vices of the fellah are firmly established traits of his mentality, and he does not discard them even if he stays for some time in town: *'wa-law makatha al-shakhṣ minhum muddatan fī Miṣr wa-Dimyāṭ lam yaktasib min al-laṭāfa qīrāṭ'* (6:8–9). Shirbīnī tells a series of stories with many examples from Arabic poetry to show that even if he is instructed and taught the simple fellah will not change his character; it is all a question of birth: *'fa'l-laṭāfa lā takhruju 'an ṭawr al-akābir wa-lā tata'addā li-'awāmm al-rīf al-arādhil khuṣūṣan danī' al-aṣl idhā idda'a al-'ilm wa'l-faḍl'* (10:28–12:26).

Not only the fellah in general, but also two specific groups among the rural population are attacked sharply by Shirbīnī, the *fuqarā'* and the *fuqahā' al-rīf*. His denunciation of the *fuqarā'* is aimed partly at dervishes in general, but in the *urjūza* in which he sums up the first half of his book he calls the object of his assault *faqīruhum* (86:20), i.e., *their* dervish, namely the dervish of *ahl al-rīf* (cf. 83:7). It is reasonable to assume that his aim was to inveigh particularly against the rural dervishes, first, because the subject is mentioned in the context of Shirbīnī's diatribes against the fellahs, and secondly, the urban Ṣūfī associations seem to have been in general more orthodox than the rural which tended to be 'latitudinarian in varying degrees and shading into heresy.' Moreover, his native village, Shirbīn, abounded in tombs of venerated Ṣūfī shaykhs and in the activity of dervish orders which, according to Mubārak, led from time to time to conflicts with the orthodox *'ulamā'* of that place.[69]

Indeed, the most frequent and most important charge against the *fuqarā'* voiced by Shirbīnī is heresy and heterodoxy. They are accused of being *zanādiqa* or *mutazandiqīn* (79:14–15, 80:17), *mulḥidīn* (79:19, 81:16), and *arbāb al-bida' al-mulḥidīn* (82:27). They deny that the Qur'ān is the word of God (80:1–6) and they are ignorant of the pillars of Islam (87:11):[70] *la ya'rifūna al-ṣawm wa'l-ṣalāt wa-lā yarawna al-ḥajj wa'l-zakāt*. They are not interested at all in the differences between the Muslim schools of law (*madhāhib*); instead they are divided, like all the fellahs, into the two factions Sa'd and Ḥarām (87:8):[71] *'wa-madhhabī yā Sa'd yā Ḥarām'*. They worship their holy men, such as Sayyid Aḥmad al-Badawī, like God. Shirbīnī explains that this is *shirk*, and although al-Badawī is to be considered a *walī*, and one may even visit his *mawlid*, as did Shirbīnī's teacher Shihāb al-Din al-Qalyūbī (32:17–19), it is permissible to pray only to God and to ask for sustenance only from Him (80:6–16).[72] Moreover, the number of holy shaykhs grows steadily, and at each of their tombs a *mawlid* is being established. Thus, when the father of Abū Shādūf died in Kafr Shamarṭāṭī and was buried on Tall Fandarūk, his tomb, known as the tomb of Abū Jārūf, became the object of veneration by the fellahs (93:27–29). To stress his disapproval of the multiplication of these holy tombs and *mawlids* Shirbīnī says that at their visits the fellahs play ball near the tomb and their animals urinate on it (94:1). Similar disapproval in a more conventional form was expressed in a poem by al-Ḥijāzī composed perhaps a few decades later than Shirbīnī's book.[73]

The beliefs and attitudes of the *fuqarā'* denounced by Shirbīnī are those which characterized the popular and 'irregular' orders, such as the Qalenderīs. These 'went out of their way to "incur censure" by wandering about with their hair, beards and eyebrows shaven and openly disregarded every precept of the Sacred Law. They would travel on foot from place to place with flags and drums, attracting crowds by their strange appearance and behaviour. They begged for a living, had no worldly interest, and took no thought for the morrow. Being mostly drawn from the lower classes, they were quite uneducated and incapable of understanding the niceties of *ṣūfī* philosophy. Their doctrine, such as it was, was pantheistic; they were said to believe in the endless repetition of events and the transmigration of souls, and to account no action unlawful . . .'[74] Each of these traits was attacked by Shirbīnī. They are called *al-darāwīsh al-mulḥidīn al-muḥallaqīn al-liḥā* (the heretic dervishes whose beards are shaved) (79:20, 81:16), and it is interesting to note that in a treatise on Egyptian guilds, whose author may well have been a contemporary of Shirbīnī, the shaving of beards is also mentioned as one of the *bida'* which have appeared in Egypt in *bilād al-dawār*.[75] On their disregard for the precepts of the Sacred Law we have cited Shirbīnī above. Their clamorous and turbulent behaviour at funerals and at *mawlids* is disparaged by Shirbīnī as well (82:13–25, 86:20, 24–26).[76] On their begging Shirbīnī has the following verse in which he quotes the rural *faqīr* (87:6):

'wa'anzil 'alā man li 'alayhi siyāda
aqul luh al-bīta wa-hāt al-'āda'

(I shall stay at the house of somebody over whom I have power, and demand from him lodging and the usual gift). It is of course originally due to this attitude that these dervishes were called *fuqarā'*, and for centuries Egypt abounded in wandering dervishes who subsisted on alms, 'which they often demand with great importunacy and effrontery.'[77] A large proportion of them were fellahs, because 'the harder life became for the cultivators, the greater the temptation to find the easy way out.'[78] Finally, Shirbīnī condemns them as infidels for not believing in resurrection, paradise, or hell, and for holding non-orthodox or even non-Islamic views about the universe, similar to those of

Abū'l-'Alā' al-Ma'arrī. They believe that the world never perishes or disappears, but there is always a sun rising and a moon setting. 'Then he (the heretic dervish who shaves his beard) says that when a man's soul leaves him on his death it enters the body of another human being or an animal, until the circle is closed and it returns to its original owner' (79:19–29).

In addition to these accusations against the *fuqarā'* Shirbīnī charges them with sexual aberrations. We have seen above that fellahs are accused by Shirbīnī of being prone to sexual intercourse with animals; similarly, dervishes were popularly believed to have homosexual relations with young boys, in many cases their followers. Shirbīnī exploits this reputation to the full in order to vilify the *fuqarā'* and satisfy the curiosity of his listeners or readers. Thus he tells various stories in which a *faqīr* desires a young boy, and seduces him by false pretences of introducing him to the pleasures of mystical revelation; and for the amusement of his audience a detailed description of homosexual intercourse is supplied (78:7–79:5, 80:19–81:14).[79] According to Shirbīnī, another of the sexual deviations of rural *fuqarā'* is incest: they have intercourse with sisters and aunts (87:13): *al-shakhṣ minhum yankiḥu al-'ammāt wa-yankiḥ al-akhawāt wa'l-khālāt.'*

It has been claimed by Nicholson and Vollers that in his *Hazz al-quḥūf* Shirbīnī 'makes a bitter attack on the learning and morals of the Muḥammadan divines', or, as Vollers put it: 'Daneben finden wir die heftigsten Ausfälle gegen die islamische Geistlichkeit, ihre Heuchelei, ihre Scheingelehrsamkeit und sittliche Entartung.'[80] This is not correct, since one can hardly call the subtle and witty satire upon Arabic commentaries, lexicography and other literature included in *Hazz al-quḥūf* 'a bitter attack' or 'die heftigsten Ausfälle' against the *'ulamā'* in general.[81] There are only two groups of Muslim clerics whom Shirbīnī attacks directly, namely the *fuqahā' al-rīf* and specific sorts of *qāḍīs*.

Faqīh rīf or *faqīh min fuqahā' al-rif* or *faqīh al-balad* is a villager engaged in all activities connected with religion. In one instance one of them calls himself *'al-fiqī* Abū 'Alī' (42:2), but Shirbīnī, unlike Lane, does not distinguish between *faqīh*, a person versed in religion and law, and *fiqī*, a man who merely recites the Qur'ān professionally or who teaches others to do so.[82] Nevertheless, the fact that a rural *faqīh* called himself *fiqī*, and that one of Shirbīnī's main criticisms of these people was, as we shall see, that they were not versed in religion and law at all, would seem to indicate the origin of Lane's distinction. However, Shirbīnī's *fuqahā' al-rīf* were not merely people who recited the Qur'ān or taught others to do so. Some of them were indeed Qur'ān teachers (31:26, 36:9–10), others arranged marriage contracts (32:13–14), some acted as *imām* (leader in prayer) (31:17), many as *khaṭīb* (preacher) (35:14, 19, 39:18), and most of them probably were also supposed to answer all questions on religion asked by the fellahs (e.g., 37:5–17). It happened that one of them was appointed *qāḍī* by a *qāḍī* of a higher rank – probably as judge for a few villages (40:18–19).[83]

The conflict between the learned *'ulamā'* of Cairo and local religious functionaries raises difficult problems in contemporary Egypt, but to judge by Shirbīnī's *Hazz al-quḥūf* this conflict is of very long standing. It finds its expression in two stories in which an urban *'ālim* who visited the village considered the behaviour of the *faqīh al-rīf* contrary to Islam, and according to his advice the rural *faqīh* was dismissed and sent away by the authorities (*'amīr al-balad'*) (36:24–27, 39:14–29).

Their principal fault, in Shirbīnī's view, is their utter ignorance. They do not even know the Qur'ān properly. One of them reads the Fātiḥa with a wrong *i'rāb* (31:16–17), and another gives wrong, and of course very funny, interpretations of the text of the Qur'ān (32:12–13). Moreover, they apparently do not know the essential Islamic creed concerning the Qur'ān: one of them asks a Cairo bookseller for an abridged Qur'ān for his pupils in the village, and another claims that he has a nice copy in the author's hand-writing *'indī maṣḥaf malīḥ bi-khaṭṭ al-mu'allif'* (36:4–15).Similarly, they teach obviously false *ḥadīths* (36:24–27), or do not read them properly (39:14–29). Nor do they know the basic matters about family law: one of them gives ridiculous instructions for the marriage ceremony (32:13–17), while another finds absurd, though quite piquant, ways to evade the rule that a man may not remarry his threefold divorced wife before her marriage to someone else has been consummated. Needless to say, he demands a high payment for such illegal procedures (37:5–17). They are completely confused about the different schools of law (*madhāhib*), a central feature of Muslim urban society at that time (36:3–4).[84] They even are indifferent to ritual instructions for prayer (86:3–4). As for the sermons of the preachers among them, they deal more with the internecine fights of the fellahs and their work than with religious admonition (35:14–25).

Moreover, their ignorance is aggravated by extreme stupidity. This is illustrated by various amusing anecdotes.Thus one of them asks about the rules for morning prayer in case the sun rises before dawn. Another attempts to settle a controversy about the right text of the Qur'ān by a compromise including elements of both versions (36:15–24). A third is so stupid as to make a serious *faux pas* while trying to bribe a *qāḍī* (40:18–22). To make fun of the stupidity of a *faqīh al-rīf* Shirbīnī reproduces a letter allegedly written by him 'in the year A. H. 1047', full of amusing nonsense (42:1–16). A school teacher, whose pupils had built a wall in front of the school-room to prevent him from entering, leaves the village in pursuit of the room which, he was told, had fled during the night, and his adventures on this hunt are told in detail. But then the stupidity of the school-teachers among the *fuqahā' al-rīf* can be accounted for: all day they are with children and all night with women (44:7–6).

To disparage the *fuqahā' al-rīf*, Shirbīnī imputes additional faults to them. One of them, whose name is *Mukhālif Allāh* (He who disobeys God), gets into ecstasy and behaves indecently and when he comes to his senses he says that he visited the heavens (37:18–38:7). Another takes part in a theft and cheats his associates (35:27–36:3). Still another *faqīh al-rīf* described as having a particularly shabby appearance is occupied in driving off dogs from his dead ass because he wants to sell the skin of the ass (36:27–37:5). Some are depicted as tall and gross, having a wide neck and coarse thighs (33:23–24, 37:25–26) and bad eating manners, too (85:26).

Like the rest of the *fuqahā' al-rīf*, the *qāḍī* in the countryside, *qāḍī al-balad*, is ignorant of the religious law (86:17–18). However, Shirbīnī does not feel much sympathy with urban *qāḍīs* either. They, too, often seem to be quite ignorant, so much so that one of them failed to distinguish between a verse from the Qur'ān and a verse of poetry (39:4–12).[85] That they are corrupt and accept bribes was a prominent aspect of their image, and Shirbīnī repeats this accusation on two occasions (40:18–22, 86:15–16).[86] Moreover, he has a number of stories about homosexual propensities of *qāḍīs* (40:13–18, 103:5–10, 223:7–13). Finally, being a Turk, one of the *qāḍīs* in Shirbīnī's stories composes inferior poetry, while his *nā'ib*, an Arabic speaking Egyptian, makes agreeable extempore rhymes (75:17–27).[87] It should be mentioned, however, that Shirbīnī's attitude towards the Turks was ambivalent. Together with this mild satire on the Turk who composes Arabic poetry, and the gentle criticism of *multazims* mentioned above, he admires the power of the Turkish rulers and approves of their measures against unruly people of the lower classes. Moreover, he stresses again and again that the Turks prepare all kinds of dishes in the most delicious fashion.[88]

IV. THE SIGNIFICANCE OF SHIRBĪNĪ'S HAZZ AL-QUḤŪF

In order to understand the social significance of Shirbīnī's *Hazz al-quḥūf*, we have to ask, first of all, the following questions: which were the literary sources of this work, and to what extent did each of them contribute to Shirbīnī's composition.

As we have said above, Shirbīnī frequently quotes from classical Arabic literature, both religious and secular. This shows that he was an *'ālim*, but such classical literature cannot be considered one of the sources of *Hazz al-quḥūf*. Almost all his quotations are marginal to the main subjects of *Hazz al-quḥūf* and most of them are short poems or aphorisms expressing some conventional wisdom.

The only literary work which Shirbīnī himself acknowledges as a source of inspiration for his *Hazz al-quḥūf* is a book by Ibn Sūdūn, who lived in the fifteenth century.[89] Shirbīnī says that in his *Hazz al-quḥūf* he has included

'*al-khalā'a wa'l-mujūn*
wa-shay' yuḥākī kalām Ibn Sūdūn.' (3:21).

From Ibn Sūdūn Shirbīnī quotes humoristic *mawwāls* in connection with specific expressions or matters (58:22, 109:11), or grotesque etymologies (100:13, 102:8, 14). However, derision and vilification of the fellah are absent from Ibn Sūdūn's composition. True, Ibn Sūdūn records a letter written by a Ṣa'īdī which is intended to mock his trite mentality and stupidity, and Shirbīnī promptly copies this letter (40:22–42:1). However, this is the only instance of a quotation from Ibn Sūdūn which is related to Shirbīnī's main theme, and even here the difference is striking. Scorn and contempt for the people of Upper Egypt was a very common attitude in Egypt throughout the centuries, and the Ṣa'īdī is the hero of many jokes and funny stories. This is a common feature of all humour and of Arab humour in particular. As Littmann puts it: 'It seems to be a common custom all over the world that the inhabitants of a certain town or village acquire the reputation of being particularly slow and dull. Therefore they are likely to be teased, and many jokes are current about them. The villages of 'Alaih and in-Nabaṭîyeh in the Lebanon and the village of Ḥalbûn near Damascus are said to have a population that is the opposite of wise'.[90] But except for the passage quoted from Ibn Sūdūn the only mention of the people of Upper Egypt is Shirbīnī's statement that they are particularly poor and therefore their food is extremely deficient (149:6–8). The object of Shirbīnī's sarcasm and derision are the fellahs of Egypt in general, and he has in mind particularly those of Lower Egypt.

Shirbīnī has drawn only little inspiration from the vast store of written popular folk tales, legends and sagas. *Alf layla wa-layla* is mentioned once as the source of the story about 'The Barber from Baghdad' (210:11 ff.) and apparently another story, 'The Champion of the Tedious' (28:7–20), is taken from the same source. Kern has found in Shirbīnī literary influences of the romances of the saga of Banī Hilāl.[91] However, all these tales which circulated among Cairo's population and which were told or read every evening in their meeting places by professional story-tellers, more or less ignored the fellah. For instance, there are no fellahs in *Alf layla wa-layla*, and only in *Sīrat Baybars*, the folk-tale most concerned with the population of Egypt, do fellahs appear occasionally, though in a definitely marginal rôle.[92] Writing a book in which fellahs are the central theme, Shirbīnī could not profit from these sources. He mentions the story-tellers, the *mukharrifīn*, and a certain *sīra* which they frequently tell (166:9–10), but no more. In one of the best nineteenth century travel accounts of Egypt, a British author recorded the following observation: 'The professed story-tellers of the cities rarely place the scene of their romantic fictions in the country. To them, what we call a pastoral is almost unknown; and as soon as they get beyond the walls of Cairo, at one bound reach the region of the marvellous and the supernatural. An Efreet is always hanging about in the suburbs, to carry to some distant city an unfortunate hero, who is invariably chosen from among the intramural population. The story-tellers love to dwell on the adventures of sons of kings, of politic ministers, of wealthy merchants, of shopkeepers, artizans, water-carriers, and even ass-drivers; but they disdain to waste the efforts of their imagination upon anything of fellâh, or rather of country origin.'[93]

The influence on Shirbīnī's writing of another kind of popular literature, the shadow play, was not greater than that of the folk-tales. In the seventeenth century, when *Hazz al-quḥūf* was written, the Egyptian shadow theatre had been flourishing for centuries.[94] Unlike the story-tellers and some collections of stories, the shadow theatre is not even mentioned by Shirbīnī. It may be that in the great number of expressions and anecdotes connected with sexual intercourse, homosexuality, sodomy, incest, excrements etc., *Hazz al-quḥūf* is following the model of the shadow-plays.[95] However, for his main theme Shirbīnī could not have found much material in the shadow plays. Among the plays which can be proved to have existed in the seventeenth century, Ibn Daniyāl's three plays and *Li'b al-manār* do not mention any fellahs.[96] As against this, a fellah plays an important role in another of the shadow plays, *Li'b al-timsāḥ*, of which quite a number of fragments in rhymes (dating from the second half of the seventeenth century) have been preserved.[97] But the central subject of this play is a fellah's attempt to exercise a craft, namely fishing, without being a member of the guild – a transgression which leads to his punishment. No hint of such a problem is to be found in *Hazz al-quḥūf*, while nothing is said in the Crocodile Play about the attributes of the fellah that are disparaged by Shirbīnī.

Thus it would seem that Shirbīnī was unable to draw material for his treatise on the fellah from written literary sources. As against this, probably quite a number of the stories and anecdotes about the fellah were transmitted orally, in one form or another, among the population of Cairo and other towns. Some of them are told up to this day, as for instance a story in which the fellah is ridiculed for not knowing urban dishes, or another which deals with the motif of the fellah and the urban lavatory. Similarly, there is the story of the glutton told by Shirbīnī about a fellah.[98] The Geniza text published by Professor S. D. Goitein shows that in the seventeenth century there existed in Egypt a story about a disputation between a fellah and a townsman, in which the differences between town and village and their relative virtues and vices were discussed. However, the unique and original contribution of Shirbīnī was to collect all these stories about the fellah for the first time, to add to the usual image of the stupid and ignorant fellah other characteristics and to explain them in detail, to observe keenly and put into writing the meeting between the fellah and the town, and last but not least, to include in his composition a vast amount of factual material about the differences and conflicts between the town and the countryside.

The question arises, of course, whether he did all this just to amuse his listeners or readers by making fun of the fellah and telling the obscene stories to divert their minds from the worries of the time? (3 : 22–25). Or had Shirbīnī an additional social motivation for attacking the fellahs so severely and deriding everything rural – rural dervishes, rural religious functionaries, rural food?

Karl Vollers, in one of the first articles written on Shirbīnī's *Hazz al-quḥūf*, has attempted to find such a social motivation for the composition of this work. He said: '. . . vermuthungsweise wage ich die Erklärung in einer socialen Wandelung zu finden, die sich in aller Stille an der Azhar, diesem mächtigen Heerde muslimischer Geistesthätigkeit seit der Zeit der Mamluken, vollzogen hat und seitdem zum Abschlusse gekommen ist, ich meine das stärkere Eindringen fellaḥischer Elemente in die lernenden und später lehrenden Kreise der Azhar und die Verdrängung der alten durch Geschlecht und Reichtum hervorragenden Familien durch jene. Der Fellaḥensohn aus Šerbin wurde ausersehen, dem Aerger der alten Classe Ausdruck zu geben und den genannten socialen Process zu dämmen, so weit es noch möglich war.'[99]

This explanation seems to be based on various false assumptions. The Azhar shaykhs from the old families would have had to be endowed with diabolic cunning and extraordinary power to be able to force Shirbīnī, the *'ālim* of fellah origin, to compose a book against the *'ulamā'* of fellah origin. Actually, it was Shaykh Aḥmad al-Sandūbī who induced Shirbīnī to write *Hazz al-quḥūf* (223 : 29, 224 : 3), and he was himself of rural origin.[100] Moreover, Shirbīnī praises *'ulamā'* of rural origin: speaking about the village of Laqāna he says that illustrious *'ulamā'* originated from it, whose merit is well known and who benefit mankind by their learning until the day of resurrection (177 : 27–28). He would not have done this had he been charged with curbing the penetration into the Azhar of *'ulamā'* of fellah origin.

Up to the middle of the twentieth century European scholars showed more interest in Shirbīnī's book than Egyptian authors;[101] since then, however, Egyptian interest in it grew tremendously. In the early 1950s Aḥmad Amīn based the article on the fellah in his Folklore encyclopedia entirely on what he found in Shirbīnī's *Hazz al-quḥūf*, which also served him to write some of the other articles in this encyclopaedia.[102]

Approximately at the same time Dr. 'Abd al-Laṭīf Ḥamza reproduced in his anthology of Egyptian literature selected passages from Shirbīnī's *Hazz al-quḥūf*, with an introduction of two pages,[103] and Dr. Shawqī Ḍayf devoted about ten pages of his book on Egyptian comical literature to Shirbīnī.[104] A shorter notice on Shirbīnī and his book is also found in Aḥmad Rushdī Ṣāliḥ's work on popular literature.[105] Moreover, while Ḥamza, Ḍayf and Ṣāliḥ were interested in the literary aspect of *Hazz al-quḥūf*, the linguistic aspect too now drew the attention of an Egyptian writer, Dr. Nafūsa Zakariyyā Sa'īd, who dealt with it in her book on the protagonists of the use of Egyptian colloquial Arabic.[106] However, the climax was attained by Muḥammad Qandīl al-Baqlī, who in 1963 published a shortened and expurgated edition of *Hazz al-quḥūf*, as the first volume of what was planned to become a series called *Qaryatunā al-miṣriyya qabl al-thawra* (Our Egyptian village before the Revolution). The introduction to this edition was written by Dr. Muḥammad Ṭal'at 'Īsā, a professor of sociology at Cairo University.[107] When this new edition had appeared, 'Abd al-Jalīl Ḥasan wrote a detailed review of it in the monthly *al-Kātib* in which he attempted a reassessment of Shirbīnī's book – one of the best articles on *Hazz al-quḥūf* written in Egypt so far.[108] One year later the book was discussed in Muḥammad 'Abd al-Ghanī Ḥasan's book on the fellah in Arabic literature published in the popular series al-Maktaba al-Thaqāfiyya,[109] and again in Ḥasan Muḥassib's study on the fellah problem in the Egyptian short-story, published in 1971 in the same series.[110] Finally, Shirbīnī's *Hazz al-quḥūf* served as the theme of a special article by Dr. 'Abd al-Raḥmān 'Abd al-Raḥīm, a lecturer at the Girls' College of al-Azhar, published in Arabic in 1973 and in English translation in 1975.[111]

This new interest in Shirbīnī was no doubt the result of basic changes in the attitude towards the Egyptian fellah which occurred in the wake of the 1952 revolution. According to the official ideology of the revolutionary regime the fellah had become one of the central pillars of Egyptian society. His organization and activation and the bettering of his material and cultural situation had become principal slogans of Egypt's new rulers. Less than two months after the revolution an agrarian reform had been inaugurated according to which land was to be distributed to the fellah, the conditions of fellahs renting land and of agricultural labourers were to be improved, and fellahs were to be organized in cooperatives. And ten years after the revolution an attempt was made to make fellahs participate in the political life by laying down the rule that in all representative bodies fellahs and workers should constitute at least fifty per cent of the membership.

This new attitude towards the fellah in official Egyptian ideology was of course reflected in the writings of Egyptian authors and publicists. In 1958 the leftist writer Anouar Abdel-Malek stated that the fellah question was the essence of the national question – *'jawhar al-mas'ala al-waṭaniyya fī miṣr huwa mas'alat al-fallāḥīn.*'[112] The fellah came to be considered as the authentic, genuine Egyptian, *al-aṣīl*. The fellahs (and the workers) are those who have a genuine interest in the revolution (*al-ṭabaqāt dhāt al-maṣlaḥa al-aṣīla fī'l-thawra*), and it is the authenticity of the revolutionary consciousness (*aṣālat al-wa'yi al-thawrī*) which 'gave the popular forces, headed by the forces of fellahs and workers, a position of actual leadership'.[113] Accordingly a change occurred in the historical image of the fellah as well, or at least such a change was desired. Thus one of the publicists wrote: 'The history of political movements in Egypt confirms that the Egyptian fellah was always ready for revolutionary action when he understood the aim. Similarly, history confirms that the assertion regarding the fellah's "*naiveté* and apathy" (*ṭība waghafla*) is a lie which Imperialism and Feudalism have tried to instil into the minds . . .'[114]

Like others, the writers dealing with Shirbīnī were imbued with this new ideology, and they do not hide the fact that they sought confirmation for their views in Shirbīnī's book. Their starting point was the idea, that the fellah is the genuine Egyptian. 'Abd al-Jalīl Ḥasan opens his discussion with the statement that as soon as the fellah will again mould his future the Egyptian people will again fulfil their authentic task (*dawrahu al-aṣīl*), i.e. participate in remoulding civilization. Baqlī states, in the introduction to his expurgated edition, that what attracted him to read the book was the 'Egyptian authenticity' of it (*'jadhabatnī ilā qirā'atihi al-aṣāla al-miṣriyya allatī ẓaharat malāmiḥuhā fī thanāyā al-kitāb'*).[115] Moreover, the fellah contains enormous revolutionary powers (*ṭāqāt thawriyya dāfi'a wa'amīqa*) which are stored up and which will work wonders when they will be freed.[116]

The belief in the genuineness of the Egyptian fellah and his enormous potential revolutionary powers corresponds with contemporary historiography which claims that in Ottoman Egypt there was a permanent struggle between Egyptians and Turks or between the native fellah and his foreign Ottoman oppressors. The National charter of 1962 made this historiographical attitude a part of the official ideology. It says: 'The French occupation (of Bonaparte) found that the Egyptian people rejected Ottoman imperialism camouflaged by the name of Caliphate . . . it found strong resistance to the rule of the Mamluks and permanent revolt against their attempts to exploit the Egyptian people.'[117] Similarly, the authors who wrote on Shirbīnī consider the oppressors and exploiters of the Egyptian fellah to have been Turks, Mamluks, and Ottomans. 'The land was a milkcow for foreigners abounding in riches for them while its native sons were denied livelihood'; 'the army of oppressors, the helpers of the Sultan . . . collect taxes from the fellah for their master'; or: 'the fellahs sweated and laboured for others, for the wild Turkish beast . . . in Istanbul and his helpers' (*al-waḥsh al-turkī al-qābi' fī al-āsitāna wa'a'wānuhu*).[118] When collecting taxes, the Ottoman Mamluks used illegal and cruel means;[119] 'The Ottomans inflicted upon the Egyptian fellahs slavery of various kinds which accompanied their sons and grandsons for generations;[120] in general, Ottoman rule was the real reason for all the calamities which struck this poor creature, for all the disasters he met and for the oppression which was his lot.[121]

It is only natural that contemporary Egyptian writers with such views on the Egyptian fellah's place in history were attracted by the only book written in pre-modern Egypt whose subject was the fellah. However, Shirbīnī's book confronted them with a difficult problem. How should they explain that a native Egyptian writer born himself in an Egyptian village mocked and despised the fellah as if he expressed the views of the fellah's Turkish and Mamluk oppressors?

Among contemporary writers who faced this problem two groups may be discerned, each solving it in a mutually contradictory way. The first group sees Shirbīnī in a favourable light. Writers of this group claim, to begin with, that Shirbīnī described the fellah's suffering in order to denounce his oppression. Such an explanation had been given already by Aḥmad Amīn in his *Qāmūs al-'ādāt*, at least as one of various possibilities.[122] Dr. 'Abd al-Raḥīm too thinks that Shirbīnī showed the injustice done to the villagers by the government apparatus and the arbitrariness and unscrupulousness of some *multazims*. They exploited their power and used illegal means in their treatment of the fellah, and Shirbīnī criticizes and condemns them for this.[123]

Moreover, in the view of this group Shirbīnī even intended to condemn the exploitation and oppression of Egyptians by the Ottomans and the Mamluks; he did this, so they say, by describing the poverty of the people and their oppression by the foreign *kāshifs* and *multazims*.[124] Dr. 'Abd al-Raḥīm even claims that Ottoman and Mamluk cruel and ruthless extortion of taxes is clearly reflected in Abū Shādūf's poem, and Shirbīnī cannot but confirm Abū Shadūf's words.[125] Such an interpretation of *Hazz al-quḥūf* corresponds with the official historiography and complements the interesting effort made recently to interpret in terms of the struggle between Egyptians and Turks or Mamluks the popular romances of that time which are being recited in cafes in Egypt to this very day.[126] It is not difficult to understand the reason for such interpretations in a period of conflict between Egyptian nationalism and foreign rule, and especially in a period of the overthrow of a Turkish speaking dynasty which ruled Egypt for a century and a half. However, with regard to Shirbīnī such an interpretation is totally mistaken. True, Shirbīnī derides a Turkish *qāḍī* who fails in his attempts to compose Arabic poetry, and he even criticizes mildly some Turkish *multazims*, but he supports unequivocally Turkish *kāshifs* who suppress rioting fellahs who revolt against the *multazims* or the *qā'imaqām*. Moreover, he frequently praises Turkish customs, especially the way in which Turks prepare their food.

Another favourable aspect of Shirbīnī's book, according to the writers of this group, is his condemnation of the fellah's cultural backwardness, their yielding to the domination of tales and superstitions which are disseminated among them to make them docile, as well as his criticism of backward systems of irrigation prevalent in the Egyptian village (Dr. 'Īsā explains anachronistically that the name Abū Shādūf was intended to indicate that the fellah used the *shādūf* instead of modern implements of irrigation!). Shirbīnī intended, says Dr. 'Īsā, to arouse the *'ulamā'*, the leaders of that time, and to remind them of their responsibility to educate society properly. Since they are the group closest to the fellah's souls, it is their duty to direct them spiritually and stir their honour and consciousness of their oppression in order to enable them to liberate themselves.[127] Thus the image of Shirbīnī in Dr. 'Īsā's eyes is that of a kind of leftist publicist, completely out of the historical context in which he lived.

This raises of course the question how such an image can be reconciled with the cynical scorn to which Shirbīnī exposes the fellah in his satire *Hazz al-quḥūf*. In the writings discussed here I have found three answers to this question, two of them so general and vague that we can dispose of them in short. Aḥmad Rushdī Ṣāliḥ claims that Shirbīnī's mockery was the expression of bitterness about the poor conditions of the fellah in which no change occurred throughout the ages;[128] but he does not explain why the victim of these conditions should be derided. Dr. 'Īsā, on the other hand, explains that Shirbīnī's biting mockery is to be understood as the release of deep pressure, occurring because he could not react to social reality by means of constructive remedies.[129] This of course does not solve the contradiction, but the anachronism of 'constructive remedies' in the context of Ottoman Egypt is amusing.

However, most writers of this group explain Shirbīnī's scorn and mockery of the fellah as camouflage to hide his real positive intentions. The first to express such a view was Aḥmad Amīn, who wrote in his folklore encyclopaedia that in Shirbīnī's time nobody could describe openly the oppression of the fellahs, and therefore 'Shirbīnī hid his description under a veil of humour and pretended to blame them.[130] Dr. 'Īsā' too explains that it was impossible at that time to describe the fellah's oppression by Ottoman rule openly and realistically, because the certain result would have been 'the breaking of the pen and cutting of the head'. Therefore, he says, 'most of the writings of that time have a symbolic tinge hiding behind the external form a deeper hidden significance'. He quotes Dr. Shawqī Ḍayf who goes even farther by stating that it was impossible to make fun of the tyrannical Ottoman rule, and therefore 'Shirbīnī turned to the popular masses and described their poverty and ignorance in a mocking and satirical style'.[131] Similarly Dr. 'Abd al-Raḥīm writes: 'Shaykh Yūsuf places the people of the countryside in a framework which in outward appearance should satisfy the authorities since it portrays the people of the countryside in such a bad light that one can hardly bear to look at them. But at the same time, the inner technique of this portrayal contains a complete picture of the injustice which surrounded this class . . .'[132]

This interpretation raises a number of interesting questions. First, as 'Abd al-Jalīl Ḥasan has rightly pointed out in his review of Baqlī's edition and 'Īsā's introduction to it, no symbolism at all can be traced in Shirbīnī's book,[133] and one may add that it is not true either that this was a prevalent literary trend at that time. Secondly, this interpretation is based on the assumption that Shirbīnī definitely sided with the fellahs against the ruling authorities. But in fact he distinguished, as we have seen, between fellahs who obey the *multazim* and his officials and refrain from causing ruin and mischief, and 'bad' fellahs who are quarrelsome and deserve severe punishment. Third, the important question must be asked, whether indeed there was in Ottoman Egypt a kind of censorship which made it impossible to criticize the Ottoman-Mamluk establishment openly. All signs indicate that no such censorship existed, neither in theory nor in practice. Shirbīnī himself condemns *multazims* who oppress the villagers and exact illegal tolls – openly and without camouflage. Moreover, very harsh words against the Turks and Ottomans could be written at that time, as shown in the guild treatise *Kitāb al-dhakhā'ir wa'l-tuḥaf fī bīr al-ṣanā'i' wa'l-ḥiraf* which was composed about the same time as Shirbīnī's book. There the Turks are described as beasts and in general inferior to Arabs.[134] Jabartī too relates that some *'ulamā'* used to tell Egypt's rulers openly and without camouflage their unfavourable opinion about them, without their heads being cut off.[135] This is not surprising, since such criticism did not endanger the rulers' position at all: the *'ulamā'* and the members of the guilds did not constitute an alternative to Ottoman rule which was based on the army, and the popular masses did not read criticism written in books or conveyed orally to the rulers, but listened to popular leaders, mainly connected with the Ṣūfī orders or messianic movements, who stimulated spontaneous eruptions as the result of concrete grievances. Finally, the camouflage theory seems to be based on the assumption that the Ottoman–Mamluk authorities were so naïve that they considered the camouflage to be Shirbīnī's real opinion without perceiving the criticism, while others (who?) understood that the scorn of the fellah is a camouflage for social criticism intended to lead to reforms. It seems to us, therefore, that the camouflage theory has no foundation whatsoever.

It probably originated in the erroneous idea that Shirbīnī acted like certain intellectuals and writers of our generation who criticized the government. A possible example may have been the experience of the semi-legal literary activity of the Egyptian left in periods of censorship; the leftist writers used to hide behind formulations whose aim their readers understood very well, while the censorship had no formal excuse to prohibit the publication of such formulations. Similarly, during 'Abd al-Nāṣir's rule writers used to hide their criticism of the Nāṣir regime behind hints the apprehension of which needed a high degree of sophistication, and the authorities tolerated such writing to let the authors release their feelings as long as the popular masses did not grasp the meaning of the hints.

In addition to these attempts to account for the contradiction between Shirbīnī's image as a social revolutionary and his scorn of the fellahs, one of the contemporary writers has tried, in an amusing and amazing way, to eliminate this contradiction by the re-editing of *Hazz al-quḥūf*. In 1963 Muḥammad Qandīl al-Baqlī published his shortened and expurgated edition of the book, but in his introduction he did not mention at all the fact that he had omitted words, passages and even pages from the original text. Only Dr. 'Īsā, in the second introduction, explained that Baqlī intended to free the book 'from blemish which is rejected by good taste'.[136] By this he probably meant the omission of words and themes which are considered unclean and indecent. Indeed Baqlī omitted every expression and every phrase relating to sex, prostitution, incest, homosexual relations, copulation between men and animals, excrements and farts, lavatories and even dung. Moreover, colloquial expressions are replaced, here and there, by literary ones. Thus, incidentally, he spoiled a great deal of the juicy flavour of the book, and many of the stories and jokes completely lost their point. However, from the point of view of our discussion it is interesting that Baqlī omitted not only what he considered obscene, but also what Shirbīnī as a champion of the fellah's case should not have written. Thus he 'freed' the book from derision of the villagers, such as mocking their dialect, their popular songs, or their torn clothes; he removed derisive expressions such as *quḥūf al-rīf*, which he replaced by *ahl al-rīf*, or a whole passage in which Shirbīnī ridicules the village shaykhs.[137] Even less than scorn was Baqlī willing to tolerate disapproval and defamation of the fellah and the villages which is copiously voiced by Shirbīnī in his book. Therefore he omitted the first two pages of the book which include, *inter alia*, an unfavourable characterization of the people of the *rīf*, reviling of the fellahs and their wives, poems and verses in which Shirbīnī compares fellahs to animals, as well as Shirbīnī's frequently uttered request from God to preserve him from agriculture (*a'ādhanā Allāh min al-filāḥa*), from the nature of a fellah, from the *rīf* in general, its ignorance, its raw food and the nature of its inhabitants.[138] Particularly severe abuse is directed by Shirbīnī against the rural religious functionaries, *fuqahā' al-rīf*; most of the stories about them have been totally omitted by Baqlī, and wherever he did not cut out the full story he just omitted *'al-rīf'*, so that the subject of the story became a *'faqīh'* or *'fuqahā'* in general.[139] The result of this cosmetic operation is a Shirbīnī more in accordance with the image of the writers of this group – an advocate of the fellahs' rights and a fighter for the betterment of their position.

Baqlī's edition of Shirbīnī has been severely criticized by writers of the second group, those who see him in an unfavourable light. In a critical review published in *al-Kātib* 'Abd al-Jalīl Ḥasan says that Baqlī's edition is an example of an erroneous and wrong system to revive the Egyptian popular tradition. Moreover, it is misleading and displays ignorance and disregard of the most elementary principles of scholarly editing and publishing. In addition, he should at least have explained the system according to which he had shortened and edited the text or even hinted that he had done so.[140]

However, 'Abd al-Jalīl Ḥasan is not content with this methodological criticism of Baqlī. The rejection of the interpretation of *Hazz al-quḥūf* by the first group of writers created an anti-thesis. In addition to 'Abd al-Jalīl Ḥasan, the writers who belonged to a second group with an opposite view are 'Abd al-Ghanī Ḥasan and Ḥasan Muḥassib. It is the opinion of these three writers that Shirbīnī's book clearly reflects the social struggle between fellahs and townsmen and between village and city, the contempt shown to villagers by townsmen, their derision by them and the townsmen's arrogance in their treatment of peasants. The book expresses the townsmen's fierce ardour to keep their privileges and their attempt to justify the fellah's calamities. Shirbīnī did not try at all to change the fellah's situation or to propagate such a change by his writing, not even indirectly through hints and hidden meanings. On the contrary, his aim was to justify this situation and to make sure that it continues, since there is no sense in changing it and no possibility to do so. Shirbīnī wants to prove by his stories that a fellah remains a fellah and that there is no chance that he will ever change. In short, Shirbīnī does not want to benefit the fellah, but to injure him. Moreover, he not only supports townsmen against fellahs, but even justifies the fellah's oppression and exploitation by the Turks and the Mamluks.[141]

There can be no doubt that this view conforms to the text of *Hazz al-quḥūf* and is free from the contradictions which we found in the interpretations of the first group of writers. Yet there remain a number of questions without answer. What was the purpose of Shirbīnī in abusing the fellah and mocking him, or in justifying his distress and oppression? Did there really exist at that time a fierce struggle between town and countryside, between fellah and townsman – a struggle which is not documented in any other sources? Why did he need to justify the continuation of the fellah's miserable situation – did anybody jeopardize its continuation?

All these questions were not touched upon at all by the writers of this school. They were, however, troubled by another kind of questions. Shirbīnī was a son of the Egyptian people – nobody doubted this basic fact. And if indeed a class-struggle was raging at that time between Egyptians and Turks, how are we to explain that Shirbīnī sides with the enemies of the Egyptian masses, and that the only Arabic literary expression of this struggle shows the Egyptian masses in such an unfavourable light? This is how Muḥammad 'Abd al-Ghanī puts the question which disturbs him: 'We do not know up to this day what the real motive was which induced Shaykh Shirbīnī to make his fierce attack on the fellah and to look down on him with contempt. If the Shaykh would have been a Turk or a member of the Turkish ruling class, we would have said that this was a racialist tendency and meanness of his character . . . But the Shaykh was an Egyptian as witnessed by everything known about him'.[142] Such questions apparently troubled other writers as well, since in their writings they make assertions intended to answer them. First, some of them claim that Shirbīnī did not write his book of his own free will. Muḥassib says that somebody whose order Shirbīnī did not dare to ignore drove him to despise and mock the fellahs, and later on he explains that he was driven to this attitude by people from the ruling class of that time.[143] This claim is based on Shirbīnī's words in the beginning of his book, namely that 'somebody whose orders I could not disregard, whom I had to obey, asked me to write a commentary' to Abū Shadūf's poem.[144] In fact it was Shaykh Aḥmad al-Sandūbī, Shirbīnī's venerated teacher, who induced him to write his book, but he did not belong to the 'ruling class' – he was an *'ālim* from rural origin like Shirbīnī himself, and it does not follow at all from Shirbīnī's words that he forced him to write against his will. Nevertheless, Dr. 'Abd al-Raḥīm expands this strange story adding his own amplifications. According to him Sandūbī refused to write a commentary on the *qaṣīd* of Abū Shādūf, apparently because of his known resistance to injustice. The *qaṣīd* expresses the feelings of an oppressed class which complains of his misery, and if he had dealt with this it would have exposed him to fearful consequences. Therefore he resorted to Shaykh Yūsuf al-Shirbīnī, who was particularly suitable because of his connections with the people of the countryside through his work as a preacher. He accepted because of two reasons. First, at that time, which was an age of stagnation, work in the intellectual field was scarce. The text shows, according to 'Abd al-Raḥīm, that Shirbīnī accepted this task for pay because of the poverty in which the *'ulamā'* lived. Secondly, his desire to ingratiate himself with the authorities. In spite of all this, Shaykh Yūsuf constantly sought to excuse himself for the entire task which he undertook.[145]

It seems to us that Dr. 'Abd al-Raḥīm's thesis lacks sufficient foundations. I have not found any hint, neither in the sources quoted by Dr. 'Abd al-Raḥīm nor in other biographies, that Sandūbī rejected the offer to write the commentary himself and, because he feared the consequences, he imposed the task on Shirbīnī. As to Shirbīnī, we have mentioned already that he did not complain at all that he had to write the book against his will. Moreover, he did not say, in the passage quoted by Dr. 'Abd al-Raḥīm, that writers in general were unemployed, but that jesters and entertainers with poor literary taste were preferred to eloquent poets. Nothing whatsoever in his book indicates that he received pay for writing it; if there are indications of his material position they point in the opposite direction. Finally, in the passage quoted by Dr. 'Abd al-Raḥīm to show that Shirbīnī wanted 'to ingratiate himself with the authorities', the authorities are not mentioned at all but 'time' and 'the people' in general, to which everybody must adapt himself.[146]

However, the thesis that Shirbīnī wrote the book against his free will was not sufficient for most of the writers of this second group; they too expected from this unique source on the Egyptian fellah to reflect the struggle between him and his Mamluk and Turkish exploiters and oppressors. To satisfy their expectations they made a distinction between the poem of the popular poet Abū Shādūf on one hand and Shirbīnī's commentary on the other hand, which, in their view, was contrary to the poem's spirit. 'The truth is', says 'Abd al-Jalīl Ḥasan, 'that the genuine hero in the book is not Shaykh Shirbīnī who reflects the task of the town but the unknown popular poet Abū Shādūf, the voice of the silent oppressed who ridicules and condemns the bad situation . . .'[147] Muḥassib adds that Abū Shādūf's poem constitutes a kind of petition containing the whole tragedy of the village and the fellah in the Mamluk and Turkish period. This enraged and frightened the rulers of that time, and therefore they imposed on one of the sharp-witted *'ulamā'*, Shaykh Yūsūf al-Shirbīnī, to deride this poem of crying pain and to laugh it to scorn.[148]

A thorough and careful reading of Abū Shādūf's poem will show that the theory about the existence of an unknown popular poet named Abū Shādūf is rather unlikely. It is much more convincing to assume that Abū Shādūf is nothing but a creation of Shirbīnī, and his poem was composed by Shirbīnī for the sole purpose of writing his humorous commentary on it. First of all, neither Abū Shādūf nor his poem are known from any other source.[149] The villages mentioned in the poem, Kafr Shamarṭāṭī and Tall Fandarūk, are not known and have not been mentioned in any historical or geographical source.[150] Moreover, these are ridiculous names, as are the names of persons mentioned in Abū Shādūf's poem: Muḥayliba, Khanāfir, Umm Waṭīf, Mukhaymir, Ibn Abū Sha'nīf, Ibn Abū Jaghanīf, etc.[151] They were invented to amuse by their sound or because of their comical associations, for the sake of the rhyme or to serve Shirbīnī's purpose of writing humorous or obscene commentaries on them; anyway, these are not names usually found in popular poetry. Similarly, it is difficult to assume that a popular poet would have described the poverty and calamities of the fellahs in a comical way as in the first parts of Abū Shādūf's poem – he would have expressed pain and complaint, as usual in a number of known popular poems.[152] In addition, if Abū Shādūf had been a popular poet he would not have derided the manner of eating of the fellahs, or told about himself that he shovels the food into his mouth, fills his cap with cheese, devours the food all at once without leaving anything for anybody else, or even eats dirty food.[153] It is quite obvious that Shirbīnī makes Abū Shādūf say these things in order to criticize and ridicule the fellah. Or take the following verse by 'Abū Shādūf': 'I shall steal from the mosque some shoes, and with their proceeds I shall eat in the village as much as I like'.[154] Generally speaking, it is not like a popular poet to mock himself as Abū Shādūf does. He says that when the tax-collectors arrive he takes refuge with the women and wraps himself up in an *'abāya* or when the villagers are recruited for the corvee Umm Waṭīf hides him in the oven.[155] On the other hand, nothing is said in the poem on the *multazims*, the army, the Turks or oppressors of any kind; the only persons about whom Abū Shādūf complains are his cousin Muḥayliba and the latter's nephew Khanāfir,[156] to show that fellahs are hostile to each other and even members of one family are quarrelling continuously.

Thus Shirbīnī neither wrote his book in order to denounce the exploitation of the fellah or the oppression of the Egyptians by Ottomans and Mamluks, nor because he was forced to do so by the rulers in order to scorn and ridicule a poem of a popular poet Abū Shādūf which was frightening them. It would rather seem to us that the background to Shirbīnī's *Hazz al-quḥūf* was indeed the penetration of a rural element into the urban class of *'ulamā'*, though Vollers' interpretation of this clash is not convincing. What we know so far is not sufficient to determine when this penetration began, in which centuries it became more intense and in which it weakened, and for what reasons. Until further study of this question, we shall have to be content with stating that throughout the centuries *'ulamā'* of village origin lived, taught and wrote books in the cities.[157] As to the eleventh/seventeenth century, we have mentioned above that one quarter of Cairo's *'ulamā'* whose biographies have been recorded by Muḥibbī were of rural origin.

Biographies of about 35 such *'ulamā'* of rural origin from the twelfth/eighteenth century are to be found in Mubārak's *Khiṭaṭ*,[158] and there are about 17 out of 93 *'ulamā'* from the nineteenth century.[159] This count includes only those who themselves were born in villages. Many more had names indicating that their forefathers had been of rural origin. Throughout centuries boys with a basic education in a village *maktab* (Qur'ān school) moved to the towns, and mainly to Cairo, in order to study at one of the *madrasas*, and many of them remained there as teachers and scholars. This, it would seem, was for a long time one of the very few ways open for urbanization, social mobility and economic advancement.

There are clear indications that this movement led to friction among the *'ulamā'*. In at least two cases recorded in biographies of *'ulamā'*, their rural origin was used in controversies or discussions by other *'ulamā'* or by towndwellers to defame them. 'Abd al Raḥmān b. 'Alī al-Tafahnī was born in A. H. 764/1362 C. E. in a small village near Damietta. When his father, a miller, died, he was taken to Cairo. There he studied, and as a result of connections with the urban elite (he married the daughter of the Head of the Cairo Merchants) he rose in the hierarchy of the *'ulamā'* and became rich. But while many people praised him for his scholarship, one of his adversaries, al-'Aynī, attacked him by saying that his father was an illiterate peasant in Tafahna, and that after he fled to Cairo he worked as an ass-driver. And another *'ālim* said to him in the heat of a discussion: O 'Abd al-Raḥmān, did you forget your dragging wooden shoes and your small cotton turban? (*anasīta qabqābaka al-zaḥḥāf wa-'umaymataka al-quṭn'*.)[160] The second example is nearer in time to Shirbīnī, although its place is Damascus. Fatḥ Allāh al-Dādīkhī was a Damascene *qāḍī* who died in A. H. 1139/1726–7 C. E. According to Murādī once a fellow *'ālim*, Shaykh 'Abd al-Raḥmān al-Manīnī, wanted to mock him because of his rural origin. He asked him: 'How many hours is it between Dādīkh and Aleppo?' He answered immediately: 'Exactly the same as between Manīn village and Damascus'. Murādī explains that he meant: 'You too are from a village, if this is what you have in mind'. And Murādī goes on: 'The same Manīnī was asked once by a known Damascene merchant named Ibn al-Zarābīlī: "Sir, when did you take off the *zarābīl*[161] from your feet", intending to mock him for being a villager. al-Manīnī replied on the spot: "When you stopped making them and working on them".'[162]

Most probably similar frictions existed among the *'ulamā'* in seventeenth century Egypt. Moreover, we have evidence from another source that *'ulamā'* of rural origin tried to keep aloof from the fellah. In one of his books 'Abd al-Wahhāb al-Sha'rānī, who lived in Cairo in the sixteenth century, reproves people who disavow their origin. He says that he knew a *qāḍī* whose mother came from the village to visit him, and being afraid of his Cairene wife, he greeted her as he used to greet strangers. Then he said: 'Give this *fellāḥa* lunch; give this *fellāḥa* dinner', and he threatened her with complete repudiation if she disclosed that she was his mother. Sha'rānī also relates a parallel case of an *'ālim* and his rustic father.[163]

It is against this background that one has to read Shirbīnī's diatribes against the fellahs, rural dervishes and the *fuqahā' al-rīf*. As we have seen, Shirbīnī does not attack *'ulamā'* of rural origin; on the contrary, he praises them, which is only natural since he was one of them. His attacks against the fellahs are to be understood as a defence against the contempt and derision on the part of *'ulamā'* from urban families, from which he and his like suffered. Shirbīnī asserts: Although I was born in a village, my relatives are not fellahs; we have nothing to do with the village except that we do business with the fellahs and quarrel with them steadily because they do not pay us their debts; we despise the rural way of life and the inhabitants of the countryside; they are stupid and ignorant of the basic tenets of religion, as well as dirty and uncouth – in contrast with us, who cherish religion and love Cairo, its manners and its way of life. The fellahs wear rags and shabby clothes, even the *fuqahā' al-rīf* among them, while we *'ulamā'* wear rich garments of smooth wool (111:1–2). Shirbīnī stresses again and again that he likes the delicious urban way of cooking dishes, not that of the villagers. The fellah is compelled to do hard physical work, while Shirbīnī stresses his own high social position and his aversion to the unrefined rural way of life. As we have seen, Shirbīnī enumerates a long list of vices and afflictions which he ascribes to the fellah, the rural dervishes and the *fuqahā' al-rīf*; his aim is to imply that he and his like are free from these vices and should not be blamed for their rural origin.[164]

The question may of course be asked, and it has been asked, why an interpretation of Shirbīnī's work is necessary at all. Does it not suffice to state that he composed *Hazz al-quḥūf* in order to amuse his contemporaries, and do not townsmen in all cultures ridicule the peasants? There can be no doubt that Shirbīnī aimed at entertaining and amusing his fellows, but this explanation cannot be the full answer. In particular it is insufficient to interpret the serious and informative parts of the book, in which Shirbīnī realistically describes various aspects of village life. Some of these descriptions too are written in a personal vein and stress the fact that Shirbīnī has nothing to do with this way of life, but they are not amusing at all. Finally, *Hazz al-quḥūf* is the only satire on the fellah known in Arabic literary history. It is not a sample of a widespread *genre*, but a unique phenomenon. It is highly probable that its author had special motives to compose such a unique work.

NOTES

1. Būlāq, Dār al-Ṭibā'a al-'Āmira, 229 pp. and again in 1284. It was later printed in Alexandria by al-Maṭba'a al-Sa'diyya by lighography in A. H. 1289/1872 C. E. (304 pp.); by al-Maṭba'a al-Amīriyya in Cairo in A. H. 1308/1890–1 C. E.; by al-Maktaba al-Maḥmūdiyya in Cairo, with no date, based on the 1308 edition, 224 pp. (we have used this edition in our references); and by al-Maktaba al-Sharqiyya in Cairo in A. H. 1322/1904–5 C. E. (259 pp.). An expurgated version, edited by Muḥammed Qindīl al-Baqlī and called *Qaryatunā al-miṣriyya qabla al-thawra* has been published recently by Dār al Nahḍa al-'Arabiyya in Cairo (no date, introduction dated July 1963).
2. A. F. Mehren, *Et par Bidrag til Bedømmelsa af den nyere Folkeliteratur i Aegypten*, Copenhagen, 1872; K. Vollers, 'Beiträge zur Kenntnis der lebenden arabischen Sprache in Aegypten', *ZDMG*, vol. 41, 1887; F. Kern, 'Neuere ägyptische Humoristen und Satiriker', *MSOS*, vol. 9, 1906; C. Brockelmann, *GAL*, II 278, S II 387; R. A. Nicholson, *A literary history of the Arabs* (1907), Cambridge, 1941, p. 450; Ben Cheneb, 'al-Shirbīnī', *EI*²; Jurjī Zaydān, *Ta'rikh ādāb al-lugha al-'arabiyya*, Cairo, 1931, vol. 3, pp. 276–7. Short parts of the book have been reprinted in transcription or translated in A. von Kremer, *Aegypten*, Leipzig, 1863, vol. 1, pp. 56 ff.; and in W. Spitta-Bey, *Grammatik des arabischen Vulgärdialectes von Aegypten*, Leipzig, 1880, Texte: Ḥikâjât, no. VIII, pp. 469–72; no. X, pp. 481–5.
3. I understand that my friend Professor Haim Blanc is engaged in doing this. I am glad to take this opportunity to express my gratitude to him for our stimulating discussions of *Hazz al-quḥūf* and for many important hints he gave me.
4. Some hints are to be found in Ben Cheneb's and Nicholson's notes, and a number of interesting ideas concerning the literary genre of *Hazz al-quḥūf* have been expressed by Kern in his article mentioned above.
5. It is interesting to note that Jurjī Zaydān is the only author who has hitherto drawn attention to this aspect.
6. A definitive study of agrarian relations in Ottoman Egypt will have to make use of Shirbīnī's treatment of this subject. Some of this corresponds to information found in Jabartī's chronicle, but it includes also much additional material.
7. Numbers in brackets represent page numbers of the al-Maktaba al-Maḥmūdiyya edition; following the page number after the colon are numbers of lines.
8. According to Evliya Çelebi, who visited Egypt at about the time when Yūsuf al-Shirbīnī wrote his *Hazz al-quḥūf*, Shirbīn had 1,700 houses, one Friday mosque (*ulu cami*), fifty mosques and one *medrese*. Near Shirbīn there was a small place called Kafr Shirbīn with 200 houses. Cf. Evliya Çelebi Seyahatnamesi, *Mısır, Sudan, Habeş* (1672–1680), Istanbul, 1938, pp. 752–3. However, many of Evliya's figures are exaggerated.
9. On p. 158:14 of our edition A. H. 1075/1664–5 C. E. is given as the year in which he made the pilgrimage to Mecca. The same inconsistency is

found in all other editions as well.

10. 32:17 and 223:29–224:2. For biographies of Qalyūbī and Sandūbī see Muḥammad Amīn al-Muḥibbī, *Khulāṣat al-athar fī a'yān al-qarn al-ḥādī 'ashar*, Cairo, A. H. 1284, vol. 1, pp. 175 and 256–7.
11. We have found no evidence for Zaydān's claim that Shirbīnī died in A. H. 1098/1686–7 C. E. nor for the contrary assertion made by Yūsuf Sarkīs in his *Mu'jam al-maṭbū'āt al-'arabiyya wa'l-mu'arraba*, Cairo, 1928, col. 1111, viz.: *'kāna mawjūdan sanata 1099'* (1687–8). Brockelmann, and after him Nicholson, state that he 'wrote in A. H. 1098/1687 A. D.'
12. See pp. 172:20–174:7; and *GAL*, S II 387.
13. Muḥibbī, *Khulāṣat al-athar*, vol. 1, p. 256.
14. 28 out of 111 Egyptian *'ulamā'* mentioned by Muḥibbī.
15. 'Abd al-Raḥmān al-Jabartī, *'Ajā'ib al-āthār fi'l-tarājim wa'l-akhbār*, Cairo, Bulāq, A. H. 1297, vol. 1, p. 65; 'Alī Pasha Mubārak, *al-Khiṭaṭ al-tawfīqiyya al-jadīda*, Cairo-Bulāq, vol. 8, A. H. 1305, p. 22; J. Jomier, 'al-Azhar', *EI²*, col. 819.
16. 9:7–10:26, 101:8–14, 110:10–11, 19–25, 147:22–149:8, 190:7–9, 197:14–23, etc.
17. See below, Section II.
18. Jabartī, vol. 2, pp. 164–5.
19. H. Shaked, 'The biographies of 'ulamā' in Mubārak's *Khiṭaṭ* as a source for the history of the 'ulamā' in nineteenth-century Egypt', in G. Baer (ed.), *The 'ulamā' in modern history, Asian and African Studies*, vol. 7, 1971, pp. 62–3.
20. Compare the similar dictum of al-Jabartī, vol. 4, p. 208:10.
21. Cf. G. Baer, *A history of landownership in modern Egypt, 1800–1950*, London, 1962, pp. 60–1.
22. See also 5:25–26.
23. About the later Mamluk period the following has been observed: 'The ties between the ulama and the merchant class were also exceedingly close. Many ulama were part-time merchants and earned part of their living from trade while many merchants were part-time scholars and teachers.' I. M. Lapidus, *Muslim cities in the later Middle Ages*, Harvard U.P., 1967, pp. 108–9. For an *'ālim* whose economic activity is described as *ṣāra yu'āmil* see, for instance, Shams al-Dīn al-Sakhāwī, *ol-Ḍaw' al-lāmi' li-ahl al-qarn al-tāsi'*, Cairo, A. H. 1354, vol. 5, pp. 47–8.
24. E. W. Lane says that the native Muslim inhabitants of Cairo commonly called themselves *awlād al-balad* – see *The manners and customs of the modern Egyptians*, Everyman's Library, London, 1944, p. 27.
25. Mubārak uses *balda* for such towns as Minūf, which had attained 20,000 inhabitants by the end of the nineteenth century, as well as for small villages, such as Ṣanāfir whose population numbered 2,000 at the same time. See Mubārak, vol. 14, p. 47:6, and vol. 13, p. 24:17.
26. Stanford J. Shaw (ed.). *Ottoman Egypt in the eighteenth century*, Harvard Middle Eastern Monographs, VII, Cambridge, Mass., 1962, p. 16 (fol. 7a of the *Nizamname*).
27. For offshoots called *kafr* see Mubārak, *passim*. For *kufūr* which have become independent see ibid., vol. 15, pp. 5 ff. A. Boinet Bey, *Dictionnaire*

géographique de l'Egypte, Cairo, 1899, p. XIX, has the following definition: 'Centre devenu indépendant d'un village dont il a généralement conservé le nom – Bourgade, Hameau souvent à proximité du village dont il dépend.' For the geographical distribution of *kufūr* see ibid., pp. 285 ff.

28. 2:4, 11:25, 13:16, 5:7, 15:16, 25, 188:2, 7, 10, 6:23, 10:23, 20:9, 22:14, 33:20, 23–4, 54:10, and *passim*.
29. 6:22, 32:19, 36:24, 28, 37:19, 39:15, 112:6, 8, 166:2, and *passim*.
30. Cf. Mubārak, vol. 12, p. 125:21–22, 23–26.
31. I. M. Lapidus, 'Muslim cities and Islamic societies', in I. M. Lapidus (ed.), *Middle Eastern cities*, University of California Press, 1969, p. 96.
32. 6:21, 14:1, 16:7, 26:19, 29:24, 26:5, 9, 17, 27:1, 201:11, 112:6, 8, 176:6, 204:25, etc. For urban (*ḥaḍarī*) and rural (*rīfī*) ways of preparing various dishes see pp. 151 ff. Cf. note 46 below. In the seventeenth-century document from the Geniza 'Townsman and fellah' published by Professor Goitein in *Asian and African Studies*, vol. 8 (1972), no. 3, p. 257 ff, the two antagonists are the Maṣrī and the Rīfī.
33. Cf. Lapidus, *Middle Eastern cities*, pp. 70, 74, 75. The Rīfī in the Geniza text is also afraid of the soldiers he sees in Cairo (Goitein 'Townsman and fellah', 10).
34. P. Kahle, 'Das Krokodilspiel (Li'b et-Timsaḥ), ein egyptisches Schattenspiel', *Nachrichten d. K. Gesellschaft der Wissenschaften zu Göttingen, Philologisch-historische Klasse*, 1915, pp. 188–359 (especially pp. 325–35). See also G. Baer, *Egyptian guilds in modern times*, Jerusalem, 1964, p. 21 and *passim*.
35. Lapidus, *Middle Eastern cities*, pp. 70, 79.
36. Ibid., p. 78.
37. Cf. Mubārak, vol. 11, p. 72:35–36.
38. Cf. Jabartī, vol. 4, p. 208:4.
39. Cf. ibid., line 9.
40. The place where the *multazim* and the *mushidd* administer their business, see 12:28, 197:25–27. The contrast between urban and rural building was mentioned right in the beginning of the disputation between the Maṣrī and the Rīfī published by Goitein.
41. Mubārak, vol. 9, p. 17:22; vol. 10, pp. 30:9, 39:12, 84:21; vol. 11, p. 84:12; vol. 12, p. 129:19; vol. 14, p. 67:22; etc.
42. Ibid., vol. 12, pp. 9:33–34, 51:31.
43. 5:19, 10:21, 8:23, 61:22–23, 6:17, 37:3. A striking difference between towns and villages in the way people dressed was observed by Leo Africanus who visited Egypt in 1517. See Jean-Léon L'Africain, *Description de l'Afrique*, Paris, 1956, vol. 2, pp. 490, 514. Cf. Goitein, 'Townsman and fellah', (5) and (6).
44. 5:20, 32:23, 37:3, 6:10–11. The Maṣrī in the Geniza text published by Goitein says (7): 'In the *rīf* even the fortunate walks barefoot'.
45. 5:18, 13:22, 70:5–6.
46. This subject is treated by Shirbīnī in great detail and his observations should be of interest to the ethnologist and anthropologist. See 151:19–152:18, 153:23–156:7, 165:1–19, 168:15–169:7, 172:2–15, 188:1–10, 209:11–15, 21. See also Goitein, 'Townsman and fellah' (11).

47. 19:12–13, 20:15, 197:23–27, 198:1–2. This aspect of the difference between townsmen and villagers is mentioned in detail in the Geniza text of the disputation between the Maṣrī and the Rīfī published by Professor Goitein. The Rīfī disapproves of the city because 'the stench from the restroom remains with you' (2), while the Maṣrī praises Maṣr because there he can visit the bathhouse, 'thus remaining always clean' (5).
48. 6:16, 10:21, 13:20–21, 20:22–25, 31:1–3, 37:29–38:1, 43:27–28, 83:28–84:3.
49. 5:29, 6:2, 10:22, 44:3. Cf. Leo Africanus, p. 490; and see *iswidād al-wajh* as a typical trait of the fellah in Ḥijāzī's poem quoted below, n. 66.
50. I. M. Lapidus in Lapidus, *Middle Eastern cities*, pp. 64–7. See also Lapidus, *Muslim cities in the later Middle Ages*, p. 90 n.
51. Lapidus, *Middle Eastern cities*, p. 56.
52. See Jabartī, vol. 1, p. 190:25–26, for a *shaykh al-balad* who sent his son as a hostage to the *multazim* because he was unable to pay the taxes (middle of the eighteenth century).
53. The son of the *shaykh al-balad* mentioned by Jabartī (see note 52) returned home as soon as his father had paid the taxes. Only his companion, an orphan, remained with the *multazim* and later had an extraordinary career.
54. Cf. P. M. Holt, *Egypt and the Fertile Crescent 1516–1922*, London, 1966, pp. 71 ff., on political instability.
55. See Baer, *Egyptian guilds*, pp. 4–6.
56. For the description of the *jarrāfa* see Stanford J. Shaw, *The financial and administrative organization and development of Ottoman Egypt 1517–1798*, Princeton, 1962, p. 228 (quoting Lancret).
57. See 20:9–21:5 for the story of the three villagers who tried to acquire power by conversing in 'Turkish'. See also 23:27–24:2. In another story the Egyptian passengers on a Nile boat between Shirbīn and Cairo hide a youth who was fleeing from his Mamluk masters without asking the reasons for his flight and even lead his pursuers astray (130:27–131:13).
58. For a description of the *'awna* see also Jabartī, vol. 4, p. 207:17–20. According to Shaw, *The financial and administrative organization*, pp. 20–1, 22–3, the cultivation of the *multazim's ūsiyya* by forced labour was an innovation of the seventeenth century. Shirbīnī may have indicated this by saying that all additional burdens to the payment of a small land-tax did not exist 'in former times' (*fī al-zaman al-mutaqaddim*) (141:19–24). The *'awna* is mentioned by Shirbīnī frequently – see 6:25, 21:6–8, 35:21–2, 144:14–145:6, 145:25–26.
59. To the best of my knowledge this term does not appear in any other source on rural life or agrarian relations in Ottoman Egypt. Probably it is identical with what Jabartī calls *kulfa* (pl. *kulaf*) – see vol. 2, pp. 133:24–25, 141:3–4, 154:3, 179:26–27; vol. 3, pp. 13–32, 199:15; vol. 4, pp. 63:31, 109:19.
60. See also 141:20–24, where Shirbīnī states that 'formerly' this obligation of the fellah did not exist.
61. 122:20–23. It should be noted that Shirbīnī considered riots and revolts of fellahs an actual possibility. So did Muḥammad 'Alī a century and a half

later; his *qānūn al-filāḥa* provided for the case of an armed revolt by a whole village or even a group of villages (cf. G. Baer, *Studies in the social history of modern Egypt*, Chicago, 1969, p. 98). Apparently Egyptians acquainted with the countryside believed in the myth of 'the submissiveness of the Egyptian fellah' as little in the seventeenth century as they did in the nineteenth.'

62. It must be pointed out, however, that Westernization primarily affected the towns and therefore again widened the gulf between town and countryside during a certain period in modern times. See ch. 2 below.
63. For relations between village and town since the beginning of the nineteenth century see G. Baer, *Studies in the social history of modern Egypt*, *passim*.
64. *Dawār* is the manor-house of the *multazim*, where crops and utensils were stored and the *multazim*'s agents and workers lived. Cf. Mubārak, vol. 12, p. 95:33. Many additional examples in Mubārak's encyclopedia show that the *dawār* served also to accommodate guests.
65. Cf. the old German verse:
Der Bauer ist an Ochsen statt
nur dass er keine Hörner hat.
66. Jabartī, vol. 4, pp. 68:30–32, 208: 5–12. For the biography of Ḥasan al-Badrī al-Ḥijāzī see Jabartī, vol. 1, p. 75:5 ff.
67. 15:11–13; see also 14:3, 22:29–23:2, and 24:11–13. Fellahs of Upper Egypt consider the inhabitants of the Delta to be greedy and stingy. Cf. H. A. Winkler, *Ägyptische Volkskunde*, Stuttgart, 1936, pp. 117, 122.
68. 29:1–6; see also 6:16, 85:17 and 14:29–15:1.
69. H.A. R. Gibb and Harold Bowen, *Islamic society and the West*, vol. 1, part 2, London 1957, pp. 184–5; Mubārak, vol. 12, pp. 128:25–27, 127:20–21.
70. Cf. also 86:22. For the neglect of prayer and disregard of the *sharī'a* by the extreme Ṣūfī orders see, for instance, A. Mez, *Die Renaissance des Islams*, Heidelberg, 1922, pp. 275–6.
71. On the importance of the *madhāhib* in Egypt's urban society at that time see below. Mubārak, vol. 4, p. 69:24–26 says that a member of the Bayyūmiyya order, when asked about his *madhhab*, would answer: '*madhhabī Bayyūmī*'. The fierce wars between the two factions among the fellahs, Sa'd and Ḥarām, and their bloody and destructive results, are vividly described by Shirbīnī in various parts of his *Hazz al-quḥūf*. In contrast with some other sources on this subject Shirbīnī makes it indubitably clear that not only artisans and nomads, but also, and perhaps predominantly, fellahs were divided into these two factions. Cf. P. M. Holt, 'Al-Jabartī's introduction to the history of Ottoman Egypt', *BSOAS*, vol. 25, 1962, pp. 38–51. By the way, this is corroborated by Mubārak, vol. 12, pp. 116–35–117:1, and vol. 13, pp. 41:23–6. Cf. also General Reynier, *State of Egypt after the battle of Heliopolis*, London, 1802, p. 58 ('The families of Fellahs and the villages are attached to one or other of these leagues'). In addition we learn from Shirbīnī that in the fights the fellahs used the name of the faction to which they belonged as a war-cry: '*yā Sa'd, yā Ḥarām.*' Cf. Jabartī, vol. 1, p. 21:29–30. For Shirbīnī's

treatment of Sa'd and Ḥarām see 5:20–23, 21:14, 84:21–24, and 87:8.

72. See also 175:12. For the deification of al-Bayyūmī by the followers of his order see Mubārak, vol. 4, p. 69:25. Cf. G. Jacob, *Beiträge zur Kenntnis des Derwisch-Ordens der Bektaschis*, Berlin, 1908, p. 2: 'Der Heilige erfreut sich auch bei den Orthodoxen eines solchen Ansehens, dass er nicht selber in die Vorwürfe einbezogen wird, die man gegen den von ihm angeblich gestifteten Derwisch Orden erhob.' (Quoted by G. Moriah, *The social structure of the Ṣūfī associations in Egypt in the 18th century*. Unpublished Ph.D. Thesis, University of London, 1963, p. 343).
73. For Ḥijāzī's poem see Jabartī, vol. 1, p. 78:30–79:2. On al-Ḥijāzī see above and note 66. Jabartī's own criticism of the *mawlids* is very similar to that of Shirbīnī and Ḥijāzī. For references, and discussion of this subject in general see M. Winter, 'The mawlids in Egypt from the beginning of the eighteenth century to the middle of the twentieth century', in G. Baer (ed.), *The 'Ulamā and problems of religion in the Muslim world. Studies in memory of Professor Uriel Heyd*. The Magnes Press, Jerusalem, 1971 (in Hebrew), pp. 79–103, especially pp. 80–83.
74. Gibb and Bowen, p. 188. Damietta was one of the original centres of the Qalenderiyya – See *Handwörterbuch des Islam*, Leiden, 1941, p. 265.
75. *Kitāb al-dhakhā'ir wa'l-tuḥaf fī bīr al-ṣanā'i' wa'l-ḥiraf*, Landesbibliothek Gotha, Arabische Handschrift No. 903, fols. 111a–112a. Cf. Baer, *Egyptian guilds*, pp. 2–3. On the *dawār* see above, n. 64, but it is not clear what is meant by *bilād al-dawār* in the Gotha MS. A possible explanation may be the countryside, i.e. where the *multazims* have their *dawārs*. On the shaving of beards among the extreme dervishes see also Mez, p. 274.
76. Cf. Jabartī, vol. 3, pp. 39–40; vol. 4, pp. 64:17 ff.; 120:17 ff.; Mubārak, vol. 4, p. 69:24; Mez, p. 274.
77. Lane, pp. 251–3. One of the principal precepts of a Ṣūfī shaykh of Shirbīn mentioned by Mubārak was *al-shiḥādha* (asking for alms). Mubārak, vol. 12, p. 127:19.
78. Gibb and Bowen, p. 202.
79. See also 81:14–26, 197:3–11; Jabartī, vol. 3, p. 40:7–8; Mez, p. 275.
80. Nicholson, p. 450; Vollers, p. 370.
81. For examples see pp. 43 ff., 114:8 f., 190:18–191:5, and *passim*. Since we are not concerned here with the literary analysis of *Hazz al-quḥūf* we cannot explore this most amusing and delightful aspect of Shirbīnī's book.
82. Cf. Lane, p. 61, n. 1.
83. Cf. ibid., p. 121.
84. Cf. Lapidus, *Middle Eastern cities*, pp. 50–51. Even a foreign visitor to Egypt at the time of the Ottoman conquest was impressed by the importance of the *madhhab* for the religious and social structure of Egyptian towndwellers. See Leo Africanus, vol. 2, pp. 517–18.
85. This seems to be an old anecdote frequently told in Arabic literature. Cf. Kern in *MSOS* (cf. n. 2), p. 38.
86. Cf. Lane, p. 118; Gotha *MS*, fol. 48a. On relations between *'ulamā'* in general and *qāḍīs* in the Arab provinces of the Ottoman Empire see Gibb and Bowen, pp. 132–3.

87. There may be a connection between the fact that most of Egypt's *qāḍis* spoke Turkish (cf. Lane, p. 116 and Gibb and Bowen, p. 122) and Shirbīnī's accusation that they had homosexual inclinations: the author of the Gotha MS, too, accuses the Turks of being sodomites. See Baer, *Egyptian guilds*, p. 14 and n. 61.
88. 148:10–13, 154:21–23, 168:27–28, 172:8–10.
89. Nūr al-Dīn Abū al-Ḥasan 'Alī b. Sūdūn, *Nuzhat al-nufūs wa muḍḥik al-'abūs*. For details see Kern in *MSOS*, pp. 31–6.
90. E. Littmann, 'Arabic Humor', *The Princeton University Bulletin*, No. 5, 1902, p. 5.
91. Kern, *MSOS*, pp. 39–42.
92. Cf. H. Wangelin, *Das arabische Volksbuch vom König aẓ-Ẓâhir Baibars*, Stuttgart, 1936, pp. 150, 156, 207.
93. Bayle St. John, *Village life in Egypt*, London, 1852, vol. 2, pp. 196–7.
94. Cf. Jacob M. Landau, *Studies in the Arab Theatre and Cinema*, Philadelphia, 1958, pp. 17 ff. G. Jacob, *Geschichte des Schattentheaters*, Berlin, 1907, pp. 34–75.
95. See Landau, pp. 9–47, *passim*.
96. See references in note 94, and G. Jacob, *Der Leuchtturm von Alexandria, ein arabisches Schattenspiel aus dem mittelalterlichen Ägypten*, Stuttgart, 1930.
97. P. Kahle, 'Das Krokodilspiel (Li'b et-Timsaḥ)' (see above, n. 34).
98. See E. Littmann, *Arabische Märchen und Schwänke aus Ägypten*, Wiesbaden, 1955, pp. 104 (no. 30), 108 (no. 39); 106 (no. 36).
99. Vollers, *ZDMG* (see above, n. 2), p. 370.
100. Muḥibbī, *Khulāṣat al-athar*, vol. 1, p. 256; Mubārak, vol. 12, p. 57.
101. One of the very few Egyptian authors who mentioned the book at all was Jurjī Zaydān (see above note 2). Zaydān dealt with Shirbīnī in eight lines, pointing out that his book included interesting social aspects, but he added that in our age writers detest expressions such as those found in Shirbīnī's book (probably meaning the obscenities). Thus he intended to explain the lack of interest in *Hazz al-quḥūf.*
102. Aḥmad Amīn, *Qāmūs al-'ādāt wa'l-taqālīd wa'l-ta'ābīr al-miṣriyya*, Cairo, 1953, pp. 310–11, Cf. also, e.g., pp. 413–14. Even before this, Aḥmad Amīn had already written a short note on Shirbīnī's book. The note was called 'Dumya fī dimna', and was republished in his collection *Fayḍ al-khāṭir*, vol. 3, 6th ed., 1965, pp. 101–6. I am grateful to Professor Haim Blanc for having drawn my attention to this note.
103. Dr. 'Abd al-Laṭīf Ḥamza, *al-Adab al-miṣrī min qiyām al-dawla al-ayyūbiyya ilā majī' al-ḥamla al-firansiyya*, Cairo, n.d., p. 209 ff.
104. Dr. Shawqī Ḍayf, *al-Fukāha fī miṣr*, n.p., n.d., pp. 91–9.
105. Aḥmad Rushdī Ṣāliḥ, *Funūn al-adab al-sha'bī*, Cairo, 1956, p. 43.
106. Nafūsa Zakariyyā Sa'īd, *Ta'rīkh al-da'wa ilā al-'āmmiyya wa'āthāruhā fī miṣr*, Alexandria, 1964, pp. 240–9. For this reference too I am indebted to Professor Haim Blanc.
107. Muḥammad Qandīl al-Baqlī (ed.), *Qaryatunā al-miṣriyya qabl al-thawra* 1. *Hazz al-quḥūf fi sharḥ qaṣīd Abū Shādūf* li'l-'allāma al-Shaykh Yūsuf al-Shirbīnī, Cairo, n.d. (introductions dated July 1963), 350 pp.

108. 'Abd al-Jalīl Ḥasan, 'Ṣawt al-ṣāmitīn ya'lū', *al-Kātib*, August, 1964, pp. 134–43.
109. Muḥammad 'Abd al-Ghanī Ḥasan, *al-Fallāḥ fī al-adab al-'arabī*, Cairo, 1965 (al-Maktaba al-Thaqāfiyya, no. 128), pp. 139–44.
110. Ḥasan Muḥassib, *Qaḍiyyat al-fallāḥ fī al-qiṣṣa al-miṣriyya*, Cairo, 1971 (al-Maktaba al-Thaqāfiyya, no. 256), pp. 15–22.
111. 'Abd al-Raḥmān 'Abd al-Raḥīm, 'Dirāsa naṣṣiyya li-kitāb Hazz al-quḥūf fi sharḥ qaṣīdat [*sic*] Abī-Shādūf', *al-Majalla al-Miṣriyya li'l-Dirāsāt al-Ta'rīkhiyya*, vol. 20, 1973, pp. 287–316 (English translation in *JESHO*, vol. 18, pt. 3, October 1975, pp. 245–270).
112. Anwar 'Abd al-Malik, 'al-Arḍ wa'l-fallāḥ fī ta'rīkhinā', *al-Masā'*, 28 August 1958.
113. al-Jumhūriyya al-'Arabiyya al-Muttaḥida, *Mashrū'mīthāq 21 Māyu 1962*, p. 38, Cf. also Adīb Dīmitrī, 'al-Thawra wa'l-ta'līm', *al-Kātib*, November 1966, p. 45.
114. Fatḥī 'Abd al-Fattāḥ, 'Kayfa yumkin daf'al-'amal al-siyāsī fī al-qarya al-miṣriyya', *al-Kātib*, February 1966, pp. 131–2.
115. 'Abd al-Jalīl Ḥasan, p. 134; Baqlī, p. 9.
116. 'Abd al-Jalīl Ḥasan, ibid.
117. *Mashrū' al-mīthāq*, p. 22.
118. Baqlī, p. 9; Muḥassib, p. 18; 'Abd al-Jalīl Ḥasan, p. 139.
119. 'Abd al-Raḥīm, p. 305.
120. Baqlī, p. 6 (Dr. 'Īsā's introduction).
121. Ḥamza, p. 40.
122. Amīn, p. 311. On the other hand, in the above-mentioned article (*Fayḍ al-khāṭir*, vol. 3, p. 105) Amīn condemns Shirbīnī for not having understood that social factors had caused the fellah's calamities.
123. 'Abd al-Raḥīm, pp. 297–8, 301, 302, 307, 311, 314.
124. Baqlī, pp. 607.
125. 'Abd al-Raḥīm, p. 305.
126. See e.g. Ghālī Shukrī, 'Buṭūlat al-muqāwama fī turāthina al-sha'bī', *al-Ṭalī'a*, December 1967, pp. 92–105, especially the conclusion on p. 105.
127. Baqlī, pp. 708 (Dr. 'Īsā's introduction).
128. Ṣāliḥ, p. 43; *'tilka al-sukhriyya kānat ta'bīran 'an al-sukht 'alā tilka al-ḥāl al-bā'isa allatī kābadahā al-fallāḥ qarnan ba'da qarn'*.
129. Baqlī, p. 7: *'ka'adāt tanfīs 'an kabt 'amīq lā yaqdir ṣāḥibuhu an yuwājih al-wāqi' al-ijtimā'ī bi'asālīb iṣlāḥiyya bannā'a'*.
130. Amīn, p. 311; cf. *Fayḍ al-khāṭir*, vol. 3, p. 105.
131. Baqlī, pp. 6–7 (Dr. 'Īsā's introduction); Shawqī Ḍayf, p. 92.
132. 'Abd al-Raḥīm, p. 301 (and see also p. 307). The English translation is 'Abd al-Raḥīm's.
133. 'Abd al-Jalīl Ḥasan, p. 137.
134. G. Baer, *Egyptian guilds*, pp. 14–15.
135. See, e.g., Jabartī, vol. 1, p. 373.
136. 'Wa'l-majhūd alladhī yabdhiluhu al-sayyid Muḥammad Qandīl al-Baqlī huwa takhlīṣ "Hazz al-Quḥūf fī sharḥ qaṣīd Abī Shādūf" min al-shawā'ib allatī yamujjuhā al-dhawq al-salīm' – Baqlī, p. 8 (Dr. 'Īsā's introduction).

137. Shirbīnī, 2:10–19, 5:18–20, 20:9, 22:14, 219:4–220:16 and many other places.
138. Ibid., 2–3:17, 5:7–14, 11:19–12:4, 84:18–19, 147:22, 159:9, 155:11–12. These are only examples; the number of omissions of this kind is much larger.
139. Ibid., 31–40; compare Baqlī, pp. 60–68.
140. 'Abd al-Jalīl Ḥasan, pp. 135, 137.
141. Ibid., pp. 136, 138, 139, 140; Muḥassib, pp. 15, 19, 22; and, in a more general and moderate way, 'Abd al-Ghanī Ḥasan, p. 141.
142. 'Abd al-Ghanī Ḥasan, pp. 140–1.
143. Muḥassib, pp. 17, 19.
144. Shirbīnī, p. 2.
145. 'Abd al-Raḥīm, pp. 297–9, 303. English formulation according to 'Abd al-Raḥīm's translation of his article.
146. Shirbīnī, pp. 3–4.
147. 'Abd al-Jalīl Ḥasan, p. 139.
148. Muḥassib, pp. 18–20.
149. This has been pointed out even by Dr. 'Abd al-Raḥīm, who in addition proved that 'part' of the verses attributed by Shirbīnī to Abū Shadūf were composed by Shirbīnī himself. Nevertheless he concludes (without proof) that Abū Shādūf really existed. See 'Abd al-Raḥīm, pp. 292–4. Ḥamza (p. 210) is more cautious: he says that Shirbīnī 'claimed' in his book that a villager named Abū Shādūf composed a poem describing the fellah. But even Aḥmad Amīn had already considered the possibility that 'perhaps' Shirbīnī himself had composed Abū Shādūf's poems (*Fayḍ al-khāṭir*, vol. 3, p. 102); similarly, Shawqī Ḍayf assumes that this was the case (*al-Fukāha fī Miṣr*, p. 91).
150. Shirbīnī, pp. 90, 93; 'Abd al Raḥīm, p. 294.
151. Shirbīnī, pp. 113, 119, 144, 181, 189, 209.
152. Cf. ibid., pp. 99–144, with Aḥmad Rushdī Ṣāliḥ, *al-Adab al-sha'bī*, Cairo, 2nd ed., 1955, p. 65.
153. See verses of Abū Shādūf's poem, Shirbīnī, pp. 159, 174, 185, 193, 197, 200.
154. Ibid., p. 206 (*wa asriq min al-jāmi' zarabīn 'idda – wa-ākul bihā min shahwatī fī al-rīf*).
155. Ibid., pp. 128, 144.
156. Ibid., pp. 113, 119.
157. For the eleventh and twelfth centuries (though not specifically relating to Egypt) see Lapidus, *Middle Eastern cities*, p. 56 and n. 10.
158. Mubārak, vol. 8, pp. 34, 51 f. vol. 9 pp. 66, 94, 95, 96; vol. 10, pp. 5, 52–3, 74, 75; vol. 11, pp. 34–5, 73; vol. 12, pp. 6, 46, 51, 144; vol. 13, p. 63; vol. 14, pp. 50 67, 70, 93–4; vol. 15, pp. 7, 35, 78; vol. 16, pp. 50, 66, 69, 70, 71, 72–3, 78, 84; vol. 17, pp. 9, 66.
159. See Shaked in *The 'ulamā' in modern history*, p. 61 (cf. above n. 19). Cf. von Kremer, *Aegypten*, vol. 2, pp. 94–5: 'Die mohammedanische Geistlichkeit rekrutiert sich häufig aus dem Bauernstande'.
160. Sakhāwī, *al-Ḍaw' al-lāmi'*, vol. 4, pp. 98–100.
161. *Zarbūl*, pl. *zarābīl*, 'ce n'est plus la chaussure des esclaves, mais celle des

chaikhs de village, qui en sont très vains'. Dozy, *Supplément*, I, 584.

162. Abū al-Faḍl Muḥammad Khalīl al-Murādī, *Silk al-durar fī a'yān al-qarn al-thānī'ashar*, Cairo-Būlāq, 1301, vol. 3, p. 276.
163. 'Abd al-Wahhāb al-Sha'rānī, *Lawāqiḥ al-anwār al-qudsiyya fī bayān al-'uhūd al-mūḥammadiyya*, Cairo, A. H. 1381/1961 C. E., p. 576. I am indebted to Dr. Michael Winter for this reference.
164. An amusing episode told by Bayle St. John in his *Village life in Egypt* seems to parallel our explanation of the motivation for the composition of *Hazz al-quḥūf.* Once the author took with him to the pyramids a 'fellah servant' from Tanta. The other servants mocked and teased 'Tantawi', and one of them told a story in which a Tantawi barber is ridiculed. To defend himself, 'Tantawi' on his part told a story deprecating the stupidity of the inhabitants of a village near Tanta called Kafr al-Ḥamīr, the Village of Asses. Bayle St. John, vol. 2, pp. 198–219.

2

VILLAGE AND CITY IN EGYPT AND SYRIA – 1500–1914

Introduction

In an important study published a few years ago, Ira Lapidus attempted to show that the conviction that city and country in Islamic society are radically opposed is exaggerated and misleading.[1] Professor Lapidus dealt in his study with all three aspects of the relation between town and country which will form the conceptual framework of this paper: (a) similarity or difference, (b) contact or isolation, and (c) conflicts or integration between towns and villages (although his argument is altogether differently structured). Concerning the first aspect, he says that in fact town quarters were village-like communities within the urban whole. Settlements of all types, from the largest metropolises to the smallest towns and villages, were clusters of distinct physical and social units. In many situations, no absolute distinction between urban and rural habitats could be drawn. Places called villages by the geographers very often had pronounced urban features. Villages were sites of periodic markets and fairs as well as centres of cloth manufacturing. Similarly, they were not deprived of the spiritual facilities of towns, such as Ṣūfī convents or Friday mosques. Villages with varied activities had differentiated populations, including landowners, *'ulamā'*, merchants and artisans. On the other hand, cities often had an agricultural component, and suburbs were used for gardening and other forms of agriculture. The composite settlements called towns included many people who differed little in their attitudes, mores, and manner of life from rural people. True, in some instances we find towns organized into religious or ethnic communities differing from rural religious (or ethnic) groups. But such urban-rural divisions were evidently exceptions to the rule of religious-communal bonds between town dwellers and the peoples of their hinterlands.

It would seem to us that there are four kinds of contact between towns and villages which should be discussed in the context of our subject: economic, political-administrative, religious-cultural contact, and contact resulting from the movement of rural people to towns (or vice versa). Economic contact between town and village is seen by Professor Lapidus mainly as landowning interests which bound village to urban families. In various countries, landowning families, who were part of the cities' bourgeoisie, resided in the villages. Political and administrative ties are not discussed. As against this, religious and cultural ties between town and village constitute a major theme of Lapidus's study. The establishment of such ties was brought about first and foremost within the framework of the Muslim schools of law, the *madhāhib*. These schools were built around the more or less formally organized *'ulamā'* study groups and reached out to include the populace at large. Family ties, and the close association of the *'ulamā'* with all quarters and classes of the population bound the people to the schools and created communities beyond parochial quarters. Moreover, the schools of law were not exclusively urban bodies: their jurisdictions extended to rural areas as well. Reciprocally, the populace of rural areas identified with and looked to the town-centred schools for social and judicial leadership. In addition, rural families often sent their sons to be educated in the cities and to dwell in the *madrasas*. Many students remained in the cities, but others returned to their villages to become prayer leaders, notaries, and judges, and to carry on local Muslim life. This, however, was not the only channel of movement between town and country. Suburban districts used to be composed of people of recent village or bedouin origin. Besides agriculturists, migrants fleeing rural hardship or looking for temporary work came to the cities. Many villagers or nomads settled there permanently, forming quarters or suburbs of their own, while others fell into an unassimilated mass of lumpen-proletarians. Among the middle and upper classes were people who came from village families to study in the *madrasas* of the capitals.

Finally, in his discussion of conflicts between town and village Lapidus states that social struggles were not formed on urban-rural lines. Village-city differences resembled conflicts between city quarters, between neighbouring villages, and conflicts which united city dwellers and villagers against other parties similarly composed. Again stress is laid on religious identification, which drew the population of a region into a single interlocking social body. Even when communal conflict was simultaneously 'urban-rural' conflict, the 'urban-rural' can still be viewed as a special variation: there were no geographically defined communities in the Muslim world. Similarly, *zu'ar* gangs (young toughs) were also found in the surrounding villages and were sometimes allied with the *zu'ar* of the city proper. In short, cities were physical entities, but not unified social bodies in contrast to villages.

It is not at all the aim of this paper to disprove the conclusions of Professor Lapidus, who studied the core regions of the Muslim world from the late tenth to the fifteenth centuries, and in particular Aleppo and Damascus in the Mamluk period.[2] What we intend to do is to show that conditions in other periods brought about a pattern of relations between town and country which was considerably different from that described in the study of Professor Lapidus. Such conditions were prevalent in Egypt and Syria during most of the Ottoman period.

Ottoman Egypt

In Ottoman Egypt people definitely drew a clear distinction between the physical character of rural and urban habitats. According to Shirbīnī,[3] town houses were high, used much wood, and their walls were overlaid with plaster and lime. They were built of red brick and cut stone. Only in towns were baked bricks used for building.[4] As against this, village houses were built of mud and dung. Even two centuries later, 'Alī Mubārak clearly distinguishes between rural and urban types of houses: houses in villages generally had one storey, and only in exceptional cases he specially mentions that some of the houses of a certain village were higher than rural houses in general or were plastered like those of the chief towns of provinces.[5] Similarly, in a disputation between the Maṣrī and the Rīfī – a Geniza text from the seventeenth century published by Professor S. D. Goitein[6] – the glaring contrast between the appearance of urban and rural houses and streets is stressed.

Like houses and streets, there was a marked difference in dress and food between fellahs and townsmen. According to Shirbīnī, fellahs wore rags or dirty and shabby clothes, and all villagers went about barefoot. Similarly, the Maṣrī and Rīfī in the Geniza text agree that townsmen wore clean shirts and turbans, while fellahs wore linen *qubṭiyyas* and woollen *jubbas*. Moreover, in the *rīf* even the fortunate walks barefoot.[7] Fellahs eat meat only on holidays, never eat butter, and none of the pastries specially favoured by townsmen, such as *kunāfa*; foodstuffs are prepared in a primitive and coarse manner in villages, while urban dishes are much more delicate.[8]

It may well be that in Ottoman Egypt too towns included people who differed little in their attitudes, mores, and manner of life from rural people. Nevertheless, Egyptian authors who lived in the Ottoman period had a clear notion that there was a distinction between a typically rural and a typically urban culture. In his autobiography *Laṭā'if al-minan*, 'Abd al-Wahhāb al-Sha'rānī (died 1565) thanks God for 'my migration, by the Prophet's blessing, from the countryside to Cairo, for his transferring me from the region of roughness and ignorance to the city of gentleness and knowledge'.[9] Shirbīnī states that the eating habits of fellahs are unrefined and vulgar (and explains in detail what he means); fellahs do not clean themselves and are coarse and unrefined in their personal hygiene and sexual habits; moreover, they have no idea about ritual cleanliness. One of the most important cultural differences between town and country was the complete ignorance of fellahs compared with some knowledge at least to be found among all townspeople. Fellahs were ignorant even of the basic precepts of Islam; they did not care for prayer or religion, and did not even know the most elementary customs and instructions concerning prayers.[10]

In this connection another conspicuous difference between town and village should be mentioned: urban women veiled their faces whenever they passed a place where they could be seen by a stranger. As against this, fellah women did not wear a veil. The following report shows that Egyptians were conscious of this clear-cut difference between village and town. Up to the 1820s al-Fashn (Minyā province, Middle Egypt) was considered to be a village (*kānat mulḥaqa bi'l – aryāf*), but Aḥmad Pasha Ṭāhir, who was appointed *mudīr* of Middle Egypt at that time, initiated an intensive building activity in this place and tried to introduce urban customs (*rataba fīhā 'awā'id mustaḥsana mimmā fī'l-banādir*). Thus he prohibited the sitting of women in the streets or their walking about without veils (*mana'a julūs al-nisā' fī'l-ḥārāt wa-khurūjahunna makshūfāt*).[11]

Egyptian villages in the Ottoman period, as in earlier times, were not deprived of Ṣūfī convents or Friday mosques, but one cannot say this with regard to all spiritual facilities of towns in general. In particular institutions of learning were completely absent from the village. Even in the 1870s, after Muḥammad 'Alī's and Ismā'īl's intensive educational activity, less than five per cent of Egypt's rural settlements had Qur'ān schools (*maktab*; see below). In Ottoman Egypt this percentage must have been even lower, and all institutions above Qur'ān school level were in towns.

In addition, the town's function as the exclusive administrative centre distinguished it clearly from the village. Soldiers, *multazims* and their stewards – in short, anybody belonging to the ruling establishment of Ottoman Egypt – lived in the town. Since these rulers and soldiers were often Turks or, more generally, from non-Arab ethnic origin, and since all kinds of non-Sunni and non-Arabic speaking *'ulamā'* or merchants lived in towns only (or passed through them), the town was the only place where people of different cultural background met. 'Cultural heterogeneity is certainly an urban characteristic and surely an essential ingredient of urbanism is the coexistence, in a densely populated small area, of many possible bands in the cultural spectrum.'[12] For Ottoman Egypt this certainly is an appropriate statement. But was it not true, as Lapidus pointed out for towns of the later Middle Ages, that villages with varied activities had differentiated populations, including landowners, *'ulamā'*, merchants, and artisans? In order to answer this question, each of these elements should be considered separately.

It would seem that in Ottoman Egypt *'ulamā'* were not at all a typical component of the village population. Quite a considerable proportion of them were of village origin, but since villages in general lacked those educational and judicial institutions which were the centres of the *'ulamā'*'s activity, most of them remained in town after the conclusion of their studies. Shirbīnī even advises men of learning not to dwell in a village lest they lose their learning (*lā taskun al-qarya fayaḍī'a 'ilmuka*). The only people in the village engaged in activities connected with religion (reciting the Qur'ān, teaching in Qur'ān schools, arranging marriage contracts, acting as *imām*s or *khaṭīb*s, and in general, answering all questions of fellahs on religion) were the so-called *fuqahā' al-rīf* – according to Shirbīnī an utterly primitive, ignorant and stupid lot who should not be mixed up with the *'ulamā'*.[13]

The consideration of the other three elements – landowners, merchants and artisans – leads us to the discussion of the economic differences, and in turn, the economic contact and connection, between towns and villages in Ottoman Egypt. To begin with landowners, there were none in the strict meaning of the term. With the exception of urban real estate and some grants (*rizaq*) which had not yet been converted into *waqfs* (*rizaq aḥbāsiyya*), the land theoretically belonged to the state and it was the custom that the tilling of a certain plot passed from father to son, though fellahs had no right in law to inherit the land their fathers had tilled. The levying of the land tax was farmed out to tax farmers (sing. *multazim*), who ruled the village or villages made over to them (*iltizām*), and exacted from them forced labour on particular plots tilled for their own private income (*ūsiyya*). Therefore they were sometimes called 'proprietors', especially by some of the French savants and administrators during Napoleon's expedition to Egypt. Proprietors or not, the *multazim*s definitely did not live in their villages but visited the villages only from time to time in order to collect the imposts. Shirbīnī says: '*iltazama ba'ḍ al-umarā' biqarya min qurā al-rīf fasāfara ilayhā liyanẓura aḥwālahā kamā huwa 'ādat al-multazimīn*'. (Fellāhs came to town in order to arrange something with their *multazim*).[14] According to de Chabrol, one of Bonaparte's savants, 'les membres du gouvernement des Mamlouks sont devenus propriétaires de presque toute l'Egypte: ils ont au moins les deux tiers des terrains cultivables.'[15] In addition to Mamluks, members of the Ottoman military units (*ocak*s), even those who were not Mamluks, were also absentee *multazim*s, living in the town: when they levied the taxes 'they sent' (a tax-collector) to their *iltizāms* (*arsalū ilā ḥiṣaṣihim yuṭālibūna al-fallāḥīn bimā 'alayhim mīn al-kharāj*).[16] At the end of the eighteenth century *iltizāms* were acquired also by members of the Cairo *'ulamā'* and merchant families al-Jawharī, Mahdī, Sharāyibī, and others.[17] The only non-urban *multazims* were Beduin shaykhs.

We have seen that although villages were not deprived of Ṣūfī convents and Friday mosques, they lacked 'the whole range of different kinds of religious buildings.'[18] Similarly one may say that, although merchants and artisans formed part of the village population, these merchants and artisans were occupied in a limited number of branches while the whole range of commerce and manufacture was found in cities only. At least one half of the professions and branches of merchants and craftsmen mentioned in our study of the Egyptian guilds were found in towns only and not in villages.[19] Among typically urban occupations one may mention the makers and sellers of luxuries (such as coffee-merchants, makers of a great variety of drugs, furriers, gilders, glaziers, goldsmiths, jewellers, pavers in marble, sellers of spices, silk-merchants, etc.); a number of services (such as door-keepers, keepers of baths, laundry men, porters, scavengers, sewermen etc.); employees and owners of urban institutions (such as the mint, the slaughter house, coffee houses etc.); professions connected with foreigners and foreign trade (interpreters, money-changers, owners of wine shops etc.); occupations related to learning (book-sellers, book-binders, engravers of seals, petition-writers, physicians); services for the army (armorers, makers of arrows and bows, powder-makers etc.); craftsmen performing at ceremonies and for amusement (such as drummers and lamp-bearers at festivals, clowns, performers of *karagöz* and a large variety of entertainers); and many more. From the *Description de l'Egypte* and Mubārak's *Khiṭaṭ* it becomes clear that a number of industrial branches were exclusively urban, such as silk-weaving and dyeing (especially in al-Maḥalla al-Kubrā), the manufacture of fabrics for veils, the production of rosewater (mainly in Madīnat al-Fayyūm) and leather tanning (with one exception of a village very near to Asyūṭ).[20]

On the other hand, it is definitely wrong to suppose that there were no artisans in Egyptian villages (or no merchants, for that matter). On the contrary, it is surprising to find how widespread rural handicrafts were in Egypt during the Ottoman era which is considered to have been a period of economic decline. Among approximately 1,000 villages described by Mubārak in his *Khiṭaṭ*, almost 200 are said to have had some kind of handicraft or manufacture (villages with flour mills only, or installations for hatching fowls' eggs by artificial heat – *ma'mal dajāj* – have not been counted). Pottery was produced in the Ottoman period all over rural Upper Egypt, especially in Qenā province; a certain kind of jug was even called *balāṣ* after a village in that province where they were made.[21] The most widespread craft in Egyptian villages was of course spinning and weaving. At the beginning of the nineteenth century observers got the impression that in every village there were some weavers, while women and children did the spinning.[22] Spinning and weaving of all kinds of woollen fabric seem in fact to have been practised at the end of the eighteenth century in almost every village, although Fayyūm province apparently was prominent in this branch.[23] Spinning of linen was done in all villages of the Delta, especially in Minūfiyya,[24] while for weaving of linen villages in Fayyūm province, as well as in the vicinity of Ṭanṭā and Samannūd, were mentioned.[25] A fabric made of wool and linen called *shadd* was made in Qallīn village (Gharbiyya) and some other villages of the Delta.[26] Some villages near Isnā specialized in cotton spinning and weaving and sold their product to Beduins.[27] Dyeing, mainly with indigo, was concentrated in Gīza province.[28] Mats, baskets, and ropes were made from *ḥalfā* and palmleaves in villages all over Egypt, although Ṭāmya village in the Fayyūm and the villages near Minūf were outstanding in this branch.[29] In some villages there were oil-presses;[30] in others natural raw material was processed: thus lime for building and for bleaching of linen was extracted all over Upper Egypt, and sal-ammoniac in Damīra, Fāriskūr, Birinbāl, and other villages in the northern Delta.[31]

Mubārak's descriptions of many Egyptian villages include notes to say that there were 'craftsmen' (*arbāb ḥiraf*) in this or that village. However, in some cases he is more explicit and mentions tin-smiths, blacksmiths, builders, masons and carpenters. In a small number of villages there were specialized craftsmen: in Salāmūn al-Qumāsh (Daqahliyya) there were specialists in making mills, who used to go from place to place, and to repair mills;[32] carpenters from Shabās al-Shuhadā' (Gharbiyya) specialized in making *sāqiyas* (irrigation wheels) and ploughs, and in Shirbīn, a village in the same province, the blacksmiths were engaged in making nails and executing light iron work for irrigation machines.[33] The special skill of Copts in Umm Khanān (Gīza) was tinning of copper vessels (*tabyīḍ al-nuḥās*); they moved all over the country and exercised their craft.[34] And blacksmiths of Manqarīsh (Banī Suwayf) were known for their skill in making a sort of pick-axe called *ṭūriyya* (pl. *ṭawārī*).[35]

All these details show that rural craftsmen were contented with producing the basic goods needed by a fellah population with a low standard of living. 'Cette industrie se borne, dans les campagnes, aux arts de première nécessité, et à la manipulation de quelques produits du sol servant à la consommation journalière . . . les villes sont toujours le siège d'une industrie plus recherchée, qui s'occupe à transformer des matières importées du dehors en objets d'un usage plus ou moins étendu'.[36] But they also show that in Ottoman Egypt the village was not dependent on the town for supply of manufactured goods, but was able to satisfy almost all its needs itself. This is one important reason for the relatively weak economic contact and connexion between town and village in Ottoman Egypt.

The second reason for the same weakness may be seen as the other side of the same coin. While the village produced most of the manufactured goods it needed, the town produced an important part of its needs for agricultural produce. In this case Professor Lapidus' statement that 'cities often had an agricultural component . . . suburbs were often used for gardening and other forms of agriculture',[37] is certainly valid for Ottoman Egypt as well. According to Evliya Çelebi, who visited Egypt in the 1670s, there were at that time in Cairo 2,060 vegetable gardens,[38] and apparently in some of them citrus fruits were grown. At the end of the eighteenth century, rice and fruits were grown in the outskirts and gardens of Rosetta, for instance, which is shown in detail in one of the studies of the French savants.[39] Towns in Ottoman Egypt were, no doubt, the source of the vegetables and fruits consumed by them;[40] thus, the supply of the city with this kind of agricultural produce did not create a strong tie between town and village.

The supply of grain, on the other hand, came from the countryside. However, at least Cairo, where more than two-thirds of the urban population lived at that time, received its grain not in the course of commercial transactions or exchange between fellahs and townsmen, but in the form of taxes paid by Egypt's villages. Most of these taxes were delivered in kind, which is clearly shown in the documents of Bonaparte's occupation kept in the archives of the French army at Vincennes.[41] This is true not only for Upper Egypt, where at the time of the French occupation the payment in kind was estimated at four-fifths of all taxes,[42] but also for most other parts of Egypt: in the archives of the French army there is a list of villages from the Delta, Middle Egypt and Upper Egypt showing the tax arrears of these villages for the years A.H. 1212 and 1213 (1797–9) – all in kind[43] – as well as a list of owners of Nile-barges (sing. *ra'īs*), the quantity of grain each of them had delivered to the government *shūnas* (warehouses for storing crops), and the names of the villages whose taxes were paid by these deliveries. The government, Mamluk *amīr*s or other *multazims*, then sold the grain to the town-dwellers.[44]

All this does not mean that there was no trade at all between villages and towns in Ottoman Egypt. Rice-growing villages in Dimyāṭ province, for instance (with the exception of Fāriskūr), paid their taxes in cash,[45] which shows that they were able to sell their crops. Similarly, fellahs in the Fayyūm sold cotton or woollen threads which they had spun to weavers in Madīnat al-Fayyūm; and like Madīnat al-Fayyum a few other small provincial towns served as commercial centres for neighbouring villages – for instance Isnā and Mīnūf.[46] But rural-urban trade was extremely limited, and even Shirbīnī's fellahs, who came to town to sell their produce, did not buy urban goods with the proceeds: they only sold their eggs or straw in order to pay taxes. Fellahs also sold water melons and dairy products, and fellah women sold dung in Cairo.[47] It would seem that the main reasons for this limitation of domestic commercial transactions were poor communication facilities and lack of security of trade routes.[48] 'L'activité du commerce intérieur de l'Egypt ne pourrait manquer de s'accroître, si l'on rendoit praticables et sûres les diverses communications d'un lieu à un autre: mais la police ne s'étend pas au délà des marchés des villes; et les moeurs des Arabes et l'ignorance des *fellâh* n'offrent aucune garantie pour la sûreté des denrées qui traversent leur territoire. Il faut, pour obtenir cette garantie, quand les marchands voyagent par terre, qu'ils se réunissent en petites caravanes; et, lorsque la saison des hautes eaux leur permet de naviguer, ils courent encore les risques d'être dépouillés par les habitans de certains villages des bords du Nil, lesquels ne vivent que des vols et des brigandages qu'ils exercent sur les bateaux chargés de marchandises qui passent à leur portée'.[49] This state of affairs was the result of a weak government and continuous internecine warfare between the rival Mamluk and Beduin factions. Moreover, for fiscal reasons the government was compelled to collect duties on commodities moving between the countryside and towns in the form of tolls levied at the entrance of the city which were farmed out to military commanders or others. Such fiscal measures too were not conducive to rural-urban commercial activity.

But not only the movement of commodities between village and town was limited; in Ottoman Egypt the movement of villagers to towns was extremely small as well. With the exception of sons of rural families who came to town to study and to dwell in the *madrasa*s, and who used to remain in the city (a movement to be discussed further on), not much urbanization can have taken place in Egypt during the Ottoman period. Shirbīnī's fellahs apparently did not come to town frequently and did not stay there for a long time.[50] 'Migrants fleeing rural hardship' did not come to the cities, as they did apparently in the period and areas discussed by Lapidus, but fled into the hills and some of them later returned to their village.[51] Some moved to other villages: 'Un fellâh qui se trouve dans l'impossibilité de satisfaire la cupidité de ses maîtres, quitte ses champs et sa maison; suivi de sa femme et de ses enfants, il va chercher dans un autre village quelques terres à cultiver et des maîtres moins avides'.[52] Landless fellahs who remain without work also moved into other villages.[53] Moreover, it was extremely difficult for the fellah to leave his village. When he fled and his refuge became known to his *multazim*, he was brought back by force and severely punished.[54] Only in cases of famine did fellahs flock temporarily into towns, where they hoped to find food.[55] Otherwise no urbanization has been recorded in any of the sources known to the present author. This corresponds to the decline of Cairo's population during the Ottoman period, from about 500,000 in 1512 to about 260,000 in 1798.[56] Even after this decline, the population of Cairo amounted to at least two-thirds of Egypt's urban population, so that one cannot speak of urbanization at other urban centres either.[57]

In fact, it would have been surprising had we found evidence of urbanization in Ottoman Egypt. During this period the urban economy of Egypt experienced a considerable decline. Cairo was no longer at the head of an empire, and Istanbul attracted artistic talents which had formerly concentrated in Cairo. The reorganization of world trade had excluded Cairo as an important commercial centre even before the Turkish conquest.[58] Under these circumstances, there existed no labour market in Cairo which would have been able to attract 'migrants fleeing rural hardship'. Moreover, from the sixteenth or seventeenth century onwards, an important change had occurred in the organization of the urban population. Recent studies have established more or less conclusively that in Fāṭimid, Ayyūbid and Mamlūk Egypt the urban population was not organized in professional guilds.[59] But in Ottoman Egypt the whole gainfully occupied town population except the higher bureaucracy, the army, and the *'ulamā'*, was moulded into an all-embracing system of such guilds under the auspices of the government.[60] A basic condition for the working of this system was the exclusiveness of each guild in its branch or sub-branch within the boundaries of a specific community. This was achieved by a variety of officially recognized monopolies and restrictive practices.[61] The existence of such monopolistic practices made the absorption of rural immigrants into the urban economy extremely difficult. Thus the lack of significant migration from village to town contributed to the relative separation between these two environments in Ottoman Egypt, for which we have found many economic reasons as well. This separation also explains, at least to some extent, the marked differences between village and town which were observed at that time in Egypt.

We have seen that one of the reasons for lack of economic contact between town and countryside was the weakness of the government. For the same reason town and countryside were rather isolated administratively as well. The only connecting link was the *multazim*, who lived in the town and ruled the village. All the functionaries of his administration were appointed by him (directly or indirectly) and were thus dependent on the tax farmer, not on any central government or power whose seat was the city. This is true not only for local functionaries who lived in the village, such as the *shaykh al-balad* (the political and agricultural chief administrator), the *khawlī* and *wakīl* (functionaries in charge of work on, and income of the *ūsīyya*), the *shāhid* (registrar of taxes, lands and fellahs in Lower Egypt), and the *ghafīrs* (local police for internal security), but also for his agents who did not live in the village, such as the *qā'imaqām* (a Mamluk in charge of village police), the *mubāshir* (the Coptic chief accountant, who operated in the village with the help of the Coptic *ṣarrāf*, the tax collector), and the *mushidd* (the executive police officer).[62] We shall see further on that from the point of view of rural-urban political ties this was an intermediate situation between effective power of a central government apparatus in the countryside (which emerged gradually in Egypt in the nineteenth century) and a system of feudal lords and *multazim*s who were Beduin shaykhs or rural notables (which existed for a long time in various parts of the Fertile Crescent). It should be mentioned, however, that in some parts of Egypt too the *multazims* were local Beduin shaykhs, and thus political contact with the city was even weaker. This was the case specifically about the middle of the eighteenth century in Upper Egypt, under the rule of the powerful Shaykh Humām of the Hawwāra tribes whose *iltizām* extended from Asyūṭ to Aswān and amounted to a yearly yield for the treasury of 150,000 *ardabb*s of wheat (one *ardabb* = 150 kilograms of wheat). All attempts of the central power in Cairo to send a *kāshif* (governor) or other *multazims* to the area under his rule were violently thwarted for a long time.[63]

In Lower Egypt, too, Beduin tribes established from time to time a semi-autonomous rule – especially the Ibn Ḥabīb shaykhs in Sharqiyya and Qalyūbiyya provinces. Although Beduin shaykhs entered into temporary alliances with this or that Mamluk faction, in general the Ottoman and Mamluk authorities in Cairo were in a state of war with them and tried to reduce their economic and political independence.[64]

If the administrative link between town and countryside was not very strong, the judicial-religious one was not either. It has been often pointed out that the Islamic city did not differ juridically from its rural surroundings.[65] It is true that it was not distinguished by the grant of privileges, as European cities were at a certain historical juncture, but its juridicial unity with the countryside was in many periods and areas theoretical only. In Ottoman Egypt the juridical connexion between villages and the city was rather weak for three reasons. First, in various areas, especially Upper Egypt, the administration of justice was independent of the network of *sharī'a* courts. The *qāḍīs* were not chosen on the basis of their training in a *madrasa*, but they were members of traditional families of '*qāḍīs*', and judgment was given according to customary law, not the *sharī'a*.[66] Secondly, even where the village *qāḍī*s were supposed to judge according to the *sharī'a*, they were in fact ignorant of its precepts (in addition to being considered a ridiculous and contemptible lot by the Cairo *'ulamā'*).[67] Finally, whenever possible fellahs had no recourse to the *qāḍī*. 'Les *fellâh* . . . louent leurs terres pour une année seulement; cet arrangement se conclut de gré à gré et sans l'intervention du qâdy. En général, toutes les fois que les *moultezim* ou les *fellâh* ont entre eux quelque confiance réciproque, ils terminent leurs affaires par devant témoins, sans appeler le qâdy; ou bien ils ne lui demandent une sentence que pour une faible partie des biens qu'ils viennent d'acquérir, afin de diminuer les frais'.[68]

Moreover, we have found no indication that in Ottoman Egypt there were strong ties between town and village within the framework of the Muslim schools of law, the *madhāhib*. True, in the early days of the Ottoman conquest, Leo Africanus, who visited Egypt in 1517, was still impressed by the importance of the *madhhab* for the structure of Egyptian urban society[69], and towards the end of the eighteenth century a fierce controversy broke out between the Shāfi'īs and the Ḥanafīs as the result of the rivalry between Shaykh al-'Arīshī and Shaykh al-'Arūsī over the post of Shaykh al-Azhar.[70] But the Ḥanafī camp in this controversy soon split into Turks and Syrians, and in general it would seem that the social importance of the *madhāhib* in urban Ottoman Egypt had declined compared with the period discussed by Professor Lapidus. For instance, *'ulamā'* used to study with teachers from the four different *madhāhib*, and some even received an *ijāza* to teach and issued *fatwās* according to all of them.[71] However that may be, there are no signs whatsoever that the *madhāhib* had any significance in the countryside. On the contrary, fellahs were not only illiterate, but so ignorant even of the basic precepts of Islam in general that there could be no question of discrimination between different schools of law.[72] But even those rural individuals who were somehow connected with religion apparently did not identify with the town-centred *madhāhib* or look to them for social and judicial leadership. According to Shirbīnī, rural *fuqarā'* (Ṣūfīs, dervishes) were not interested at all in the differences between the schools of law; instead they were divided, like all fellahs, into the two factions Sa'd and Ḥarām.[73] Similarly, *fuqahā' al-rīf*, i.e. villagers engaged in all activities connected with religion, such as reciting the Qur'ān, teaching, arranging of marriage contracts, leading in prayer and preaching, were completely confused about the different *madhāhib*.[74] It should be mentioned, in this context, that these *fuqahā' al-rīf* apparently were not appointed by a central religious authority, but by the *multazim* (*amīr al-balad*, as Shirbīnī pointed out).[75] Finally, the village *qāḍī*s too were ignorant and rather unimportant, as we have seen above.

It may well be that the decline of the *madhāhib* was connected with the enormous expansion of the Ṣūfī orders in Egypt during the Ottoman period. By the eighteenth century almost everybody was a member of such an order, fellahs and townsmen, common people and *'ulamā'*, members of all social classes and groups. In our context it would be interesting to find out whether the *ṭarīqa*s constituted a framework within which significant ties between town and village were established. However, no definite answer can be given to this question. On one hand there was a contrast between the urban and the rural Ṣūfī orders: while the former tended to be influenced by the *'ulamā'* and their outlook and practice did not deviate greatly from Islamic orthodoxy, the latter tended to be 'latitudinarian in varying degrees and shading into heresy'.[76] Thus, in so far as urban and rural orders were different organizations with a different character, urban-rural ties were hardly established through their framework. On the other hand, evidence shows that in some cases the *ṭarīqa*s in fact furthered contact between villages and the city. Thus, Sha'rānī and other Ṣūfī shaykhs took it upon themselves to instruct fellahs in religious matters, either by living among them or when they came to Cairo.[77] Or take for instance the following story told by Jabartī. In A. H. 1172/1758 died in Cairo the Ṣūfī shaykh 'Abd al-Wahhāb al-Marzūqī al-'Afīfī. He was born in Minyat 'Afīf village (Minūfiyya) and in his youth came to Cairo, where he studied and later acquired the customs of the Ṣūfīs. He was venerated by shaykhs and amīrs, and after his death his sons and novices built a mausoleum in Cairo. They established a yearly pilgrimage (*mawsim*) to this place where a great number of people assembled, among them many fellahs from the villages.[78] Like al-'Afīfī, many of Cairo's distinguished Ṣūfīs came from the villages.[79]

Indeed, *'ilm* or Ṣūfism was the only channel by which a very thin stream of the rural population reached the city (mainly Cairo). As in earlier centuries, in Ottoman Egypt too rural families (often with some religious background) sent their sons to be educated in the city and to dwell in the *madrasa*s, and many of them remained there and joined the corps of the *'ulamā'*. According to Muḥibbī's biographical dictionary for the eleventh/seventeenth century *Khulāṣat al-athar*, about one quarter of Cairo's *'ulamā'* during that period (28 out of 111) were born in the Egyptian countryside. The first known Shaykh al-Azhar, Muḥammad al-Khirshī (d. A. H. 1101/1690) was born in a village called Abū Khirāsh in Buḥayra province.[80] Biographies of about thirty-five such *'ulamā'* of rural origin from the twelfth/eighteenth century are to be found in Mubārak's *Khiṭaṭ*.[81] These counts include only those who themselves were born in villages; many more had names indicating that their forefathers had been of rural origin.

Thus, with this exception of a small and limited movement of villagers (not necessarily fellahs) to the city as Ṣūfīs or to become *'ulamā'*, ties between town and country in Ottoman Egypt were rather weak. Village and town were not integrated into an interlocking social body – neither economically nor politically, adminstratively or religiously. All the same, there were few social struggles on urban-rural lines. Basically, this was the result of the fact that the city in Islamic Egypt, and not only in Egypt, never developed into an autonomous league of citizens or attained corporate status or rights. It was not independently administered by its inhabitants but by the central government, which created the administrative apparatus of the city and appointed all its important functionaries.

A permanent conflict existed between the Ottoman-Mamluk urban establishment and Beduin shaykhs at various times and places in Ottoman Egypt. As against this, no rural notables achieved power to such an extent that they could challenge the rule of the Cairo-based Mamluk *multazim*s. To judge by Shirbīnī's experience, the conflict between these rural notables and the fellahs made them view the *multazim*s as their allies. Clear evidence in his book shows that Shirbīnī was a member of a typical family of such rural notables. Although he criticizes the *multazim*s here and there for oppressing the fellahs and making unlawful demands on them, he nevertheless states his firm view that the good fellah should obey the *multazim* and his assistants and refrain from causing ruin and mischief. Fellahs who riot or revolt against their *multazims* or *qā'imaqām* should be punished severely.[82] In our view, Shirbīnī and other sources also show conclusively that there was indeed a persistent conflict in Cairo between *'ulāmā'* of rural origin and those who came from urban families,[83] but it would be wrong to say that this was the dominant conflict among Cairo's *'ulamā'*. Moreover, there was apparently no serious conflict between the *'ulamā'* of Cairo and *'ulamā'* living in the countryside, mainly because not many of them really lived in villages, as we have seen above.

In Ottoman Egypt ethnic or religious conflict took the form of conflict between town and village only to a limited extent. On one hand, the fellah viewed the city as the abode of an urban establishment of soldiers and *multazims* who spoke Turkish and thus differed from Egypt's rural population.[84] On the other hand, these Turks called all Arabic-speaking Egyptians 'fellāḥīn'. When in Ṣafar A. H. 1220 (May 1805) the popular masses of Cairo (*al-'āmma*) assembled and demanded to depose the Ottoman Pasha and appoint Muḥammad 'Alī as *vali* of Egypt, the Turkish Pasha declared that he would not quit his office 'by order of the fellāḥin' (*bi'amr-il-fallāḥīn*).[85] Lane says that 'the Turks often apply this term [El-Felláḥeen] to the Egyptians in general in an abusive sense'.[86] However, the antagonism between the Arabic-speaking Egyptian population and the Turkish-speaking rulers existed not only as an urban-rural antagonism, but also within the city itself. Thus a sixteenth or seventeenth century manuscript originating in the Egyptian guild of barbers or physicians accuses the Ottomans of having practised discrimination against *awlād al-'arab*. The treatise is full of hatred of the Turks and states that Arab shaykhs of guilds are superior to Turkish ones and Arabic-speaking people in general to Turks.[87] Moreover, there was no religious conflict between town and village: both the city and the countryside had a Sunni Muslim majority and a Coptic Christian minority.

Finally, fellah revolts in Ottoman Egypt were not aimed expressly at the town. True, the *kāshif*s, *multazim*s, or *qā'imaqām*s against whom the fellahs revolted came to them from the city, but the revolts were mainly the results of oppressive taxes or other demands made by these rulers, and it is not at all certain whether the fellahs considered them as representatives of the town as a social unit.[88] This ambiguity is probably the result (at least partly) of the relative isolation between town and country which has been a recurring theme in the foregoing pages. Thus it would seem that in Ottoman Egypt social struggles on urban-rural lines were rather limited not because town and country were socially interlocking but, on the contrary, because there was so little contact and so few connections between them.

Nineteenth century Egypt

The nineteenth century was the era of the beginnings of modernization in Egypt, and it is widely believed that modernization narrowed the gap between town and village. This may be fully true for the twentieth century,[89] and partly for the nineteenth, in so far as the contact between town and countryside is concerned. However, the difference between village and city certainly grew in this early stage of modernization. On one hand, the village was not yet influenced significantly by modernization and most traditional differences persisted. Thus, as we have seen above, even towards the end of the nineteenth century Mubārak distinguished clearly between rural and urban types of house and considered a divergence from this model exceptional.[90] In 1862 Egyptian villages were described as follows by a very sensitive observer: 'The villages look like slight elevations in the mud banks cut into square shapes. The best houses have neither paint, whitewash, plaster, bricks nor windows, nor any visible roofs. They don't give one the notion of human dwellings at all at first, but soon the eye gets used to the absence of all that constitutes a house in Europe . . .'[91] True, there were periods of agricultural prosperity in nineteenth century Egypt, and apparently 'very impressive additions to the agricultural *per capita* product were achieved over the nineteenth century'.[92] It is however extremely doubtful whether this narrowed the gap between urban and rural levels of material well-being: a great part of the agricultural income was not spent in the village because large landowners lived in the cities. This is true not only for members of the Muḥammad 'Alī family, officials, *'ulamā'*, merchants, Copts who owned large estates and foreigners, but also for village notables who moved to cities for economic and political reasons from the 1860s onwards, and even for a number of Beduin shaykhs who at that time became large landowners.[93]

On the other hand, modernization and Westernization were just sufficient to make their impact on the cities and thus to widen the gulf between town and countryside. 'As the cities become Westernized, the countryside does not. This probably increases the gap between city and country in some respects, certainly the gap between the elite of city folks and the rural people without any education'.[96] The same has been observed for other parts of the Middle East as well: 'Il en résulte entre villes et campagnes un extraordinaire déséquilibre social et économique et qui va sans cesse croissant. Les premières se sont mises rapidement à l'école de l'Europe; on trouve dans la plupart d'entre elles une bourgeoisie riche et instruite, parlant souvent une ou deux langues européennes et qui par son genre de vie paraît entièrement occidentalisée. Quelles relations communes peut-elle avoir avec la masse paysanne qui n'évolue pas?'[97] In both quotations education is stressed, and in this sphere the gap probably widened more than in any other during the nineteenth century. At the beginning of the century religious education was the only kind of education available. Although religious education too tended to concentrate in towns, especially all institutions above the level of the *maktab*, the Qu'rān school, quite a considerable proportion of the *maktabs* were located in the countryside. We have no figures for the beginning of the century, but about 1870 the distribution was as follows:[98]

	Number of maktabs		Number of pupils	
Cairo	295	24.1%	9,883	22.4%
Alexandria	46	3.8%	3,284	7.4%
Eighteen towns	244	20.0%	7,950	18.0%
Provinces	638	52.1%	23,082	52.2%
Total	1,223	100.0%	44,199	100.0%

As against this, the network of newly established secular schools in nineteenth century Egypt was almost completely restricted to the towns, mainly to Cairo and Alexandria. According to Edouard Dor's 'Statistique des écoles gouvernementales, confessionelles et Européennes', 33 out of 78 of these schools were in Cairo (42.3 per cent), 26 in Alexandria (33.3 per cent) and 19 in other towns (24.4 per cent) – including only three in very small towns.[99] From the time of Muḥammad 'Alī up to 1887, 93 primary schools (*écoles primaires*) had been established by the government, but most of those founded in the days of Muḥammad 'Alī were closed again before his successors assumed power. In 1887 only 23 remained extant, nine in Cairo, two in Banī Suwayf, one in Alexandria, one in each of nine provincial capitals, and two in two other small towns. None of the schools established in villages had survived by 1887. During the same period three preparatory schools (*écoles préparatoires*) had been established, all of them in Cairo, but only one had survived, and 36 *écoles supérieures et spéciales*, 34 of them in Cairo, but only eight had survived in 1887, all of them in Cairo.[100] As to confessional and foreign schools, the following statistics have been published for the year 1875:[101]

	Teachers		Boarders		Day Students	
	number	per cent	number	per cent	number	per cent
Cairo	220	50.2	545	53.4	3,183	39
Alexandria	138	31.5	273	26.8	3,662	45.8
Other towns	32	7.3	83	8.1	490	6.1
Remainder	48	11.0	120	11.7	653	8.2
Total	438	100.0	1,021	100.0	7,988	100.0

The full significance of these figures for the overwhelmingly urban bias of the educational development of Egypt in the nineteenth century can be grasped only if one keeps in mind the percentages of the urban population at that time. These were as follows, according to the 1882 and 1897 censuses and revised figures for these two years:[102]

Percentages of total population of Egypt

	1882 Census	revised	1897 Census	revised
Cairo	5.5	5.0	5.9	6.1
Alexandria	3.4	2.9	3.3	3.2
Other towns of more than 20,000 inhabitants	2.6	4.9*	4.4	5.7*
Total towns of more than 20,000 inhabitants	11.5		13.6	
Revised calculation for 23 large towns		12.8		15.0

*main large towns.

Thus Cairo and Alexandria in particular, and large towns in general, had a disproportionately high share in the newly established schools in nineteenth century Egypt. This educational gap resulted in a widening cultural gap between a partly Westernized urban layer of the population and the rural masses.

Like education, the newly established health services also tended to concentrate in Egypt's towns, mainly Cairo and Alexandria. In his geographical encyclopaedia 'Alī Pasha Mubārak claims that under the rule of the Muḥammad 'Alī family health services in the countryside had considerably improved, and that instead of the services of the barbers and old women there is 'now' (in the 1880s) a hospital in each *mudīriyya* and a physician in each *qism*.[103] It is true that by the 1870s there was a hospital in each *mudīriyya*. However, in each of these hospitals there were between 25 and 50 beds (in Madīnat al-Fayyūm only 10), which was hardly a considerable improvement for populations ranging from 200,000 to 500,000 per province. As against this, Cairo's hospitals had 1,303 beds (or 48.0 per cent of all hospital beds in Egypt) for a population of about 330,000, and Alexandria 640 beds (23.6 per cent) for a population of about 160,000. Thus over 70 per cent of the hospital beds served less than 8 per cent of the population.[104] Similarly, it was scarcely true that by the 1880s there was a physician in each *qism*; according to the census there were 11 districts out of 99 without a physician. However, Cairo had 24 doctors employed by the government (15.7 per cent of the total number in Egypt) and Alexandria 12 doctors (7.8 per cent), while Minūfiyya province, for instance, had only 7 doctors (4.6 per cent) although its population exceeded that of Cairo and Alexandria combined, Qenā (3.9 per cent) and Banī Suwayf 5 doctors (3.3 per cent). Among the 214 doctors who were not in government employment 67 (31.3 per cent) were in Cairo and 45 (21.0 per cent) in Alexandria.[105] Thus even if the few doctors in the provinces were an innovation of the nineteenth century, compared with developments in this sphere in Cairo and Alexandria they constituted a negligible quantity – the more so as their impact on village life seems to have been minimal. An illuminating example of this is a visit of the doctor from Qenā to Luxor described by Lady Duff-Gordon in letters written in April 1864. 'He was very unhappy that he could not supply me with medicines; none are to be bought above Cairo, except from the hospital doctors, who sell the medicines of the Government, as the Italian at Assiut did . . . Today Ali Effendi-*el-Hakeem* came to tell me how he had been to try to see my patients and failed; all the families declared they were well and would not let him in. Such is the deep distrust of everything to do with the Government . . . They all said, ". . . he would send us off to hospital at Keneh, and then they would poison us . . ." '[106] Thus the early stages of emerging health services, like those of educational development, seem to have widened the difference between city and countryside in Egypt.

A further aspect of Westernization was the influx of foreigners into

Egypt. At the end of the eighteenth century there were in Egypt no more than a few hundred Europeans, including Greeks. During the rule of Muḥammad 'Alī the number of Europeans grew to about ten thousand. The great influx of Europeans occurred during the time of Sa'īd and Ismā'īl, especially in the early 1860s, as a result of the great financial and commercial opportunities connected with the cotton boom and the manifold projects of these two rulers. By 1872 their number amounted to at least 80,000, of whom more than half (about 47,000) lived in Alexandria, about 20,000 in Cairo, more than 7,500 in the towns along the Suez Canal (Port Said, Suez, Ismailia) and only the very small number making up the rest in other provinces of Egypt.[107] As a result of this influx, which continued throughout the rest of the century, parts of Cairo and Alexandria were built or rebuilt after the model of Paris and supplied with water, gas, and electricity; and some groups among the inhabitants of these cities adopted European dress. Nothing comparable happened in the Egyptian villages. Though some of the foreigners settled in provincial towns as owners of cotton gins, almost none settled in villages except for some Greek merchants. Among more than 1,000 villages included in Mubārak's encyclopaedia, the residence of foreign merchants is mentioned in less than ten. The result was a further widening of the gap between the urban and rural population. If in Ottoman Egypt cultural heterogeneity was an urban characteristic, in nineteenth century Egypt this trait which distinguished towns from villages was certainly strengthened.

So far we have argued that, on one hand, the village was not yet influenced significantly in the nineteenth century by modernization and thus traditional differences did not diminish; on the other hand, modernization and Westernization made their impact on the cities and thus widened the gulf between town and countryside. However, the impact of the West intensified the divergence between town and village in Egypt in yet another way. We have seen that in the Ottoman era handicrafts were practised in a rather large number of Egyptian villages. During the nineteenth century rural handicrafts in Egypt seem to have declined considerably. Mubārak frequently says that a certain village in the past was famous for this or that industry, but that by now the industry has ceased to exist (*thumma baṭala dhālika*). The industries concerned are weaving, fabrication of indigo and ammoniac, pressing of sugar-cane and others.[108] Thus the villages became more exclusively agricultural and from this point of view too more different from towns than before. The decline of rural handicrafts was the result of the growing competition of urban Egyptian and foreign industries whose impact was felt in the villages from the nineteenth century onwards because of their closer ties with the market. While in Ottoman Egypt weak economic contact between town and village was concomitant with a relative independence of the village in the supply of manufactured goods for itself, in the nineteenth century closer ties and increasing dependence involved greater economic differences between the two environments.

The development of closer economic ties between town and village was indeed one of the important changes which occurred in rural-urban relations in nineteenth century Egypt. This was the result, in the first place, of the transition from subsistence agriculture to cash crops. In particular cotton and sugar cane became principal crops of Egyptian agriculture. Cotton exports rose from 100,000–300,000 *qinṭār*s (1 *qinṭār* = 45.4 kilograms) to 4–6.5 million in the 1890s. By the end of the century Egypt had become an importer of grain. This process brought with it stronger connections of villagers with urban merchants, urban industrialists (for instance, cotton ginners) and urban financial institutions. An important corollary of this transition was the tremendous expansion of transport in the nineteenth century. Before that time, owing to the complete absence of roads, wheeled traffic was unknown – the first carriage seen in Egypt was brought from France at the end the eighteenth century. Although Egypt had an internal waterway, the Nile, river navigation was severely restricted by natural obstacles, piracy, tolls and other impediments. Improved transport was introduced by foreigners in the nineteenth century to meet international, not domestic needs, but by the turn of the century modern transport had reached the greater part of the countryside. Light agricultural railways were built by private enterprise, mainly in the Delta and Fayyūm, and the ramified railway made it possible to move Egypt's main export crops from the remote parts of the country. By 1913, Egypt was as well provided with railways as any country in the world relative to its inhabited area, and, relative to its population, it was better off than most.[109]

The transition to cash-crops and the expansion of transport had yet another result which strengthened the ties between town and countryside, namely the emergence of a number of provincial towns. At the beginning of the century Cairo was the only town in Egypt with more than 20,000 inhabitants, but by 1907 there were nineteen (and a few others came very near this limit). Particularly during the third quarter of the nineteenth century, mercantile centres of agricultural areas expanded as the result of the tremendous agricultural development at that time. Thus Ṭanṭā became the principal market of a large area of cotton plantations and in 1856 it was connected to the railway network. The number of visitors to the annual fair, the *mawlid al-Sayyid al-Badawī*, was estimated in the 1860s and 1870s at half a million, as against from 100,000 to 150,000 in the first half of the century. Similarly, Manṣūra profited by the railway connection which was established in 1865. In the 1860s the sales of cotton, wool, flax, fruit, rice and oilseed in Manṣūra amounted to about a quarter of the yield of Lower Egypt. Like Ṭanṭā in Gharbiyya province and Manṣūra in Daqahliyya, Damanhūr became an agricultural centre in Buḥayra, and three fairs were annually held at this place. The most impressive development, however, was that of Zaqāzīq, which had been founded by Muḥammad 'Alī in 1836–7. Foreigners who settled here established cotton gins and other workshops, and the place became an important centre of the cotton trade. In the early 1860s the railway connection was established. By the end of the century the number of its inhabitants amounted to 35,000.[110]

As a result of the transition to cash-crops, money taxes gradually replaced payment of taxes in kind, and from 1880 cash payments alone were recognized by law.[111] This transition to a money economy caused the penetration of money-lenders into the village. In Ottoman Egypt the urban money-lender was out of place in the rural subsistence economy; when the fellah could not pay his taxes he came to some kind of arrangement with the *multazim* or the *ṣarrāf*, the tax farmer or tax collector.[112] Exceptions apparently were found in the areas of rice-growing (a cash crop) in the Northern Delta, which may explain what Shirbīnī has to say on this subject.[113] Two developments in the nineteenth century considerably furthered the increase in fellah indebtedness to urban money-lenders: first, since in the course of that century fellahs had become the owners of their land, they could now be granted credit on its security; and secondly, the legal sanction given to the acquisition of land by foreigners and the establishment of Mixed Courts in 1875 brought about the introduction of mortgages as known in the West, which were not recognized previously by Ottoman Law.[114] In many cases the urban merchant, the money-lender, and the absentee landlord were the same person.

According to a recently published paper by Xavier de Planhol, 'rent capitalism' and 'a system in which the city dominated the countryside' largely predated Islam but was adopted by it. 'It was also nurtured by the instability and hazards of pluvial cultivation, which forced the peasants in poor years to apply for loans from the city lenders; this in turn usually led to absentee ownership of large estates.'[115] As we have seen, this statement is certainly not applicable to Ottoman Egypt. True, there was no 'pluvial cultivation' in Egypt, but irrigation by the Nile flood was no less unstable and hazardous. Nevertheless, there was no rent capitalism with indebtedness of peasants to city money-lenders or absentee ownership of large estates, although the city dominated the countryside economically. Moreover, in the rain-fed agriculture of the Ottoman Fertile Crescent there was no rent capitalism either. The mistake is the result of equating the economic domination of the countryside by the city with capitalist exploitation. The same mistake is made by Planhol's critic, I. Harik. In a contribution to the same volume, Harik points out that 'economic domination of rural areas by urban-based groups, such as merchants, money-lenders, and absentee landlords . . . is a relatively modern phenomenon, concomitant with the emergence of a domestic market and demand for cash crops . . . It was the state, not urban interests, which dominated rural areas before the advent of a market economy'.[116] But was not the state, at least in Ottoman Egypt, an 'urban based agency'? Harik is perfectly right when he says: '. . . grain upon which the city population depended for livelihood was transferred to the major cities not as a commercial transaction but in the form of taxes paid in kind to the government . . . Also grain which was obtained by *multazims* from their *uhdahs* was sold in the urban market where most of the *multazims* lived.'[117] If this is not economic domination by an urban based agency – what is? How else was the fellah dominated by the state than by exploitation through the urban based *multazims*? Thus urban economic domination is not necessarily identical with rent capitalism, as implied by Harik.[118] The contrast between the nineteenth century and the period preceding it is not between urban economic domination of the village and its absence, but rather between rent capitalism, strong ties between cash-crop producing villages and urban merchants, and exploitation of indebted fellahs by urban money-lenders and absentee landlords on one hand, and economic domination of the fellah by the state through urban-based tax farmers, combined with relative isolation between town and countryside, on the other hand.

Not all villages or areas in Egypt underwent the process described in the preceding pages to the same extent. First, Upper Egypt differed considerably from Lower Egypt in this respect. The greater proximity of Lower Egyptian villages to the principal mercantile and economic centres of the country brought with it greater economic opportunities and faster changes. Thus, even in 1880 the law recognizing cash alone for payment of taxes still met with opposition in Upper Egypt, where peasants feared that their produce would find no markets.[119] In general, the greater isolation of Upper Egyptian villages kept the Ṣa'īdī fellah poorer than his counterpart from the Delta.[120] Secondly, certain villages established particularly strong ties with the city, for specific reasons. Thus Mubārak tells us that among the inhabitants of Banī 'Adī village (Asyūṭ province) there were many sheep and grain merchants doing business in Cairo, as well as merchants selling the produce of the oases (dates, rice, indigo) in Cairo. There were also other strong economic connections between this village and Cairo. The reason for such extraordinary ties between this Upper Egyptian village and Cairo may well be the strong tradition of a steady stream of students from Banī 'Adī who went 'since old times' (*min qadīm al-zamān*) to the Azhar where at least thirty of them were studying when Mubārak wrote his work. The shaykh of the hostel (*riwāq*) of the Ṣa'īdīs was always a native of Banī 'Adī, as well as many teachers, authors, and shaykhs.[121] This traditional religious contact may well have paved the way for strong economic connections emerging as the result of economic changes in the nineteenth century.

We have seen above that such a movement of sons of certain rural families to the *madāris* of the towns had taken place for centuries. However, most of them had remained in town after the completion of their studies. It would seem that in the nineteenth century more of them than before returned to their villages after finishing their studies. This is attested by many examples in Mubārak's biographies of Egyptian *'ulamā'*.[122] Together with greater economic and administrative contact, this was an important reason for an ever-increasing penetration of orthodox Islam into the countryside. This process has been described in detail by Mubārak with regard to the fellahs of tribal origin living in al-Hilla near Ṭahṭā (Girgā province). In the course of the nineteenth century many of them established Qur'ān schools, built mosques and appointed *imāms* and *khaṭībs* for the services to be held in them, and sent their boys to study at al-Azhar.[123] Comparison of sources for the seventeenth, the nineteenth, and the twentieth century indicates a steady growth of the number of mosques in Egyptian villages.[124] Unfortunately we have no descriptions from the nineteenth century to show how exactly the growing penetration of Islamic orthodoxy into the countryside worked, but later sources may give us some idea. In Silwa (Aswān) an *'ālīm* came yearly to the village and people flocked to him for advice on religious matters, such as the details of prayers, or whether certain sayings or deeds were considered to be religiously approved or disapproved. A preacher coming from the city told the villagers that the customs they practised on the death of a person were non-Islamic, and they took a vow not to practise them any more.[125] In other villages too, greater influence of orthodox religion and greater efficiency of the administration led to a decrease in violence and other popular customs connected with mourning rites.[126] Moreover, since Muḥammad 'Alī's time even Ṣūfī orders came under stronger supervision of a centralized framework.[127] One could ask, of course, whether all this caused not only an intensified religious connection between the village and the town, but also the narrowing of the cultural gap between these two environments – in contradiction to what we have found above. The answer is that the cultural gap between villagers and that part of the urban population on which Westernization made no impact narrowed, since orthodox Islam together with a low educational level and its corollaries became their common denominator. In the meantime, however, the difference grew between the village population and another part of the urban population which was influenced by the various aspects of Westernization which we have analysed above. An exact quantitative evaluation of these processes is impossible, but our guess is that, generally speaking, in the nineteenth century the gap widened and in the twentieth it narrowed (among other reasons, because large scale urbanization led to ruralization of large parts of the great cities).

A further aspect of growing religious connections between town and country was the incorporation of the village into the network of *sharī'a* courts. As we have seen, in Ottoman Egypt either *sharī'a* courts did not exist in the countryside, especially in Upper Egypt, or the peasants disregarded them and had recourse to the *multazim* and his agents or traditional '*qāḍī*s' who judged according to customary law. In the nineteenth century *sharī'a* courts were established in many villages, not only in the Delta,[128] but also in Middle Egypt,[129] and even in such villages as Benbān, Edfū, Armant, Qurna, Ibrīm, Halfa and Abū Hor in Aswān and Qenā provinces (Upper Egypt).[130] Qāḍīs or *nā'ib*s were appointed in such villages as Birinbāl (Daqahliyya), Banī Mazār (Mīnyā), Dirr (Isnā), Dashnā (Qenā), Duwayr (Asyūṭ), Sanbū (Asyūṭ), Ṭama (Girgā), al-Qanayāt (Sharqiyya), al-Mansha'a (Girgā), and others.[131] As against this, the traditional *qāḍī* of al-Hilla, for instance, who judged according to customary law, was deposed and made an assistant of the tax collector.[132]

All this was part of a legislative and administrative activity whose aim it was to integrate the village into the new centralized state of Muḥammad 'Alī and his successors. Early in 1830 Muḥammad 'Alī published the *qānūn al-filāḥa* which contained detailed instructions concerning agricultural work and the functions of various officials in the villages, as well as penalties for crimes and offences committed, among others, by fellahs and village shaykhs. In 1842 he published the *lā'iḥat al-jusūr* dealing with offences connected with the maintenance of dikes, and his *qānūn 'āmm* of 1844 included again 26 articles dealing with agricultural crimes and offences.[133] Throughout the century a ramified legislation concerning the ownership and transfer of land was enacted.[134] Moreover, Egypt's rulers attempted, in various ways, to incorporate the local village shaykhs into the administrative network of the state. Since the abolition of *iltizām* by Muḥammad 'Alī, the village shaykh was appointed by the central government, and in the first half of the century tax assessment and the draft of fellahs for public works and army service were added to his functions. Some of his judicial and fiscal functions were later transferred to the newly established specialized government agencies, but others were added to his burden.[135] From 1833 onwards, village shaykhs were appointed as governors of districts, and after a set-back Sa'īd resumed this policy on a larger scale. Ismā'īl even began to appoint village shaykhs to the office of *mudīr* (governor of a province) in addition to a number of other administrative posts they held. Moreover, in 1866 he set up an Assembly of Delegates (*Majlis Shūrā al-Nuwwāb*) which was composed mainly of village shaykhs. In addition to integrating them into the government administration, Egypt's rulers, especially Sa'īd and later the British, did all they could to break their independent political power.[136] There can be no doubt that all these legislative, administrative and political acts greatly contributed to the establishment of a closer contact between city and village in nineteenth century Egypt.

Another political-military factor working in the same direction was the conscription of fellahs into the army. Mamluk-Ottoman tradition did not ascribe any military capacity to the settled native Egyptians, who were accordingly never recruited into the army. But after the failure of Muḥammad 'Alī's attempt to man the infantry of his *Nizam-i cedid* by Negro slaves captured in the Sudan, he started in 1822 to recruit Egyptian fellahs.[137] From then onwards and throughout the century Egyptian fellahs always served in the army and thus came into contact with places and people outside their village, especially in Egyptian towns. The number of fellahs concerned was at that time relatively small, but nevertheless even this limited contact was of significance for reducing the isolation of the Egyptian village. In particular it probably contributed to some extent to urbanization, signs of which began to appear at that time.

However, the extent of urbanization in the nineteenth century should not be exaggerated. True, between 1821 and 1907 the number of towns in Egypt with more than 20,000 inhabitants increased from one to nineteen, but the percentage of their inhabitants in the total population increased only from 8.6 to 13.7.[138] Moreover, this was no sustained growth, but in fact in three different periods different towns or groups of towns grew, in many cases mainly at the expense of other towns. Thus in the second quarter of the century only Alexandria grew, largely at the expense of Cairo, Rosetta and Damietta; during the third quarter small mercantile centres of agricultural areas emerged, but Egypt's two largest towns, Cairo and Alexandria (and, for that matter, the urban population as a whole) grew relatively less than the total population; finally, during the last quarter of the century, it was mainly Cairo which grew tremendously and increased its share in the urban and total population of Egypt. In the decade 1897–1907 there was deurbanization in Egypt.[139]

In view of the growing economic, religious and administrative ties between town and country in Egypt throughout the nineteenth century, this low rate of urbanization requires an explanation. It was caused by a number of evident reasons. First, Egypt entered the modern age at the beginning of the nineteenth century with a relatively large proportion of town-dwellers: Cairo comprised 7–10 per cent of Egypt's total population, while in 1800 the percentage of the total population living in towns of 100,000 or over in England and Wales and the Netherlands was 7, in France 2.7, in Russia 1.6 and in Germany 1.0. This has been explained by Charles Issawi by the absence of a strong rural-based feudal system, prevailing rural insecurity, more favourable treatment by the government of townsmen than of peasants, and pilgrim and transit traffic.[140] Secondly, the nineteenth century in Egypt was a period of intensive agricultural development, as we have shown above. Since at that time the rate of population increase was still relatively low, there was a shortage of manpower in agriculture during most of the century. This was one reason for the lack of urban development, and indeed during periods of agricultural expansion urbanization slowed down or ceased altogether (third quarter of the nineteenth century, and first decade of the twentieth).[141] Connected with this, to some extent, was the lack of industrial development in nineteenth century Egypt. After the failure of Muḥammad 'Alī's industrial experiment,[142] his factories were liquidated by his successors. Those which survived after they had been transferred into private hands made no headway, since they had to pay a large variety of burdensome taxes. A group of new factories established by Ismā'īl turned out to be uneconomic and was liquidated in 1875. Foreign capital, in general, was interested in public utility companies rather than in industry. As to local Egyptian capitalists, they shunned industrial investment because taxes discriminated against them (foreigners were exempted by the capitulations) and because of the great risk involved as the result of a small market and competition of European products. Protective customs duties could not be introduced because of the capitulations, and later because of strong opposition on the part of Lord Cromer, the British Consul General who in fact ruled Egypt. In addition, although no considerable local modern industry developed to compete with the traditional crafts, the latter were seriously affected by changing habits of consumption and the growing influx of foreign goods. As early as 1863, many branches of local crafts which flourished in Cairo in former times (e.g. copper vessels) had succumbed to European competition. By the end of the century the same fate had befallen ivory, wooden lattice work, engraving in wood or metal, production of saffian, embroidery, and tapestry. Indigo dyeing had been almost entirely superseded by aniline dyes imported from Europe. A similar process was observed all over the country. In Alexandria, in the 1880s local industry dwindled from day to day. Damietta, once famous for its leather and textile products, had ceased to be of any industrial importance. In the past, Banī Suwayf had been famous for carpet-making, which largely died out during that period. Asyūṭ's weaving industry and the manufacture of red leather in that town declined to such an extent, that by the end of the first decade of the twentieth century scarcely anything was left of them.[143]

We have seen that one of the reasons for the lack of rural to urban movement in Ottoman Egypt was the emergence of a system of guilds holding a monopoly each in his branch. Similarly the low rate of urbanization in the nineteenth century was partly the result of the fact that, contrary to the assumption of many writers, the guilds did not decline or disappear at the beginning of that century, but only at its end. Until the 1880s a ramified system of guilds existed in Cairo and many other towns, comprising almost the whole indigenous gainfully occupied population. The shaykhs of the guilds controlled and supervised the guilds' members' activities; they were made responsible for misdemeanour of their guilds' members; they supplied labour and services to the government and private employers; they were responsible for the payment of taxes by the guilds' members and collected these taxes; they fixed maximum wages for them; and it was their function to restrict the number of persons exercising a certain trade. The reason for its long survival was, first of all, the interest of the government in maintaining the guild system, since it fulfilled functions which the government was unable to fulfil at that stage. Secondly, the guilds did not disintegrate as a result of class struggle among various strata of its members, which were not rigidly distinguished or economically and socially differentiated. Egyptian guilds were neither suppressed by law nor did they disintegrate as a result of internal differentiation, nor were they superseded by the emergence of a modern industrial society. Their decline and disappearance during the last quarter of the nineteenth century and the first decades of the twentieth were mainly the result of the impact of Europe, of the influx of European goods and of Europeans settling in Egypt who began to disregard the shaykhs of the guilds as suppliers of labour. During the 1880s and the 1890s the government published a whole series of decrees providing for professional permits to be issued by official authority, not by the guilds' shaykhs, and in 1890 the complete freedom of all trades was announced. Finally, towards the end of the century, Egypt's administration was reorganized so that the state could do without the intermediate link of the guilds, and step by step their administrative, fiscal and economic functions shrank until they lost most of them.[144]

The decline of the guilds towards the end of the century greatly facilitated the emergence of a free labour market and thereby laid the foundation for modern urbanization. Fellahs running away from oppression during the time of Muḥammad ʻAlī found refuge, as they did in Ottoman Egypt, not in the towns but in villages.[145] Similarly, under ʻAbbās, the entire population of certain villages hid in the hilly desert or in caves from conscription, and during Saʻīd's reign there were villages whose male inhabitants, owing to conscription for forced labour, 'are almost constantly on the move out of their village'.[146] As late as July 1879 the British Vice Consul Borg reported from Qalyūbiyya: 'Indeed, I hear from different sources that the oppression received at their (the shaykhs) hands is such, that the fellaheen often abandon their smallholds and become labourers to the Zawats and Europeans in the hope of obtaining protection against their sheikhs'.[147] Thus, in most of the nineteenth century, 'migrants fleeing rural hardship' generally did not come to the cities. This changed in the 1880s and 1890s when the free labour market emerged. Moreover, by that time population had begun to increase faster, and no shortage of labour existed any more as it had done earlier in the century. By 1907 there lived in Cairo about thirty thousand people born in Asyūṭ province. Many of Cairo's porters were from Mūsha village (Asyūṭ), many of the water carriers from Dār al-Baqar (Gharbiyya), and a great part of the building workers were recruited in Tirsa (Gīza). In Suez there was a whole quarter called *ḥārat al-Ṣa'āyida*, the quarter of people from Upper Egypt.[148] In the course of the twentieth century this trend grew to enormous proportions.

In the nineteenth century, as in Ottoman Eygpt, there were few social struggles on urban-rural lines. Unlike some European countries, Egypt's dominant social class was not divided into a country-based gentry and an urban bourgeoisie. This was true, as we have seen, for Ottoman Egypt, and remained so in the nineteenth century, notwithstanding basic changes which occurred in the economy. In the course of the century members of the bureaucracy who lived in the towns became large landowners, mainly by receiving land grants from the rulers. On the other hand, village notables who had become large landowners were appointed as government officials and moved to towns.[149] Sometimes these landowner-officials also entered other economic spheres, especially as contractors for supplies for the government, transport, and the like.[150] At the same time rich merchants began to acquire large estates, both because agricultural development made investment in land a profitable business and because landownership had become the most important criterion of social status. Two outstanding cases, those of the al-Hajīn and al-Ṭarazī families, have been related in detail by Mubārak.[151] Others were the al-Shanāwīs and Mutawallī Bey Nūr of Manṣūra; Sayyid Aḥmad Bey al-Dīb, Rizqallāh Bey Shadīd, and the Abāẓas of Zaqāzīq; Maḥmūd Pasha Sulaymān of Asyūt; and Muḥammad Bey Abū Ḥusayn and many others of Cairo.[152] As a result of this interpenetration, the Egyptian upper class was not divided by social struggles between urban and rural interests.

But was not the Egyptian army divided on urban-rural lines? The question arises of course in connection with the 'Urabī revolt which preceded the British occupation of Egypt. In some of the Western literature on this chapter of Egyptian history, 'Urābī and his fellow officers who led the revolt are called 'Fellah officers'.[153] The obvious reason for this attribute is the fact that many of them were of rural origin.[154] In addition, Turks used to call all Egyptians 'fellahs' in a derogatory manner, as we have mentioned above; and 'Urābī says in his autobiography that when he was imprisoned one of the leading Circassian officers called him and his colleagues fellahs as a reviling designation for Egyptians.[155] However, 'Urābī himself did not pretend to fight for fellahs against town-dwellers; his antagonists are 'Circassian amīrs' or 'Circassian officers' or 'Mamluks', and he considers his own party as 'Egyptians' or 'patriotic officers' (*al-ḍubbāṭ al-waṭaniyyūn*), but never 'fellah officers'.[156]

Compared with Ottoman Egypt, fellah revolts seem to have become more frequent in the days of the Muḥammad 'Alī. Such revolts broke out in 1807–8, 1812, 1816, in every year between 1820 and 1826, and again in 1838 and 1846. Fellahs revolted against taxation, conscription for the army and forced labour, and Muḥammad 'Alī's monopolistic practices.[157] The greater frequency of these revolts was probably not only the result of the improvement of our sources for the nineteenth century compared with those for earlier times. The abolition of the traditional system of the *iltizām* and the liquidation of the Mamluks as a ruling class by Muḥammad 'Alī deeply undermined continuity and led to unrest. Thus, when former *multazim*s attempted to make the fellahs work on their *ūsiyya* land as they had formerly done, the answer often was: 'Find someone else, I'm busy. What remains to you in this land? Your days are past, now we are the Pasha's fellahs'.[158] On the other hand, the fellahs' expectations must have been greatly disappointed when the change involved tighter control by the government and heavier pressure to pay taxes and to supply forced labour for public works, in addition to the innovation of conscription to the army. The Mahdist flavour of most of the ensuing revolts shows that at that time popular Islam still was very strong in the Egyptian village and that the penetration of orthodox Islam, which strengthened religious ties between town and countryside in the course of the century, had not yet progressed very far. As in earlier times, it is not at all certain whether the revolting fellahs considered the oppressing rulers as representatives of the town as a social unit. But unlike Ottoman Egypt, we have unequivocal evidence that the government identified the rebels as fellahs or villages, and throughout the first half of the nineteenth century legislation provided for the possibility of revolts of peasants or villages, but not of any other social group. As a result of the numerous peasant revolts during the 1820s, a law which was promulgated in 1830 (*qānūn al-filāḥa*) dealt with this problem in particular. Paragraph 26 of that law deals with the case of villagers attacking a government official or their shaykh because he demanded taxes, and details the punishments and the procedures of paying indemnities in the event that they killed him. Paragraph 27 states:

> In the event of an armed revolt by a whole village where the village does not obey the representative of the *ma'mūr* or the *ḥākim*, the *ma'mūr* is required to proceed to the village himself. If he is also not obeyed, he is required to lay siege to the village, to capture its head shaykhs and to send the chief instigator of the revolt to Fayzoğlu [a place of exile in the Sudan] for five years. The other instigators will be sent to hard labor for the same period. The other shaykhs and the fellahs will be punished by 400 stripes of the *kurbāj* [whip] each. If some one from a neighbouring village comes to the aid of the rebellious village, he will be conscripted into the army if he is a young man; if he is an older person he will be sent to hard labor in the port of Alexandria for three years. If shots were fired and there were wounded or killed, the punishments listed in paragraph 26 would go into effect.[159]

Similarly, the criminal-administrative law promulgated immediately after Sa'īd's ascension again includes special clauses fixing punishments in the event of peasant revolts or disobedience. One of these clauses states:

> In the event of a *shaykh al-balad* conspiring with the fellahs or of one fellah conspiring with the others against the *nāẓir* [inspector] of the village or the shaykh and attacking him with clubs or arms: in the case of blows alone without the use of firearms, the shaykh or the fellah at the head of the rebels is to be punished by 200 stripes and each of the fellahs by 100 stripes. If they used firearms the set punishments for such cases would go into effect.[160]

Thus it would seem that the transition from relative isolation between town and countryside in Ottoman Egypt to economic and political integration of the village in a common framework with the city in the nineteenth century was accompanied by a period of increased friction and social struggles between the village and the markedly urban government.

Syria and Palestine

While Egypt forms a more or less monolithic unit, Syria and Palestine consist of a great variety of social patterns. Partly because of this reason, research into the social history of Syria and Palestine has not advanced to a stage at which detailed descriptions can be given, let alone conclusions drawn. What we propose to do, therefore, is to find out the principal patterns of urban-rural formations in Syria and Palestine during Ottoman rule, the basic differences among them and between each of them and what we have found for Egypt, and the influence of these differences on various aspects of urban-rural relations in each case.

By far the largest towns of Ottoman Syria were Aleppo and Damascus. Towards the end of the eighteenth century, the number of their inhabitants was estimated at about 200,000 and 100,000 respectively, i.e. together more than Cairo, which means that Syria at that time was at least twice as urbanized as Egypt. The relations between Aleppo and Damascus and their respective agricultural vicinity was probably somewhat closer than that of Cairo and the Egyptian countryside, which may have been the result of a different spatial pattern: while in Egypt there was only one predominant large town, in Syria there were two. But the extent of the hinterland of each of these towns was rather limited: in Damascus it did not much exceed the Ghūṭa and the Ḥawrān, while in Aleppo 'in the eighteenth century the limit of other than sporadic agriculture was approximately thirty miles southeast of Aleppo. Beyond this limit extended the domain of the Bedouin'.[161] One sign of these closer ties than in Egypt was a steady movement of peasants to these towns, although some of the limitations for such a movement which we have found in Egypt existed in Syria too.

> Many were nomads and peasants led to migrate into the city on account of economic distress . . . On the part of the peasant the insecurity of the villages from raids caused many to in-migrate to lose themselves in the anonymity of the urban masses. Since the trades were closely controlled by guilds . . . it was difficult for a recent in-migrant to attain a position of prestige. He was relegated to the low-class quarters, where he often engaged in agriculture or husbandry under the mantle of the city's protection.[162]

Volney, too, mentions this steady flow of peasants into the large Syrian towns in order to escape the rapacity of their rulers or the danger of famine – since towns were always better provided for in case of shortage of grain than villages. This, he says, was one of the main causes for the large population of these towns.[163]

Otherwise the pattern of relations between Aleppo and Damascus and their rural dependencies was the nearest to the Egyptian pattern among the different Syrian ones. However, the economic ties between Damascus and the surrounding villages seem to have been relatively strong. In addition, the composition of the urban élite was somewhat different: there were no Mamluks in the Syrian towns, and therefore the indigenous notables were more powerful. But both in Cairo and in the Syrian towns this élite included Ottoman officers, *'ulamā'* and *ashrāf*, and rich merchants, and in both areas there was a large extent of interpenetration among these elements. In the eighteenth century members of this élite in Aleppo and Damascus were the *multazims* of the villages surrounding these towns. By that time taxes used to be farmed for longer terms than a year, a system called *malikâne*. From the beginning of the eighteenth century villages near Damascus became *malikâne* of the principal families of the Damascus *'ulamā'*, such as the Murādīs, the family of the Ḥanafī *muftī*, or the 'Ajlānīs, a family from which the *naqīb al-ashrāf* was frequently chosen, especially in the days of 'Ali al-'Ajlānī who devoted much energy to the agricultural administration of these villages.[164] In this way the Damascus notables dominated the supply of grain to the town and were able to manipulate its price. Similarly, Burckhardt stated that in the late eighteenth century 'most of the villages round Aleppo were then in their [the *ashrāf*'s] possession, they command the landed interests . . .'.[165] Thus, as in Egypt, agricultural produce was delivered to the town in the form of taxes or of the profit of the tax farmer, rather than exchanged with urban products.

Unlike Egypt, the *iltizām* persisted in Syria throughout the nineteenth century. Nevertheless, during that time Syrian agriculture and urban-rural relations underwent similar changes as those observed in Egypt. In various areas farm specialization in certain cash crops was introduced; close commercial ties emerged between towns and neighbouring farming regions or artisan centres and farm regions which provided them with raw material (processes observed by European authors specifically in Damascus and Aleppo); as in Egypt, part of the home industries of the peasants was ruined, except in remote regions; and merchants and money-lenders gradually made themselves masters of the newly emerging commercial activities of the peasants and became owners of their land. One of the reasons for this process was the fact that the impoverished peasant could not leave the village to seek a living in town because by 1840 industrial production was sharply declining and the peasant was therefore forced to hang on to his farm, thus falling prey to the usurer. Moreover, a large number of city dwellers returned to the villages, thus creating a rural surplus population by the first half of the century. According to K. M. Bazili, the Russian Consul General in Beirut, Aleppo's population declined from 150,000 in the 1820s to 80,000 in the 1840s, and during the same period the population of Damascus decreased from 120,000 to 80,000. This was due to the ruin of weaving and other industries under the impact of European products.[166] It would be interesting to find out whether this similarity with Egyptian development extended to other spheres as well, such as political and religious connections between the two towns and their hinterland, but material at present at our disposal does not enable us to do so.

A completely different picture emerges from a study of three smaller towns of Northern Syria, Antioch (Anṭākiya), Hama (Ḥamāh) and Latakia (al-Lādhiqiyya), which has been made by the French geographer Jacques Weulersse and published in two of his works.[167] The dominant characteristic of the relations between these towns and their vicinity was the ethnic or religious differentiation between the urban and rural population. While the village population was mainly 'Alawī (a heterodox sect on the fringes of Islām), and, in Hama province, also Ismā'īlī (extreme Shī'ite), the town population of Hama was Sunnī Muslim, of Latakia Sunnī Muslim and Christian (mainly Greek Orthodox), and of Antioch Sunnī Muslim but, in addition, mostly Turkish-speaking. It would seem that this situation represents an extreme crystallization of a general trend analysed by Weulersse. The rural element, he says, remains faithful to its ancient gods as the result of its remoteness, ignorance, and tradition, and resists the invasion of new creeds. On the other hand, young and active but persecuted communities instal themselves in the countryside to evade the danger of proximity to the ruling power and in order to develop in security. As against this, urban life did not emerge as the result of spontaneous concentration of autochthonous forces, but through artificial implantation by foreign masters. If you ask a town-dweller about the origin of his family, only very rarely will he admit rural origin, and never that he himself came from a village. Usually he will say that he originated from another town, or bedouin snobbery will make him proclaim that he came from the desert.[168]

The result, as described by Weulersse, is a deep chasm between town and village. 'Dans tous les pays, citadins et ruraux se différencient par leur genre de vie et leurs coutumes; mais ici ils forment deux peuples absolument différents, non seulement en manières extérieures, mais également en nature profonde et même en origine . . .' 'En dehors des cités, ni instruction, ni justice, ni assistance publique, ni médecine, ni voirie, ni travaux d'aucune sorte; pas même d'activité religieuse profonde . . .'[169] Not only are the differences enormous, but also contacts and connections are minimal. As we have seen, Weulersse mentions the lack of kinship relations between the towns and their rural vicinity, as against 'constant demographic exchange' among towns, even remote ones. Economically too the towns and the villages live apart. The peasants themselves produce their habitation, their furniture, their tools and most of their clothes, and only the ploughshare, the iron part of the spade, some clothes, and some minor goods are bought from the town. Urban craftsmen practically don't work for villages, only for towns. Nor has the village population been integrated politically or administratively; in the provinces the whole government apparatus, police, justice and finance, is in the hands of the 'great families of the towns'. Religious isolation is self-evident in a region whose dominant characteristic is the religious divergence between towns and villages. One might add that, in contrast with Egypt, modernization did not eliminate the gap as a result of orthodox penetration into the countryside, but rather widened it because of the growing self-consciousness and self-assertion of minority groups, in this case of villagers against townsmen. Growing hostility and opposition between these two groups is indeed envisaged by Weulersse.[170]

There can be no doubt that Weulersse has put his finger on an important factor influencing rural-urban relations in Northern Syria, and thus drawn our attention to the existence of one specific pattern of these relations. Unfortunately, he deems that he has done more than that, namely found an absolute rule valid for all of Syria or even 'l'Orient' in general. 'En Syrie', he says, 'il y a scission brutale; dès qu'on franchit la porte des villes on tombe dans un monde social différent et inférieur, celui des fellahs. Point de commune mesure: jamais un fellah ne deviendra un citadin; il restera derrière sa charrue et ses fils de même. Et cela presque avec la rigueur d'une loi de caste.'[171] None of the great metropolises of Syria is 'vraiment caractéristique' for urban-rural relations, whereas the three smaller towns which he has chosen as 'an example' are 'particulièrement typiques'.[172] More than that: after having chosen that 'typical example', he continues to speak about 'l'Orient'.[173] In addition, Weulersse does not limit any of his statements in time, and he implies that they are valid without such limitation. In fact they apply to the area in which 'Alawī peasants live, and particularly to the period of the nineteenth and early twentieth century. But as has happened to some scholars after having studied intensively one area or one period, Weulersse attributes to his findings much wider and more general significance than they have.[174]

A third area, with a different pattern of rural-urban relations, was the hill-country of Lebanon and Palestine. Up to approximately the middle of the nineteenth century this area differed from all the other areas with which we have dealt so far in one principal feature of its social structure: with few exceptions, the countryside was economically and politically dominated by families of notables who lived in the countryside itself, not in towns, and whose position was hereditary. Lebanon was divided into twenty-four *muqāṭa'āt* (sing. *muqāṭa'a*) and each of these had a ruling family, *muqāṭa'ajī*, except for three families each of whom ruled more than one *muqāṭa'a*: the Junbalāṭs, the Abū al-Lam's and the Nakads. All these families of *muqāṭa'ajī*s resided in villages: the Junbalāṭs in Mukhtāra or Ba'dharān, the Arslāns in Shuwayfāt, the Abu al-Lam's in Bikfayyā, the 'Imāds in al-Bārūk, the Ḥubayshs in Ghazīr, the Khāzins in 'Ajaltūn, Ghūsṭā, Rayfūn, Mazra'at Kafr Dabyān and other villages in Kisrawān. Only the Nakads resided in Dayr al-Qamar, which was a small town. The rule of the *muqāṭa'ajī* was hereditary, and the region over which his governmental rights extended was called *'uhda*. He was responsible for order and security, as well as for agricultural production. A major function of the *muqaṭā'ajī* was the financial administration of his *'uhda*: he collected taxes from his subjects and turned them over to the *amīr* or *ḥākim*, the central and superior ruler of the Lebanon. The *muqāṭa'ajī* was exempted from the land tax on his own private holdings, which amounted often to a high proportion of the land of the *muqāṭa'a*. The fellah's relationship to the *muqāṭa'ajī* and his faction was a bond of allegiance and loyalty called *ismiyya* (or *sumiyya*).[175] In Palestine no central and superior ruler intervened between the Ottoman *vali* and the *multazīm*s, but otherwise conditions were very similar. Both Jabal Nāblus and the Judean Hills were divided into *nāḥiya*s which were administered by local shaykhs. These were appointed by the Ottomans, who were however restricted in their choice to the family or families which held an almost hereditary right to the post. The shaykhs of most of the important families built castles or fortresses for themselves in the villages in which they resided: the Jarrārs in Ṣānūr, the 'Abd al-Hādīs in 'Arāba, the Banū Ghāzīs (Rayyāns) in Jammā'īn, the Jayūsīs in Ṣūfīn and Kūr, the Barqāwīs in Shūfa, the Samḥāns in Rās Karkar, the Saḥwīls in 'Ibwayn, the Abū Ghōshs in Qaryat al-'Inab, etc. Taxes were paid to the central government through these shaykhs, and the fellahs showed their loyalty to them by supporting them in their quarrels and clashes with their rivals.

The reason for the different pattern of this third area is obvious: the mountainous countryside of Lebanon and Palestine was much less accessible to the urban-based government or the urban élite than the plains in the neighbourhood of Damascus or Aleppo or than the flat Nile valley. Therefore local rural notables were able to assert themselves as tax farmers and rulers of their village or area of villages, and even maintain this privilege in their families as a hereditary right. In this area, indeed, the economic domination of the village by the city began only in the nineteenth century, as against Egypt and the Syrian plains where it existed much earlier.

One important consequence of the lack of economic domination of the town, and the residence of the 'upper class', the tax farmers, in the village, was the higher standard of material well-being in this rural area than in the villages of the Syrian plains or the Nile valley, or, in other words, the smaller difference in material well-being between the rural and urban population, compared with Egypt or Syria. This is true at least for rural Lebanon, which has been characterized by its 'picturesque prosperity' or 'continuity of well-being from the earliest times' but apparently also for Palestine. We have seen that in Egypt, at the time of a famine, fellahs flocked into towns where they hoped to find food. In Palestine a different situation seems to have been prevalent. This is what

Mrs. Finn writes: 'A remarkable instance occurred during the scarcity and famine in 1854, when the war had raised the prices of provisions, and when the effendis of the city, by buying up the wheat stores, had caused extreme distress, esp. to the poor Jews. A fellah then resolved to do what in him lay to mitigate the sufferings of the poor, and, though he himself was not rich or powerful, to reduce the price of corn. He brought his little store of wheat, a single camel load, into the market of Jerusalem, and, spreading his own *aba* (cloak) on the ground, emptied the grain out of the sacks, crying aloud to the poor to come and buy . . . .'[176]

On the other hand, the greater administrative isolation of rural areas in Lebanon and Palestine resulted in the greater conservation of local customs in the countryside, especially in the field of law. In Lebanon, the *muqāṭa'ajī* and the *ḥākim* performed judicial functions. The *muqāṭa'ajī* heard cases and imposed punishment of various kinds, and in the *ḥākim*'s court criminal cases and cases concerning property were tried. The *muqāṭa'ajī* also carried out judgements given by the clergy (mainly in matters of personal status, such as marriages or inheritance).[177] Moreover, the law of personal status of the predominantly rural Maronites and the totally rural Druzes differed significantly from the *sharī'a* which was applied in the towns. The most important difference was the law of inheritance. Maronite law permits a testator to dispose freely of a large part of his estate (one-half to two-thirds, as against one-third according to Muslim law), and sometimes even of the whole estate. Even after Muslim law was introduced by Bashir II, Maronite fathers often transmitted their estates to one or some of their children only during their lifetime. 'C'est ainsi que les familles de la Montagne ont pu conserver les anciennes propriétés de leur aïeux, jusqu'à nos jours'.[178] Similarly, according to Druze customary law a testamentory disposition was valid whether it concerned part or the whole of an estate and whether it was made in favour of an heir or non-heir. Such a testamentory disposition, for instance, was one of the reasons for the enormous wealth of Shaykh Bashīr Junbalāṭ.[179] Both the Maronite and the Druze law of inheritance tended to conserve the power of the notable families of the Mountain. Although Palestinian fellahs were predominantly Muslim, here too rural law differed considerably from urban judicial systems. In Jerusalem, for instance, there was a dual court system: the *sharī'a* courts and a mixed court consisting of the Pasha, the notables and a few Christians. As against this, in the villages the customary law (*'urf*) was preferred which was administered by the village *shaykh*s and *ikhtiyāriyya* (elders). In southern Palestine it was called *sharī'at Khalīl* (Abraham's law) – in contrast with *sharī'at Muḥammad*. For instance, blood money (*diyya*) according to *sharī'at al-Khalīl* was 4,000 piastres for a man and 2,000 for a woman, while the town *qāḍī* imposed much higher amounts, sometimes reaching 30,000 piastres. Fellahs claimed that a city verdict was not binding since it did not follow *'urf* procedure (' "Seraglio (palace) law" is "no law" '). The *qāḍī* of the *sharī'a* court and the secular courts recognized the jurisdiction of *sharī'at Khalīl* in the villages and even pressed the Pasha to impose its judgements on villagers who tried to elude them, but this legal system was exclusive to the rural areas and town-dwellers did not refer to it. It would seem that this customary law was common to Muslim and Christian villages; in the latter it was called *ḥukm 'ashā'irī*.[180]

Political and economic domination by village-based families of notables had a marked influence on the formation of rural-urban conflicts in Palestine and Lebanon. First, in contrast with Egypt, there were practically no fellah revolts against their *multazim*s or *muqāṭa'ajī*s up to the middle of the nineteenth century. Wherever fellahs were involved in conflicts (mainly as the result of the aggravation of the tax burden), they followed their shaykhs in their struggle against the central government or, in Lebanon, against the superior *amīr*.[181] Most probably this was the result of the close allegiance and loyalty of the fellahs to their rulers, who resided among them and were their leaders in the factional strife – the most prominent political feature of this area at that time. However, at the end of the 1850s a great revolt of peasants against their *muqāṭa'ajī*s broke out in Kisrawān in the northern central part of Lebanon.[182] It is interesting to note that in Lebanon a peasant revolt occurred in the period of transition in which the rule of the *muqāṭa'ajī* families deteriorated and new economic and political conditions emerged; as we have seen, in Egypt too the period of transition between the *iltizām* system and Muḥammad 'Alī's new order brought about a sharp intensification of peasant revolts. However, while in Egypt these revolts definitely had the flavour of a rural-urban conflict, at least as seen from the point of view of the urban-based government, this was not at all the case in Kisrawān. The revolt of the peasants was directed exclusively against the *muqāṭa'ajī* family of the Khāzīns, who lived in the villages of Kisrawān; the only concern of the town in the revolt was a certain amount of support given to the peasants by the town-based clergy and by the inhabitants of some small towns in Kisrawān. There can be no doubt that this difference had a decisive influence on the outcome of the revolt. As against the Egyptian revolts, the revolt of Kisrawān's peasants was successful: the Khāzins were driven out of Kisrawān, their estates were expropriated and, most important, the achievements of the rebellious peasants in the course of the revolt were in fact maintained after its end.

The rural character of the dominant social class in Lebanon had yet another implication for the formation of rural-urban conflicts. As we have seen, in Egypt no division occurred between a country-based gentry and an urban bourgeoisie – neither in the Ottoman period nor in the nineteenth century. This was primarily the result of the fact that both the *multazims* and the capitalist landowners of modern times lived in the town. Since the Lebanese *muqāṭa'ajīs* did not, a conflict between them and an emerging urban bourgeoisie was much more plausible than in Egypt. In fact signs of such a conflict appeared at the period of transition from the traditional system to a new order, i.e. the first half of the nineteenth century, both in southern and in northern Lebanon. In the south the Amīr Bashīr II, who attempted to limit the power of the *muqāṭa'ajīs*, stimulated the growth and development of the towns of Dayr al-Qamar and Zaḥleh as a counterpoise to the hitherto exclusive predominance of the Druze lords. Dayr al-Qamar rose from a population of about 1,300 in 1812 when Burckhardt visited it, to about 8,000 inhabitants, mostly Christians, and became famous for its silk manufactures. Its merchants became rich, built luxurious houses and Druze landed property in the neighbourhood passed into their hands. They 'assumed an air of independence and superiority', as a sign of their emancipation from Druze control. This finally led to clashes with their former feudal superiors, the Druze shaykhs of the Abū-Nakad family and other *muqāṭa'ajīs*. Zaḥleh's inhabitants, whose number increased to 12,000, traded in wool and farmed in the Biqā' – formerly the domain of the Druze lords. In the late 1850s they had risen in rebellion against the Druze *amīrs*, had appointed a municipality of their own, and formed an alliance against their rivals, the Druze *muqāṭa'ajīs*, with Dayr al-Qamar. However, in the course of the violent disturbances in Lebanon in 1860 these two towns suffered severely and much of their former prosperity was liquidated.[183] In the north a similar conflict developed between the Khāzins, the *muqāṭa'ajīs* of Kisrawān, and the inhabitants of the town of Zūq Mikhāyil, north of Beirut, most of whom were Greek Catholics. Their relative prosperity, derived largely from the silk trade and silk processing, had made them independent of the shaykhs. As a result of the antagonism between them and the Khazīns, they declared their support for the rebellious peasants.[184] Thus, for a short time the Lebanese rural lords clashed with an emerging urban bourgeoisie; things changed as a result of the liquidation of the power and privileges of these lords in 1861 and subsequent economic and political changes in the Lebanon which resembled to a large extent those of Egypt and Syria described above.

We have said above that Syria and Palestine consist of a great variety of social patterns; how great this variety was can be seen from a comparison between two towns in the hill-country of nineteenth-century Palestine – which according to our scheme was only a sub-region of the area representing the third pattern. The following comparison between rural-urban relations in the Jerusalem and the Nāblus area is based on a detailed and thorough study of Palestine in the first half of the nineteenth century, whose main theme is the feud between the Qays and Yaman factions.[185]

The principal difference between the two towns was the fact that, while the importance of Nāblus was limited to its immediate vicinity, Jerusalem's sanctity to the three monotheistic faiths gave it an importance transcending the area of the Judean hills. Jerusalem's population of about 15,000 to 16,000 comprised about 5,000 Muslims, 7,000 Christians and 3,500 Jews, while almost all of the 8,000 to 9,000 inhabitants of Nāblus were Muslims. The notable families of Jerusalem – the Khālidīs, Nusaybas, Nashāshībīs, 'Alamīs, Ḥusaynīs, Dajānīs, Jārallāhs and Anṣārīs – had lived for hundreds of years in the city and many of them held religious offices; as against this, the leading families of Nāblus – al-Nimr, Ṭūqān, and 'Abd al-Hādī – were partly of rural origin and had arrived in the town as late as the middle of the seventeenth and the beginning of the eighteenth century.

As a result of Jerusalem's religious importance and its prominent place in the Ottoman administrative hierarchy, the city had several institutions which did not exist in Nāblus. After the Ottoman restoration it was raised to the rank of *mutaṣarriflik*, and in 1854 to an *eyalet*. From 1841, the region was governed by an Ottoman Paşa, and a *majlis idāra* (advisory council) was established. In Jerusalem resided a Greek Orthodox Patriarchate, a Latin Patriarchate (re-established in 1847) and in 1841 an Anglican Bishopric was founded. In 1838 a British consulate was founded, followed by the French and Prussian in 1843, the Austrian in 1849, and the Spanish in 1854. As against this international importance of Jerusalem, Nāblus was characterized by its function as an administrative centre for the surrounding mountain area. A family of village notables aspiring to control Jabal Nāblus firmly had to move to the town. Thus the fact that the 'Abd al-Hādīs moved to Nāblus perhaps played a decisive part in their being appointed governors by Ibrāhīm Paşa.

Jerusalem's strictly urban character and its foreign administration tended to widen the gap between the city and the surrounding rural area, while the more independent and local nature of government in Nāblus necessitated close relations between the town governors and the rural population. In contrast with the governor of Jerusalem, the ruler of Nāblus was dependent on the acquiescence of the *nāḥiya shaykh*s: thus, when they opposed the rule of the Ṭūqāns, the latter were prevented from collecting taxes from the rural areas. On the other hand, in Nāblus *nāḥiya shaykh*s were able to gain control of the town's government, which did not happen in Jerusalem.

The different town-village relations in the two areas found various expressions. We have seen above that in the Jerusalem area there was a sharp contrast between rural and urban law, *sharī'at Khalīl* and *sharī'at Muḥammad.* In the Nāblus area, on the other hand, unwritten customary law (*al-qaḍā' al-'urfī*) was valid both in the city and the countryside, and one of the urban notables, Shaykh 'Abd al-Hādī, was known as an *'urfī* judge as far away as the Judean hills. The most remarkable difference, however, was the different part each of the two towns played in the Qays and Yaman feuds and other factional strife of the countryside, Nāblus' notables led the factional wars and took an active part in them, and fighting sometimes even occurred in the city. The town quarters were split along factional lines: city-dwellers joined in the village skirmishes, and in the city itself they tried to sabotage the efforts of their rivals. Not so in Jerusalem, which was never the scene of fighting in the factional wars. The city's quarters were not divided between opposing groups, and the city's notables neither led the fighting nor did they, or any other townspeople, play any active part in it. The paşa's helplessness in face of the factional strife, and his inability to suppress it by force, compelled him to negotiate with the leaders of the opposing sides. The forum of these negotiations was the *majlis al-idāra*, in which the notables possessed great power and influence. Since the paşa needed the help of the notables to govern, they were able to turn the factional strife to their own advantage. Just as they were bribed by the consulates, the monasteries, patriarchates and others to advance their respective interests in the *majlis*, so they were used by the village faction leaders in the same way. Thus the Laḥḥāms, 'Abd al-Raḥmān 'Amr and especially the Abū Ghōsh family had their allies in the *majlis*. Although it sometimes seemed that the 'effendi's too were split into Qays and Yaman, the city's participation in the factional strife was secondary and unconnected with the Qays-Yaman schism of the fellahs.

Conclusion

The study of urban-rural relations in Middle Eastern history has suffered in the past from too much generalization. Most authors who have dealt with this question have attempted to achieve a general model of what happened in this regard in 'the Islamic world' of 'les relations entre les villes et les campagnes d'Orient', or about 'city and country in Islamic society'. It is our conviction that this is an impossible task. In this paper, we have tried to show the enormous variety which existed in these relations, the changes which occurred in this respect in one country (Egypt) in the course of its history from Mamluk to modern times, as well as differences between towns as near to one another as Jerusalem and Nablūs.

These differences were not the result of one single cause or even of a definite set of circumstances, but rather of the interplay of geographical, political, economic, social, cultural and historical conditions. Each of these conditions influenced urban-rural relations, and some became in specific periods and places a predominant factor.

To begin with, it is due primarily to the geographical peculiarities of Lebanon and certain parts of Palestine that rural-urban relations in these areas differed from those in other regions of the Middle East. The mountains of Lebanon and of the interior of Palestine kept these areas apart from the urban-based power of the central government and thus local rural notables were able to assert themselves as tax farmers and rulers of their village or area of villages, and even maintain this privilege in their families as a hereditary right. As a result this was the only region in Egypt and Syria in which the town did not dominate the villages politically and economically.

However, each of these two major geographical types comprised a great variety of urban-rural relations, which was caused, first of all, by different socio-political structures and characteristics of different towns. In Palestine, Jerusalem's religious importance involved a demographic and administrative situation which separated it from its rural neighbourhood, while in Nablūs the urban population did not differ very much from the surrounding villagers and the rural notables were able to gain control of the town.[186] In some of the smaller towns of Northern Syria there existed a sharp ethnic and religious differentiation between the urban and rural population, which resulted in a deep chasm between town and village. On the other hand, the larger towns of the Syrian interior plains, Aleppo and Damascus, apparently had stronger ties with their respective agricultural vicinity – compared not only with Northern Syria and Lebanon, but also with the Nile Valley. This may have been the result of the different spatial pattern (two towns in the Syrian interior against one predominant city in the Nile Valley). But in the Ottoman period at least socio-political conditions contributed to the difference as well. In Egypt the imported Turkish-speaking Mamluks who resided in Cairo were the tax farmers and rulers of the villages, while the countryside near Damascus had become *malikâne* of notables, merchants and *'ulamā'*. This difference in the social character of the tax farmers or owners of the villages resulted in stronger political, economic and religious ties between Damascus (and perhaps also Aleppo) and its rural hinterland than those which existed in Egypt at that time. It is interesting to note that for the turn of the century, when Cairo's *'ulamā'* had increasingly become *multazim*s, many more cases of relations between Cairo and fellahs from the Egyptian countryside are being recorded by Jabartī than for earlier periods.[187]

This last example shows that socio-political characteristics of towns may change, and indeed political, economic and social change in specific areas resulted in different urban-rural relations in different periods. The influence of such changes has been investigated in this paper mainly with regard to Egypt, and in order to draw general conclusions similar and perhaps even more detailed investigations of other areas will have to be made. This limitation should be borne in mind in view of the following summary.

Egypt's political history from Mamluk times to World War I seems to indicate that in periods of a strong and centralized government urban-rural ties become closer, while the weakening of government tends to separate the countryside from the city. Compared with Mamluk Egypt, during the time of Ottoman rule the power of the central government certainly deteriorated, especially during the seventeenth and eighteenth centuries. As we have seen, this was a period of relatively weak political ties between Cairo and the Egyptian countryside. As against this, the new centralized state established by Muḥammad 'Alī and his successors displayed a ramified administrative and legislative activity attempting to integrate the village into the body politic; at least partly these attempts were crowned with success.

Economic changes throughout these three periods brought about parallel results. During the Ottoman period the urban economy of Egypt experienced a considerable decline. This had two effects: first, villages became less dependent on urban crafts, and second, there was practically no urbanization at that time. In the nineteenth century, on the other hand, Egypt's economy not only grew quantitatively, but underwent a transition from subsistence agriculture to cash crops, accompanied by a tremendous expansion of transport. As a result, urban money-lenders and merchants penetrated into the village and a system of 'rent capitalism' was established which considerably strengthened economic and other ties between town and countryside.

At the beginning of this paper, we divided our discussion into three sets of relations between village and city: similarity or difference, contact or isolation, and conflict or integration. In this summary, we have dealt so far only with the impact of different conditions on the second set. In the paper we have tried to show that the same conditions did not necessarily effect the first set in a parallel manner. In other words, growing contact was not necessarily accompanied by growing similarity between town and village, but in most cases rather by the opposite: with greater differences between them. This is true particularly for the nineteenth century, when economic and cultural differentiation between the two environments widened. However, not all aspects of the first set always went together (in some parts of Syria and Lebanon cultural and religious differences went together with economic similarity), and growing contact is not always accompanied by greater differences (for instance, this rule is probably not true for the twentieth century).

Finally, concerning the third set, we have seen that there were very few social conflicts in Egypt and Syria which were formed on urban-rural lines. In fact, there was only one instance of such a conflict, in Lebanon. This was certainly no accident: only Lebanon, and to some extent Southern Palestine, had a hereditary aristocracy residing in the countryside. When this feudal system deteriorated about the middle of the nineteenth century, an urban bourgeoisie emerged in the small towns of Lebanon and clashed with the traditional *muqāṭa'ajī* families. As we have seen, even this conflict was of short duration. However, it should be stressed that the lack of urban-rural conflict in the Middle East was not the result of an integrated society comprising town and countryside, but rather of a social structure in which the village was dominated by one or other urban élite.

NOTES

1. Ira M. Lapidus, 'Muslim cities and Islamic societies', in Ira M. Lapidus (ed.), *Middle Eastern cities*, Berkeley & Los Angeles, 1969, pp. 47–74.
2. Ira M. Lapidus, *Muslim cities in the later Middle Ages*, Cambridge, Mass., 1967.
3. Yūsuf al-Shirbīnī, *Hazz al-quḥūf fi sharḥ qaṣīd Abī-Shādūf*, al-Maktaba al-Maḥmūdiyya, Cairo, n.d., pp. 112, 166. For details on this source see above.
4. P. S. Girard, 'Mémoire sur l'agriculture, l'industrie et le commerce de l'Egypte', *Description de l'Egypte, Etat moderne*, Tome seconde, première partie, Paris, 1812, p. 593. Cf. W. S. Blackman, *The fellāḥīn of Upper Egypt*, London, 1927 (1968), p. 154.
5. For references see above, p. 40, notes 41 and 42.
6. S. D. Goitein, 'Townman and fellah, a Geniza text from the seventeenth century', *Asian and African Studies*, vol. 8, no. 3, 1972, pp. 257–61, (1).
7. See above, p. 11, and Goitein, ibid., (5), (6) and (7).
8. See above, pp. 11–12, and Goitein, ibid., (11) and (12).
9. 'Abd al-Wahhāb al-Sha'rānī, *Laṭā'if al-Minan*, quoted in M. Winter, 'Sha'rani and Egyptian society in the sixteenth century', *Asian and African Studies*, vol. 9, no. 3, 1973, pp. 313–38.
10. See above, pp. 10–11.
11. 'Alī Pasha Mubārak, *al-Khitat al-tawfīqiyya al-jadīda*, Būlāq A.H., 130–5/1886–89, vol. 14, p. 76.
12. John Gulick, 'Village and city: cultural continuities in twentieth century Middle Eastern cultures' in Ira M. Lapidus (ed.), *Middle Eastern cities*, p. 144.
13. See above, pp. 9, 20–22.
14. Shirbīnī, pp. 12, 18, 29.
15. M. de Chabrol, 'Essai sur les moeurs des habitans modernes de l'Egypte',

Description de l'Egypte, Etat moderne, Tôme second (2e partie), Paris, 1812, p. 481. This is a typical example for the use of the word 'propriétaire', for *multazim*.

16. 'Abd al-Raḥmān al-Jabartī, *'Ajā'ib al-āthār fī'l-tarājim wa'l-akhbār*, Cairo – Bulaq, A.H. 1297/1880, vol. 3, p. 140.
17. Ibid., p. 166; vol. 4, pp. 233–4; vol. 1, p. 204; etc.
18. Professor O. Grabar in Lapidus, *Middle Eastern cities*, p. 78.
19. Cf. 'List of Egyptian guilds', G. Baer, *Egyptian guilds in modern times*, Jerusalem, 1964, pp. 166–76.
20. Girard, pp. 594, 601–2, 609; Mubārak, vol. 17, p. 61.
21. Girard, pp. 591 ff; Cf. Blackman, pp. 135–54; Mubārak, e.g. vol. 9, pp. 82, 90. For *balāṣ* see Girard, p. 593, and cf. Blackman, p. 142.
22. M. Michaud and M. Poujoulat, *Correspondance d'Orient*, Paris, 1834, vol. 7, p. 57 (written in 1831).
23. Girard, pp. 595–6. Mubārak mentions in detail some of the villages in Fayyūm which were most famous for the production of woollen fabrics (vol. 12, p. 20; vol. 14, p. 36; vol. 15, p. 69).
24. Girard. p. 599.
25. Ibid., pp. 597, 600.
26. Ibid., p. 600.
27. Mubārak, vol. 8, p. 60.
28. See, for instance, ibid., vol. 9, pp. 14, 61.
29. Girard, pp. 603–4; see also Blackman, pp. 155–61; and Mubārak, *passim*.
30. Mubārak mentions oil pressing in six villages only, and Girard (pp. 605–8) does not say where this craft was practised.
31. Girard, pp. 594, 613; Mubārak, vol. 11, p. 57.
32. Mubārak, vol. 12, p. 44.
33. Ibid., p. 115; Hekekyān Papers, vol. 3, British Museum Add. 37450, fol. 231 (written January 1847).
34. Mubārak, vol. 15, p. 35.
35. Ibid., vol. 16, p. 50.
36. Girard, pp. 590, 617.
37. Lapidus, 'Muslim cities and Islamic societies', p. 64.
38. *'Mısır içinde iki bin altmış bağ bostan ve gaytan vardır'*, Evliya Çelebi, *Seyahatnameşi, Mısır, Sudan, Habeş (1672–1680)*, tenth volume, Istanbul, 1938, p. 359. Evliya's figures should not be taken by any means as accurate statistics. For the guild of gardeners in Cairo see André Raymond, *Artisans et commerçants au Caire au xviiie siècle*, vol. 1, Damascus, 1973, p. 309. Fowl's eggs were hatched in Cairo in special incubators (*ma'mal farrūj*) on a large scale (ibid., p. 311).
39. M. Jollois, 'Notice sur la ville de Rosette . . .', *Description de l'Egypte*, Tôme second (2e partie), pp. 339–40. For a Cairo *amīr* who sold fruit from his gardens see Jabartī, vol. 2, p. 151.
40. Cf. Iliya F. Harik, 'The impact of the domestic market on rural-urban relations in the Middle East', in R. Autoun and I. Harik (eds.), *Rural politics and social change in the Middle East*, Bloomington and London, 1972, pp. 342–3.
41. Service Historique de l'Armée, Château de Vincennes, sous-série B^6

(hereafter: Vincennes), no. 81, *passim.*

42. Le comte Estève, 'Mémoire sur les finances de l'Egypte', *Description de l'Egypte, Etat moderne*, Tôme premier, Paris, 1809, p. 322.
43. Vincennes, no. 162, pp. 46–8.
44. Ibid., no. 82; no. 162, pp. 39–40; Jabartī, vol. 1, p. 305; vol. 2, p. 226.
45. Vincennes, no. 162, p. 30.
46. Girard, pp. 597–8, 600, 621, 625–8; E. W. Lane, *Description of Egypt*, vol. III, British Museum, Add. 34082, pp. 12–13 (written 1825–6).
47. Shirbīnī, pp. 22, 27, 200, 209; Jabartī, vol. 2, pp. 143, 154; Raymond, vol. 1, pp. 208, 351.
48. Cf. Harik, ibid., p. 343.
49. Girard, pp. 628–9; Raymond, vol. 1, p. 246.
50. Shirbīnī, pp. 6, 13–14, 30, 34.
51. Ibid., pp. 84, 125.
52. Michel-Ange Lancret, 'Mémoire sur le système d'imposition territoriale et sur l'administration des provinces de l'Egypte . . .' *Description de l'Egypte, Etat moderne*, Tôme premier, p. 250.
53. Ibid., p. 244; Jabartī, vol. 4, p. 109.
54. Jabartī, vol. 4, p. 207.
55. Ibid., vol. 1, p. 26; vol. 2, pp. 83–4; Raymond, vol. 1, pp. 87, 104. For a similar situation in the 19th century see Robertson Smith to Vivian, Cairo, 14 March 1879 and Report by Mr. Beaman on the state of the Nile villages, Cairo, 15 March 1879, Public Record Office (P.R.O.), F.O. 141/131.
56. Cf. J. Abu-Lughod, *Cairo, 1001 years of the city victorious*, Princeton, 1971, pp. 22, 37, 52, 57, and notes to these pages. As against this, the same author has frequently stated that Cairo has been attracting migrants from rural areas throughout its history. This has been explained by higher urban than rural mortality rates which created vacancies to be filled by a 'floating population'. However, this hypothesis needs proof. See J. Abu-Lughod, 'Varieties of urban experience: contrast, coexistence and coalescence in Cairo', in I. Lapidus (ed.), *Middle Eastern cities*, pp. 167–8. Table 2 (p. 169) is adduced as proof that there was migration to Cairo 'much earlier' than 'the present century', but its figures relate only to 1917, 1947, and 1960. For the decline of Cairo's population in the 18th century see also Raymond, vol. 2, p. 812, but recently Raymond has made more detailed studies of Cairo's population figures.
57. On the poor state of Egypt's provincial towns of the Delta at the end of the eighteenth century see du Bois-Aymé et Jollois, 'Voyage dans l'intérieur du Delta', *Description de l'Egypte, Etat moderne*, Tôme second, première partie, pp. 97, 105, 108, 114.
58. Abu-Lughod, *Cairo*, pp. 50–1.
59. See sources quoted in G. Baer, 'Guilds in Middle Eastern history', in M. A. Cook (ed.), *Studies in the economic history of the Middle East*, London, 1970, pp. 12–14; S. M. Stern, 'The constitution of the Islamic city', and C. Cahen, 'Y a-t-il eu des corporations professionnelles dans le monde musulman classique?', in A. H. Hourani and S. M. Stern (eds.), *The Islamic city*, Oxford, 1970, pp. 25–63; Lapidus, *Muslim cities*, pp. 96–101. In view of this conclusion the present writer would revise some of his

formulations in Part I of his *Egyptian guilds*.

60. For detailed discussion see G. Baer, *Egyptian guilds*, *passim*.
61. Ibid., pp. 105–9, and below, Part Three, Ch. 2.
62. Information on functionaries of the *iltizām* according to M. Sharon, *Agrarian relations in eighteenth century Egypt*, unpublished Seminar paper, Jerusalem (1962), pp. 14–20. Sharon's summary is based mainly on Jabartī, Lancret, and Estève.
63. Ibid., p. 10, based on Jabartī, vol. 1, pp. 187, 206, 343–5; Girard, p. 510. For other cases of Beduin *multazims* see Mubārak, vol. 8, p. 28 (Abū Manā', Qenā province); and for fellahs who had become clients, tenants, or even some sort of slaves of Beduins see ibid., p. 82, and Girard, pp. 512–13.
64. On the Ḥabā'iba see Jabartī, vol. 1, pp. 345–9. See also on these tribes and on the relation between Cairo and the tribes in general Stanford J. Shaw (ed.), *Ottoman Egypt in the eighteenth century, the Niẓâmnâme-i Mısır of Cezzâr Ahmed Pasha*, Cambridge, Mass., 1962, pp. 8–9 of the Turkish text (pp. 26–8 of the translation).
65. See G. Baer, *Studies in the social history of modern Egypt*, Chicago and London, 1969, p. 190 and sources quoted there.
66. See, for instance, Mubārak, vol. 17, p. 22 (relating to Girga province). This situation lasted in the villages described by Mubārak up to Muḥammad 'Alī's time.
67. Cf. Shirbīnī, p. 86 (also p. 40).
68. Lancret, p. 258. This situation has been well summarized by Janet Abu-Lughod as follows: 'Prior to the nineteenth century there was a wide discrepancy between the degree of local autonomy granted *legally* to rural or provincial communities (virtually none) and the amount actually enjoyed by them, which often was quite extensive, given the weaknesses at the center and the absence of administrative and physical techniques facilitating control'. J. Abu-Lughod, 'Rural migration and politics in Egypt', in R. Antoun and I. Harik (eds.), *Rural politics and social change*, p. 327.
69. Jean-Léon l'Africain, *Description de l'Afrique*, Paris, 1956, vol. 2, pp. 517–18.
70. For a detailed description of this episode see Jabartī, vol. 2, pp. 53–4.
71. See e.g. Jabartī, vol. 2, p. 25, and many other biographies. This question needs of course a more detailed examination and explanation; but see below.
72. See above, p. 21.
73. Shirbīnī, p. 87.
74. Ibid., p. 36.
75. Ibid., pp. 36, 39.
76. H. A. R. Gibb and Harold Bowen, *Islamic society and the West*, vol. 1, part 2, London, 1957, pp. 184–5.
77. Winter, p. 327. Cf. also Jabartī, vol. 1, p. 300.
78. Jabartī, vol. 1, pp. 220–1, Cf. J. W. McPherson, *The Moulids of Egypt*, Cairo, 1941, pp. 174–5 (quoting Murray).
79. See, for instance, Muḥammad Amīn al-Muḥibbī, *Khulāṣat al-athar fī*

a'yan al-garn al-ḥādī-'ashar, Cairo, A. H. 1284, vol. 3, pp. 134–5. Cf. Winter, p. 328.

80. Jabartī, vol. 1, p. 65; Mubārak, vol. 8, p. 22; J. Jomier, 'al-Azhar', *EI*², vol. 1, col. 819.
81. For references see above, p. 46, note 158.
82. See above, p. 29.
83. See above, p. 36–7.
84. See above, pp. 8, 14, etc.
85. Jabartī, vol. 3, pp. 329–30. This has led some authors to the erroneous assumption that 'forty thousand fellahin converged upon the Cairo courts in 1805 . . .' – see J. B. Mayfield, *Rural politics in Nasser's Egypt*, Austin and London, 1971, p. 25. See also below, Ch. 3.
86. E. W. Lane, *The manners and customs of the modern Egyptians*, London, Everyman's Library, 1944, p. 27. For an additional example see Raymond, vol. 2, p. 787.
87. *Kitāb al-dhakhā'ir wa'l-tuḥaf fī bīr al-ṣanā'i' wa'l-ḥiraf*, Gotha, Arabische Handschrift No. 903. Cf. Baer, *Egyptian guilds*, pp. 2–3, 14–15.
88. On fellah revolts in Ottoman Egypt see Baer, *Studies in the social history of modern Egypt*, pp. 95–6, and below, Part Four, Ch. 2.
89. A detailed discussion of the twentieth century is beyond the scope of this paper. Recently much has been written on this problem, especially by contributors to the volumes edited by Lapidus and by Autoun and Harik. Most authors are in fact convinced that the gap narrowed or even disappeared. Jacques Berque differs: 'The divergence between town and country was intensified' (*Egypt, Imperialism & Revolution*, London, 1972, pp. 622–3). No proof or explanation whatsoever is given for this statement, nor does the author define the period to which it relates. We assume, however, that the twentieth century or part of it is meant, since the statement is found in a chapter dealing with the period of World War II and after.
90. See above, note 5.
91. Lady Duff Gordon, *Letters from Egypt, 1862–1869*, London 1969, p. 56.
92. Patrick O'Brien, 'The long-term growth of agricultural production in Egypt, 1821–1962', in P. M. Holt (ed.), *Political and Social Change in modern Egypt*, London, 1968, p. 193.
93. G. Baer, *A history of landownership in Modern Egypt 1800–1950*, London, 1962, pp. 39–70; Id., *Studies in the social history of modern Egypt*, p. 57.

(Notes 94 and 95 have been omitted)

96. Charles Issawi in Lapidus (ed.), *Middle Eastern cities*, p. 154.
97. J. Weulersse, 'La primauté des cités dans l'économie syrienne', *Congrès International de Géographie*, Amsterdam, 1938, section IIIa: Géographie Humaine, p. 239.
98. Compiled on the basis of V. Edouard Dor, *L'instruction publique en Egypte*, Paris, 1872, Appendice, pp. 379–80.
99. Ibid., pp. 381–2. Dor's table has no date; it probably relates to the same time as the former one, i.e. about 1870.

100. Compiled on the basis of Yacoub Artin Pacha, *L'instruction publique en Egypte*, Paris, 1890, Annexe C, pp. 175–202.
101. J. Heyworth-Dunne, *An introduction to the history of education in modern Egypt*, London, n.d. [1939], Appendix A, p. 444.
102. See Baer, *Studies in the social history of modern Egypt*, pp. 134–5, 136, 143. There are indications that in the field of education the urban-rural gap continued to widen even in the twentieth century, but the evidence is not conclusive.
103. Mubārak, vol. 7, p. 22. *Mudīriyya* and *qism* are province and district, respectively, but mean also the capitals of these administrative units.
104. Ministère de l'Intérieur, *Statistique de l'Egypte*, Année 1873, Cairo, 1873, p. 234 (for population figures cf. p. 20). Our percentages disregard figures for Sudanese towns which are included in the table.
105. 'Report on the Medical and Sanitary Administration of the Government of Egypt by Surgeon-Major Greene', Cairo, 7 February 1885, enclosure in no. 19, *Reports on the State of Egypt and the Progress of Administrative Reforms*, Egypt No. 15 (1885), C.-4421, pp. 73–6.
106. Lady Duff Gordon, pp. 156–7.
107. *Statistique de l'Egypte*, 1873, pp. 19–21.
108. Mubārak, vol. 9, pp. 65, 79, 98; vol. 11, p. 57; vol. 12, pp. 2, 7; vol. 13, p. 41; vol. 15, p. 79; etc.
109. Charles Issawi, 'Asymmetrical development and transport in Egypt, 1800–1914', in W. R. Polk and R. L. Chambers (eds.), *Beginnings of modernization in the Middle East, the nineteenth century*, Chicago and London, 1968, pp. 394–7.
110. See Baer, *Studies in the social history of modern Egypt*, pp. 134–5, 138–40, 147.
111. Id., *A history of landownership*, p. 34.
112. Estève, pp. 318–9; Chabrol, p. 488.
113. Shirbīnī, pp. 83, 125–6; cf. also Raymond, vol. 2, p. 720.
114. For detailed discussion of this process see Baer, *A history of landownership*, pp. 34–8. In addition to sources mentioned there see also Lady Duff Gordon, p. 182.
115. Xavier de Planhol, 'Regional diversification and social structure in North Africa and the Islamic Middle East: a geographic approach', in R. Antoun and I. Harik (eds.), *Rural politics and social change*, p. 104.
116. 'Introduction', ibid., p. 6.
117. I. Harik, 'The impact of the domestic market on rural-urban relations', ibid., pp. 341–2.
118. Ibid., pp. 338, 345, 362–3.
119. *Despatch from H. M. Agent and Consul General in Egypt, forwarding Consular Reports on the state of the country*, Egypt No. 3 (1880), C. 2606, pp. 4, 7, 8.
120. Baer, *Studies in the social history of modern Egypt*, pp. 215–6.
121. Mubārak, vol. 9, pp. 94–7.
122. For references, as well as discussion of this point, see H. Shaked, 'The biographies of 'ulamā' in Mubārak's *Khiṭaṭ* as a source for the history of the 'ulamā' in nineteenth-century Egypt', in G. Baer (ed.), *The 'Ulamā' in*

modern history, Asian and African Studies, Vol. 7, Jerusalem, 1971, pp. 62–3.

123. Mubārak, vol. 17, pp. 22, 25.
124. For Shirbīnī and Mubārak see above, p. 9; cf. Blackman, pp. 30–1 (speaking even of Upper Egypt): 'A mosque is to be found in every village, and in many places there are three or four such buildings'.
125. H. Ammar, *Growing up in an Egyptian village*, London, 1954, p. 78.
126. Cf. J. Berque, *Histoire sociale d'un village égyptien au xxème siècle*, Paris – The Hague, 1957, p. 42. 'Islamization, reinforcing the significance of the essentials of orthodox Islam for everyday village life' has been observed among the resettled Nubians. See Hussein M. Fahim, 'Change in religion in a resettled Nubian community, Upper Egypt', *IJMES*, April 1973, pp. 163–77. For similar trends in modern Sudan see H. B. Barclay, *Buurri al Lamaab, a surburban village in the Sudan*, Ithaca, N.Y., 1964, pp. 145, 271–2.
127. P. Kahle, 'Zur Organisation der Derwischorden in Ägypten', *Der Islam*, vol. 6, 1915, p. 152; Gibb and Bowen, vol. 2, p. 199; and see discussion of this point in M. Berger, *Islam in Egypt today*, Cambridge, 1970, pp. 69–70.
128. For villages in Daqahliyya, Gharbiyya and Minūfiyya see Mubārak, vol. 11, p. 18; vol. 14, p. 65; vol. 15, pp. 89 and 18; vol. 16, p. 47.
129. For Banī Suwayf and Minyā see ibid., vol. 11, p. 83 and vol. 16, p. 55.
130. Ibid., vol. 11, p. 2.
131. Ibid., vol. 9, pp. 37, 97; vol. 11, pp. 2, 14, 69; vol. 12, p. 54; vol. 13, p. 40; vol. 14, p. 125; vol. 15, p. 79.
132. Ibid., vol. 17, p. 22.
133. For details see Baer, *Studies in the social history of modern Egypt*, pp. 109–113.
134. Cf. id., *A history of landownership*, pp. 1–12, and *passim*.
135. Id., *Studies in the social history of modern Egypt*, p. 45.
136. Ibid., pp. 5–6, 54, 221, 57; 55–6, 58. Since we have dealt with all these developments in great detail in the works given as reference, we are summarizing them here only very shortly.
137. For details see D. Farhi, 'Niẓām-ı Cedid – military reform in Egypt under Meḥmed 'Alī', *Asian and African Studies*, vol. 8, no. 2, 1972, pp. 153 ff., 178.
138. Baer, *Studies in the social history of modern Egypt*, pp. 134–5, 147. According to our revised estimate, the population of 23 important towns in Egypt grew during that time from 9.5 to 14.3 per cent of the total population, which does not make a basic difference.
139. Ibid., pp. 136–46; 148.
140. Charles Issawi, 'Economic change and urbanization in the Middle East', in I. Lapidus (ed.), *Middle Eastern cities*, pp. 102–5.
141. Baer, *Studies in the social history of modern Egypt*, pp. 138, 144.
142. For analyses of this failure see A. E. Crouchley, *The economic development of modern Egypt*, London, 1938, pp. 72–6; M. Fahmy, *La révolution de l'industrie en Egypte et ses conséquences sociales au 19e siècle (1800–1850)*, Leiden, 1954, pp. 98 ff.; H. Rivlin, *The agricultural policy of Muḥammad 'Alī in Egypt*, Cambridge, Mass., 1961, pp. 198–200.

143. For references see Baer, *Egyptian guilds*, pp. 138–9.
144. Ibid., *passim*.
145. See, for instance, Barnett to Canning, 16 March 1845, P.R.O., F.O. 78/623.
146. B. St. John, *Village life in Egypt*, London, 1852, vol. 2, pp. 84–5; Hekekyan Papers, vol. 7, British Museum Add. 37454, fol. 365a.
147. *Correspondence respecting the affairs of Egypt*, Egypt No. 1 (1880), C. 2549, p. 49. Zawats are notables and high officials. Fellahs working on their and Europeans' estates were exempt from forced labour.
148. Mubārak, vol. 10, pp. 31, 100; vol. 12, p. 93; vol. 16, p. 90.
149. For details see Baer, *A history of landownership*, pp. 13–15, 17, 45–60.
150. See for instance, the interesting biography of 'Alī Bey al-Badrāwī, Mubārak, vol. 12, pp. 49–50; cf. Rogers to Stanton, Cairo, 3 November 1871, F.O. 141/75, part 3.
151. Mubārak, vol. 3, pp. 54–5; vol. 15, p. 26.
152. For details on their landed property and urban business see A. Wright and H. A. Cartwright, *Twentieth century impressions of Egypt*, London, 1909, pp. 384, 389, 481–2.
153. Cf. e.g. W. S. Blunt, *Secret history of the English occupation of Egypt*, New York, 1922, pp. 99 ff.; Sir Edward Malet, *Egypt 1879–1833*, London, 1909, p. 128; J. M. Landau, *Parliaments and parties in Egypt*, Tel-Aviv, 1953, p. 85 ff.; or, among the most recent works, A. Schölch, *Ägypten den Ägyptern. Die politische und gesellschaftliche Krise der Jahre 1878–1882 in Ägypten*; Freiburg i. Br., n.d. [1972 or 1973], *passim* (but he puts 'fellachische' in inverted commas).
154. Schölch, p. 316, n. 22 and 24; p. 323, p. 112.
155. Aḥmad 'Urābī, *Mudhakkirāt 'Urābī* (two volumes), Cairo, n.d. (foreword by Liwā' Muḥammad Najīb), vol. 1, p. 62.
156. Ibid., pp. 45, 59, 62, 65, 124, etc.
157. For details and references see Baer, *Studies in the social history of modern Egypt*, pp. 96–9. For the revolt of 1807–8 see Jabartī, vol. 4, p. 62; details of the revolts in 1812 and 1816 are given in Rivlin, p. 113, and of the revolt in 1838 ibid., p. 207. See also below, Part Four, Ch. 2.
158. Jabartī, vol. 4, p. 207.
159. Fīlīb Jallād, *Qāmūs al-idāra wa'l-qaḍā'*, Alexandria, 1890, vol. 3, p. 354.
160. Ibid., vol. 2, p. 98, and A. von Kremer, *Ägypten*, Leipzig, 1863, vol. 2, p. 62. The stress on the *shaykh al-balad* has to do with the rebellious mood that manifested itself among these shaykhs in some districts of Egypt towards the end of Muḥammad 'Alī's rule and in the time of 'Abbās. See Baer, *Studies in the social history of modern Egypt*, p. 54, and sources mentioned there.
161. H. L. Bodman, Jr., *Political factions in Aleppo, 1760–1826*, Chapel Hill, North Carolina, 1963, p. 8.
162. Ibid., p. 63. Another impediment to fellah migration to Damascus was the opposition of tax farmers.
163. C. F. Volney, *Voyage en Egypte et en Syrie pendant les années 1783, 1784 et 1785*, *Oeuvres Complètes*, Paris, 1864, p. 292.
164. Muḥammad Khalīl al-Murādī, *Silk al-durar fī a'yān al-qarn al-thānī*

'ashar, Cairo, 1291–1301, vol. 4, pp. 129–30; vol. 3, p. 207.

165. Quoted by Bodman, p. 100.
166. See I. M. Smilianskaya, 'The Disintegration of feudal relations in Syria and Lebanon in the nineteenth century' in Charles Issawi (ed.), *The economic history of the Middle East*, Chicago and London, 1966, pp. 227–47. For the acquisition of the land near Damascus by members of the Damascus elite in the 1870s see also 'Report by Vice-Consul Jago on the trade and commerce of Damascus for the year 1879', Damascus, 13 March 1880, U.K., F.O., *Diplomatic and Consular Reports CRC*, no. 26 (1880), pp. 1003–6. I am grateful to Dr. Gad Gilbar for having drawn my attention to this report and supplied me with a photographic copy of it.
167. J. Weulersse, 'La primauté des cités dans l'économie syrienne' (see above, note 97), pp. 233–9; and id., *Paysans de Syrie et du Proche Orient*, Paris, 1946, pp. 87–8.
168. Id., *Paysans de Syrie*, pp. 72, 86, 87.
169. Id. 'La primauté des cités', p. 235; *Paysans de Syrie*, p. 88.
170. The present position of the 'Alawīs in the Syrian army and state, and their conflict with the urban Sunnī Muslims, is indeed explained by some observers, *inter alia*, by their rural origin.
171. Id., 'La primauté des cités', p. 235.
172. Ibid., p. 233; Id., *Paysans de Syrie*, p. 87.
173. Id., 'La primauté des cités', p. 233; *Paysans de Syrie*, pp. 87–8.
174. Jacques Weulersse has written an excellent monograph on the 'Alawī region: *Le pays des Alaouites*, Tours, 1940. It should be noted, by the way, that even his findings are represented in a somewhat exaggerated way. Thus he says (*Paysans de Syrie*, p. 87) that the villagers around Antioch are 'alaouites et arabes', but a map in his book (ibid., p. 75) shows clearly that among the villages in the hinterland of Antioch there was quite a large number of Turkish ones.
175. See, for example, lists of villages owned by the Junbalāṭs, Yūsuf Khaṭṭār Abū Shaqrā, *al-Ḥarakāt fī Lubnān*, Beirut, n.d., pp. 7, 93–4. For the *iqṭā'* system of Lebanon see I. Harik, *Politics and change in a traditional society, Lebanon 1711–1845*, Princeton, 1968, pp. 38, 42, 63–4, 68 and *passim*. For the description of the rural residence of a *muqāṭa'ajī*, the Junbalāṭ castle in Mukhtāra, see, e.g., D. Urquhart, *The Lebanon: a history and a diary*, London, 1860, vol. 1, pp. 183–214. A list of residences of Lebanon's notables is found in T. Touma, *Paysans et institutions féodales chez les Druses et les Maronites du Liban du xviime siècle à 1914*, vol. 2, Beyrouth, 1972, p. 439. The social and economic function of the *muqāṭa'ajīs* has been analysed in the excellent work of D. Chevallier, *La societé du Mont Liban à l'époque de la révolution industrielle en Europe*, Paris, 1971.
176. Urquhart, p. 4; Mrs. Finn, 'The fellahheen of Palestine – notes on their clans, warfare, religion, and laws', *PEFQS*, 1879, p. 40.
177. Harik, pp. 62–3; Ibrahim Aouad, *Le droit privé des Maronites*, Paris, 1933, pp. 120–1.
178. Aouad, pp. 240–4.
179. Abū-Shaqrā, p. 86.
180. Mrs. Finn, 'The fellahheen of Palestine' pp. 38–9, 44–5; J. Finn, *Stirring*

times, London, 1878, vol. 1, pp. 216, 220; Ph. Baldensperger, 'The immovable East', *PEFQS*, 1906, p. 15; Yūsuf Jirjis Qadūra, *Ta'rīkh madīnat Rāmallāh*, New York, 1954, pp. 29, 40; as quoted in M. Hoexter (see below, note 185).

181. See below, pp. 290–2.
182. By far the best study of this revolt is Y. Porath, 'The peasant revolt of 1858–61 in Kisrawān', *Asian and African Studies*, vol. 2, 1966, pp. 77–157. The following conclusions are based largely on Porath's study. See also below, Part Four, Ch. 2.
183. Colonel Churchill, *The Druzes and Maronites under the Turkish rule*, London, 1862, pp. 103–8, 181, and *passim*. Cf. also Abū Shaqrā, p. 33; and J. L. Burckhardt, *Travels in Syria and the Holy Land*, London, 1822, p. 193 (for the population of Dayr al-Qamar in 1812).
184. Porath, 'The peasant revolt of 1858–61 in Kisrawān', p. 86.
185. Miriam Hoexter, 'The role of the Qays and Yaman factions in local political divisions – Jabal Nāblus compared with the Judean hills in the first half of the nineteenth century', *Asian and African Studies*, vol. 9, no. 3, 1973, pp. 249–311. With the author's permission, we have heavily drawn on this excellent study. We have not repeated here its detailed documentation.
186. It is most probable that similar relations developed elsewhere as well. Unfortunately, material on the smaller towns is extremely scarce; but without further study of the character of these small towns we will not be able to arrive at a comprehensive analysis of urban-rural relations in the Middle East.
187. For instance, fellahs from the villages of Shaykh Aḥmad al-Sharqāwī came to Cairo to be judged and married by him. See Jabartī, vol. 3, p. 61. See also ibid., pp. 92, 94, 134, 150, 166, 177, 180, 181, 189, 196, 199, 202, 204, 209, 241. No cases of this kind are recorded by Jabartī in vol. 1 and 2 of his work.

3

VILLAGE AND CITY IN THE MIDDLE EAST – DICHOTOMY OR CONTINUUM?

In recent years the question of the relations between village and city in the Middle East has become a subject of frequent discussions. A volume published in 1972 on a conference dealing with rural politics and social change in the Middle East bears witness to the fact that the controversy continues. 'A suggestion which stimulated lively methodological discussion during the Conference was that rural-urban conditions be viewed as a continuum, not a dichotomy'.[1] Such a suggestion or similar views seem to have gained ground among scholars dealing with the history or sociology of Islamic countries. 'Abu-Lughod agrees that to view rural and urban as polar concepts or even as opposite ends of a continuum leads to a misinterpretation of the Egyptian evidence'.[2] '. . . rural and urban categories are likely to assume less importance for analysis. While these terms served a useful purpose in the past they never really acquired precise and distinct meaning'.[3] ' "Rural" and "urban" are another pair of such megaconcepts badly in need, and nowhere more than in Middle Eastern studies, of some kind of disaggregation. A number of people here have stressed that they do not form a dichotomy, which is at least the beginning of wisdom. As Peters said rather more exactly, "city" and "village" don't confront one another as units.'[4] Very similar generalizations have been voiced recently in other studies. Thus we read: 'To understand all the realities of geographical structure in the Muslim world, we should eschew the urban-rural dichotomy . . .' 'The urban-rural antithesis . . . has become increasingly untenable as more varieties of urban experience come within our purview'.[5]

In a paper on urban-rural relations in Ottoman Egypt and Syria,[6] we tried to deal with this problem by means of a concrete analysis of a limited area during a definite period. Two points emerged from this analysis. First, one has to differentiate between three sets of urban-rural relations: similarity or difference, contact or isolation, and conflict or integration. It became clear that there is no necessary parallelism between these different sets of relations: sometimes extremely weak contacts were concomitant with lack of conflicts, but under different circumstances isolation created temporary conflicts; at a certain period, the widening of differences was accompanied by growing contacts, but not with urbanization; and cultural or religious differences between towns and their rural surroundings sometimes went together with economic similarity between the two environments. Secondly, even in so limited an area and period there were extreme differences in urban-rural relations. This was due to the geographical peculiarities of Lebanon and certain parts of Palestine, to different socio-political structures and characteristics of different towns, and to political, economic and social change in specific areas which resulted in changes in urban-rural relations. Under these circumstances any generalization must necessarily be wrong. This is true for some of the above-mentioned quotations, exactly as it is true for the opposite thesis, formulated by Gibb and Bowen as follows: '. . . the contrast which exists between the rural community and the city in every society was rarely more striking than in the medieval Islamic world . . . it was a contrast of civilizations'; and by Weulersse in the following words: '. . . les relations entre les villes et les campagnes d'Orient présentent . . . des caractéristiques originales: l'antagonisme entre citadins et ruraux y atteint un degré tel que l'on peut presque parler de deux populations différentes. . . .'[7] We suspect that everybody generalizes from the conditions in the specific period or area with which he is familiar; what is needed is a detailed analysis of the differences and the reasons leading to these differences.

One specific issue of the complex of rural-urban relations is the question of the domination of the countryside by the city. In the volume mentioned above this question is being discussed by two authors, Planhol and Harik, each of them holding a different view. According to the paper by Xavier de Planhol, 'rent capitalism' and 'a system in which the city dominated the countryside' largely predated Islam but was adopted by it. 'It was also nurtured by the instability and hazards of pluvial cultivation, which forced the peasants in poor years to apply for loans from the city lenders; this in turn usually led to absentee ownership of large estates'.[8] This statement is certainly not applicable to Ottoman Egypt. True, there was no 'pluvial cultivation' in Egypt, but irrigation by the Nile flood was no less unstable and hazardous. Nevertheless, there was no rent capitalism with indebtedness of peasants to city money-lenders or absentee ownership of large estates, although the city dominated the countryside economically. Moreover, in the rain-fed agriculture of the Ottoman Fertile Crescent there was no rent capitalism either. The mistake is the result of equating the economic domination of the countryside by the city with capitalist exploitation. But the same mistake is being made by Planhol's critic, I. Harik. Harik points out that 'economic domination of rural areas by urban-based groups, such as merchants, money-lenders, and absentee land-lords . . . is a relatively modern phenomenon, concomitant with the emergence of a domestic market and demand for cash crops. . . . It was the state, not urban interests, which dominated rural areas before the advent of a market economy'.[9] But was not the state, at least in Ottoman Egypt, an 'urban-based agency'? Harik is perfectly right when he says: '. . . grain upon which the city population depended for livelihood was transferred to the major cities not as a commercial transaction but in the form of taxes paid in kind to the government . . . Also grain which was obtained by *multazims* from their *uhdahs* was sold in the urban market where most of the *multazims* lived'.[10] If this is not economic domination by an urban-based agency – what is? How else was the fellah dominated by the state than by the exploitation through the urban-based *multazims.* Thus urban economic domination is not necessarily identical with rent capitalism, as implied by Harik.[11] The contrast between the nineteenth century and the period preceding it is not between urban economic domination of the village and its absence, but rather between cash-crop producing villages and urban merchants, and exploitation of indebted fellahs by urban moneylenders and absentee landlords on one hand, and economic domination of the fellah by the state through urban-based tax farmers combined with relative isolation between town and countryside – on the other hand.

Anybody claiming that the categories of village and city are irrelevant for the analysis of the social history or the social reality of the Middle East will have to find an explanation for the recurring consciousness of an urban-rural dichotomy in the writings of Arab authors, in oral tradition, and in attitudes as reflected in interviews with researchers and as expressed in informal talk. It is this aspect which has been disregarded so far in the discussion on urban-rural relations, and to which I intend to contribute some remarks on this occasion. Anthropologists and sociologists dealing with these relations will certainly have to take into account the way in which they are seen by the people concerned themselves.

Writers in Ottoman Egypt and other Arab provinces were definitely conscious of differences and conflicts between city and countryside as well as between fellah and townsman. Writing in the sixteenth century, 'Abd al-Wahhāb al-Sha'rānī, the Egyptian Ṣūfī shaykh and writer, frequently expresses the contrast which existed at that time between Cairo and the countryside, and the tendency of certain *'ulamā'* to conceal or disavow their rural origin.[12] In the seventeenth century Yūsuf al-Shirbīnī composed his *Hazz al-quḥūf fī sharḥ qaṣīd Abī-Shādūf*, whose main theme is the difference between the fellah and the townsman and the conflicts between them.[13] From the same century we have a Geniza text on 'the Maṣrī and the Rīfī', written in a similar vein.[14] In the eighteenth century Muḥammad Khalīl al-Murādī tells us various stories about polemics among *'ulamā'* concerning the rural origin of some of them.[15] A few decades later the historian al-Jabartī and the *'ālim* and poet Ḥasan Badrī al-Ḥijāzī whom he quotes frequently, enumerate what they consider to be the characteristic peculiarities which distinguish the fellah from the townsman.[16]

But even in the twentieth century we frequently find such confrontations in Egyptian literature. In the 1930s the Egyptian authoress Ibnat al-Shāṭi' published a number of books on the Egyptian fellah in which she complains that everything is done for the city whose inhabitants enjoy all rights, while the village is neglected, overburdened with taxes and humiliated.[17] Khālid Muḥammad Khālid, who wrote in the early 1950s, went even further. In one of his books he claims that millions of villagers in Egypt consider Egyptian towns and their inhabitants to be the cause of all the calamities which have befallen Egypt.[18] An interesting book, from this point of view, is a recent novel by the Egyptian writer, 'Abd al-Ḥakīm Qāsim, whose subject is the Egyptian village and the changes which it underwent after the revolution. Notwithstanding these changes, in the author's view the gap between city and village has widened in recent years. A fellah who comes to Ṭanṭā, a large town in the Delta, feels as if he came to a strange country and to a hostile environment.[19] The feeling that the gap between town and village has widened seems to have been widespread in Egypt in the 1960s. Thus the author of an article on village education published in 1965 concludes that, as the result of revolutionary progress, the town has left the village far behind (*qad jāwazat* (*al-madīna*) *al-rīf bi-marāḥil*), and he warns Egyptian society of the serious consequences of the continuing isolation of the town from the countryside.[20]

Differences and conflicts between peasants and townsmen are deep-rooted in the consciousness of the population of Palestine as well. This feeling is reflected, for instance, in the common proverbs of Palestine collected by Sa'īd 'Abbūd in the 1930s.[21] Among those dealing with the fellah, the following are noteworthy: *el-fallāḥ fallāḥ walaw akal ish-shūrbā bi'sh-shawkeh* (the fellah remains a fellah, even if he ate the soup with a fork); and *il-fellah quffet tuffāḥ w'il-madanī quffet jadarī* (the fellah is a basket full of apples, and the townsman is a basket full of smallpox), and 'Abbud explains: just as the townsman despises the fellah and ridicules him, so does the fellah make fun of the townsman. These seem to be socially significant attitudes to this very day. In a study of the professional elite in Samaria towns (West Bank) carried out by scholars from Tel-Aviv University in the 1970s, it was found that 'rural origin, in these towns, is a mark of lowly social status. . . . Research has revealed that considerable tension exists between the "white collar" people who are of urban origin and those of rural origin: the former tend to emphasize the inferiority of the latter, and the latter, on their part, seek to establish for themselves a proper status in the city and collaborate with one another (and with other groups of rural origin) for the achievement of this purpose.'[22]

To sum up: the discussion whether urban-rural relations in the Middle East are a 'dichotomy' or a 'continuum' seems to be rather futile. Instead of generalizing from specific conditions, the time has come to acknowledge the fact that in the Middle East we find areas and periods of similarity, contacts, and integration between town and countryside, as well as areas and periods of differences, isolation and conflict between village and city. There still is much to be done to analyse the different conditions and attitudes and their specific causes.

NOTES

1. Richard Antoun and Ilya Harik, editors, *Rural Politics and Social Change in the Middle East*, Bloomington and London: Indiana University Press, 1972, p. 10.
2. Ibid., p. 11.
3. Ibid., pp. 12–13 (both quotations from the editors' introduction).
4. Ibid., p. 463 (comments of Clifford Geertz).
5. I. Lapidus and J. Abu-Lughod in I. Lapidus (ed.), *Middle Eastern Cities*, Univ. of California Press, 1969, pp. 67, 159. Cf. L. Carl Brown (ed.), *From Madina to Metropolis*, Princeton, 1973, p. 39.
6. See above, Part One, Ch. 2.
7. H. A. R. Gibb and H. Bowen, *Islamic Society and the West*, vol. 1, part 1, London, 1950, p. 276; J. Weulersse, *Paysans de Syrie et du Proche Orient*, Paris, 1946, p. 85.
8. Antoun and Harik (ed.), p. 104.
9. Ibid., p. 6.
10. Ibid., pp. 341–2.
11. Ibid., pp. 338, 345, 362–3, etc.
12. Cf. M. Winter, 'Sha'rānī and Egyptian society in the sixteenth century', *Asian and African Studies*, vol. 9 (1973), no. 3, pp. 324–9.
13. See above, Part One, Ch. 1.
14. S. D. Goitein, 'Townsman and fellah – a Geniza text from the seventeenth century', *Asian and African Studies*, vol. 8 (1972), no. 3, pp. 257–61.
15. Muḥammad Khalīl al-Murādī, *Silk al-durar fī a'yān al-qarn al-thānī 'ashar*, Cairo, Būlāq, 1291–1301 H, vol. 3, p. 276.

16. ʻAbd al-Raḥmān al-Jabartī, *ʻAjā'ib al-āthār fī'l-tarājim wa'l-akhbār*, Cairo, Būlāq, 1297H, vol. 4, p. 208.
17. Ibnat al-Shāṭi', *al-Rīf al-miṣrī*, Cairo, 1936, pp. 14, 94, 126–8, etc. id., *Qaḍiyyat al-fallāḥ*, Cairo, n.d. (1938–9), pp. 53, 101, 108, 153.
18. Khālid Muḥammad Khālid, *Min hunā . . . nabda'*, Nazareth, 1959, p. 73.
19. ʻAbd al-Ḥakīm Qāsim, *Ayyām al-insān al-sabʻa*, Cairo, 1969, p. 119 and *passim*. I am grateful to my student Mr. ʻAdnān al-Saʻdī for this reference.
20. ʻAbd al-Khāliq al-Sahāwī, ʻal-Taʻlīm wa'l-thaqāfa fī al-rīf', *al-Kātib*, March 1965, p. 111.
21. Saʻīd ʻAbbūd, *5,000 arabische Sprichwörter aus Palästina*, Berlin 1933, p. 142, nos. 3122–3128, especially 3123 and 3125.
22. S. Shamir, R. Shapira, E. Rekhess, S. Tibon, I. Stockman, *The Professional elite in Samaria*, Tel-Aviv, Shiloah Center, 1975, p. 79. Our quotation is from the English *Summary of Findings* published by the Shiloah Center in March 1976, p. 23, except for the passage in brackets which we have added according to the Hebrew original.

Part Two

THE VILLAGE SHAYKH IN PALESTINE

1

THE OFFICE AND FUNCTIONS OF THE MUKHTĀRS

The office of *mukhtār* was first established by the Ottoman Law of Vilayets of 1864.[1] According to this law, every group of people (*sınıf*) in a village should elect two mukhtārs, but a group of less than 20 houses was entitled to elect only one. The term *sınıf* does not specify the character of these groups, which means that the Ottoman legislator intended the existing traditional groups to be represented by the holders of the new office. These were the *ḥamūlas* (clans) and religious communities. Though this was contrary to the territorial character of the Law of Vilayets, the Ottoman government was apparently compelled, at that stage of the reforms, to base the administration partly on traditional units, as it did in the towns with respect to the guilds. In any case, the principle that mukhtārs represent groups within the village continues to hold up to our days, though from time to time a tendency emerges to appoint only one mukhtār for the whole village as a territorial unit. Thus, as early a law as the Law of Vilayet Administration of 1871 provided for the possibility that a village might have only one mukhtār if this was sufficient for the administration of the village.[2]

The appointment of mukhtārs made slow progress during the last third of the nineteenth century. By the beginning of the twentieth century the process had been completed in theory, but not in practice.

The temporary law of general vilayet administration published by the Young Turks in 1913, as well as its amendment of 1914, reiterated the stipulation that every village should have a mukhtār, and that if there were different groups in the village each was entitled to a mukhtār of its own.[3] These laws were in force when Palestine was occupied by the British army and the British Mandate was imposed. In 1934, however, the Mandatory Municipal Corporations Ordinance repealed the Ottoman laws of local administration and left village administration without a legal basis. Though mukhtārs continued to be appointed as if the Law of Vilayets was still in force, the enactment of a new law became necessary. In 1940, the High Commissioner appointed a committee which presented a detailed and extremely illuminating report in 1941.[4] Among other recommendations, the committee reiterated the suggestion to confine the number of mukhtārs, if possible, to one for every village. According to data presented to the committee, villages of less than 1,000 inhabitants had in fact, as a rule, only one mukhtār, but villages between 1,000 and 5,000 had more than two and villages with more than 5,000 inhabitants had from 4 to 11 mukhtārs. A great number of mukhtārs in one village, rather than satisfying rival claims, may result in keeping alive the flame of party rivalry – asserted the committee. Only in very large villages, or in places with different religious communities, did the committee justify the appointment of assistants to mukhtārs, but nowhere of more than one major mukhtār.[5] A new Mandatory Ordinance to regulate village administration was finally issued in 1944, but it left things more or less as they were before: every village would have a mukhtār or some mukhtārs and assistant mukhtārs – as required by the size of the village or other conditions.[6]

After the termination of the Mandate, the 'West Bank' was annexed by the Hashemite Kingdom of Jordan, which replaced the 1944 Ordinance by a new, practically identical law of 1954. According to this law, too, the number of mukhtārs in each village was flexible,[7] but the office of assistant mukhtār was no longer provided for in Jordanian legislation of rural administration. Instead, so-called 'village committees', or 'makhtara committees', were established to assist the mukhtār in the performance of his functions. Candidates for membership in these committees were to be named by the mukhtār and confirmed or rejected by the Governor of the Province (*mutaṣarrif al-liwā*), who was also to determine the number of the members of the committee (generally two to three). Whenever the government was reluctant to appoint additional mukhtārs, the establishment of such a committee was recommended instead. It was a device to grant representation to various components of the village population without creating a top-heavy administration. The number of such committees in the West Bank, prior to 1967, amounted to more than thirty.[8] Anyway, the tendency to organize village administration on a territorial base was scarcely successful. In practically all villages which include more than one important *ḥamūla*, each *ḥamūla* of this kind is represented by a mukhtār of its own.[9]

A major innovation of the Law of Vilayets was the introduction of formal election of the mukhtār. According to that law the mukhtārs were to be elected for one year (with the right to unlimited re-election) by males of their group over 18 years who paid more than 50 piastres as direct taxes. The Kaimakam had only to confirm the election.[10] In fact, the mukhtār was rarely elected in this democratic fashion. True, evidence from the Jerusalem Sancak shows that late in the nineteenth and early in the twentieth century, elections for the office of mukhtār took place. But only very few participated in these elections, probably only the chiefs of the main families in the village.[11] Apparently the reality was less formal and nearer the following description given by the Committee on Village Administration: 'In practice, however, election in the ordinary sense did not take place. They were in fact the nominees of the local administration, which, although account was taken of the wishes of the people when appointments were made, put the interests of the Government first, following the principle of direct control.'[12]

As we have seen, the Law of Vilayets was in force up to 1934, and only in 1942 did the High Commissioner issue an order providing for the appointment of the mukhtār and his dismissal by the Governor of the Province, no mention being made any more of an election. In fact, however, not many elections to the post of mukhtār seem to have been held in Mandatory Palestine even prior to the new order. Usually the mukhtārs were appointed and dismissed by the District Officers, and if the latter took into account the view of the village notables, they did not do so in any formal way.[13] This situation was finally legalized in the 1944 Ordinance, which did not provide for elections at all.[14]

Election of the mukhtār by male villagers over 18 years was reintroduced by the Hashemite Kingdom of Jordan, the successor state of the British Mandate in the West Bank. Regulations for such elections were to be issued by the Governors, who also retained the right to dismiss a mukhtār if they had good reason to do so.[15] In fact, such regulations were issued for both Nablus and Hebron provinces in 1955. They differed in one major provision: the Governor of Nablus allowed village notables of this province to agree – according to a clearly defined procedure – on one candidate for the post of mukhtār and thus to make the election redundant. In such a case, only the objection of more than a quarter of the adult male villagers would enforce the holding of elections.[16] In addition to this system of election by agreement, many mukhtārs continued to be appointed by governors without election, as in Mandatory times; but even in these cases the governors probably took into account the trends of village opinion.[17] This system seems to have been the prevalent one during Jordanian rule of the West Bank. A breakdown of cases of new mukhtārs in the files of the Jordanian administration of the West Bank shows the following distribution:

Election and Appointment of Mukhtārs in the West Bank, 1949–1967

	Total new muktārs		Appointment without elections		Agreement without elections		Elections by majority	
Province	number	per cent	number	per cent	number	per cent	number	per cent
Nablus	49	100.0	25	51.0	17	34.7	7	14.3
Hebron	120	100.0	73	60.9	30	25.0	17	14.1
Total	169	100.0	98	58.0	47	27.8	24	14.2

It is remarkable that the percentage of mukhtārs elected in Nablus and Hebron is practically identical. Thus it would seem that the option opened by the Governor of Nablus – nomination through agreement by notables – substituted direct appointment by the authorities rather than elections by majority.

Village opinion was of course not the only consideration of governors who appointed or dismissed mukhtārs. But among the reasons given for the dismissal of mukhtārs in the West Bank between 1949 and 1967 the most frequent was disagreement between the mukhtār and his *ḥamūla* (or most of its members) or deterioration of relations among the villagers.[18] This shows that village opinion had an important influence on the deliberations of the government in this matter. However, in many villages the office of mukhtār was customarily inherited within a certain family.[19] In a memorandum submitted by the Banī ʻAwda *ḥamūla* from Ṭamūn village in June 1955 to the Prime Minister of Jordan and many other addressees they claimed that the backwardness of the village was due to the fact that the makhtara was inherited within one family which, in the view of the petitioners, was not interested in the welfare of the village.[20] In Ṣūrīf the office of one of the mukhtārs was held by one family (brothers and sons) for decades, a fact which was advanced as a strong argument by the nephew of a dismissed mukhtār who aspired after the office himself (ʻ *ʻilman bi'anna al-makhtara al-shāghira mundhu al-qidam hiya liʻā'ilatina* . . .ʼ).[21] Often the son of a mukhtār officiated as acting mukhtār when his father became old or sick and was then appointed to the office when the father died.[22]

In addition to these considerations, the economic and social position of the mukhtār was taken into account, as well as his education.[23] However, almost half of the dismissals of mukhtārs in the West Bank between 1949 and 1967 were accounted for by administrative, political and security reasons, such as lack of cooperation with the government, neglect of the functions of the office, harm to security, shielding of criminals and smugglers, etc. The best recommendation for an aspirant to the office of mukhtār was cooperation with the government, while any connection with 'one of the parties' (which were all opposition parties) was explicitly given by the Governor of Hebron as a good reason to reject a candidate.[24]

By and large, the stabilizing factors seem to have outweighed the motives for replacing mukhtārs with others. In 89 villages of Nablus District there were, in 1957, 134 mukhtārs of whom only 23 (17.2 per cent) were replaced by others in the course of eight years, until 1965, while 111 (82.8 per cent) remained in their office. In 21 villages of Hebron Province, more than half the mukhtārs retained their position from 1949 to 1960 (and almost half up to 1963), in spite of changes in the administration, innumerable complaints of mukhtārs submitted to the Jordanian administration as the result of village conflicts, serious security problems, stormy political events, and natural mortality.[25]

Thus, the Palestinian mukhtār belonged to the kind of office holders whose administrative functions were performed within a unit of traditional society, such as the *ḥamūla*, the village community, or the professional guild. In order to guarantee its effective control, the government always retained the right to appoint and dismiss these functionaries. However, since they acted within a traditional framework, it was compelled to take into consideration the view of influential leaders of these units and the custom that the office of their heads was inheritable within specific families. The relative weight of these factors differed according to different conditions. The more remote a place was from central government, the greater was the autonomy of traditional units and therefore the importance of social tradition and the influence of the community leaders in choosing the administrative chief of the unit. In the appointment of the *'umda* in centralistic Egypt, the say of the government was always relatively more decisive than in the appointment of mukhtārs in the hilly areas of the Fertile Crescent, where the *ḥamūla* leaders had greater influence. Similarly, Westernization strengthened the central government: in Egypt, British occupation did away with the large autonomy which rural notables had enjoyed in the time of Ismā'īl, and Mandatory rule in Palestine never acknowledged *de facto*, and after 1942 not even *de jure*, the principle that the mukhtār be elected by his village or *ḥamūla*.[26] Finally, even where elections were held before the middle of the twentieth century, they were never formal popular democratic elections, but rather informal consultations of notables with the aim of reaching agreement and electing a chief by acclamation.

Ever since the creation of the office of the mukhtār, one of his principal functions, if not his principal function, was to maintain order and security in the village. The 1864 Law of Vilayets stipulated that the guardians of the villages, such as *bekcis* (field wards), *korucus* (forest watchmen) and others, were subject to the orders of the mukhtār. In the Law of Vilayet Administration of 1871, the functions of the mukhtārs were ennumerated in detail. They were obliged to inform the Ottoman official in charge of a group of villages of any violent conflicts or murders in their villages and to assist in delivering the culprits into the hands of the government. In addition, they were to supervise the activity of the field wards and forest watchmen as well as other guards appointed by the council of elders in the village.[27] As we have seen, these regulations remained in force until 1934 in theory, and in fact until they were replaced by the Village Administration Ordinance of 1944. Meantime, the security functions of the mukhtārs were confirmed in several other Mandatory laws, such as the Police Ordinance which reiterated the duty of the mukhtārs, in conjunction with village notables, to appoint *ghafīrs* (guards), the Ordinance of Criminal Procedure which provided for the mukhtār to accompany police officers in the exercise of their duties in the village, or the Firearms Ordinance which entitled the mukhtār to require the production of firearm licenses and of firearms and ammunition.[28] In this context, a passage from a report on the Palestine police force written in 1930 by H. L. Dowbiggin is of special interest. He said that 'the police will . . . look to the Headman as their principal means for getting information as to what is going on in the village . . . The inspecting officer should make a point of asking the Headman if the Police are treating them with every consideration and with the respect due to their rank . . . The Headman, if questioned, may have some ideas as to how the patrol system might be organised to better advantage . . .'[29]

The Village Administration Ordinance of 1944 again stressed the security functions of the mukhtār and did not leave any doubt that these were his major functions. Article 40, which deals with the mukhtār's duties, opens with his obligation to maintain order and security in his village, to inform the police about criminals, vagabonds, foreigners, or suspicious persons who are found in the village, or of any intention to commit an offence which may come to his knowledge. It then goes on to state that it is his duty to send information as soon as possible to the nearest police station of every serious offence or accident or death due to unnatural causes occurring in the village, and also to report every case of the use of false weights or measures. The Jordanian Law of Village Administration of 1954 adopted these articles verbatim.[30] In addition, the Jordanian mukhtārs were obliged, according to special legislation, to assist the Attorney General.[31]

Additional duties connected with security were imposed on the mukhtārs of the West Bank during the period of Jordanian rule as the result of the special military situation of the Kingdom. For guarding the villages, special police were appointed who were paid by the villagers.[32] But while the mukhtārs were ordered to man and finance this unit, a military officer was appointed as responsible commander of the guard, which frequently caused friction.[33] The mukhtārs were also responsible for the payment for arms supplied to the villages, for storing the arms, for preventing the inhabitants from going too near the border, and for fighting infiltrators, spies and smugglers.[34] Various duties of a similar character were assigned to the mukhtārs by the laws concerning the National Guard and National Service.[35] In addition, the mukhtārs were supposed to recruit villagers for public works with security implications, such as digging trenches, erecting security fences or paving roads,[36] but often the help of the police or the army was needed to put the work into practice.[37]

All these duties were the result of an external security situation, but internal security conditions of the villages occupied the attention of the mukhtārs as well. Thus one of their concerns was to prevent fights between different villages. The Mukhtār of Jab'a village, for instance, explained to the Governor of Hebron, in a memorandum dated January 21, 1957, that one of the reasons for the hostility against him which prevailed in his village was the time-honoured custom of the villagers to raid neighbouring villages and plunder them, an activity against which he, the mukhtār, had taken severe measures.[38]

It would seem, therefore, that the security concerns of the mukhtār were not only an important part of his functions, but that they increased and ramified in the course of time and of different regimes. These duties confronted the mukhtār with difficult problems. Unlike the traditional village shaykh,[39] the modern mukhtār had neither the social prestige and authority nor the armed retainers to enable him to maintain order and to punish criminals. Since Mandatory times, the complaint has been voiced that numerous duties and functions had been imposed on the mukhtār, but that, in fact, he had no executive authority over the village population.[40] Apparently the 1944 and 1954 laws attempted to overcome this disadvantage by conferring on the mukhtār the authority of a police officer, but it is extremely doubtful whether this measure achieved its aim. The weakness and helplessness of the mukhtār in implementing his authority over his villages has been described very well in Richard Antoun's study of the Jordanian village Kufr al-Mā.[41] He says that if members of the clan refuse to pay their dues to the mukhtār, he is powerless to force them to do so. Moreover, for social reasons, he is extremely reluctant to use the governmental authority vested in him against recalcitrant clansmen or even other villagers. By virtue of his office, he can call on the support of such government officials as subdistrict officer or police chief, but he seldom does so. Antoun reports that in the twelve-month period in which he stayed in the village (November 1959–November 1960), the mukhtār of Banī Yāsīn requested the intervention of government authority only twice; in one case, when the mounted police arrived, he apologized and told them that the dispute had been settled amicably by the villagers themselves. Similarly, in the above-mentioned memorandum of the Mukhtār of Jab'a dated January 1957, he frankly admitted that he had concealed and hushed up a murder case 'in order not to arouse fraternal strife'.[42] The mukhtār fears alienation of his *ḥamūla* and violation of the prevalent conception that the village is the proper framework of social control, of mediation and punishment, rather than government administration, courts, and police.

Such an attitude, and sometimes perhaps also avarice and greed, gave rise to frequent complaints that the mukhtārs did not discharge their security and police duties properly. In the files of the Jordanian administration of the West Bank, one can find many petitions accusing mukhtārs of having received hush-money to disregard thefts, of having shielded relatives who had committed offences, of having hidden fugitive criminals, of having concealed murder cases, of having freed persons who had been rightfully arrested, etc.[43] Frequently, mukhtārs were reported to have tried to delete names from the lists of military conscripts.[44] In all these respects, there existed a remarkable similarity between the Palestinian mukhtār and the Egyptian *'umda*.[45]

Nevertheless, concern for village security remained the main responsibility of the Palestinian mukhtār, as it did in Egypt of the *'umda*. In Egypt, this function of the *'umda* was abolished in villages where police stations had been established. In less centralized Palestine, such a development has not yet taken place, but mukhtārs have begun to voice the demand that a police station be established in their village.[46] This may have been the first sign that in Palestine too, sooner or later, the office of mukhtār may disappear.

Though concern for security was the principal function of the mukhtār, it certainly was not the only one. When the office of mukhtār was created in the nineteenth century, the Ottoman administration intended it to fulfil an important purpose in its system of taxation. Prior to the era of reform, taxes were collected by the traditional village shaykhs who served as *multazim*s (tax farmers) or sub-*multazim*s.[47] The replacement of the village shaykh by the mukhtār as tax collector was designed to put an end to the *iltizām* which was legally abolished in 1839 and again in 1856.[48] Indeed, in the 1864 Law of Vilayets, the mukhtār was made the agent of the government for the purpose of collecting taxes in the village, while the Council of Elders was to supervise the distribution of the tax burden among the villagers; and the 1871 Law of Vilayet Administration reiterated the duty of the mukhtārs to collect taxes in accordance with the decision of the Council of Elders and government instructions.[49] However, these laws alone were not enough to bring about the desired changes in practice. *Iltizām* persisted as the prevalent system of tax collection until World War I,[50] and the mukhtārs generally did not collect the taxes.[51] It should be noted, however, that in the early years of the twentieth century, Ottoman administration in the Sancak of Jerusalem made an attempt to do away with *iltizām* by encouraging the mukhtārs to compete with the *multazims* at the *muzāyada* (the auction of tax farming) and to farm the taxes themselves in the name of their villagers. They would have to distribute the tax burden among the villagers and they or the villagers would sign a contract stating the amount of taxes to be paid, which then would be collected by the *mudīr al-naḥiya* (the official in charge of a sub-district).[52] According to another description of this system, it was not the mukhtārs but the village notables or the Council of Elders (*ikhtiyāriyya*) who distributed the tax burden among the villagers,[53] as laid down in the Law of Vilayets. The laws of vilayet administration published by the Young Turks in 1913 and 1914 confirmed the duty of the Council of Elders in the villages to distribute the tax burden among the villagers.[54] But whoever distributed the tax burden, Ottoman government in Palestine did not succeed, prior to World War I, in abolishing the *iltizām* by substituting the mukhtārs for the *multazims*.

The British occupation of Palestine did not do away immediately with the collective responsibility of the village for the payment of taxes. For some years to come, the mukhtārs and the village elders used to sign an obligation of the village as a whole and afterwards to distribute the burden among its inhabitants. Only in 1922 was the collective tax liability of the village abolished, and taxes were collected, from then onwards, from each peasant individually. The mukhtārs became the representatives of the regional tax authorities and collected the taxes from the peasants according to individual assessments.[55] A similar change had taken place in Egypt seventy years earlier, in Saʿīd's days. In Egypt, new duties of the *ʿumda* in the sphere of taxation replaced the old function of distributing the tax burden.[56] The same happened in Palestine in the 1920s. Thus he was required (together with the village elders) to nominate candidates for membership in the committee for tithe assessment; to inform the government when the crops had been gathered and were ready for tax assessment; he was made responsible, together with the village elders, for the crops stored in the barn or the threshing-floor; and if the committee for the assessment of the taxes had not acted within a time-limit fixed by law, the mukhtār and the village elders were entitled to perform the assessment themselves.[57] In addition, the mukhtārs were required, according to laws promulgated in the 1920s and 1930s, to assist the government tax collectors in sequestrations and confiscations; to certify the ability of tax defaulters to pay taxes due; to keep safe goods which had been confiscated; to certify statements of petitioners for exemption from rural property tax; to prepare lists for collection of animal tax; to register flocks exempted from payment of animal tax; to help in procedures of confiscation in connection with animal tax, etc.[58]

There can be no doubt that these numerous and variegated functions in the sphere of taxation conferred on the mukhtār in the 1920s and 1930s a central position in Palestine's village economy. British Mandatory administration tended to reduce this position and these functions of the mukhtār. After the British occupation of Egypt, in the 1880s, the Egyptian *'umda* had been deprived of his function to assess and collect taxes.[59] Similarly, the Mandatory Ordinance of 1944 did not any longer consider these activities to be the explicit duty of the mukhtārs. Among the manifold functions of the mukhtār enumerated in article 40 of this law, tax collection is mentioned only indirectly in paragraph 3 as follows: '. . . to assist the officers of Government in the execution of their duty, including the collection of revenue.' The Jordanian law of 1954 adopted this provision word for word.[60] The assistance to government officials consisted of course mainly in information and registration. Thus the mukhtārs were required, under Jordanian rule as in Mandatory times, to transfer tax assessments and demands to the tax-payers, to keep registers of taxation of buildings, and to serve as members of committees conducting live-stock censuses for the purpose of taxation.[61]

In fact, however, the mukhtārs did much more than just assist officials of the inland revenue department. First, they participated as members in the committees which assessed the property and solvency of the villagers and thus they took part in preparing the lists of persons who were subject to taxation.[62] In the years 1944–51, the mukhtārs of some villages in Samaria prepared lists of villagers according to the following classification: persons without property, persons with property who live in the village, and landowners without houses who do not usually live in the village but are liable to taxation.[63] After the tax had been assessed, the mukhtārs had many ways of influencing decisions on exemption from taxation because of crop failure, animal diseases, loss of land, emigration, or just individual hardship.[64] All these activities enabled the mukhtārs, of course, to influence the burden of taxation imposed on individual villagers. Indeed, villagers frequently voiced complaints and accusations of discrimination and favouritism against mukhtārs.[65]

But the mukhtār had other means as well to turn his office to his own economic, social, and political advantage. Thus, for instance, at the time of Jordanian rule, the distribution of government aid and relief was added to his regular duties. This aid was of two kinds: development subsidies for afforestation, amelioration of land, etc., and relief for refugees, poor people, and inhabitants of border villages. To judge by complaints found in the files of the Jordanian administration, it would seem that the mukhtārs were able to benefit both from preparing the lists of villagers entitled to aid and from the distribution itself. They were accused of deleting from the lists names of persons entitled to aid and adding names of their relatives or fictitious names,[66] of accepting bribes for including persons in the lists, or preparing defective lists because of family strife.[67] Frequently, it was claimed that the money remained with the mukhtār and was not distributed at all, or that the mukhtār distributed reduced quantities of goods and food and mixed them with inferior materials.[68] Many of such claims and accusations turned out to be false, but they would not have been launched had it not been likely that the mukhtārs turned these functions to their own economic, social or political advantage. Opportunities to do this were one reason why villagers fiercely competed for the office of mukhtār although the prestige attached to it had considerably declined. A similar situation seems to have existed in Turkey: it has been pointed out that the fact that the Turkish muhtar distributed government aid to villagers was the main reason for his high status among them and for the great demand for this office in Turkish villages.[69]

As against the mukhtār's functions in the sphere of taxation and as distributor of government aid, which entailed opportunities of making material and social profit, a large number of administrative duties was imposed on him which constituted a heavy burden with no attached advantages at all. Since the 1871 Law of Vilayet Administration, the mukhtār was supposed to transmit information from the government to the villages and vice versa. He was required to publish in his village laws, regulations and ordinances, to inform defendants that they must appear in court and the authorities when they would be able to appear, to inform the competent authorities of births and deaths in the village, in particular of deaths of persons with heirs who were minors or absent, and so on.[70] In Mandatory times, the mukhtār continued to serve as a source and a channel of information for the government on events in the village and for the village about the demands of the government. In this respect the 1944 Ordinance adopted, with small changes, part of the provisions of the 1871 Law of Vilayet Administration, and the Jordanian law followed the former word for word.[71] Many Jordanian laws, especially those concerned with taxation and agriculture, mention the mukhtār as the conveyor of government instructions to the villagers. In addition, from time to time the mukhtārs were supplied with official circulars containing such matters as conditions of loans to agriculturists and similar information.[72] In the past the mukhtār's position as the principal source of information in the village had considerably enhanced his prestige and social status. But the development of modern means of communication enabled a growing number of villagers to go to town and to obtain information through other sources, such as newspapers, radio and television, and today a large proportion of villagers in Palestine are literate. The mukhtār continues, of course, to transmit government instructions to the villagers, but as a result of these developments, his position as a source of information declined and the prestige connected with this position was severely damaged.

While the 1871 Law of Vilayet Administration required no more than periodic information about births and deaths, the Mandatory government introduced the obligation of mukhtārs to keep registers of births and deaths in the village.[73] The 1944 Ordinance and the 1954 Law did not specify the kind of registers the mukhtār was supposed to keep, but the Personal Status Law of 1966 made it clear that the mukhtār's duty was to register births and deaths and even details about the health condition of the villagers.[74] Since this constituted a profitless burden for the mukhtārs, they frequently neglected this duty. The files of the Jordanian administration include numerous memoranda demanding of mukhtārs to comply with the instructions to keep these registers and accusing them of ignorance and obduracy for neglecting to do so.[75]

Other administrative burdens too were imposed on the mukhtār in the Mandatory and Jordanian periods. The laws of 1944 and 1954 required the mukhtār to do his best to guard railways, telegraph and telephone communications, roads, forests, and other government property, and to notify the government of any damage occurring to such property. Similarly, he was required to inform the authorities about antiquities which were discovered in his village and to conserve them, as well as to maintain monuments and historical sites.[76] When the Hashemite Kingdom introduced parliamentary elections, the village mukhtārs were required to participate in committees for preparing the lists of voters and to publish those lists. Similarly, they were supposed to prepare and keep lists for local elections.[77] Thus, concerning the functions of the mukhtār, the Mandatory and Jordanian periods correspond to the period of British domination in Egypt (1882–1922) in which many new duties were imposed on *'umda* as the result of the reorganization of the administration – partly the same duties as those mentioned above.[78] It was felt then that this burden surpassed the capabilities of the *'umda*, and indeed from the 1920s onwards, many of these functions were transferred to the appropriate government departments.[79] This stage of development had not yet been reached in the West Bank when Jordanian rule ended in 1967.

There was, however, one administrative duty from which mukhtārs were able to derive considerable material and other profit, by legal means or otherwise. This was their authority to issue certificates and affidavits of various kinds. The first time this duty was mentioned was in the 1871 Law of Vilayet Administration, which entitled the mukhtār to issue affidavits for persons who had applied for transit certificates.[80] In Mandatory times this authority of the mukhtār was also originally confined to the same purpose,[81] but the 1944 Ordinance on Village Administration extended it and demanded of the mukhtār to keep a seal to be affixed to all certificates and documents which require a seal. This provision, like most other provisions of this Ordinance, was reiterated verbatim by the Jordanian Law of 1954.[82] The need to confirm certificates by affixing the mukhtār's seal and signature was indeed considerably extended in the Jordanian period, and villagers were very frequently compelled to have recourse to the mukhtār to verify their documents. For instance, without the mukhtār's signature and seal, no claim to an inheritance would be accepted by the *Sharīʿa* Court, since the mukhtār kept the registration of both personal status and landownership, and the final division of the estate (*maḍbaṭat ḥaṣr irth*) again needed the mukhtār's signatures.[83] Similarly, the mukhtār's signature was required for marriage contracts, as well as for the issuing of identity cards and passports.[84] A certificate of character signed by the mukhtār was needed by villagers on innumerable occasions, such as enlistment in the army, any legal procedure, or any petition presented to the authorities.[85] Of particular importance was the requirement that the mukhtār's signature and seal be attached to documents concerning ownership of land and real estate.[86]

This manifold dependence of villagers upon the goodwill of the mukhtār could of course be easily exploited by him for extortion and blackmail. Thus Hilma Granquist tells us, in her book on ʿArṭās in the 1930s, that on the occasion of a procession to fetch the bride, the people had to wait outside the bride's village. When asked why this happened, the bridegroom explained: 'Because she [i.e. the bride] was young and the civil head of the village [the mukhtār, G.B.] must give his stamp; we gave him sugar and coffee and money'. In this way, explains Miss Granquist, the mukhtār was bribed to give his permission, although the bride was only eleven years old, i.e. below the legal age to marry.[87] In order to prevent such misuse of authority the laws of the village administration provided for legal fees to be collected by the mukhtār for confirming documents.[88] Nevertheless, villagers frequently complained that mukhtārs refused to put their seal to their documents, for no good reason,[89] and a special circular was distributed among the mukhtārs warning them not to misuse their seal.[90] But the temptation was too strong and the application of pressure on the villagers by the mukhtārs too easy to be restrained by circulars. To cite only two plain instances from the Jordanian files: when the Red Cross began in 1948 to distribute relief to refugees in Taffūḥ, the mukhtār demanded L.P.1.5 (an enormous sum at that time) from every refugee to issue the certificate he needed for benefiting from relief; and in 1954, the mukhtār of Ṭamūn received four Dīnārs per person from a group of people in order to certify that they had not been in prison, though he knew well that the opposite was the truth.[91]

As against his manifold administrative duties, the Palestinian mukhtār lacked most of the social functions which had been performed by the traditional village shaykh and which were attached to the office of the Egyptian *'umda*. The traditional village shaykh in Palestine was the acknowledged arbitrator of the villagers' conflicts and their judge, who was entitled to fine and punish them in accordance with rural custom, called in Southern Palestine *Sharī'at al-Khalīl* (while in the towns *Sharī'at Muḥammad* was in force).[92] Similarly, the Egyptian *'umda* judged villagers who had committed certain offences, fined them up to a certain limit, and arbitrated land disputes and other conflicts. His judicial functions were reduced in the 1890s, after the British occupation, and abolished altogether in 1930, and his task as an arbitrator of village disputes was not mentioned any more in the 'Umda Law of 1947, but in fact he continued to perform these functions up to the middle of the twentieth century, though to a smaller extent than before. The Palestinian mukhtār was never charged with these duties by law and did not exercise them in practice, except in limited periods and areas. Both the 1864 Law of Vilayets and the 1871 Law of Vilayet Administration considered arbitration of disputes among villagers as the province of the village elders, not the mukhtār, while trial and punishment were not mentioned at all in connection with any authority on the village level.[93] These principles persisted in later legislation of village administration. Thus the vilayet laws of the Young Turks of 1913 and 1914 again charged the council of village elders and the Nāḥiya council with arbitration of disputes inside the village and between villages; Mandatory legislation transferred this authority to the village councils, whose creation was planned at that time; and the Jordanian law made no changes in these provisions.[94]

The reason for this difference between the authority of the Palestinian mukhtār and the Egyptian *'umda* was a different historical background. The office of the Egyptian *'umda* developed from the position of the traditional shaykh, whose social functions the *'umda* inherited together with his other duties and powers. Only gradually was the *'umda* absorbed into the modern network of administration, which attempted to introduce the principle of a division between the judicial and the executive power. The office of the Palestinian mukhtār, on the other hand, was created in opposition to the position of the traditional shaykh, with the aim of weakening his position or evading him. From the beginning, it was part of the administrative structure of the Ottoman reform period, and therefore the mukhtār was charged with executive duties, but not with judicial powers. Traditional arbitration, which could not be abolished by decree, and which had its advantages even in the new context, was left in the hands of the council of elders – a traditional institution with sufficient prestige to perform it, as it had done, at least partly, in the past. But the traditional shaykhs were explicitly deprived of their judicial authority, including arbitration, in order to weaken the autonomy of the influential chiefs of powerful families.

In fact it would be an exaggeration to claim that the village mukhtār in Palestine had nothing to do with arbitration among villagers. There were, of course, strong and prestigious mukhtārs whom villagers asked to settle their disputes, even without legal authority to do so. However, it is certainly not incidental that in the files of the Jordanian administration such cases appear in the southern parts of the Hebron hills only, an area with strong tribal traditions. Thus the Mukhtār of Dūrā was appointed as arbitrator in a dispute between two Dūrā villagers about a plot of land.[95] Occasionally, mukhtārs were appointed arbitrators, or at least they named arbitrators, in disputes between different villages. For instance, in December 1954, the Mukhtār of Ḥalḥūl was appointed as arbitrator in a dispute about lands between Khirbat Jālā and Bayt Umar, and in January 1961, the Mukhtār of Dūrā in a similar dispute between Ḥalḥūl and Bayt Kāḥil.[96] Because of the unofficial character of such activities, they are of course reflected only very sparely in the official correspondence. When the mukhtār performed arbitration, he did so in general in cooperation with other persons in the village, notables of various families, religious functionaries, etc. In the only case of arbitration in Kufr al-Mā recorded in Antoun's book in which the mukhtār played any role, he did so together with the *imām* and one of the *ḥamūla* elders.[97]

Another function of mukhtārs in Palestine, as in Egypt, was that of extending hospitality to foreigners passing through the village and especially to government officials. This duty was not established by law either, but resulted from a tradition which was formed at a time when the village shaykh was the richest and most influential person in the village who controlled the *maḍāfa*, the place where strangers were accommodated. The Egyptian *'umda* inherited this function from the village shaykh and was responsible for extending hospitality to all strangers who happened to come to the village, until in recent generations his material position deteriorated to such an extent that he could no longer perform this duty properly.[98] The Palestinian mukhtār was supposed to entertain in particular government officials, usually not overnight, and he was helped in performing this duty by the members of his *ḥamūla*.[99]

To conclude, one of the principal changes brought about in the position of the mukhtār by the British mandate was the abolition of the collective responsibility of the village for paying the taxes, thus depriving the mukhtār of his function to distribute the tax burden among the inhabitants of the village. In addition, the administration was gradually organized according to modern principles and thus the collection of taxes, formerly the function of the village shaykh and the mukhtār, became the duty of officials specially appointed for this purpose. On the other hand, the mukhtār was charged, at that time, with a large number of duties which constituted a heavy burden without conferring on him effective executive authority and without rendering any equivalent personal or material profit.

Generally speaking, the growing efficiency of government administration in the course of the last 200 years left the mukhtār with smaller opportunities to turn the office to his personal profit. However, some of his new duties reinforced his position and enabled him to derive advantage for himself. Among these were the preparation of lists of villagers' property and the distribution of government aid. In particular, the growing ties of the villagers with the outside world and the authorities increased their need of all kinds of documents and verifications of their identity, their personal status, their integrity, their property, their inheritance and so on. The function of the mukhtār to supply these documents was a source of considerable power, a fact which became increasingly evident during Jordanian rule in the West Bank. But this, no doubt, was only a period of transition. The establishment of village councils and the growing integration of villages in a centralized administration will certainly strengthen the control over the mukhtār and thus complete his transformation into a regular government official of the lowest grade.

NOTES

1. *Düstur*, vol. 1 (Istanbul, 1289), pp. 618–20; G. Young, *Corps de droit Ottoman*, vol. 1 (Oxford, 1905), pp. 42–2 (hereafter: Law of Vilayets).
2. *Düstur*, ibid., p. 638, art. 59; Young, ibid., p. 59 (hereafter: Law of Vilayet Administration).
3. Palestine Royal Commission, *Memoranda prepared by the Government of Palestine* (London, 1937), pp. 80–81 (hereafter: *Memoranda*).
4. Palestine. *Report of the Committee on Village Administration and Responsibility* (Jerusalem: Government Printing Press, n.d. [1941]) (hereafter: *Report on Village Administration*).
5. Ibid., pp. 17, 43.
6. Art. 36 (1) of Village Administration Ordinance No. 23 of 1944, Supplement No. 1 to *The Palestine Gazette*, No. 1352 of 17 August 1944 (hereafter: 1944 Ordinance).

7. Art. 22 (1a) of Law No. 5 of 1954 (hereafter: Law of 1954).
8. See, for instance, Governor of Hebron to Commander of Hebron District concerning Khirbet al-Majd, 1 February 1962, and concerning Khirbet al-Burj, 6 February 1962, Israel State Archives (hereafter I.S.A.) 1160/4/1; Director of Police, Hebron, to Governor of Hebron, 23 July 1966, concerning 'Ashīrat al-Sharā'una in Dayr Sāmit, I.S.A. 826/12/8/11/33; Governor of Hebron to Sālim Musallam 'Abd al-Raḥmān 'Īsa al-'Adm of Bayt Ūlā, 12 November 1958, I.S.A. 826/8/4/33; Governor of Hebron to 'Abd al-Fattāḥ Aḥmad Muṣṭafā and others from Jab'a, 10 April 1954, I.S.A. 1318/27/8/33; Letter of Qā'imaqām Ṭul-Karm concerning mukhtār and committee of Rās 'Aṭiyya, 4 March 1962, I.S.A. 1502/9; Correspondence between Governor of Nablus and the Mudir of Salfīt concerning makhtara committee of Salfīt, September 1955, I.S.A. 771/23.
9. See also R. Antoun, *Arab Village: A Social Structural Study of a Trans-Jordanian Peasant Community* (Bloomington: Indiana University Press, 1972), pp. 89, 91–2.
10. Law of Vilayets (1864), arts. 54–5, 62–6.
11. For a description of these elections, based on the minutes of the *Maclis-i Idare* of Jerusalem found in the Israel State Archives, see Haim Gerber, 'Ottoman Administration in the Sancak of Jerusalem, 1890–1908' (in Hebrew) in *Hamizrah Hehadash*, vol. 24, no. 1–2, pp. 12–13.
12. Report on Village Administration, p. 7.
13. Ibid., pp. 43–4.
14. Articles 36–39 of the 1944 Ordinance.
15. Law of 1954, Arts. 22 (1b); 25 (1).
16. See Circular of Governor of Nablus, n.d. [1955], I.S.A. 1160/9/1.
17. It is difficult to imagine how mukhtārs functioned if indeed they were often 'appointed by the *qā'immaqām* without any regard for the wishes of the *hamula*', as claimed by Lutfiyya with regard to Baytīn, a village in the West Bank, under Jordanian rule. His statement that 'the popular vote has not been officially accepted as the way in which such matters are to be decided' is equally inexact. See A. M. Lutfiyya, *Baytīn, a Jordanian Village* (The Hague: Mouton & Co., 1966), p. 79.
18. See, for instance, for Ṣūrīf in 1953 I.S.A. 1160/9/1 and 1318/18/1/16/10/1; for Ṭamūn in 1955 I.S.A. 675/18; for Ṭamūn in 1965 I.S.A. 4/1 and 3362/3; for Jab'a in 1958 I.S.A. 1318/27/8/33; for Samū' in 1962 and Idnā in 1963 I.S.A. 1160/4/1.
19. For instance, the al-Najjāda family in 'Arab al-Ka'ābina, I.S.A. 2865/11/19/33, the Abū Ḥamiyya family in al-Shuyūkh, I.S.A. 2865/4/15/33; the Imṭayr family in Ẓāhiriyya, I.S.A. 2865/6; the 'Īsā and Mūsā families in Banī Na'īm, I.S.A. 2865/3/1; the 'Aql family in Sa'īr, I.S.A. 1318/2/1/13/10/1; the Darwīsh family in 'Aṣīra al-Shimāliyya, I.S.A. 3362/3; etc.
20. Banī 'Awda to Prime Minister and others, June 27, 1955, I.S.A. 675/18.
21. Letters to the Governor of Hebron Province, 1 May and 17 June 1965, I.S.A. 2865/1.
22. See, for instance, for Sebasṭiya, November 1966, I.S.A. 771/15; Qiṣra, May 1950 to November 1951, I.S.A. 785/25; Nūbā, February to August 1952,

I.S.A. 2865/14/21/33; Wādī Fūqīn, September 1964, I.S.A. 91/5; as well as part of the instances mentioned in note 19. A field investigation by the author in the Ṭul-Karm District conducted in April 1969 showed that this was common practice in that area.

23. For the economic and social position of the village mukhtār in Palestine see below.
24. Circular of Governor of Hebron, 1955, I.S.A. 1160/9/1.
25. Figures based on comparison of lists of mukhtārs for Nablus District in 1957, I.S.A. 1502/9, with lists for June 1965, I.S.A. 771/14 and of lists for Hebron District in 1949, I.S.A. 1318/20, with similar lists for Hebron Province dated 15 October 1960 and 7 August 1963, I.S.A. 1318/3/7/1.
26. On the Egyptian village shaykhs and *'umdas* see G. Baer, *Studies in the Social History of Modern Egypt* (Chicago and London: The University of Chicago Press, 1969), pp. 30–61. On appointment and election of guild shaykhs, see G. Baer, *Egyptian Guilds in Modern Times* (Jerusalem: Israel Oriental Society, 1964), pp. 69–72, and Part Three, Chapter 3 below. The Iraqi Law of Village Administration of 1957 found a compromise: the government appoints the *'umda* from among those recommended by the males of the village. See Muḥammad Ḥilmī Murād (ed.), *Qawānīn al-idāra al-maḥalliyya fī al-duwal al-'arabiyya* (Cairo: Arab League Publications, 1962), p. 511, article 3 of the law.
27. Law of Vilayets, art. 57; Law of Vilayet Administration, art. 60.
28. *Report on Village Administration*, p. 50, arts. 3, 4, and 5.
29. Ibid., p. 56.
30. 1944 Ordinance, art. 40, paras. 1, 2, 7, and art. 42; Law of 1954, art. 26, paras. 1, 2, 7, and art. 28.
31. Law of Criminal Court No. 76 of 1951, art. 9, *Official Gazette* No. 1071 of June 16, 1951; Law of Criminal Court No. 9 of 1961, art. 9 (1), *Official Gazette* No. 1539 of 16 March 1961.
32. See, for instance, Qā'imaqām to Mukhtār of Saffārīn, 5 November 1952, I.S.A. 1624/14; Governor of Nablus to Mukhtārs of Bayt Fūrīk, 28 February 1965, and to Mukhtārs of Būrīn, 8 March 1965, I.S.A. 771/14; also the whole file I.S.A. 1513/2.
33. For instance: Governor of Hebron Province to Commander of Hebron Area, 27 October 1953; I.S.A. 1160/9/1; Mukhtār of Jab'a to Commander Ṣūrīf guard, 15 August 1953, I.S.A. 1318/27/8/33.
34. See, for instance, Commander of Ṭul-Karm Area to the officer commanding Qalqīlya and the Officers of the Bāqa, Kafr Ṣūr and Shwayka Guard Stations, 5 August 1956, I.S.A. 1426/1; Villagers of Jab'a to Governor of Hebron, July 2, 1953, I.S.A. 1318/27/8/33; Commander of Hebron District to Commander of Ṣūrīf Guard, 2 September 1962, and to Governor of Hebron Province, 18 January 1964, I.S.A. 1160/4/1; Minutes of Meeting of Mukhtārs on 29 August 1963, ibid.
35. National Guard Law No. 7 of 1950, arts. 9 and 16, *Official Gazette* No. 1010 of 9 February 1950; Law of Compulsory National Service No. 102 of 1966, arts. 8 and 14, *Official Gazette* No. 1966, 27 November 1966; Temporary Law of Compulsory National Service No. 18 of 1967, arts. 45, 46, and 48, *Official Gazette* No. 1988 of 1 March 1967.

36. Commander of Regiment 332 to Commander of Hebron Area, 25 February 1962, I.S.A. 1318/4/4/1; Hasan 'Alī Ḥasan to Governor of Nablus Province, 26 September 1965, I.S.A. 731/18; Mukhtār of Kafr Ṣūr to the Qā'imaqām, 7 October 1955, and reply dated 12 October 1955, I.S.A. 1624/12; I.S.A. File 1566/19 dealing with the paving of the 'Azūn-Kafr Tilth road in 1951–2; I.S.A. File 1426/5 on paving the Dayr al-Ghuṣūn-'Atīl-Bāqa al-Sharqiyya road in the years 1950–1965; Qā'imaqām of Ṭul-Karm to mukhtārs of 'Alār and Ṣaydā, 7 July 1956, I.S.A. 1421/5; etc.
37. Qā'imaqām of Ṭul-Karm to Police of the area, 25 February 1962, I.S.A. 1426/6; Mukhtār of Shuwayka Village to Commander of Ṭul-Karm Area, August 7, 1951, I.S.A. 1426/5.
38. I.S.A. 1318/27/8/33.
39. On the differences and relations between the mukhtār and the traditional village shaykh in Palestine, see below.
40. *Report on Village Administration*, p. 16.
41. Antoun, pp. 92–3.
42. See note 38 above.
43. See, e.g. correspondence concerning the Mukhtār of Qiṣra dating from the end of 1942 and the beginning of 1943, I.S.A. 786/14; Muḥammad 'Abd al-Razzāq Musallam to Governor of Hebron Province, 21 November 1951, I.S.A. 1318/18/1/16/10/1; Ṣādiq Muḥammad Aḥmad Najīb to Commander of Nablus Area, 19 December 1961, I.S.A. 3369/24; Commander of Hebron Area to Governor of Hebron Province concerning Mukhtār of Ḥalḥūl, 29 August 1963, I.S.A. 1160/9/1.
44. Commander of National Guard in Hebron to Attorney General, 31 December 1952, concerning Mukhtār of Ṣūrīf, enclosed in letter of Commander of Hebron Area to Governor of Hebron Province, 5 January 1953, I.S.A. 1318/18/1/16/10/1; Governor of Hebron Province to 'Abd al-Fattāḥ Aḥmad and others, 29 March 1954, I.S.A. 1318/29/8/33; Commander of Regiment 333 to Governor of Hebron Province, 8 September 1962, and Commander of Hebron Area to Governor of Hebron Province, 17 September 1962, concerning Mukhtār of Banī Na'īm, I.S.A. 2865/3/I.
45. Cf. Baer, *Studies in the Social History of Modern Egypt*, p. 46 and note 88.
46. Mukhtārs and notables of Mukhayyam 'Askar al-Jadīd to Commander of Nablus Area, 19 August 1965, I.S.A. 771/14.
47. See Iḥsān al-Nimr, *Tārīkh Jabal Nāblus wa'l-Balqā'*, vol. 2 (Nablus, 1961), pp. 184–6, 233; Amnon Cohen, *Palestine in the 18th Century* (Jerusalem: Magnes Press, 1973), pp. 8, 50, 83, 123, etc.; Miriam Hoexter, 'The Role of Qays and Yaman Factions in Local Political Divisions,' *Asian and African Studies*, 9 (no. 3, 1973), pp. 252–3.
48. Cf. Baer, ibid., p. 65.
49. Law of Vilayets, arts. 56 and 59; Law of Vilayet Administration, arts. 60 and 108.
50. Baer, ibid., pp. 65–6.
51. Gerber, p. 13.
52. Ibid., p. 31.

53. C. T. Wilson, *Peasant Life in the Holy Land* (London, 1906), pp. 80–81.
54. *Memoranda*, p. 83, arts. 16 and 27.
55. A. Granovsky, *Das Steuerwesen in Palästina* (Jerusalem, 1933), p. 155.
56. See Baer, ibid., pp. 40–41, 45.
57. Granovsky, pp. 152–154.
58. *Report on Village Administration*, pp. 50, 52 (the laws concerning animal tax had existed in the Ottoman period as well).
59. Baer, ibid., pp. 42, 45.
60. 1944 Ordinance, art. 40 (3); Law of 1954, art. 26 (3).
61. Law No. 57 of 1951, art. 6, *Official Gazette* No. 1062, 16 April 1951, p. 990; *Supplement to Official Gazette*, No. 1081/1, 25 September 1951, p. 276; Law No. 30 of 1955, arts. 9(2) and 10(5), *Official Gazette* No. 1226, 16 May 1951, pp. 482 and 484; Law No. 42 of 1951, arts. 5 and 9, *Official Gazette* No. 1057, 1 March 1951, pp. 799–800; Law No. 5 of 1952, arts. 5 and 9, *Official Gazette* No. 1100, 16 February 1952, pp. 80–81.
62. Correspondence between Mudīr of Ṭūbās and Governor of Nablus, 1961–3, I.S.A. 741/15; Petition of Villagers of al-Majd al-Sharqiyya to Governor, 26 April 1962, I.S.A. 826/19/2/11/33; Minutes of Meeting of Mukhtārs on 18 September 1951, I.S.A. 1624/1.
63. I.S.A. 1395/4 (Kafr Ṣūr); 1395/1 (al-Nazla al-Sharqiyya); 1624/14 (Saffārīn); 1566/12 (Shuwayka); 1463/12 (Khirbat Ijbāra).
64. Minutes of Meeting of Mukhtārs, 29 August 1963, I.S.A. 1160/4/1; Mukhtārs of Bayt Lidd to Qā'imaqām of Ṭul-Karm, 17 November 1962, I.S.A. 1566/20; Mukhtār Iktāba to Qā'imaqām of Ṭul-Karm, 10 January 1961, I.S.A. 1426/8; Mukhtārs of Bayt Lidd to Qā'imaqām of Ṭul-Karm, 17 March 1951, 23 February 1952, 23 November 1952, I.S.A. 1395/8; Mukhtār of Ṭīra to Qā'imaqām of Ṭul-Karm, 8 October 1949, I.S.A. 1395/5; Mukhtār Zībād to Minister of Interior, Governor of Nablus Province and Qā'imaqām of Ṭul-Karm, 12–24 September 1962, I.S.A. 1624/9; Mukhtār Fir'awn to Qā'imaqām, 20 May 1962, I.S.A. 1395/12; Villager of Bāqa al-Sharqiyya to Qā'imaqām, 3 October 1962, I.S.A. 1632/3; etc.
65. Villagers from Iktāba to Qā'imaqām, 16 June 1957, I.S.A. 1426/8; Villager of Bayt Lidd to Qā'imaqām, 6 January 1950, I.S.A. 1395/8; Aḥmad Khalīl al-Najjār, representative of a family in Ẓāhiriyya, to Governor of Hebron Province, 3 January 1953, I.S.A. 1160/17/22; Notables of 'Ashīrat al-Sarrātīn in Bayt Ūlā to Governor of Hebron Province, 29 March 1967, I.S.A. 826/8/4/33.
66. Commander of Hebron District to Commander of Hebron Area, 24 October 1963, I.S.A. 1160/4/1; Notables of the Zaydāt Ḥamūla in Banī Na'īm to Governor of Hebron Province, September 1962, I.S.A. 2865/3; Muḥammad Jibrīn Mīṭā to Governor of Hebron Province, 29 March 1966, I.S.A. 2865/10; Villagers of Bayt Ūlā to Governor of Hebron Province, 6 October 1951, I.S.A. 826/4; Baṣma Abū Laṭīf of Jab'a Village to Governor of Hebron Province, 6 October 1951, I.S.A. 1318/27/8/33.
67. Complaint about Mukhtār of Banī Na'īm to Governor of Hebron Province, 6 October 1951, I.S.A. 1160/4/1; Muḥammad 'Abd al-Razzāq Musallam of Ṣūrīf to Governor of Hebron Province, 21 November 1951, I.S.A.

1318/18/1/16/10/1; Complaint about Mukhtār of Jab'a, enclosed in Report of Commander of Hebron Area to Governor of Hebron Province, 15 December 1956, I.S.A. 1318/27/8/33.

68. Complaints about Mukhtār of Ṣūrīf, 4 January 1954, I.S.A. 1318/18/1/16/10/1; Complaints about Mukhtār of Jab'a, October 1956, I.S.A. 1318/27/8/33; Villager of Ḥabla to Vice Governor of Nablus Province, 21 October 1946, I.S.A. 1345/3.
69. Richard B. Scott, *The Village Headman in Turkey, A Case Study* (Ankara: Institute of Public Administration for Turkey and the Middle East, 1968), p. 29, note 55.
70. Law of Vilayet Administration, art. 60.
71. 1944 Ordinance, art. 40(4), (6), etc.; Law of 1954, art. 26(4), (6), etc.
72. See, for instance, *al-Difā'* (daily), 14 September 1953.
73. Cf. Public Health Ordinance of 1940, *Report on Village Administration*, p. 51, art. 10.
74. 1944 Ordinance, art. 40(10); Law of 1954, art. 26(10); Personal Status Law No. 32 of 1966, *Official Gazette* No. 1927, 11 June 1966, pp. 1012–1015, arts. 27, 28, 34, 50, 55, 57.
75. For instance: Complaint of Ṭul-Karm physician that mukhtārs supply incorrect lists of births and deaths, 17 May 1953, I.S.A. 1581/2; Qā'imaqām of Ṭul-Karm to Governor of Nablus Province including minutes of Meeting of Mukhtārs, 22 January 1958, I.S.A. 1624/1; Minister of Health to Minister of the Interior, 23 June 1958, I.S.A. 1502/9; Commander of Nablus Province to Governor of Nablus Province, 8 March 1961, I.S.A. 771/15.
76. 1944 Ordinance, art. 40(8), (9); Law of 1954, art. 26(8), (9).
77. Temporary Electoral Law No. 24 of 1960, arts. 7, 10, 14 (c), 15(b), *Official Gazette* No. 1494, June 11, 1960; Superintendent of Police, Nablus, to Commanders of Police Stations in Nablus Town, Nablus District, Ṭūbās District, and Salfīt District, 16 and 22 August 1966, I.S.A. 771/21; Correspondence of Commander of Nablus Area, Mid-September 1965, I.S.A. 3362/3. Commander of Ṭul-Karm Area to Commander of Guard Station Dayr al-Ghuṣūn, including detailed instructions how to conduct the elections, 25 October 1965, I.S.A. 771/13.
78. Cf. Baer, ibid., p. 43.
79. Ibid., pp. 43–5, and table on p. 45.
80. Law of Vilayet Administration, art. 60.
81. *Report on Village Administration*, p. 52, art. 12.
82. 1944 Ordinance, art. 40(5); Law of 1954, art. 26(5).
83. Qāḍī of Hebron to Governor of Hebron Province, and Governor of Hebron Province to Mukhtārs of Bayt Umar, 28 November 1961, I.S.A. 826/3. See also Governor of Hebron Province to 'Abd al-'Atīt Salmān from Dayr al-'Asal, 8 March 1965, I.S.A. 826/11.
84. See, for instance, Governor of Hebron Province to Mukhtārs of villages, 11 December 1964, I.S.A. 1160/4/1 etc.
85. For a list of laws and orders including relevant provisions, as well as for many examples, see our full study.
86. Ordinance of Land Registration No. 3 of 1952, art. 7, *Official Gazette*

No. 1123, 1 October 1952, p. 371; Law No. 42 of 1953, art. 8, *Official Gazette* No. 1134, 16 February 1953, p. 56. See also Commander of Hebron Area to Governor of Hebron Province, 24 October 1963, I.S.A. 1160/4/1; Ḥasan Maḥmūd Abū 'Ayyāsh of Bayt Umar to Qā'imaqām of Hebron District, 18 March 1951, I.S.A. 826/3.

87. H. Granquist, *Marriage Conditions in a Palestinian Village*, vol. II (Helsingfors: Akademische Buchhandlung, 1935), p. 63.
88. 1944 Ordinance, art. 44; Law of 1954, art. 30; Payments to Mukhtārs Ordinance No. 62 of 1964, *Official Gazette* No. 1803, 1 November 1964, p. 1565.
89. See, for instance, Muḥammad 'Awda Mūsā al-Ḥalā'iqa from Shuyūkh village to Governor of Hebron Province, 27 November 1952, I.S.A. 2865/4/15/33; Muḥammad Aḥmad Sulaymān from Taffūḥ to Governor of Hebron Province, 25 February 1952, I.S.A. 826/24/6/22; Letters from Villagers of Salfīt to Governor of Nablus Province, 22 January 1955, 11 February 1955, and 13 December 1958, I.S.A. 771/23.
90. Governor of Hebron Province to Mukhtārs, 3 May 1964, I.S.A. 1160/9/1.
91. Elders of Taffūḥ Village to Governor of Hebron Province, 27 September 1950, I.S.A. 826/24/6/22; Mudīr of Ṭūbās to Governor of Nablus Province, 18 February 1954, I.S.A. 675/18.
92. Cf. Mrs. Finn, 'The Fallahheen of Palestine – Notes on their Clans, Warfare, Religion, and Law', *Palestine Exploration Fund Quarterly Statement* (*PEFQS*), 1897, pp. 38–9, 44–5; Yūsuf Jirjis Qaddūra, *Tārīkh Madīnat Rāmallah* (New York, 1954), pp. 29, 40; *Report on Village Administration*, p. 6; J. Finn, *Stirring Times* (London, 1878), vol. 1, pp. 216–220; P. Baldensperger 'The Immovable East', *PEFQS*, 1906, p. 15; al-Nimr, p. 185.
93. Law of Vilayets, art. 59; Law of Vilayet Administration, art. 107. It is interesting to note that corresponding to these Ottoman reforms, Ismā'īl decreed in 1871 in Egypt the establishment of special 'Judicial Councils' in large villages to take over the judicial functions of the shaykhs, but apparently the implementation of this decree was rather limited. See Baer, ibid., p. 41, note 66.
94. *Memoranda*, p. 83; arts. 26 and 27; 1944 Ordinance, Part IV, arts. 31–35; Law of 1954, Part III, arts. 18–21 (art. 35 of the 1944 Ordinance was deleted in the 1954 Law).
95. Governor of Hebron Province to Mukhtār of Dūrā, 16 April 1963, I.S.A. 2871/22.
96. Instructions of Governor of Hebron Province, 30 December 1954 and 23 January 1962, I.S.A. 2871/1/13.
97. Antoun, pp. 66–8.
98. See Baer, ibid., pp. 39, 46, 52–3.
99. Cf. Antoun, pp. 91–2. In Palestine the *maḍāfa* usually was maintained by the village or the *ḥamūla*, while in Egypt the *'umda* himself used to keep the *maḍyafa* on behalf of the government. For details and sources, see G. Baer, *The Arabs of the Middle East: Population and Society* (Tel-Aviv: Hakibbutz Hameuchad, second edition, 1973), p. 180 (in Hebrew).

2

THE ECONOMIC AND SOCIAL POSITION OF THE MUKHTĀRS

As we have seen, the office of *mukhtār* was first established by the Ottoman law of Vilayets of 1864.[1] Prior to that date the villages of Palestine were governed by so-called *shaykhs*. The smallest official administrative unit was a *nāḥiya* – a group of villages, headed by a *shaykh al-nāḥiya* who was formally appointed by the Ottoman governor of the province. Officially he served as *multazim* – tax farmer – of the *nāḥiya* and he was supposed to keep peace and order, but in fact his authority was much larger. In the villages belonging to his domain, he had military power, arbitrated the disputes of the fellahs and inflicted punishment upon offenders; in short, he acted as a semi-autonomous ruler. The position of shaykh was the hereditary privilege of specific families and on the whole the central government was unable to change this situation. Most of these families had fortified their small palaces, situated strategically on the top of the hills which served as the centre of their government. Their fellahs enjoyed their patronage and protection and, in return, supported the shaykhs in whatever way they needed support. The *shaykh al-nāḥiya* used to appoint an unofficial representative in every village called *shaykh al-qarya*, who was supposed to help him collect the taxes; his remuneration was one-quarter of the profit of the *shaykh al-nāḥiya's* three per cent, i.e., 0.75 per cent of the taxes which he collected.[2] In the course of the eighteenth century the power of these local shaykhs had increased considerably and they had become virtually independent of the central government.[3]

In the nineteenth century the Ottoman government tried to break the power of these shaykhs in order to establish a centralized administration with effective power all over the realm. At the time of the Egyptian occupation, Ibrāhīm Pasha executed some of the prominent shaykhs who had revolted against Egyptian rule in 1834, and he established a post called *nāṭūr* to be occupied by nominees of the central government in the villages.[4] Although this post did not survive the Egyptian occupation, the Ottomans apparently thought that the position of the shaykhs had been weakened sufficiently to establish direct rule in the villages. One of the ways to accomplish this was the Law of the Vilayets, which attempted to replace the village shaykh by the mukhtār. While the shaykh was a traditional political leader with judicial and military power over his clientele – the fellahs of his village or villages – the mukhtār was no more than a government official of the lowest grade, subordinate to his superiors in the hierarchy of the government administration.

This difference has been well illustrated by Richard Antoun in his study of Kufr al-Mā in ʻAjlūn. In the nineteenth century, the importance of the shaykh was accentuated by the absence of any centralized administration in the area. The Ottoman governor of the ʻAjlūn district lived in Derʻā. Considering the conditions of communications and transportation, appeal to him against the rule of the shaykh was out of the question. Moreover, Ottoman authorities found it easiest to deal with the single authority who could collect taxes and maintain some sort of order. The shaykh was recognized as the political overlord of the area by his own followers, by the bedouins who opposed him, and by the Ottoman government who sought his aid:

> The elders of Kufr al-Ma in speaking about Kleb Wazir, the last of the Tibne shaykhs, were unambiguous about the nature of his overlordship, saying 'he used to loose and bind' (*kan yafiq*[5] wa yirbut). And the *mukhtar* (present day village mayor) was always compared invidiously with the shaykh of Tibne. He was only another man 'from among the peasants' (*min al fellāhīn*).[6]

As long as Ottoman rule persisted, the government never fully succeeded in replacing the shaykh by the mukhtār. The power of the shaykhs diminished but their influence did not disappear before World War I. In the writings of Mrs. Finn, published in the 1870s, she does not mention the mukhtārs at all, and on the other hand she stresses the power of the traditional shaykhs in the villages.[7] In the 1880s, Oliphant writes on the Carmel area: 'Where a sheik is supreme, as at Dalieh, he has practically the fortunes of the villagers in his hands . . .'[8] And even in the early years of the twentieth century Wilson says:

> The head of a village is called a *Sheikh* (literally, 'an old man'). As a rule there is only one sheikh, but occasionally there is more than one. Till recent times there was a great deal of real authority attaching to the office, extending even, in rare cases, to the power of life and death. The policy of the Ottoman Government of late years has been to

> abolish such offices, as far as any effective authority is concerned, so that except in very out-of-the-way places, where the central power is still comparatively ineffective, the position of a sheikh is very largely a sinecure, and carries with it but little of the old prestige; nevertheless, an able man, especially if he be rich and of an influential family, has still a good deal of indirect power. Many cases of petty crimes are never taken to the Government but settled locally; and I have even known the same course pursued in a murder case. In serious matters several of the more prominent Sheikhs of the neighbourhood will be called in to advise or adjudicate, and their decision will be binding. When a sheikh dies, the sheikhs of the adjacent villages meet together to choose his successor, the office not being hereditary. As a matter of fact, however, unless there were anything specially to disqualify him, the oldest son of the late sheikh would succeed his father.[9]

Thus administrative functions had been transferred to the new mukhtārs, but the shaykhs continued to exert influence in the villages. In many cases this influence was exerted indirectly, sometimes, indeed, through the newly appointed mukhtārs, many of whom were bound to the shaykhs of the important families by kinship ties or economic relations. In particular, the shaykhs continued to exercise their traditional function of arbitration.[10] Only after the establishment of the British Mandate did the effective power of the shaykhs disappear from the villages and the central government – and to some extent urban notables – acquired influence and authority in their stead. The mukhtār served to convey the new influence and authority to the village.

It is interesting to note that in Egypt the modern shaykh and *ʿumda* did not differ from the traditional village shaykh to such an extent as in Palestine, and he never was appointed to counter the influence of a traditional power in the village.[11] This difference was the result of the fact that in Egypt the traditional shaykh never achieved such a large measure of autonomy as in Palestine and other Asian provinces of the Ottoman Empire. Even in the eighteenth century, when central power in Egypt had weakened considerably, the village shaykhs did not fulfil the function of *multazims*, as did their opposite numbers in the Fertile Crescent: the tax farmers and even the tax collectors were imposed on the villages from outside. The village shaykhs were dependent on the urban *multazims*, were appointed by them and executed their orders. Only the shaykhs of some powerful bedouin confederacies achieved any kind of political and economic autonomy, but not the village shaykhs.

One of the reasons for this difference was no doubt the ease with which central government was able to reach every village in Egypt, and the topographical incapacity of the villages to fortify and defend themselves. As a result the central government did not see any need to undermine the position of the village shaykh, but rather used him for its own purposes – as the *multazims* had used him for theirs in the past. Thus the post of the modern village shaykh was a continuation of the traditional one, not opposed to it as in Palestine.

In most countries of the Middle East, the village headmen did not receive any direct remuneration from the government, although they fulfilled the function of a government official. Neither the Egyptian *'umda*, nor the Turkish *muhtar* received a salary or other direct payments from the government.[12] In Syria the payment of salaries to mukhtārs was provided for in Law No. 136 of 29 October 1952 but was not immediately implemented.[13] Only in the Sudan does the village headman receive a salary, but such a low one that it suffices solely for the accommodation of guests.[14]

Mandatory Palestine was, therefore, an exceptional case, since here the mukhtār received a salary fixed in accordance with the size of the village: from 12 Palestinian Pounds yearly for villages of less than 100 inhabitants to £P100 for villages of more than 6,000 inhabitants. When a village had more than one mukhtār, these sums were divided among them.[15] Whether or not the rate of remuneration was sufficient for the adequate execution of the mukhtār's duties was the subject of a long controversy in Mandatory Palestine.[16] Anyway, the Village Administration Ordinance of 1944 confirmed the mukhtār's right 'to receive such fees or remuneration as the High Commissioner may by rule prescribe,' and the Jordanian Law for the Administration of Villages of 1954 copied this provision word for word (except for replacing the High Commissioner by the Minister of the Interior).[17]

However, while the Mandatory administration implemented this provision, the Jordanian government did not. In the early years of Hashemite rule the mukhtārs used to remind the authorities that their salaries were long overdue.[18] But before long the mukhtārs were informed that, for the time being, the government was unable to pay them.[19] An inquiry, undertaken by the Minister of the Interior in 1956–7, resulted in the conclusion that the total of the mukhtārs' salaries amounted to 40,000 Dinars, and that the government was unable to bear this burden. On the other hand, no additional taxes could be imposed to finance the payment of these salaries. As a result, so the inquiry said, people refrain from accepting the office of mukhtār.[20] Again and again officials recommended the resumption of payment of salaries to mukhtārs, but the government did not heed their advice. From time to time the claim was voiced that the mukhtārs compensated themselves by collecting all kinds of illegal and exorbitant payments for their services and that they misused their position for furthering their personal material interests.[21]

In the early 1950s some mukhtārs agreed to work temporarily

without remuneration[22] – which shows that they indeed did derive such profits from their positions that the burden of being mukhtār was worth their while even without a salary. But apparently the situation was not the same everywhere. Some mukhtārs tried to make arrangements to receive a salary from the village.[23] In one case it was reported that the villagers agreed to collect a sum of money for the mukhtār.[24] Similar arrangements were operative in Kufr al-Mā (East Bank) when Antoun made his study there in the 1960s. He reported that the mukhtārs received their remuneration from their clans (*ḥamūla*), generally in kind. Every landowner in the clan was obliged to give him two *rotls* of wheat or barley annually for every *qīrāṭ* of land. The mukhtār usually collected this grain in kind on the threshing ground after the harvest. In years of poor harvest he received less. Some people paid the mukhtār in cash.[25] To be sure, payment of mukhtārs' salaries by the village was not peculiar to Palestine or Jordan. In Turkey the *muhtar* receives a small annual salary from the village budget, as determined by its Council of Elders – depending on the tradition, wealth and activities of the village.[26] In the Syrian village of Tel Ṭuqān too, the owners of land and shops pay the mukhtār's salary, and in the North-Iraqi village of Araden every villager provides three days of work for the mukhtār.[27]

However, the main reason why the mukhtār was able, under certain circumstances, to function even without receiving a salary, was that he collected from the villagers various fees for services which he rendered them, and that, in addition, he turned his office to his own material advantage in various legal and illegal ways. Like his salary, the authority for the payment of these fees was contained in government orders of 1920, as well as in various laws subsequently promulgated, especially rules concerning taxes.[28] Thus the mukhtārs received two per cent of the tithe which they collected within three months of the assessment, and the same rate was confirmed in further tax ordinances of the 1920s.[29] The Village Administration Ordinance of 1944 reconfirmed that the mukhtārs were entitled to receive fees in accordance with specific orders and laws, and the Jordanian law of 1954 reiterated the same article.[30] A special Jordanian law of 1964 fixed maximum rates for such fees, and thus tried to prevent the misuse and arbitrary exploitation of the mukhtār's authority for his own material advantage. For endorsing an official document or verifying certificates, the mukhtār was entitled to collect 100 *fils*, and for signing a marriage certificate he was allowed to charge 500 *fils*.[31]

But, in addition to these legal fees, the mukhtār was able to use his position to collect exorbitant and illegal payments, and sometimes it was the income from this source which made the mukhtārship profitable. Complaints that mukhtārs exploited the villagers in this way are as old as the position of the mukhtār itself. In Mandatory times mukhtārs were accused specifically of collecting large payments for issuing certificates of landownership[32] and, during the Jordanian era, for all kinds of documents and certificates, before 1964[33] as well as later on.[34] Many of these accusations turned out to be false, but there can be no doubt that so many complaints would not have been launched had it not been likely, *a priori*, that the mukhtār collected fees exceeding the legally fixed maximum limit. The same is true with regard to other accusations that the mukhtār turned his office to his own material advantage.[35]

During the Jordanian era mukhtārs of some villages were also accused of having profited by selling *mushā'* land of the village.[36] *Mushā'* land, which was held collectively by the village, amounted on the eve of World War I to about 70 per cent of the total area in Palestine. During the Mandatory period land settlement was carried out – involving the splitting up of *mushā'* land and its registration in the name of individual owners. But not all *mushā'* lands were distributed, and on the eve of World War II , *mushā'* land still amounted to about one-quarter of the whole area. According to the Ottoman Land Code land cannot be registered collectively in the name of a village, and indeed this was not done in Mandatory Palestine. Instead it was usual to register *mushā'* in the name of the Treasury or the High Commissioner, to be kept in trust for the benefit of the village. When Village Councils were established, the Village Administration Ordinance of 1944 provided for these village councils to become a juridic person, and made the following proposition concerning *mushā'* lands:

> Upon the establishment of a Village Council, the High Commissioner may give directions for vesting in the Village Council all or any lands in the village area which are then owned by the Government of Palestine or are the property of the village or are held in trust for the village and thereupon the lands to which the directions relate shall vest in the Village Council and shall be registered accordingly in the Land Registry free of charge.

The Jordanian law of 1954 copied these provisions verbatim.[37]

The mukhtārs, therefore, had no official standing with regard to *mushā'* land but, since they were the only official representatives of villages in which no councils had been established, they often succeeded in acquiring control over property held collectively by the village and not owned privately. Even in the Mandatory period *mushā'* land was apparently sometimes distributed to villagers by the mukhtārs.[38] The files of the Jordanian administration in the West Bank show that some mukhtārs continued to control *mushā'* land in their villages. For instance in Ṣaydā, a village of the Tulkarm sub-district, *mushā'* land was not registered in the *Tabu* (cadaster), but the treasurer of the district officer kept a list in which the land was registered in the name of the mukhtār as the representative of the villagers – which made its transfer to the village council difficult.[39] Such situations apparently enabled the mukhtārs to sell *mushā'* land or at least to initiate its sale. For instance, in 1960, the mukhtārs of 'Atīl asked the Qā'imaqām for permission to sell to one of the inhabitants of the village a piece of *mushā'* – unused land, as they said.[40]

As a result the mukhtārs were accused time and again of attempts to sell the *mushā'* of the village, or of actually having made transactions with such lands. In 1955, for instance, a group of villagers from Ṭamūn in Samaria complained about the mukhtār 'Abdalla al-Rashīd al-Muṣṭafā, accusing him of an attempt to sell 400 dunam *mushā'* to Ya'aqūb 'Abd al-Hādī from Nablus. In addition, he was accused of preventing the *ḥamūla* from tilling its *mushā'* land, and from distributing it among its members – all this with the aim of enabling strangers to acquire the village lands.[41] Similarly, the mukhtār of Zībād was accused of having sold two pieces of *mushā'* belonging to the village.[42] As we said above, such complaints and accusations were not necessarily justified, but they show that the existence of *mushā'* land in the village enabled the mukhtār to turn his position to his profit, and that villagers believed that he did so in fact. We may add that elsewhere too, for instance in Egypt and Persia, collective holding of land by the village, and its periodical redistribution, were the source of great power in the hand of the village headman.[43]

Did all these sources of income of the mukhtār in Palestine contribute to making him a wealthy man compared with his fellow-villagers? There can be no doubt that the traditional village shaykh in Palestine generally was the wealthiest man in his village. He farmed the taxes of the village, often owned most of the village lands, and his political power assisted him in consolidating his material superiority. There are many indications that this cannot be said of the mukhtār, who gradually replaced the shaykh in many of his functions. Nevertheless, he usually was quite wealthy. According to the Law of Vilayets of 1864, he could not be elected mukhtār unless he owned property paying at least 100 *qurūsh* in direct taxes.[44] If he owned no such property, his election was declared invalid, as happened to a candidate in Silwād village early in this century, or else he was required to present a guarantor capable of mortgaging property worth 20,000 *qurūsh*.[45]

Unfortunately we have no data on the wealth of mukhtārs in the Mandatory period. To judge by their social status (see below), one may assume that compared with Ottoman times their material position had worsened. Both Mandatory and Jordanian laws on village administration no longer required mukhtārs to be owners of property, or payers of taxes above a minimal sum.[46] All this, however, is only circumstantial evidence.

Evidence from the files of the Jordanian administration, and from interviews, yields a quite variegated picture. Some mukhtārs were among the greatest landowners in the village, or owners of land in nearby *khirbes*, in the Ghor (Jordan Valley) or in Transjordan (the East Bank).[47] Quite a few among them were owners of other property, great merchants, owners of garages, etc.[48] According to lists published in the *Official Gazette*, mukhtārs frequently were among the directors and shareholders of companies, especially agricultural and bus companies. But there were also many mukhtārs engaged in some business on a smaller scale, in addition to agricultural work. They were owners of small booths in markets or small work-shops in their villages.[49] On the other hand, among the mukhtārs whose letters of resignation are found in the files of the Jordanian administration, quite a few were engaged in jobs requiring a certain level of education, such as clerical jobs, journalism, or teaching.[50] Nevertheless, it appears that many of the mukhtārs were men who had passed the working age, and owned sources of income which needed no work. In general, it is often said that the economic situation of the mukhtār is better than that of most other villagers. This definition seems to be true for the mukhtārs or village shaykhs of other Middle Eastern countries as well.[51]

In the times of the Jordanian rule in the West Bank, the view was expressed that it was unseemly for a mukhtār to work as a road-worker.[52] Nevertheless, there was a mukhtār who worked as a stone-mason.[53] Moreover, there were apparently mukhtārs who in the past had been labourers, and who by their own initiative had climbed the social ladder. The biography of a mukhtār of this type is related by Antoun. One of the two mukhtārs of Kufr al-Mā had first worked as an unskilled labourer, a watchman, a fisherman, a ploughman, a plasterer, and a helper to a blacksmith. Later, in 1936, he participated in the Arab rebellion against the British, which 'involved some degree of smuggling, extortion, and thievery.' In 1939 he was jailed, and on his release in 1941 he worked for the British Army. With the outbreak of the Palestine War, he enlisted in the Arab Legion. In 1951 he returned to Kufr al-Mā, 'where he worked as fellah until 1957 when he was chosen unanimously by his clan to represent it as mukhtār.'[54] Thus initiative and connections with the authorities were extra social assets for those who aspired to become mukhtār. As a result of the mobility of the twentieth century, the growing connections of the village with the outside world and its ramifying administrative needs, new types of people rose to the mukhtārship from lower layers of the society which in the past had had no access to this post.

In contrast with Turkish and Egyptian legislation, Jordanian legislation (following Mandatory law) did not postulate literacy as a condition for the mukhtārship.[55] However, in his instructions concerning elections of mukhtārs, issued in 1955, the Governor of Hebron made literacy a condition for candidates.[56] The Governor of Nablus required literacy of mukhtārs of specific villages, but not as a general rule.[57] Nevertheless, before 1967, there were in the West Bank a number of mukhtārs who signed documents with a thumb-print. Usually a mukhtār would have had some years' schooling, but very often his education was insufficient for correspondence with the authorities or for the keeping of registers, and he needed clerks or educated sons of assistants.[58] Whoever had a secondary education would not be satisfied with a position as mukhtār, but would aspire to higher posts.[59]

The authorities were of course interested in appointing young educated men to the post of mukhtār – men who would be able to carry out government instructions intelligently, develop the village, and disregard factional strife in the village.[60] As against this, the notables and traditional society in the village were suspicious of such trends. Some of the notables expressed the view that educated people are mostly young and inexperienced men, and that villagers prefer the old and experienced, even if they are illiterate.[61]

Authors of books on Arab society in Palestine in the 1940s reflected the impression that, in general, the mukhtār was either the head of the *ḥamūla* himself, or a younger confidant, such as his son or 'one of the heads of the families,' in short one of the most prominent notables.[62] It is interesting to note that the 1941 *Report on Village Administration* yields a different picture. According to views expressed before the authors of the Report, the mukhtār was said to be ill-educated, rarely a man of local standing or importance and generally inefficient. Although the authors of the Report did not subscribe to this indictment as being a fair one for general application, they agreed with the following statement made in a police report of 1930: 'The Mukhtār . . . is not today, in the majority of cases, the best man in the village.' They disagreed with those who had represented this state of affairs as due to inadequate remuneration. In their view, the real reason for the failure to attract the best men to the post of mukhtār was to be found in the low status of the office, and in the general failure of the government to take steps towards the enhancement of the prestige of those appointed to it. The mukhtār's position was more that of an agent of government than of a functionary exercising a degree of independent authority. He had a large number of duties imposed upon him, but practically no powers in relation to the people of the village he was supposed to represent. 'It is no doubt on account of this lack of authority in the internal administration of the village, and because he is so much more the Government maid-of-all-work than a prototype of traditional leadership, that his office tends in some areas to be regarded with contempt, and to be shunned by persons of education, standing and influence.'[63]

It would seem to us that the contradiction between these two groups of authors was the result of the existence of different types of mukhtārs, none of which was really a general prototype. The first type was the traditional one, reflected in the characterization by Shimoni and Waschitz. This was the eminent head of the *ḥamūla*, wielding power and authority in the village, the heir of the village shaykh of 150 years ago, the greatest landowner in the village, whose office was inherited by members of his family.[64] The second type is the mukhtār who executes the orders and wishes of the influential notables, or *ḥamūla* heads, who control affairs from behind the scenes, while the mukhtār himself has no great prestige – except as the tool of those who have. This type is very common in the West Bank, as well as in other Middle Eastern countries, such as Turkey and Syria.[65] The third type is a fellah, without prestige based on traditional criteria of wealth or family background, who succeeds in being appointed or elected because of his initiative or connections with the authorities, and who hopes that the opportunities of getting personal profit out of the position will recompense him for its burdens. This type is reflected in the Mandatory *Report on Village Administration*.

No doubt there were intermediate types and variations according to the economic, social, and political situation of the mukhtārs and the villages. The mukhtārs reflect to a large extent the balance of powers which differs from village to village.[66] But it seems to us that the first type disappears gradually, and the prestige of mukhtārs of the other types declines because of the widening cracks in the *ḥamūla* edifice of the village, the increase in the education of larger layers of the village society who no longer respect illiterate, poor or powerless mukhtārs, and because of greater opportunities which have opened up outside the village for villagers with initiative and schooling.

Indeed, the general trend characterizing the development of the position and power of the village headman in Palestine during the last 200 years is a declining line. The first stage of this decline consisted of the undermining of the position of the traditional village shaykh, and the appointment of mukhtārs, in the course of the nineteenth century. By this process the village headman was deprived of military power, judicial authority and the capability to extend his patronage over his village clientele. As a result, the newly appointed mukhtārs were inferior to the traditional shaykhs concerning the control of landed property, the splendour of their places of abode and their wealth in general.

The second stage was brought about by the changes in the position of the mukhtār introduced by the British Mandate. One of the principal changes during this period was the abolition of the collective responsibility of the village for paying taxes, thus depriving the mukhtār of his function of distributing the tax burden among the inhabitants. In addition, the administration was gradually organized according to modern patterns and thus the collection of taxes, formerly a function of the village shaykh and the mukhtārs, became the duty of officials specially appointed for this purpose. On the other hand, the mukhtār was charged at that time with a large number of duties, which constituted a heavy burden without rendering any equivalent personal or material profit.[67] This was one reason for the diminishing prestige and social status of the mukhtārs as reflected in the official report of the early 1940s.

The third stage, i.e., Hashemite rule in the West Bank, brought with it first of all the abolition of the payment of a salary to mukhtārs. However, other developments disrupted the mukhtārs' position at least as severely as that. The introduction of elections to the office of mukhtār,[68] as well as the gradual establishment of village councils, were only administrative reflections of deeper social processes. These trends consisted of the emergence of a group of people in the villages with primary or even secondary education, who criticized and opposed the traditional and illiterate mukhtārs. In addition, new vistas opened up outside the village which made the office of mukhtār profitable only to a relatively low layer of villagers.

NOTES

1. *Dustur*, vol. I, Istanbul 1289, pp. 618–20; G. Young, *Corps de droit Ottoman*, vol. I, Oxford 1905, pp. 42–4. (Hereafter: Law of Vilayets).
2. Iḥsān al-Nimr, *Tārīkh Jabal Nāblus wa'l-Balqā'*, vol. 2, Nablus 1961, pp. 184–6, 233, 409. Since the *shaykh al-qarya* had no official standing, he is not mentioned in Ottoman official documents.
3. See A. Cohen, *Palestine in the 18th Century*, Jerusalem 1973, index: *shaykh* and *passim*; M. Hoexter, 'The Role of Qays and Yaman Factions in Local Political Divisions,' *Asian and African Studies*, vol. 9, No. 3, 1973, pp. 253, 284–5, 295.
4. R. A. S. Macalister and E. W. G. Masterman, 'Occasional Papers on the Modern Inhabitants of Palestine,' III, *PEFQS*, 1906, pp. 39–40.
5. *Sic*. The correct form probably is *yafikk*.
6. Richard T. Antoun, *Arab Village. A Social Structural Study of a Transjordanian Peasant Community*, Indiana University Press, Bloomington – London, 1972, pp. 17–18.
7. Mrs. Finn, 'The fallahheen of Palestine – Notes on their Clans, Warfare, Religion, and Law,' *PEFQS*, 1897, pp. 38–9.
8. Lawrence Oliphant, *Haifa or Life in Modern Palestine*, Edinburgh and London, 1886, p. 195.
9. C. T. Wilson, *Peasant Life in the Holy Land*, London, 1906, pp. 80–1.
10. Cf. Palestine, *Report of the Committee on Village Administration and Responsibility*, printed at the Government Printing Press, Jerusalem, n.d. (1941), p. 7. (Hereafter *Village Administration*).

11. For the Egyptian village shaykh see G. Baer, 'The Village Shaykh 1800–1950,' in *Studies in the Social History of Modern Egypt*, The University of Chicago Press, Chicago and London, 1969, Ch. 3.
12. Ibid., pp. 47–8 and ff. For Turkey, see Richard B. Scott, *The Village Headman in Turkey – A Case Study*, Institute of Public Administration for Turkey and the Middle East, Ankara, 1968, p. 13 and note 7.
13. See 'Uthmān Khalīl, *al-Tanẓīm al-idārī fi al-duwal al-'arabiyya*, League of Arab States, Cairo, 1957, p. 139.
14. H. B. Barclay, *Buurri al Lamaab: a Suburban Village in the Sudan*, Ithaca, N.Y. 1964, p. 46.
15. *Village Administration*, p. 15. The legal basis for the payment of salaries to the mukhtārs was a notice issued on 7 July 1920 and published in *Official Gazette*, No. 24 of 25 July 1920. See ibid, p. 45.
16. Ibid., pp. 15–16.
17. Art. 44 of the Village Administration Ordinance No. 23 of 1944, Supplement No. 1 to *The Palestine Gazette*, No. 1352 of 17 August 1944, (Hereafter: *1944 Ordinance*); and art. 30 of Qānūn Idārat al-Qurā, Law No. 5 of 1954, *Official Gazette*, No. 1167 of 1 February 1954 (Hereafter: *1954 Law*).
18. For instance, Memorandum of the Notables of Ṭamūn to the Governor of Nablus, 3 December 1952, Israel State Archives (Hereafter: ISA) 675/18.
19. *al-Difā'*, 4 May 1951; Report on Meeting of the Mukhtārs, 18 September 1951, ISA., 1624/1.
20. Minister of the Interior to Prime Minister, 8 July 1956, and Governor of Nablus to Minister of Finance, 3 January 1957, ISA 1318/9/1/7/1'ח.
21. Governor of Hebron to Minister of Interior, 28 January 1961, ISA, 1318/3/7/1/'ח, and 11 July 1962, ISA, 1318/15/8/1/'ח.
22. See, for instance, Maḥmūd Sālim and Muḥammad Ḥamdān al-Darīdi from Bayt Lidd to the Qā'imaqām of Ṭulkarm, 6 November 1951, ISA, 1624/10.
23. Governor of Nablus to the Qā'imaqām, 29 October 1951, ISA, 1624/10; Members of the Village Committee of 'Atīl to the Qā'imaqām of Ṭulkarm, 9 February 1951, 1426/9; Village Committee of Dhanāba to the Qā'imaqām, 5 February 1952, 1632/24; correspondence concerning the village of Ṣūr, January 1952, 1345/9.
24. Correspondence concerning 'Arab al-Zubaydāt, January 1954, ISA, 771/20.
25. Antoun, p. 92 and *passim*.
26. Scott, p. 13 and note 7.
27. L. E. Sweet, *Tel-Toqaan: A Syrian Village*, Michigan, 1960, p. 190; A. Ishow, 'Un village irakien, Araden,' in *Cahiers de l'Orient Contemporain*, October 1966, p. 9.
28. *Village Administration*, p. 45.
29. A. Granovsky, *Das Steuerwesen Palästinas*, Jerusalem, 1933, pp. 150, 155.
30. *1944 Ordinance*, art. 44; *1954 Law*, art. 30.
31. Law No. 62 of 1964, *Official Gazette*, No. 1803 of 1 November 1964, p. 1565. Antoun (p. 166, note 68) considered this to have been an 'official change in the economic basis of the mayorship,' which 'created the potential for radical change in the traditional political institutions of the village.' We

cannot agree to this interpretation, since the collection of fees for services rendered by the mukhtār had been established in Mandatory times and reconfirmed by earlier Jordanian laws.

32. *Village Administration*, p. 45.
33. See, for instance, Maḥmūd Aḥmad Sulaymān to Governor of Hebron, 17 December 1950, ISA, 1160/17/22; Elders and Notables of Ṣūrīf village to Minister of Interior, 9 October 1953, 1160/9/1/'מ ; Aḥmad Sulaymān Shaykh Da'ūd of Qufīn village to the Qā'imaqām, 8 August 1950, 1624/7; etc., etc. See also, *al-Difā'*, 26 February 1953.
34. See, for instance, 'Uthmān Aḥmad Abū Fāra, Mukhtār of Ṣūrif village to Governor of Hebron, 2 November 1965, ISA, 2865/1; Governor of Nablus to Commander of Nablus Police, concerning the mukhtār of Ammātin, 10 February 1966, 771/22; etc.
35. Hundreds of such complaints can be found in the Jordanian files kept in ISA. For some more details see our full study.
36. On mushā' see G. Baer, *Introduction to the History of Agrarian Relations in the Middle East 1800–1970*, Tel Aviv, 1971, pp. 67–71; A. Granott, *The Land System in Palestine*, London, 1952, pp. 213–48.
37. *1944 Ordinance* and *1954 Law*, art. 6, paras. (1) and (4).
38. I have not yet been able to verify this statement – made in a recent study – because the relevant document in ISA has been mislaid.
39. Correspondence between Mudīr Qaḍā Ṭulkarm and the Governor of Nablus, 23 June and 6 July 1966, ISA, 1624/2.
40. Mukhtārs of 'Atil to Qā'imaqām, 18 July 1960, ISA, 1345/20.
41. Complaints of villagers from Ṭamūn, 18 January and 15 March 1955; Commander of Nablus area to Governor of Nablus, 3 April 1955; Governor of Nablus to Minister of the Interior, 7 April 1955, ISA, 675/18.
42. Villagers of Zībād to Governor of Nablus, 20 June 1966, ISA, 771/18.
43. Cf. Baer, 'Village Shaykh,' p. 47; A. K. S. Lambton, *Landlord and Peasant in Persia*, Oxford University Press, 1953, p. 301; K. A. Wittfogel, *Oriental Despotism*, Yale University Press, 1957, p. 118.
44. *Law of Vilayets*, art. 64.
45. Protocol of Meclis-i Idare of the Sancak of Jerusalem, ISA, 1327/1740 and 1322/413. I am grateful to Dr. Haim Gerber for this information.
46. *1944 Ordinance*, art. 38; *1954 Law*, art. 24.
47. Correspondence with Governor of Hebron concerning mukhtār of al-Shuyūkh, 15 March 1952, ISA, 2865/4/15/33/'ח ; Amīn Abū Fāra, Mukhtār of Ṣūrif, to Governor of Hebron, 1 May 1965, 2865/1; Correspondence concerning Zayn al-Dīn Ḥanūḥān, Mukhtār of Ḥalḥūl, 4 July 1964 and 17 June 1965, 826/23/9/33/'ח ; etc.
48. The mukhtār of Salfīt, for instance, was a partner in a bus and taxi company and the owner of a garage in Nablus. See Commander of Nablus Area to Governor of Nablus, 10 January 1959, and Mudīr Nāḥiyat Salfīt to Governor of Nablus, 19 January 1959, ISA, 771/23; similarly, the directors of the Bayt Kāḥil bus company were members of mukhtār's family – see Letter to Governor of Hebron, 2 January 1962, 826/10/5/33/'ח .
49. For instance, Muḥammad Ḥasan Da'das, Mukhtār of 'Askar al-Jadīd, correspondence with Governor of Nablus, 7 August 1966, ISA, 771/12; the

mukhtār of Silwān owned two shops and a magazine in East Jerusalem, see *Ha'aretz*, 22 April 1969. However, mukhtārs engaged in small business of this kind generally were those of villages situated near towns or mukhtārs of refugees.

50. Commander of Hebron Area to Governor of Hebron, concerning mukhtār of Kafr al-Burj, 28 June 1964, ISA, 826/21/1/11/33/'ח ; Governor of Hebron to Commander of Hebron Area concerning mukhtār of Bayt al-Kūsh al-Fawqā, 12 December 1966, 826/16/6/11/33/'ח ; Mukhtār of Salfīt, Ḥasan Ḥasūn al-Zayd, to Governor of Nablus, 7 January 1954, 771/23.
51. Scott, pp. 34–5; Baer, 'Village Shaykh,' p. 52, note 129; Sweet, p. 190; Ishow, p. 9.
52. Mukhtārs of refugees to Qā'imaqām of Ṭulkarm, 13 August 1950, ISA, 1566/14.
53. Commander of Hebron area to Governor of Hebron concerning mukhtār of Samū', 30 December 1963, ISA, 1160/4/1.
54. Antoun, p. 30.
55. Scott, p. 15; Egyptian 'Umda Law of 1975, part 2, art. 3, para. 5, *al-Ahrām*, 12 May 1957. In Egypt only the 'Ezba Shaykhs were exempted from the requirement of literacy. Scott points out that in Turkey this obligation is often evaded. The Iraqi Law of Village Administration, 1957, found a compromise: the *'umda* must know how to read and write 'as far as possible' (*ḥasb al-imkān*). See Muḥammad Ḥilmi Murād (ed.), *Qawānīn al-idāra al-maḥalliyya fī al-duwal al-'arabiyya*, League of Arab States, Cairo, 1962, p. 512.
56. Stencilled Circular, no date (1955), ISA, 1160/9/1/'מ.
57. Governor of Nablus to Commander of Nablus area, 9 April 1953, and Announcement of Mudīr Salfīt concerning elections of mukhtār, 20 May 1965, ISA, 771/23.
58. Ismā'īl Muṣṭafā al-Ḥīḥ of Ṣūrīf village to Governor of Hebron, 6 January 1953, ISA, 1318/18/1/16/10/1/'ח ; Ḥājj Muḥammad Ibrāhīm al-Dardūn of Dayr al-'Asal al-Fawqā to Governor of Hebron, 13 August 1961, and Yūsuf 'Alayān al-Shawāmra of Dayr al-'Asal al-Fawqā to Governor of Hebron, 13 August 1961, 826/11.
59. For similar conclusions about the Turkish *muhtar*, see Scott, pp. 13 (note 6) and 15.
60. See, e.g., Commander of Hebron Section to Commander of Hebron Area, 16 September 1963, ISA, 1160/4/1 (concerning Īdnā village).
61. See, for instance, Notables of al-Jahālīn to the Qā'imaqām of Hebron, 13 November 1949, ISA, 1318/20/18/33/'ח.
62. Y. Shimoni, *Arvei Eretz-Yisrael*, Tel Aviv, 1947, pp. 173, 177; J. Waschitz, *Ha'aravim be-Eretz-Yisrael*, Merhavia, 1947, p. 21.
63. *Village Administration*, pp. 15–16.
64. See description of such a type of *muhtar* in Turkey by Scott, pp. 21–2. In Egypt too such an *'umda* could be found here and there, but the type has become extremely rare.
65. See, for instance, Scott, p. 18; and J. Weulersse, *Paysans de Syrie et du Proche Orient*, Paris, 1946, p. 226.

66. Cf. Mübeccel B. Kiray, 'Some notes on elected headmen and mayors in different communities of Turkey,' in *Local Government and National Development*, Institute of Public Administration for Turkey and the Middle East, Ankara, 1968, pp. 113–17.
67. See above, Part Two, Ch. 1.
68. Ibid.

Part Three

THE TURKISH GUILDS

1

ADMINISTRATIVE, ECONOMIC AND SOCIAL FUNCTIONS

INTRODUCTION AND GENERAL REMARKS

A discussion of Turkish guild history becomes meaningless if it does not take as its point of departure that a guild is a professional organization. This means that a guild is neither an organization which is not grouped according to professional criteria, nor just another name for groups of artisans or merchants about whose organization nothing definite is known. One may be justified in speaking about the existence of guilds if within a certain area people occupied in a branch of the urban economy constitute a unit which fulfils economic, fiscal, administrative and social functions. A further condition is the existence of a framework of officers or functionaries chosen from among the members of such a unit and headed by a headman.

Apparently, there were no guilds with such attributes in Turkey until the fifteenth century. Scholars who have studied that era have found no proof for the existence of guilds at that time.[1] Although the *ahi* movement, the popular organization of Anatolia in the thirteenth and fourteenth centuries, recruited its members mainly among craftsmen, the association as such was non-professional.[2] Unfortunately, most writers dealing with the early history of Turkish guilds have included in their writings long descriptions of the *ahi* movement and *fütüvvet* literature without making it unequivocally clear that they were not talking about professional guilds.[3]

It is not known exactly when and where professional organizations first appeared in Turkey. Taeschner assumed that the transition from the free *fütüvvet* associations to a system of professional guilds occurred at the beginning of the sixteenth century.[4] He may well have been right: for from the end of the century we have a number of documents which show that by that time the guild must have been a well-established institution. First of all, we have the *Surname* of Murad III, a description of the procession on the occasion of the circumcision of his son Mehmed in the year 1582.[5] But, although many different crafts and professional groups are enumerated, there is no explicit mention of the existence of heads or officers of these organizations. There can be no doubt, however, that in the 1570s, and certainly in the 1580s, various professions in Istanbul possessed such an organization, headed by chiefs called *kethüda* who were assisted by officers called *yiğit başı*. This is borne out by a series of firmans collected by the Turkish historian Ahmet Refik.[6] We learn from a firman of the year 981/1573 that, at that time, a *kethüda* and a *yiğit başı* had been specially appointed for the guild of the *varakçılar* (gilders) in order to guarantee a regular supply of gold and silver leaf to the Sultan's court at reasonable prices.[7] *Kethüda*s, *şeyh*s, and *yiğit başı*s are mentioned in firmans of the 1580s concerning the Istanbul guilds of flour merchants and bakers, tanners, boatmen, makers of pins and needles, sellers of sweets, woollen drapers, leather merchants, dealers in candlesticks, and founders.[8]

Information about guilds in the sixteenth century is rather sporadic, but from the seventeenth century onward it becomes so copious as to support the conclusion that by that time the entire population of Istanbul had become organized in an elaborate guild system. It has, indeed, been the unanimous observation of writers on this subject that all walks of life were encompassed in this system, much more so than in any western country.[9] They differ only with regard to the exceptions from this rule. Taeschner, for instance, thought that no one was exempt from belonging to a guild: 'Das Zunftwesen [war] damals die Form . . ., durch die allein auch der Einzelmensch, der ja sonst im orientalischen Staatswesen gar nicht fassbar war, erfasst werden konnte, weshalb auch die Regierung ein Interesse an diesen Zünften hatte. So waren alle Untertanen des Reiches, auch die Beamten, die Soldaten und die Geistlichkeit zunftmässig eingeteilt . . .'[10] We have not found any confirmation in the sources for this somewhat astonishing view that soldiers and officials also were organized in guilds. Therefore, the following formulation by Mantran seems to be more accurate: 'Toutes les classes, tous les individus composant la population stambouliote, à l'exception des Janissaires, des Sipahis, des fonctionnaires et employés du gouvernement, ou du palais, et des étrangers, sont embrigadés dans les corporations.'[11] In any case, the common source of both conclusions that the whole population of Istanbul was organized in guilds was Evliya Çelebi's enumeration of the guilds as they passed in procession on the occasion of their muster by Murad IV (1623–40).[12] It must be asked, however, whether Evliya's description of the all-embracing character of this system reflects the reality of daily life in seventeenth century Istanbul, or whether this was a theory used only on ceremonial occasions.

In order to answer this question, it may be useful to divide Evliya's guilds into two: one group which does not generally figure in other sources dealing with the function of the guilds in everyday life,[13] and the other group, whose functions are reflected in numerous other sources. The first group includes the following:[14] (*a*) The *ulema*, including *kadıs*, *hatibs*, and many other religious functionaries or people belonging to Islamic institutions, such as mystics, students of the *medreses*, *şerifs*, etc., enumerated, amongst others, in Section III of the procession.[15] (*b*) Workers in state factories and day-labourers.[16] (*c*) Farmers and peasants (residing in towns).[17] (*d*) Entertainers of all kinds and members of the so-called 'immoral guilds', such as prostitutes, pickpockets, etc.[18] The fact that these guilds do not generally figure in documents on the guilds' administrative, economic or social functions does not mean that they did not exist. We have no grounds for doubting Evliya's account of their forming a professional organization headed by *şeyhs*, *kethüdas*, and other officers, and thus fulfilling at least the function of constituting a unit for the purpose of general control and supervision by the state, performed through their muster on the occasion of ceremonial processions, and perhaps by other means as well. For this purpose, indeed, the entire urban population was comprised in the guild system, except the higher bureaucracy and the army. However, in many other respects, the guild organization of professions of this group apparently had no significance, while it was of crucial importance for the public life of the second group.

This second group includes, first and foremost, artisans and craftsmen of all branches of industry. Secondly, it includes merchants of all kinds. Too much stress has been put by modern authors on the division of the guilds into merchants, on one hand, and craftsmen, on the other. Such a distinction may be useful for the orientation of the economic historian, but it certainly had no fundamental significance in the economic and social reality of the seventeenth and eighteenth centuries, or even the nineteenth. Most artisans in the bazaar sold their own products, and it would be very difficult indeed to decide whether many of them were 'craftsmen' or 'merchants'. In addition to these artisan-merchants, merchants proper also had their guilds, complete with *kethüdas*, *yiğit başıs*, etc.[19] In some cases, the merchants of a specific market were incorporated in one guild, as, for instance, those of the Galata *bedesten*.[20] But since many merchants dealing in specific goods were concentrated in one market, this may have been just another name for the guild of a certain branch of merchants.

Thirdly, this second group includes guilds of persons engaged in transport and services. To give only a few examples, there were guilds of the Bosporus boatmen (*peremeciler*), water carriers (*sakalar*), the fire brigade (*tulumbacılar*), public weighers (*kantarcılar*), porters (*hamallar*), etc.[21] Their classification as persons engaged in transport and services is again of course one of the modern historian, and has no significance whatever from the point of view of the life of these guilds or their function.

Finally, one should include in this group of professions for which the guild organization was of paramount significance all those connected with medicine. This includes physicians, oculists, surgeons, pharmacists, etc.[22] Physicians in Middle Eastern countries had strong conceptual traditions connected with their profession, as well as strong guild organizations.[23] It is this second group mainly which will figure in the following study of the functions of Turkish guilds.

A universal system of guilds consistently divided into professional groups (at least for the purpose of control by the government and of ceremonies) necessarily includes groups with extremely different sizes of membership.[24] According to Evliya, whose figures should be considered only rough approximations, there were in Istanbul such large guilds as those of watchmen (12,000 members), merchants of the Black Sea (8,000, or, according to another manuscript, 7,000 with 2,000 store houses), tallow-chandlers (5,500 workers), and saddlers (5,000 with 1,084 shops), and such small guilds as those of map-makers (15, with eight shops), sling-makers (five, with three shops), merchants of almond oil (seven, with three shops), and even the one-man one-shop 'guild' of a painter-fortuneteller.[25] The section of building guilds included, on one hand, guilds of 4,000 carpenters, 3,000 builders, and 10,000 day-labourers, and, on the other, 12 upholsterers (with ten shops), ten litter-makers (one shop), and the one-man 'guild' of the maker of torturing instruments. The number of members in most guilds was, of course, between these extremes.[26]

The reason for the existence of so many small guilds was the extreme tendency for occupations to split into guilds of specialized branches.[27] According to Evliya, there were in the seventeenth century about twenty different guilds of cooks and sellers of various dishes, about eleven guilds of fishermen, separated according to the system which each used for fishing and the different kinds of nets they used, and 64 guilds of makers of different musical instruments.[28] A firman from the eighteenth century informs us of the existence in Istanbul of a guild of weavers of ribbons for the fire-brigade (*tulumbacı şeridi dokuyan esnaf*).[29] Even in the nineteenth century there were fourteen different guilds of shoemakers grouped according to the community of the craftsmen and the kind of shoes they made,[30] and White said that the tailors' trade was subdivided into nearly as many branches as there were kinds of apparel.[31] As we have remarked with regard to Egypt, the extreme subdivision of trades and occupations into separate guilds was mainly the result of administrative considerations of government, since in order to maintain close supervision over guild members it was necessary for the head of the guild to know his members personally.[32]

FUNCTIONS

(1) *The guilds as an administrative link*

The most important function of the guilds throughout the centuries was their service as an administrative link between the government and the urban population. As long as the state was unable to create a bureaucracy on a large scale or to carry out censuses it was compelled to use intermediate units in order to establish relations between the government and the individual. In Turkey, as in Egypt, the guilds were among the most important of these units.

First of all, they accomplished the general supervision of the town population, since people employed in each craft and profession were registered through the guilds and their heads. For such registration we have Evliya's evidence relating to seventeenth century Istanbul as well as documents from the nineteenth century, such as the *İhtisab Ağalığı Nizamnamesi* of September 1826 and the regulations for boatmen (*kayıkçılar*) of 24 December 1874.[33] The guild *kethüda*s therefore were in a position to convey government orders and announcements to their members and to make certain that the instructions of the authorities were carried out. Throughout the whole period with which we are dealing, the *kethüda*s were charged with supervising the implementation of government orders regarding industry, commerce, and services, such as the regulations for boatmen (*peremeciler*) concerning the production, sale, and traffic of boats in the year 985/1577 and those for porters of the year 1143/1730, the prohibition to produce certain luxury goods in which gold and silver were used (1128/1716), the order to the Muslim makers of *kavuklar* (wadded caps) to refrain from producing headgear worn by Jews (1141/1729); instructions concerning the height, shape, material, and use of new buildings erected after the destruction of the old ones by fire (1210/1795), the exclusion of European style medical shops from the Muslim quarters of Istanbul (1221/1806), the prohibition to make sharp-pointed shoes (1222/1807), and many similar orders.[34]

In some cases, government supervision was carried out through the guilds and other units of the population at the same time. Thus in 1222/1807, when it appeared that non-Muslims (Greeks, Armenians, and Jews) were imitating Muslims in the way they dressed, and, contrary to tradition, were wearing green fabrics, the *kadı* assembled the *kethüdas* of the guilds of makers and sellers of various kinds of textiles as well as the heads of the communities concerned (the Greek and Armenian Patriarchs and the Jewish *Hahambaşı*) and warned the former not to sell green fabrics to non-Muslims and the latter to see to it that their flock did not dress in the Muslim fashion.[35]

Nor was the government content with just charging the *kethüdas* with the implementation of its instructions; individual guilds also were required to supply guarantees that official orders would be carried out. For instance, in 1766 a baker was punished for using false weights, and he was allowed to resume his business only after the guild had given a guarantee that he would not repeat his misdeed.[36]

Moreover, the guild usually was required to issue a guarantee for the good character of each of its members, providing the government with a kind of indirect control over each individual in the urban population. The existence of such guarantees for the boatmen of Istanbul is documented for a period extending from the end of the sixteenth century to the end of the nineteenth.[37] The guild of makers or casters of lead supplied a guarantee for the reliability of its members (document dated 1114/1703), and according to the above-mentioned *Ihtisab Ağalığı Nizamnamesi* of September 1826, the *kethüda* and *yiğit başı* of every guild was required to furnish the Istanbul *ihtisab ağası* with a guarantee for the guild and its members.[38] Similarly, the *şehbender* (chief) and *muhtars* (assistants) of the guild of Muslim merchants called *hayriye tüccarı* issued guarantees for the honesty and good character of all the merchants belonging to this guild. They were responsible to the government for ensuring that none of them had acquired his *berat* (patent) by fraud.[39]

The *kethüda* (or *kâhya*) represented not only the authorities to the guild, but also the guild before the authorities. Thus, for instance, we learn from a document dating from 996/1588 that the *kethüda* and officers of the guild of workers in bronze, brass, and copper complained to the *kadı* of soldiers who interfered with the work of the guild members and molested them and violated guild traditions in various ways.[40] In nineteenth century Seres, the chief *kâhya* (*kâhyalar başı*) was the spokesman for all the guilds, and it was his task to submit to the government the decisions of the grand council (*kâhyalar meclisi*), as well as complaints against government officials and other communications from the guilds. In special cases, the communication was submitted by a delegation consisting of the *kâhyalar başı*, two *kâhyas* and two workers, elected in an extraordinary meeting of the *kâhyalar meclisi* together with three masters from each guild. However, as in Egypt, this seems to have been a secondary function. For the most part the *kethüda* was the agent of the government rather than the spokesman of the guild: we have found only a few examples of the latter function, almost all of them from

Seres where guild organization was exceptionally strong and autonomous.[41]

(2) *Guilds and taxation*

One of the most striking differences between the activities of guilds in Istanbul and Egyptian guilds was the absence of fiscal functions among the former. In Istanbul most urban taxes were collected by the *ihtisab ağası* (*muhtesib*) through agents called *kol oğlanları*.[42] Neither in the documents reproduced by Refik and Nuri, nor in secondary sources using additional documents, have we found traces of the four aspects of the guilds' fiscal function, about which copious information exists concerning those of Egypt: (1) assessment of the amount of taxes to be paid; (2) distribution of the tax quota among members of the guild; (3) the *şeyh*'s responsibility for payment of the taxes by individual members of the guilds; and (4) the collecting of taxes by the guild *şeyhs*.[43]

This statement must be qualified by some information relating to the early nineteenth century. White tells us that in his time part of the earnings of the Istanbul porters was given to their *vekil* and used by him both to provide food and lodging and for the payment of government taxes.[44] Similarly, according to the *Ihtisab Ağalığı Nizamnamesi* of September 1826, the *kethüda* of the gardeners collected 88,500 *kuruş* yearly as *imdadiye* for the Imperial dockyards at Istanbul (*tersane-i âmire*). These regulations also imposed upon *kethüda*s in the great market of Istanbul some duties connected with tax collection, but made it clear that elsewhere this was not carried out through guilds.[45]

On the other hand, according to the same regulations, the *şehbender*s, *muhtar*s and *kethüda*s of some guilds of merchants and grocers were responsible for payment of the customs dues of imported material sold by them.[46] This is remarkable, since in general, even in Egypt, customs were not among the payments made through the guilds or guaranteed by the guild. Equally interesting is the information that the *şeyh* of the booksellers' guild collected from its members the sum to be paid for the rent of their shops – five to seven piastres per month each – and transmitted it to the administration of the Imperial foundations, but White, who is the source for this information, implies clearly that the *şeyh* did not collect the tax they paid to the government. In connexion with the payment of rent through the guild, it should be mentioned that in the eighteenth century the guild or its *kethüda* apparently occasionally guaranteed payments of rent by members, as documented in a firman concerning the printers' guild dated 1142/1729.[47]

(3) *Control of the quality of products and of weights and measures*

In Istanbul, as in many Arab countries (Syria, Tunis, Morocco, and

Algeria), control of the quality of goods made or sold by artisans and merchants was one of the main tasks of the guilds. In this respect only Egypt was an exception.[48] But neither in the Arab countries nor in Istanbul was this control an exclusive affair of the guilds; rather it was the responsibility of government authorities who used the guild system as an instrument for supervising the implementation of its instructions in this respect. The instructions were issued by the government, as, for example, detailed regulations concerning the quality and measures of various goods and services included in the *kanunname* of 1091/1680, and the (undated) instructions concerning the measures of bath towels.[49] The guild officers, i.e. the *kethüda* and *yiğit başı*, and its elders, the *ihtiyarlar*, were charged with supervising the implementation of such instructions. Thus a firman to the *kethüda*, *yiğit başı*, and *ihtiyarlar* of the makers and sellers of knives dated 1138/1725–6 required them to make sure that they were made of genuine steel (*halis çelikten*), not of wrought iron (*karademirden*). Similarly, a firman dated 1106/1695 demanded that the *yiğit başı*s of the furriers see to it that traditional standards were kept. It was the task of the *kethüda*s to confirm the stamps impressed on weights and on textiles as shown in a firman to the weighers dated 1200/1785–6; and the *kethüda*s of the guilds concerned were ordered in 1206/1792 to prevent the use of adulterated dyes.[50] In certain cases a *kethüda* or a *baş kethüda* was especially appointed for this purpose. Thus, with the spreading use of tobacco a *kethüda* of the tobacconists was appointed in 1138/1725 to prevent the adulteration of tobacco practised by some Jewish merchants; and similarly a *kethüda* was appointed in 1163/1750 for the makers of roof-tiles to supervise the adherence of the members of this craft to regulations concerning the measures of their roof-tiles.[51] An interesting case was that of the Istanbul shoemakers. By the middle of the nineteenth century the quality of shoes sold in the market of Istanbul had considerably deteriorated; this was explained by the extreme independence of the various guilds that took part in the process of producing shoes (workers, cobblers, menders, etc.), each of whom had its own *kethüda*, whereas formerly the *kethüda* of the shoemakers of the Grand Bazaar (*büyük arastenin hafaflar kethüdası*) had served as a head *kethüda* (*baş kethüda*) of all the guilds and supervised the quality of their work. In order to restore the original state of affairs, a *baş kethüda* for 14 specified guilds of shoemakers of all kinds was appointed according to a document dated 6 *Cemaziyelâhir* 1277/20 December 1860.[52]

However, the guild's control of the quality of goods made or sold by its members and by others was rather limited. The guild was supposed to be alert to detect fraudulent practices and goods of inferior quality, but it could not itself take any action. It could only denounce the culprit to the authorities and leave the punishment to them. This was the case whether or not the culprit was a member of the complaining guild. According to a document dated 29 *Zilhicce* 1206/18 August 1792 the *kethüda*, yiğit *başı* and *ihtiyarlar* of the guild of Istanbul weavers appeared before the *kadı* and complained about the illegal supply of inferior material by a certain silk merchant. The latter promised the *kadı* not to supply such material again, and in view of this his punishment was postponed. Similarly, according to a document dated 16 *Şevval* 1138/17 June 1726 the guild of sword makers denounced one of its members to the *kadı* for making hilts from inferior wood and painting them black to imitate ebony. He was severely warned by the *kadı* not to do this again.[53] Another interesting example is a case of copper vessels made of inferior material and unfit for use, brought before the *kadı* in 1131/1718–9 by the *kethüdalar* of the tin and copper merchants. The *kadı* ordered that the vessels be thrown into the sea, and appointed a person to execute this order.[54] Thus it was the *kadı*, rather than the guild, who in the last resort took effective measures to implement the regulations concerning the quality of goods made or sold by artisans or merchants. This fact conforms to other conclusions about the guilds' judicial functions to be dealt with later on.

(4) *Fixing of prices* (narh) *and wages*

As we have seen, instructions concerning the quality of goods were issued by the authorities, and the authorities punished makers or sellers of goods of inferior quality. The guild only controlled implementation of the official instructions and denounced the offenders. The actual prices of goods also were fixed by the government, and those who sold at higher prices were punished by the authorities. In addition, most of the implementation of these orders was in the hands of the official market inspector and was not a function of the guilds, whose concern with preventing overcharging was extremely small and rather indirect. The explanation of this difference is obvious: it was in the guild's interest that none of its members, and even less outsiders, should adulterate materials made or sold by it, produce or sell goods of inferior quality, or exercise fraudulent practices, but it was primarily in the interest of the authorities, as defenders of the consuming population, that the guild's monopoly should not be abused for raising the prices of goods needed by the people.

Despite the changes that occurred in this respect throughout the centuries, the fixing of maximum prices (*narh*, in Arabic *tas'īr*) was always the prerogative of the authorities, not the guilds.[55] Generally it was the *kadı* and the *ihtisab ağası* who were charged with this task, and the list of fixed maximum prices then was transmitted to the guilds as an order.[56] In the middle of the nineteenth century this function was transferred to the *şehremaneti* (prefecture) established at that time, but the custom for its decisions to be transmitted as orders to the guilds was maintained.[57] Such instructions were issued periodically – according to a document dated 29 *Safar* 1139/26 October 1726, once in each of the year's four seasons.[58] The explanation that the *narh* was directed against the abuse of monopolies by the guilds is explicitly given in another document dated 1 *Rebiyülevvel* 1194/7 March 1780.[59]

In view of this situation, the fact that the authorities punished offenders against the *narh* needs no particular elaboration. This emerges clearly, for instance, from the provisions of the 1840 and 1851 Ottoman penal codes. Article 19 of the 1851 code says that he who relapses into this offence for the fourth time should be exiled and expelled from the guild, but this was a law laid down by the government, and not an internal regulation of the guild.[60] An interesting case was that of the *Ahi Baba* of the Istanbul tanners, who in 1726 was dismissed by the government from his position as head of the guild because of an infringement of the *narh* regulations.[61]

Not only were the fixing of prices and punishing of offenders in official hands, but also the control of the implementation of the *narh*. A typical example is an order of March 1780 in which the *kadı* was charged with continually supervising implementation of the *narh* regulations by secret and open scrutiny.[62] Many other documents on the functions of the *kadı* and the *ihtisab ağası* imply the same, and none of the documents known to us include cases in which guilds controlled such an implementation or denounced offenders.

All this does not mean, however, that the guilds had no connexion whatever with the *narh*. First, the officials who fixed maximum prices of goods did so in the presence of the *kethüda*s of the guilds concerned.[63] Secondly, from time to time certain guilds asked the government (the *kadı*) to enforce maximum prices of materials supplied to them by wholesalers or transporters, as did the coal-dealers in 1147/1734 and the butchers in 1151/1738.[64] Thirdly, there was an indirect connexion between the guilds and the *narh*. Before the middle of the nineteenth century, all official activities concerning price fixing would have been practically impossible without the functioning of the guilds as an administrative link between the government and the population. Whenever the guilds lost their grip over the urban population, for instance as a result of the penetration of Janissaries into the artisan and merchant class, the government encountered difficulties in implementing the *narh* and punishing offenders against its regulations.[65] Finally, under the economic and administrative circumstances which prevailed until a century ago, a prerequisite for fixing prices and implementing the *narh* was the guilds' monopoly of producing and/or selling specific goods.[66]

Like the instructions concerning the quality, weights and measures and prices of goods, orders laying down wage scales also were issued by the government. Many firmans were issued as a result of attempts by carpenters and other craftsmen and workers engaged in building to exploit a boom caused by fires to demand higher wages. In these firmans, addressed to the *kadı* and the *mimar başı*, detailed wage scales were fixed, and offenders were threatened with heavy punishment.[67] In general the guilds were not mentioned in these firmans, but again, this does not mean that they had nothing to do with wage fixing. Their task is made clear by one of these firmans, dated *Zilhicce* 1229/December 1814, where it is stated explicitly that the master carpenters and decorators, as well as the *kethüda*s of the building trades, were assembled at the *şer'î* court where details of the wage scale were announced to them, and they were threatened with heavy punishment in case of non-compliance. Thereupon the representative of the guilds declared their compliance and undertook not to demand higher wages in future.[68] Thus it was the guilds' function to carry out the government's orders concerning wages in the same way that they were responsible for implementation of regulations regarding quality and the weights and measures of goods.

(5) *Supply of services and labour*

It was an important function of Turkish guilds to provide the government with needed services and labour. The principal difference between Turkish and Egyptian guilds in this respect seems to have been that while the latter were required primarily to furnish the government with manpower for building, transport and public works, the services of Turkish guilds were needed mainly to recruit their members as civilian auxiliaries for the army in time of war.[69] This, according to Nuri, was partly the result of the decline of the state's financial power; as long as it flourished, its own enterprises employed craftsmen, but after its deterioration these services were supplied to the army by the guilds of Istanbul, Edirne and Bursa.[70] It seems to have been one of the principal aims of the guild processions to muster this manpower.

In case of war, where an officer of the Janissaries or of another unit was appointed as *Ordu-yu hümayun Ağası*, the firman by which he was appointed included the number of guild members to be recruited and the place where they were to assemble. In order to perform his task he would have recourse to the *kadı*, who assembled the *kethüda*s, *yiğit başı*s and veteran masters of the guilds concerned at the *mahkeme* (Law Court) and conveyed to them the contents of the firman.[71] After further consultations with the guild, those who were selected for the army were sent to the *mahkeme*.[72] Naturally, only a small part of a guild was recruited, and those who remained at home had to supply means for keeping the recruits and their families, as well as for hiring agents or deputies to run their businesses. The sums supplied in this manner were recorded in the *kadı*'s register.[73] After the destruction of the Janissary corps in 1826 and the establishment of professional artisan units, guild members no longer were recruited into the army.[74]

Later in the nineteenth century the heads of some guilds apparently turned into labour contractors. In Egypt[75] and Turkey, among the guilds in which this seems to have become a rule, there was, first and foremost, the guild of porters. A contemporary observer wrote of the Istanbul porters in the early 1840s: 'The number of porters at each station is determined by the *vekil*, who regulates the employ of hands to the demand, so that all may gain a fair livelihood. No *hamal* can ply at any station without the assent of this *vekil* . . . Divisions of men, working at each station, generally lodge together in the outskirts of the city and suburbs, and pay a fixed sum monthly to their *vekil*, who provides food and lodging . . .'[76] Thus even in the later stages of their history some functions of supply of labour and services were retained by the guilds.

(6) *Supply and distribution of goods*

In addition to supplying labour and services, the guilds also fulfilled certain functions connected with the supply and distribution of goods. These may be divided into two main categories. First, corresponding to the guilds' task of furnishing labour and services to the government, they also were made responsible for the supply of certain goods to the authorities. Very early documentation for this function is found in a firman dated 26 *Cemaziyelâhir* 981/23 October 1573, according to which a *kethüda* and a *yiğit başı* were especially appointed for the guild of *varakçılar* in order to guarantee the regular supply of gold and silver leaf of standard quality to the Sultan's court at reasonable prices.[77] During the sixteenth and seventeenth centuries, such items of information are very scarce, and we have not found any in Nuri's collection of documents. They appear again in the eighteenth century. Thus, according to a firman dated 1140/1727 the head of the guild of shipowners (*gemiciler kethüdası*) was made responsible for the regular supply of timber to Istanbul. In 1167/1754 and in 1196/1782 respectively the head of the quarrymen (*taşcılar*) was requested (among others) to ensure the supply of stones for the restoration of the Bayazid mosque and the supply of marble for the restoration of the mosque of Mehmed II; and an order of 1168/1755 made the heads of the furriers' guild (*kürkçüler*) responsible for preventing the furs brought to Istanbul from being sold secretly at exorbitant prices instead of being sent to the Sultan's Court.[78]

Another function connected with the supply of goods, that of distributing raw material needed by artisans and craftsmen, seems to have been quite an important task of the guilds. This is how Taeschner described this function:

> So wissen wir, dass die Zunft als Ganzes den *Einkauf der Rohstoffe* besorgte und für eine gerechte Verteilung an die einzelnen Meister sorgte. Vor allem wurde darauf gesehen, dass nicht einige wenige wohlhabende Meister das Rohstoffmaterial ganz an sich brachten, so dass die minderbemittelten Meister leer ausgingen; vielmehr wurde zunächst eine allgemeine Verteilung vorgenommen, und erst vom Überschuss konnten die wohlhabenderen Meister ihre Wünsche nach mehr Arbeitsmaterial befriedigen, – ja, sie waren sogar dazu verpflichtet, damit der Händler mit seiner Ware nicht sitzen blieb und dann vielleicht nicht wiederkam.[79]

Unfortunately, Taeschner does not disclose his sources for this statement. Nevertheless, there can be no doubt that at least for some guilds and for specific periods his description is true. Thus, a firman dated 1001/1593 provided for the distribution of wood brought to Istanbul by the *kethüda* of the sawyers to the members of this guild. Similarly, in 1018/1609 the *kethüda* and *yiğit başı*s of the linen-drapers were ordered to distribute the linen and cotton cloth imported into the town among their guild, and the same instruction was given to the *ustalar* (masters) and *ihtiyarlar* (elders) of the furriers in 1168/1755 with regard to furs. Finally, according to a document dated 21 *Cemaziyelevvel* 1180/25 October 1766 and other documents of the same period from the *sicil* of the *kadı* of Istanbul, the leather brought by the tanners to Istanbul was assembled in the *lonca* (lodge – also called *tacirhane*) of the leather merchants and there distributed among them by the *kethüda*, the *yiğit başı* and the *ihtiyarlar* of their guild at current prices.[80] Nuri says that all wares imported into Istanbul were brought to a place called *kapan* (originally *kaban*), a mart furnished with public steel yards for wholesale commodities. There they were distributed by a *naib* (delegate of the *kadı*), a secretary and the *kethüda*s, *yiğit başı*s and *ihtiyarlar* of the guilds concerned.[81]

(7) *Judicial functions and arbitration of disputes*

So far we have dealt mainly with the activities of the guild as a link between the government and the craftsmen, merchants and workers. However, the distribution of raw material among guild members represents another aspect of the guilds' functions, namely the regulation of relations among the artisans and merchants themselves. The most important of these functions were the arbitration of disputes among members of the guilds and provision for mutual help.

We have seen that usually it was not the guilds or their officers who punished craftsmen, merchants, or workers for economic offences, but the *kadı* and the *muhtesib*.[82] In addition to the examples mentioned above, this is shown by an order dated 1139/1726–7, according to which the *kethüda* of the carpenters was required to make sure that no sawdust gathered in their workshops and no fire was lighted there. He was required to inform the *kadı* if this order was violated, but not to punish offenders.[83] Similarly, the *şehbender* of the guild of Muslim merchants called *hayriye tüccarı* was supposed to verify whether members of the guild had perpetrated a crime or offence, but the actual punishment was effected by the official authorities.[84]

There were, however, some important exceptions to this rule. First, Evliya Çelebi tells us that the guild of shoemakers had its particular officers, 'appointed by an Imperial Rescript of Sultan Suleiman, who exempted them from the jurisdiction of all other commanding officers. They punish their culprits themselves, even by death, and bury them in the precinct of their establishment.' They had received this privilege as a reward for their support of Süleyman against the Janissaries.[85] Apparently, it was not the only privilege which the shoemakers enjoyed.[86] Another guild with similar privileges was that of the tanners. According to a firman dated 1773 granted to the *Ahi Baba* of the tanners of Kırşehir, the guild had the right to punish its members for crimes with the bastinado, temporary prison, prevention of exercising their craft, and other punishments.[87] Probably it was no coincidence that we have information on the existence of such privileges among the shoemakers and tanners; these two were among the few guilds which strictly preserved various traditions and enjoyed a great extent of autonomy for a long time.[88]

Other guilds enjoying a large extent of autonomy were those of the Macedonian town of Seres. It is not surprising, therefore, that they too punished delinquent guild members. One aspect of the guild autonomy in Seres, as in Damascus, was the existence of a common chief under whom the whole town guild system was united. Exactly as in Damascus, it was this common chief who was authorized to punish guild members for their offences.[89] According to the procedure current in Seres a culprit was judged by the *lonca*, the guild-council, and after the verdict was confirmed by the *kâhyalar meclisi*, the assembly of guild heads, the sentence was executed by the *kâhyalar başı*, the common chief of all the Seres guilds.[90]

The foregoing relates to economic offences or crimes for which heavy penalties were fixed and which in general were dealt with by the *kadı*. There were, however, other judicial functions which were always carried out by the officers of the guilds. Thus the guild head or its officers dealt with disciplinary misdemeanours of guild members who did not obey their superiors, and even applied corporal punishment when necessary.[91] If a member acted contrary to the guild's traditions, he could be banned from the guild by its officers and council and thus be deprived of the right to exercise his craft or trade.[92] This applied also to idleness, drunkenness, and other offences against religious precepts.[93]

Finally, it was the task of the heads or councils of practically all the guilds to arbitrate disputes among their members – often in order to prevent the intervention of the *kadı*, i.e. of the authorities.[94] In this, the Turkish guilds resembled the Egyptian ones, where the arbitration of disputes among guild members was one of the most general and persistent functions of the *şeyh*s.[95]

(8) *Provident fund and mutual help*

A provident fund and other arrangements for mutual help seem to have been an important feature of the Turkish guilds' activities, in contrast to the situation in Egypt, where only the shoemakers made such arrangements.[96]

According to Nuri, every Turkish guild had a fund for mutual help called *teavün sandığı* or *esnafin orta sandığı*. It was under the supervision of the guild's *kethüda*, yiğit *başı* and *ihtiyarlar*, and its accounts were examined at the *lonca*, where means to increase its income were discussed. The income consisted of voluntary contributions, regular contributions by guild members collected weekly or monthly, and special payments made by the masters on the occasion of the promotion of their *çırak*s (apprentices) to the rank of *kalfa* (journeyman) or of their *kalfa*s to the rank of *usta* (master). Until the beginning of the twentieth century a master of the guilds of the Uzunçarşı in Istanbul contributed 50 *kuruş* whenever a *çırak* of his became a *kalfa* and 300 *kuruş* when a *kalfa* became *usta*.[97]

The guilds also owned common property in the form of copper vessels which were donated by the guardians of apprentices on the occasion of their promotions. These vessels were held as foundations by the guilds, and they were rented out for celebrations. Evliya relates that Sultan Süleyman, to show his favour to the goldsmiths, granted them as a *vakıf* a thousand plates and five hundred kettles and pans. The renting out of such vessels was prohibited in the *Nizamname* of 1826–7.[98]

The guilds' funds and the income derived from them served various purposes. Accumulated capital was lent to members in need of money, for instance those wishing to enlarge their businesses. The interest from such loans (at the rate of one per cent) was assigned to charity, such as the distribution of rice among poor members or other destitute persons, assistance to sick members, and funerals of members who lacked sufficient resources for this purpose. In addition, income from the guilds' funds was used for religious purposes, such as the recitation of the Qur'an in the mosque of Eyüb during the month of Ramazan.[99]

Unfortunately, Nuri's information on funds for mutual help in the guilds of Istanbul does not include any detailed or specific example. However, many details of this kind are found in the sources available on the guilds of Seres. There the guilds' funds were kept in the form of foundations called *esnaf vakfı*, *esnaf sandığı* or *vakıf sandığı* (previously: *esnaf kisesi*). They were managed by the guilds' heads, who also were called *mütevelli*, probably because they fulfilled this function. The *mütevelli* was responsible to the *lonca*, to whom he had to submit yearly statements. The accounts then were examined by the *lonca*, and afterwards were open to inspection by every master of the guild. The fund was divided into six 'bags' (*kese*, *torba*):

(1) the satin bag, for keeping *hüccet*s (deeds) of the guild's *vakıflar* and the relevant correspondence; (2) the green bag, for keeping *vakfıye*s and *tapu* (cadaster) documents belonging to the guild's real estate; (3) the plaited bag, for cash; (4) the red bag, for documents relating to interest-bearing funds; (5) the white bag, for receipts and confirmed annual accounts; and (6) the black bag, for unrealizable vouchers and various documents.

Details concerning the budget of the fund of the wool-carders' guild (*hallaclar*) in Seres for the year 1289–90 (1872–3) show that out of a total of 21,910 *kuruş* the largest items contributing income were rents (7,650 *kuruş*), interest (7,900 *kuruş*) and voluntary contributions (2,700 *kuruş*). The expenditure included payment for shops bought (2,050 *kuruş*), all kinds of charities, allotments for education and ritual purposes (e.g. *hacc*, sacrifice, Qur'an reading, etc.), repairs of bridges and roads, the management of the *vakıf*s, and various other activities.[100]

Some Turkish guilds also provided for mutual help in other ways. The members of a guild or all the owners of a *gedik* (right to a shop) belonging to a specific profession were mutually responsible for each other's debts, and paid the taxes of destitute guild members. We have evidence of this function for the guild of makers and sellers of snuff (undated document), certain merchant guilds (document from the end of the eighteenth century) and the guilds of Seres (nineteenth century).[101]

Whether this principle of mutual help was a survival from the Society of Virtue (*fütüvvet*), whose members 'lived almost communistically',[102] remains to be established by further research. In any case, this aspect of guild functions seems to have been much more important in Turkey than in the other countries of the Middle East and North Africa,[103] but we have not yet found a convincing explanation for this difference.

(9) *Social functions*

In addition to their administrative and economic functions, the Turkish guilds constituted social units, and it may well be that among their members a feeling of loyalty developed, a certain esprit de corps. But since we have no means of testing the existence of such feelings by the methods of modern social research, and because of the absence of literary sources, we must content ourselves with the examination of outward signs of guild solidarity.

In Seres, the members of each guild had their particular dresses, worn from the day of their promotion from apprentice to journeyman (*kalfa*).[104] Elsewhere, however, there was no difference between the dress of most of the guilds (with few exceptions), but only between that of the official classes on one hand and the common people (including *esnaf* and *âhadınas* or *avam*) on the other.[105]

The Egyptian guilds symbolized their trades only in a very concrete manner, by displaying the tools themselves and not, like the European guilds, by adopting heraldic signs or pictures.[106] In this respect, Turkish guilds did not differ, as is shown by numerous miniature representations,[107] as well as by literary descriptions of their processions.[108] In nineteenth-century Seres each guild had its own flag and standard-bearer. On top of the flagstaff there was a crescent, and beneath it, fastened to a small cord, was the symbol of the guild. The quilt makers, for instance, had a small satin-made quilt measuring 15–20 square centimetres, the farriers had a small silver horse-shoe, the makers of slippers had a nice little pair of child's shoes, the barbers a barber's basin, the confectioners a small sugar-loaf made of paper, and the farmers had a bunch of corn.[109]

Symbols of this kind, or the tools themselves, were displayed at various processions held by the guilds from time to time, whenever they attended the festivities arranged by the Sultans on the occasion of the birth or circumcision of their sons, or whenever the Sultans felt the necessity to muster them for other reasons. Such processions are described in several *surnames*, as well as in Evliya's account.[110] The participation of the guilds in these processions was perhaps not the most important, but certainly the most conspicuous, of their social activities.

Less ostentatious but more frequent were the common prayers held by each of the guilds of the Istanbul markets early in the morning before the opening of their shops. In the Grand Bazaar there was a special place for this purpose called *dua meydanı*.[111] Similarly, until the beginning of the twentieth century, the Ankara tanners had a special café where they prayed every morning.[112]

Important occasions for reinforcing the solidarity of the guilds were yearly excursions to the countryside (*tenezzüh*, *teferrüc*, also *sohbet*).[113]

In Seres, each guild assembled once a year outside the town behind the fortress for a picnic called *ziyafet-i ictimaı* which lasted for one day and included amusements, prayers, and meals. Another yearly festivity of the Seres guilds, held at the same place, lasted for three days and was therefore called *üç günler*. It was arranged by the *kâhyalar meclisi* and attended by all 24 guilds of the town as well as by the notables and the common people of all the villages in the vicinity. On this occasion also meals were served, religious ceremonies were held, and amusements were arranged. Finally, the third day of the *bayram*, the festival following the fast of Ramazan, was called in Seres *esnaf günü* (guilds' day). On this day receptions were held at the various *lonca*s, and members of the guilds visited and congratulated each other.[114]

In the early period of Turkish guild history the pilgrimage, or *hacc*, also was an important occasion for the social activity of the guilds. It was one of the principal functions of the *şeyhs* of Turkish guilds to accompany members who departed for the *hacc* or returned from it.[115] While in Egypt this remained the most important of the regular public ceremonies in which all the guilds participated,[116] in nineteenth century Turkey the connexion between the guilds and the *hacc* seems to have weakened considerably. Nevertheless, when a member of a Seres guild made the pilgrimage to Mecca, the flag of his guild was brought to the Grand Mosque of the town, where a special ceremony was held. Next morning, the departing pilgrims were accompanied by a procession of their respective guilds and their flags. Similar processions met them on their return.[117]

Among the particular ceremonies of specific guilds, the most famous was that of the goldsmiths held every 20 (or 40) years for a duration of ten (or 20) days and nights in the meadow of Kâğithane, the valley of the Sweet Waters of Europe at the top of the Golden Horn. On these occasions, goldsmiths from all over the Empire assembled, met the Sultan, and performed various ceremonies, *inter alia* a procession at which they exhibited on wagons and litters a large variety of precious articles made or sold by them. The saddlers also met at the same place every 20 years.[118]

In the context of the guilds' social functions, the proposition that they encouraged qualities of honesty and sobriety has often been discussed.[119] It has been claimed that the guilds did this through their affiliations with the *tarikat*s: 'The social function of the corporations was enhanced . . . by their religious affiliation, usually to one of the great religious orders . . . This religious personality encouraged the qualities of honesty and sobriety . . .'[120] This seems to be based on Nuri's statement that the guilds were connected with the *turuk-u aliye*, who developed among them qualities of *doğruluk* (righteousness) and *kanaatkârlık* (contentment).[121] But this connexion is highly doubtful. Nuri frequently reiterates the claim that members of certain *tarikat*s were all from the same guild or that there was a connexion between the guilds and the *tarikat*s,[122] but he does not cite any documents as proof. The detailed account of the Melâmî *şeyh*s who practised various crafts[123] does not prove any connexion, and even indicates that there was no such tie and that in the same *tarikat* different crafts were represented, and that the Melâmîs often practised the craft only as a cover for their *sufi* activity. Moreover, he talks about crafts, but not about guilds.[124] In any case, Nuri leaves no doubt that in his view it was Islam and the religious education which developed favourable qualities among the artisans and merchants, and not some institution peculiar to the guilds.[125]

Again, there were exceptions. In Seres the ceremony of transition to the rank of master included a sermon delivered by the *kâhya* to the candidate in which the commendable qualities required of a master were enumerated: faithfulness, integrity, respect to guild masters and members and to customers, honesty, consideration of other people's interests, obedience to the sovereign, veneration of the *ulema*, kindness to other people, love of children, helpfulness, and the consideration of apprentices and journeymen as the master's children.[126] Similar qualities apparently were required of apprentices of the tanners of Kırşehir in the eighteenth century.[127] However, these were guilds which had maintained the traditions particularly well, and their case does not justify the generalization that all guilds encouraged such qualities.

CONCLUSION

This study of the various functions performed by Turkish guilds in the course of about three centuries shows clearly that the guild system was closely connected with the government. One of its principal *raisons d'être* was to serve as an administrative link between the authorities and the town population and as a means of supervision and control of this population by the rulers. Moreover, the scope left to the guilds to fulfil this task independently was rather narrow. Instructions, such as those concerning control of the quality of goods or wage scales, were issued by the authorities, and it was the guilds' duty only to carry them out. In cases of infringement, the culprits were punished by the *kadı*, not the guilds. The all-embracing character of this system, which included extremely different elements of the urban population, also indicates that the impetus for its functioning did not come from below but rather that it was moulded from above.

The involvement of the guilds with the government often has been considered as a sign of their degeneration. This view is based on a comparison between the guilds of the seventeenth, eighteenth and nineteenth centuries with the free, popular and relatively autonomous *fütüvvet* and *ahi* associations of earlier times. But since the latter were not professional organizations, one cannot speak about the degeneration of the guilds as such. What happened was that at a certain juncture, apparently during the first half of the sixteenth century, there occurred a transition from free associations to professional guilds, probably under the auspices of the official authorities. Part of the newly established guilds, but not all of them, kept some of the traditions of the old free associations, and many of the social functions of the guilds apparently were based on these.

Guilds differed considerably with regard to their relative autonomy and the maintaining of social traditions. The shoemakers and tanners, for instance, in contrast with most other guilds, enjoyed judicial privileges, and at the same time maintained many of the social traditions, such as the encouragement of honesty and sobriety. It is important to stress these differences in order to avoid generalizations. In addition, there were differences between guilds of Istanbul and those in the provinces. To judge by the detailed accounts we have of the guilds in Damascus and Seres, the provincial guilds enjoyed greater autonomy; in both places there was a common guild chief with judicial powers, and their *kâhya*s served them as genuine representatives *vis à vis* the official authorities. Their social traditions also seem to have been stronger than in most guilds of Istanbul.

There were a number of differences between the Istanbul guilds and those of other countries in the Middle East, especially Egypt. Guilds in Istanbul performed no fiscal functions, but, on the other hand, undertook the distribution of raw materials among their members and kept funds for mutual help. On the other hand there were many common features. An evaluation of the significance of the differences and parallels between the guild functions in the two areas will be possible only as a result of further research into other aspects of their guild history and of their economic and social history in general.

NOTES

1. F. Taeschner, 'Futuwwa', *EI²*, vol. II, p. 967; F. Babinger, *Mehmed der Eroberer und seine Zeit* (München, 1953), p. 491: 'Gar nichts verlautet bislang über fachgenossenschaftliche Vereinigungen, Zünfte der Handwerker, wie sie im Osmanenreich des 16. und vor allem des 17. Jahrhunderts aus Schilderungen erweisbar sind.'
2. F. Taeschner, 'Akhi', *EI²*, vol. I, pp. 321–3. However, on the basis of Ibn Baṭṭūṭa's evidence, Professor Cahen assumes that beginnings of professional grouping of the *ahi*s may have existed in the fourteenth century or even earlier. See C. Cahen, *Pre-Ottoman Turkey* (London, 1968), pp. 199–200.

3. This is a general affliction of writings on Islamic guilds. See G. Baer, 'Guilds in Middle Eastern history', in M. A. Cook (ed.), *Studies in the Economic History of the Middle East*, London, 1970, pp. 11–30.
4. F. Taeschner, 'Das Zunftwesen in der Türkei', *Leipziger Vierteljahrsschrift für Südosteuropa*, vol. V (1941), p. 178.
5. J. von Hammer, *Geschichte des osmanischen Reiches*, vol. IV (Pest, 1829), pp. 126 ff., pp. 626–9. Cf. Osman Nuri, *Mecelle-i umur-u belediye*, vol. I (Istanbul, 1922) (Nuri in later references), pp. 591–4. In this extremely important work many documents from the Ottoman archives are quoted verbatim. It is not correct that Nuri treats mainly the origin and early developments of the guilds until the beginning of the sixteenth century and examines only rapidly later periods, as claimed by R. Mantran, *Istanbul dans la seconde moitié du XVIIe siècle* (Paris, 1962), p. 349 n. 1.
6. Ahmet Refik, *Onuncu asır-ı hicrîde Istanbul hayatı* (Istanbul, 1333) (Refik X in later references). Refik's collections include a large number of important documents for Turkish guild history.
7. Refik X, pp. 155–7.
8. Refik X, pp. 141, 169, 170, 171, 178–9, 180–1, 185, 188. The various officers of the guilds, as well as the structure of the guilds in general, are dealt with below in Ch. 3.
9. Cf. e.g. H. Schurtz, 'Türkische Basare und Zünfte', *Zeitschrift für Socialwissenschaft*, vol. VI (Berlin, 1903), pp. 695–9.
10. Taeschner, 'Zunftwesen', p. 180.
11. Mantran, *Istanbul*, p. 357.
12. Evliya Çelebi, *Seyahatnamesi*, vol. I (Istanbul, 1314), pp. 512–669 (Evliya in later references). This part of Evliya's work is included in two translations by J. von Hammer, a German one called *Constantinopolis und der Bosporus, örtlich und geschichtlich beschrieben* (Pest, 1822), vol. II, pp. 398–521 (very much shortened), and an English one called *Narrative of Travels in Europe, Asia, and Africa in the Seventeenth Century, by Evliya Efendi*, vol. I, pt. 2 (London, 1846), pp. 104–205. It is true that this translation too is 'nach einer lückenhaften Handschrift ungenau und unvollständig übersetzt' (Taeschner, 'Zunftwesen', p. 180 n. 14). But it is not only much better than the German one, but also in some parts more complete than the Turkish printed edition itself, which was prepared from a manuscript at least as lacunal as that from which the English translation was made. For instance, guilds nos. 163 to 218 (pp. 149–63 of the English translation) are missing from the Turkish printed edition (see p. 563), as are guilds nos. 230 to 302 (pp. 169–88 of the translation – see p. 569 of the Turkish text).
13. Some guilds of this group are mentioned also in a similar description of a muster of the guilds written by the Armenian traveller Eremya Çelebi which took place 20 years later, in 1657. See Mantran, pp. 353–4.
14. All authors who mention the organization of these groups as guilds refer to Evliya or to Nuri, pp. 500–1, which is a summary of Evliya's enumeration. See, for instance, H. A. R. Gibb and H. Bowen, *Islamic Society and the West*, vol. I, pt. 1 (London, 1950) (Gibb and Bowen in later references), p. 290.

15. Evliya, pp. 521–30; Hammer, *Narrative of Travels*, pp. 110–6.
16. Evliya, pp. 560, 616, 628; Hammer, *Narrative of Travels*, pp. 145, 222, 231 (nos. 152, 480, 646). It is interesting to note that the only source for the existence of guilds of day labourers in Egypt is also Evliya's description of the procession of the Egyptian guilds on the occasion of the *ru'ya* ceremony. See Evliya Çelebi, *Seyahatnamesi*, vol. X, *Mısır, Sudan, Habeş (1672–1680)* (Istanbul, 1938), p. 363 (Evliya, *Egypt*, in later references). Cf. G. Baer, *Egyptian Guilds in Modern Times* (Jerusalem, 1964) (Baer, *Egyptian Guilds* in later references), pp. 5, 13, 30.
17. Evliya, pp. 534, 556; Hammer, *Narrative of Travels*, pp. 119, 141 (nos. 62, 132). None of the sources for Egypt has mentioned a guild of farmers – except Evliya, in very general terms. See Evliya, *Egypt*, p. 359. It should be mentioned, however, that farmers (*çiftçiler*) were in 1250/1834–5 one of the twenty-four guilds of Seres (Nuri, p. 692). The Macedonian town of Seres was occupied by the Turks in 1368 and remained in their hands until 1913, when the Bulgars entered it. After the second Balkan war, Seres became Greek, as a result of the Bucharest Treaty of 10 August 1913. In the course of its changing hands, it was burnt down and the old city was completely destroyed. A description of the guilds of Seres in the nineteenth century by Esad Bey, a native of that town who moved to Istanbul after the Balkan wars, is published by Nuri on pp. 690–716 of his work.
18. Evliya, pp. 517–9, 625–7, 632 ff.; Hammer, *Narrative of Travels*, pp. 108–9, 228–9, 233 ff. In sources on Egypt too these guilds have been mentioned in connexion with public ceremonies or in comprehensive lists of guilds rather than as units fulfilling administrative, economic or social functions.
19. See, for instance, Nuri, pp. 669–70 (leather merchants); p. 673 (merchants of the Wallachia trade), etc.
20. Evliya, p. 618; Hammer, *Narrative of Travels*, p. 224 (no. 504). Cf. for Egypt, 'merchants of the Sūq al-Daqīq market'; 'merchants of Khān al-Khalīlī', etc. Baer, *Egyptian Guilds*, p. 27.
21. Refik X, pp. 170, 201; Nuri, pp. 594, 610, 640, 666–7; Ch. White, *Three Years in Constantinople* (London, 1845), vol. III, pp. 323 ff. White's excellent observations are an indispensable source for the history of the Turkish guilds, but it has not yet been used systematically for this purpose. One must, however, distinguish carefully between his original observations and those passages which he copied from Evliya.
22. Evliya, pp. 530–4; Hammer, *Narrative of Travels*, pp. 116–9; Nuri, pp. 649–50.
23. An Egyptian manuscript dating from the end of the sixteenth or the seventeenth century, called *Kitāb al-dhakhā'ir wa'l-tuḥaf fī bīr al-ṣanā'i'wa'l-ḥiraf*, whose author probably was closely connected with the guilds of barbers and physicians and which therefore reflects admirably their concepts and organization, has been studied in detail in Baer, *Egyptian Guilds*, pp. 2–3, and *passim*.
24. See observation by Nuri, p. 595.
25. Evliya, pp. 520, 551, 559, 596; 548, 580–1, 601, 611; Hammer, *Narrative of Travels*, pp. 109 (no. 15), 133 (no. 111), 143 (no. 145), 207 (no. 390);

131 (no. 107), 196 (no. 335), 212 (no. 425), 219 (no. 458).

26. Evliya, pp. 627–8. Hammer, *Narrative of Travels*, pp. 230–1, nos. 604, 605, 646; 632, 636, 638. For parallel observations on Egypt see Baer, *Egyptian Guilds*, p. 25.
27. Cf. Schurtz, p. 698; Taeschner, 'Zunftwesen', p. 180. For Egypt cf. Baer, *Egyptian Guilds*, p. 26.
28. Hammer, *Narrative of Travels*, pp. 151–5, 158–60 (both groups are missing from the Turkish printed text); pp. 226–8; Evliya, pp. 622–5.
29. Nuri, p. 558 (firman dated *Cemaziyelâhir* 1192/July 1778).
30. Nuri, p. 571 (document dated 6 *Cemaziyelâhir* 1277/20 December 1860).
31. White, vol. I, pp. 8–9.
32. Cf. Baer, *Egyptian Guilds*, p. 32.
33. Mantran, p. 357; Nuri, p. 341; D. Nicolaïdes, *Doustour-i-Hamidié, appendice à la législation ottomane* (Constantinople, 1878), pp. 289–91.
34. Refik X, pp. 201–3 (no. 10); Ahmet Refik, *Hicrî on ikinci asırda İstanbul hayatı* (Istanbul, 1930) (Refik XII in later references), pp. 108–9, 54–6, 133 (nos. 140, 79, 133); Id., *Hicrî on üçüncü asırda İstanbul hayatı* (Istanbul, 1932) (Refik XIII in later references), pp. 9–11 (no. 9); Nuri, pp. 649–51, etc.
35. Nuri, p. 502.
36. Nuri, pp. 638–9.
37. Refik X, p. 170 (no. 34); Nicolaïdes, ibid.
38. Refik XII, pp. 36–7 (no. 55); Nuri, p. 341.
39. Document dated *Rebiyülâhır* 1257/May–June 1841, Nuri, pp. 682, 685.
40. Nuri, pp. 622–3.
41. Nuri, pp. 697, 701; for Egypt see Baer, *Egyptian Guilds*, p. 84.
42. Nuri, pp. 329 ff.; Mantran, pp. 144, 304–5, 307–15, etc.
43. Baer, *Egyptian Guilds*, pp. 88–93. In Damascus the situation apparently was intermediate between that of Istanbul and Cairo: the Damascus guilds sometimes were charged with fiscal functions, and sometimes taxes were collected through the *ḥāra* system. See Baer, 'Guilds in Middle Eastern history'. However, in many other Turkish towns taxation was one of the main functions of the guilds. See below, Chapter 4.
44. White, vol. III, p. 325.
45. Nuri, pp. 349–51. According to the résumé of an undated *règlement* for the corporations, reproduced (without reference) by G. Young, *Corps de droit ottoman* (Oxford, 1906), vol. V, pp. 288–9, monthly taxes were collected by the *kâhya*s according to an 'appended list' (missing from Young) and transmitted to the Prefecture. Unfortunately this information is rather vague.
46. Nuri, pp. 375, 684.
47. White, vol. II, p. 158; Refik XII, pp. 104–5 (no. 134).
48. Baer, *Egyptian Guilds*, pp. 96–7.
49. Nuri, pp. 404 ff.; 303.
50. Nuri, pp. 559; Refik XII, pp. 19–20 (no. 29); Nuri, pp. 609–10; Refik XIII, p. 3 (no. 3).
51. Nuri, pp. 569–70; Refik XII, pp. 169–70 (no. 202).
52. Nuri, pp. 570–72.

53. Nuri, pp. 608–9, 303.
54. Nuri, p. 639.
55. White, vol. II, p. 254, says that the committee of six Armenian elders chosen by the *esnaf* of the sandal *Bezesten* determined factory and market prices, but these were minimum prices to protect the interests of the guild, and their goods were not vital consumer goods.
56. Nuri, pp. 302, 350, 419–20 ff., 443–8, etc. Cf. M. Z. Pakalın, *Osmanlı tarih deyimleri ve terimleri sözlüğü* (Istanbul, 1946 *et seq.*), vol. II, p. 656.
57. Nuri, pp. 359–61, 643, Pakalın, vol. II, p. 657.
58. Nuri, p. 549.
59. Nuri, pp. 419–20; Pakalın, vol. II, p. 656; cf. Gibb and Bowen, pp. 282–3. The *narh* was gradually abolished in the 1860s. See Nuri, p. 459; Pakalın, vol. II, p. 657, and cf. Baer, *Egyptian Guilds*, pp. 102–3.
60. Nuri, pp. 640–2; cf. Ahmed Lûtfı, *Mirat-i adalet* (Istanbul, 1304/1876–7), pp. 127–46, 150–76. A similar interpretation should be applied to the following statement by Taeschner: 'Unterbietungen wie auch Überforderungen wurden streng bestraft, bisweilen mit Schliessung der Werkstatt und mit Ausschluss aus der Zunft'. Taeschner, 'Zunftwesen', p. 186. Cf. also Pakalın, vol. II, pp. 655–6, and Baer, *Egyptian Guilds*, pp. 101–2.
61. Nuri, p. 549.
62. Nuri, pp. 419–20.
63. Nuri, p. 641; Mantran, pp. 325–7; cf. Baer, *Egyptian Guilds*, p. 101.
64. Refik XII, pp. 129–30, 141 (nos. 157 and 172).
65. Cf. Nuri, pp. 619, 622.
66. Nuri, p. 644. The guilds' monopolies and restrictive practices are dealt with below, in Chapter 2.
67. See, e.g. Refik XII, pp. 70, 155–6 (nos. 96, 186).
68. Refik XIII, pp. 20–23 (no. 18).
69. Cf. the following with Baer, *Egyptian Guilds*, pp. 93 ff. For an exception regarding Egypt see p. 41 n. 2. As to Turkey, we have also found instances in which the Turkish guilds were required to supply craftsmen for civilian needs: thus a firman to the *kadı* of Gelibolu dated 1001/1592–3 included an order to the *yiğit başı* of the carpenters of that town, all Christian Greeks, to supply 13 carpenters, mentioned by nạme, for the building of a palace. See Ahmet Refik, *Hicrî on birinci asırda İstanbul hayatı* (Istanbul, 1931) (Refik XI in later references), pp. 5–6 (no. 10).
70. Nuri, p. 628.
71. Nuri, p. 629; Pakalın, vol. II, p. 729. For an example of such a firman, dated 19 *Receb* 1108/11 February 1697, with details about the required recruits, see Nuri, pp. 630–2 (cf. Gibb and Bowen, p. 322). For a further list of recruited members of guilds dated 1809–10 see Nuri, pp. 634–5. At that time additional officials of the state were concerned with the recruiting of guild members to the army, such as the *mimar başı*, the *su nazırı*, and the *lağımcı başı* (see ibid., pp. 635–6).
72. Nuri, pp. 633–4.
73. Nuri, pp. 630, 633–5; cf. Evliya, p. 527; Hammer, *Narrative of Travels*, pp. 114–15. The occurrence of an interesting similar arrangement in Egypt

is related by 'Abd al-Raḥmān al-Jabartī, *'Aj'āib al-āthār fī'l-tarājim wa'l-akhbār* (Cairo-Bulaq, 1297/1870–1), vol. III, p. 6. When Bonaparte approached Cairo in July 1798 the guilds furnished the means for those who were recruited in order to combat the invaders.

74. Nuri, p. 636.
75. Cf. Baer, *Egyptian Guilds*, p. 99.
76. White, vol. III, p. 325.
77. Refik X, pp. 155–7 (no. 16).
78. Refik XII, pp. 97, 178, 180, 232 (nos. 125, 216, 218, 271).
79. Taeschner, 'Zunftwesen', p. 186.
80. Refik XI, pp. 8, 40 (nos. 14, 77); Refik XII, p. 180 (no. 218); Nuri, pp. 669–70; Refik XII, p. 230 (no. 270 for the year 1196/1781).
81. Nuri, p. 799.
82. Cf. Gibb and Bowen, p. 288.
83. Nuri, p. 559.
84. Nuri, p. 685.
85. Hammer, *Narrative of Travels*, p. 209. (This information is missing from the published Turkish text – cf. Evliya, p. 598.) The Egyptian guild of shoemakers also exercised this privilege – see Baer, *Egyptian Guilds*, p. 83.
86. See White, vol. I, p. 99. For the special position of the shoemakers' guild in various countries of the Middle East see Baer, *Egyptian Guilds*, pp. 63–4.
87. Taeschner, 'Zunftwesen', pp. 183–4.
88. Cf. Nuri, p. 537.
89. Cf. Ilyās Qudsī, 'Nubdha ta'rīkhiyya fī'l-ḥiraf al-dimashqiyya' ('Notice sur les corporations de Damas'), *Actes du sixième Congrès International des Orientalistes*, deuxième partie, Section 1: *Sémitique* (Leiden, 1885), p. 11.
90. Nuri, p. 697.
91. Nuri, pp. 611, 613.
92. Nuri, p. 638.
93. Nuri, p. 713; cf. Young, vol. V, p. 288.
94. Nuri, pp. 576, 694, 697; cf. Taeschner, 'Zunftwesen', p. 183.
95. Cf. Baer, *Egyptian Guilds*, pp. 113–14.
96. Ibid. pp. 114–16.
97. Nuri, pp. 576, 579–80.
98. Nuri, pp. 347, 580–1, 597, 708; Evliya, p. 570 (where the number of plates is given as 10,000); Hammer, *Narrative of Travels*, p. 188; cf. Baer, *Egyptian Guilds*, p. 115.
99. Nuri, p. 580. Cf. also pp. 704 and 707.
100. Nuri, pp. 704–6.
101. Nuri, pp. 656–7, 672–3, 713. The *gedik* will be discussed below, in Chapter 2.
102. Gibb and Bowen, p. 286.
103. Cf. Baer, *Egyptian Guilds*, p. 115 nn. 8 and 9. It seems to be significant that nothing is said about a fund or other arrangements for mutual help in Qudsī's detailed account of the Damascus guilds.
104. Nuri, p. 708.
105. Cf. Nuri, pp. 503–5 (documents from the eighteenth and the beginning of

the nineteenth century). Cf. also the miniatures mentioned in note 107 below.

106. Baer, *Egyptian Guilds*, p. 123.
107. See, for instance, R. Ettinghausen, *Turkish Miniatures from the Thirteenth to the Eighteenth Century* (UNESCO, New York, 1965), Pls. 20 and 27; Mazhar S. Ipsiroglu, 'Das Buch der Feste', *Du* (Zürich), December 1963, pp. 57 ff., especially the plates depicting the guilds of makers of ropes, of sailors and of tailors.
108. See, for instance, Evliya and Hammer, *Narrative of Travels*, *passim*; *Surname-i Vehbi* as quoted by Nuri, pp. 588–91; Mouradgea d'Ohsson, *Tableau général de l'Empire ottoman*, as quoted by Gibb and Bowen, p. 287 n. 1; etc.
109. Nuri, pp. 692–3. Cf. also p. 713, where a specific flag of each guild is mentioned in connexion with the pilgrimage.
110. See above, and Baer, *Egyptian Guilds*, pp. 117–18.
111. Nuri, p. 563.
112. Schurtz, pp. 704–5.
113. Nuri, p. 580; Taeschner, 'Zunftwesen', p. 187, where the author quotes details about such excursions in Çankırı as related by Hasan Uçok and reproduced in French by E. Borrel in *Revue des Études Islamiques*, vol. X (1936), pp. 309 ff. Other occasions of social gatherings of the guilds are mentioned by Mantran, p. 365, but no sources are given.
114. For more details see Nuri, pp. 698, 700–1, 714; for expenditure on such festivities included in the budget of the guild of wool-carders for the year 1872–3 see pp. 705–6.
115. Nuri, p. 561.
116. Cf. Baer, *Egyptian Guilds*, pp. 116–17.
117. Nuri, pp. 713–14.
118. Evliya, pp. 484, 570; Hammer, *Narrative of Travels*, pp. 86, 188–9; Nuri, pp. 582–3.
119. Baer, *Egyptian Guilds*, p. 113; *Middle Eastern Studies* (London), vol. II, no. 3, p. 275; vol. no. 1, p. 107; vol. no. 3, p. 321.
120. Gibb and Bowen, p. 277.
121. Nuri, p. 603.
122. Nuri, pp. 552, 613–14.
123. Nuri, pp. 553–6; cf. Gibb and Bowen, p. 286.
124. Mantran (p. 362) also maintains: 'Que des corporations aient conservé des liens avec des ordres mystiques n'est pas niable', but he too does not prove this assertion, and what he says further on rather disproves it. Detailed analysis of the situation in Egypt has led us to the conclusion that, in spite of many points of contact, the two frameworks, which had different functions, seem to have co-existed on different levels, a large part of the population belonging to both at the same time. The same seems to have been the case in the Maghrib. See Baer, *Egyptian Guilds*, pp. 125–6.
125. Nuri, pp. 603–8.
126. Nuri, p. 710. Cf. Baer, *Egyptian Guilds*, pp. 52–3.
127. Taeschner, 'Zunftwesen', p. 183.

2

MONOPOLIES AND RESTRICTIVE PRACTICES

Professional organizations of the urban population headed by a headman and officers chosen from among their members emerged in Turkey at the end of the fifteenth or the beginning of the sixteenth century. During the seventeenth and eighteenth centuries they were moulded into an all-embracing system which served as an administrative link between the government and the urban population, and fulfilled various economic and social functions. A basic condition for the working of this system was the exclusiveness of each guild in its branch or sub-branch within the boundaries of a specific community. This was achieved by a framework of rules, partly unwritten but officially recognized and partly laid down in official regulations or orders, by which a variety of monopolies and restrictive practices was established. It is the aim of the following study to analyse this framework of rules and practices in detail.[1]

Monopolies and restrictive practices were called *hasır* or *inhisar*, the full term being *inhisar-i beyi ve şira*.[2] These included restrictions concerning the number or the kind of people allowed to perform a trade or a profession, as well as limitations imposed on production or on commerce. Restrictions of this kind were considered necessary and beneficial to society. As against this, another kind of monopolistic practice, namely hoarding or cornering (*ihtikâr*), was condemned and prohibited by the government.[3] It is the first kind of restrictions and their connection with the guild system which will be the subject of our study.

On the basis of numerous firmans issued to different guilds Nuri states in general that if a craftsman or merchant wanted to become independent and open a shop, he needed the agreement of the *kethüda* (the head of the guild), the *yiğit başı* (the assistant of the guild's head) and the *ihtiyarlar* (the veterans of the guild).[7] As illustrations to this rule Nuri reproduces a number of firmans dating from the eighteenth century. Thus, an order to the weavers of ribbons for the fire-brigade dated cemaziyelâhir 1192/July 1778 stated that he who intended to exercise this craft was required to equip himself with a *tezkere* (certificate) issued by the *kethüda* of the guild.[5] Joiners who wanted to open a shop needed the agreement of the *kethüda* and the *ihtiyarlar* (firman dated 1139/1726–7).[6] Similar regulations apparently existed at that time outside Istanbul as well. For instance, according to a frequently published firman dated 1187/1773 the guild of tanners in Kırşehir supplied its members with diplomas which were a necessary requirement for opening a shop.[7] Evidence for the persistence of this practice in the nineteenth century is found in various sources. White says about the Istanbul greengrocers that 'no stall can be established without permission of the company's officers, sanctioned by a magistrate', and that 'no hamal (porter) can ply at any station without the assent of this vekil (deputy head of the guild)'.[8] According to a document of 6 cemaziyelâhir 1277/20 December 1860 the shoemakers of the Istanbul Grand Bazaar received a *tezkere* from their *usta başılar*, to be signed with the seal of the *kethüda* of the Bazaar (*Büyük Arasta Kethüdası*). Only the owner of such a *tezkere* was allowed to exercise his craft.[9]

All the above-mentioned documents are from the eighteenth or nineteenth centuries; no earlier evidence for the requirement of the guild's sanction for the exercise of a trade has been published hitherto. There are two possible explanations for the absence of earlier documents for such a control: (a) the lack of publication of such documents may be fortuitous, and further research will reveal them; (b) in earlier centuries this control was a custom, an unwritten rule, and only in the eighteenth century it was incorporated in the official system and therefore appeared in firmans or other official documents.

One of the major purposes of the control of the establishment of new shops and the employment of new workers in transport and services was to implement restrictions of the number of shops or people occupied in various trades and crafts. For this kind of restriction in Istanbul we have evidence from the sixteenth to the nineteenth century; usually they were imposed by the government and the guilds were required to carry them out. Thus a firman dating from the year 990/1582 ordered the *kethüda* of the boatmen on the Istanbul-Mudanya line to see to it that their number did not exceed thirty – the reason given in the firman being that otherwise the *kethüda* would not be able to be responsible for them to the government.[10] The number of the weavers of cloth of gold was restricted at the end of the sixteenth and again at the beginning of the seventeenth century in order to diminish the demand for gold.[11] Detailed restrictions of the number of shops in every sub-branch of sellers of various kinds of furs are included in a firman dated 1168/1755 – the purpose in this case being to facilitate the supply to the Court and the control of prices.[12] An order dated 1206/1791–2 laid down the number of wholesale-traders in various branches and various parts of Istanbul.[13] At about the same time the number of Muslim merchants engaged in foreign trade was restricted to 40 in Istanbul and to 10 in each of the other important commercial towns.[14] According to the regulations called *Ihtisab Ağalığı Nizamnamesi* of the year 1242/1826–7 the number of guild members and the number of apprentices in each of the following occupations was to be determined by the *Şeriat* Courts and by representatives of the *Ihtisab*: porters, boatmen, bath attendants, and watchmen.[15] White says that the number of retail fishmongers, most of whom were Greek, was limited (in the early 1840s) to 45 shops – a rule which secured more vigilant inspection.[16] Other trades and crafts with a limited number of shops or of people engaged in them were, at that time, greengrocers, water-carriers, booksellers ('some forty'), seal engravers (fifty), and porters at each station.[17] White remarked, moreover, that the number of shops in all trades was limited.[18]

It was not enough to limit the number of shops, workshops or workers in every guild in order to control the craft or the trade; it was also necessary to prevent the establishment of 'wild' enterprises, 'illicit' competition with guild-merchants by hawkers or the penetration of 'unorganized' labour into transport or services. Thus, for instance, the guild of confectioners complained in the year 990/1582 to the *kadı* that recently the number of *koltukçular* (hawkers, pedlars) selling sweets had grown and they demanded the prohibition of this illicit trade. A firman to this effect was issued.[19] Similarly, the dealers in Morocco leather demanded (in 1610?) to put an end to the secret trade of the *koltukçu taifesi* in this commodity, and again this was ordered by the authorities.[20] One kind of outsiders who tried to break the guild monopoly were Jews. A firman granted in the year 1019/1610 to the druggists in response to their request ordered the *kadı* to prevent the Jews from selling coffee to the army, a recent practice which had not existed before.[21] Similarly, the makers of gold and silver thread of Istanbul, Salonika and Bursa had enjoyed a monopoly for a long time, until some Jews began secretly to produce silver thread. This was prohibited by a firman, but they disregarded the prohibition and as a result they were banished in the year 1113/1701 to Salonika.[22] As late as the nineteenth century it was thought necessary to forbid itinerant Jewish dealers of stationery to expose their goods in the streets within the walls.[23] Another element of outsiders challenging the guild's monopolies were irregular soldiers or marines, such as the *Levends*, who at certain stages began to penetrate various crafts and trades.[24] Thus it appears from a firman dated şevval

1113/March 1702 that some *Levends* had established a new slaughterhouse; it was claimed that they had done harm both to the old established guild of butchers and to the consumers (by raising prices). They were forbidden to go on with this activity.[25] Another firman issued some ten years earlier had prohibited the establishment of 'wild' new tanneries in Istavroz near Üsküdar by former workers of the main tannery of Istanbul at Yedikule. In this case too it was claimed that the 'wild' enterprise competed with the old established tannery of Üsküdar by raising the price of hides and thus harmed the *vakıf* of Valide Sultan from which the premises of the tannery were rented. The prohibition was issued in response to a complaint by the Ahi Baba (head), *ihtiyarlar* and members of the Üsküdar guild of tanners in the year 1104/1692.[26] Many other similar documents have been published. For instance, the boatmen of Rumeli Hisar anchorage tried to maintain their monopoly by removing competitors from outside (1040/1630); slave-dealers demanded to put an end to 'illicit' slave dealing by unqualified people selling slaves (or so-called slaves) outside the slave market (1046/1637); or people who were not members of the guild of makers or casters of lead and who had not been apprentices to masters of this guild were strictly forbidden to work in lead and to sell their goods, which they did in shops of dealers in small wares (firman dated 1114/1703).[27] It should be stressed that both the limitation of the number of shops and of people engaged in a craft or trade and the prohibition of outsiders from competing with the guilds were enforced by the government; they were part of a guild system maintained and controlled from above and serving the purposes of the state.[28]

A similar kind of restriction forming part of the Istanbul guild system was the limitation of each guild to producing and/or selling specific goods only. This had two purposes: (a) to prevent clashes with other guilds; (b) to preserve morals, religion, tradition, and to guard economic interests. The first of these two purposes was served, for instance, by a firman issued in the year 1018/1609–10 as a response to a complaint of the makers of vinegar that all kinds of other guilds such as makers of semi-solid sweet, grocers and makers or sellers of sweetmeats had recently embarked upon production and sale of vinegar. The firman strictly prohibited this transgression.[29] Two documents dating from the year 1039/1629 include a prohibition of Akserai soap-merchants from selling wax – which is *âhar esnafın metai* (the merchandise of another guild). Similarly, fruiterers were forbidden to sell cheese, the exclusive right of grocers.[30] Complaints of guilds against the infringement of their privileges by other guilds seem to have been a frequent feature in the seventeenth century. Spice merchants of Galata complained of sellers of caviare and fish for selling products reserved for spice-merchants (1039–40/1629–30); candle-makers complained of butchers for selling tallow – contrary to all regulations (1070/1659); the shoemakers of Üsküdar protested against the transgression of the *eskiciler* (cobblers) who had embarked on buying and selling old slippers which had been the privilege of the former guild (1070/1660).[31] In zilkade 1071/June 1664 the *kethüda, yiğit başı* and *ihtiyarlar* of the weavers of *boğası* and the weavers of *dimi* (two kinds of textiles) appeared before the *kadı* and declared that in future the weavers of *boğası* would not produce *dimi* and *vice versa*.[32] Finally, one more example from the eighteenth century: as a result of a complaint by the guild of bakers of bread the guild of makers of *çörek*, *halka* and *gâhi gevrek* (shortbread shaped as ring, biscuits) was forbidden, by a firman of the year 1115/1703, to bake bread.[33]

Various other purposes of the limitation of each guild to producing or selling specific goods manifest themselves in the following examples. In some cases the reason was purely to keep traditions and to prevent changes of fashion. Thus in rebiyülâhır 1222/June 1807 an order was issued to the *kadı* of Istanbul, to be conveyed to the *kethüda* and members of the guilds of shoemakers and cobblers, that it was strictly forbidden to produce and sell shoes with pointed toes – a recent innovation. The prohibition was also supported by the argument that this innovation had led to the rise of prices of shoes.[34] Another reason was the distinctive fashion of the different religious communities; limitations of the sale or the production of a particular dress to a specific community found its expression in official orders when there were attempts to break the tradition. Thus a firman of the year 1141/1729 informs us that the makers of *kavuk*, a head gear particular to Muslims, had recently begun to produce a cap similar to the *şabka* of the Jews. This was forbidden, since the sale of these caps to Muslims and their wearing it made it difficult to distinguish between Muslims and non-Muslims.[35] Similarly, in 1222/1807 it appeared that non-Muslims (Greeks, Armenians and Jews) were imitating the Muslims in the way they dressed and, contrary to traditional usage, were wearing green fabrics. Thereupon the *kadı* assembled the *kethüdas* of the guilds of makers and sellers of various kinds of textiles as well as the heads of the communities concerned and warned the former not to sell green fabrics to non-Muslims and the latter to see to it that their flock did not dress in Muslim fashion.[36] In the last example the restriction was of the buyer, i.e. the kind of people to whom a certain guild was allowed to sell, rather than of the kind of goods to be sold. Similar limitations were imposed sometimes for economic reasons. Thus it was ordered in 1196/1782 that hides of animals slaughtered in Istanbul should be supplied to the Yedikule tanneries only – not to the newly established ones of Üsküdar, Tophane, Kasımpaşa, Hasköy and Eyüp; the reason given was that the premises of the Yedikule tanneries were rented from the *evkaf* of the

Ayasofya and a decline in the business of these tanneries would be detrimental to the income of the Ayasofya.[37]

The last mentioned example indicates still another kind of restrictions connected with the Ottoman guild system, namely the geographical concentration of the guilds. 'Members of a guild . . . had their shops all together in one street or quarter'.[38] Evliya Çelebi's account of the Istanbul guilds includes many instances illustrating this rule.[39] Thus the smiths of small boot nails had their 102 shops all at a certain place in the neighbourhood of the mosque of Sultan Mehmet; the file-makers' 55 shops were all at the Long Market; the pearl-merchants were all established at the gate of the old Bezestan; the cage-makers' shops (about one hundred) were all in the neighbourhood of Sultan Bayezid; the guild of makers of instruments for shoemakers had their eighty shops in a particular market near the old Bezestan; the printers' guild was concentrated near a place called Sırthamam; the toy-makers had one hundred shops, all in Eyüp; etc.[40] The booksellers were concentrated in a special market between Bayezid and the old Bezestan as late as in the nineteenth century.[41]

Apparently there were always attempts to infringe these rules, at least since the beginning of the eighteenth century. This is shown by a large number of firmans and other orders and instructions aiming at confining trades or guilds to specified places. As early as in the year 1119/1707 a firman reiterated former firmans and documents prohibiting the sale of leatherwork outside the Sarachane.[42] A firman of zilhicce 1138/July 1726 included instructions confining the printers' guild to a certain place called Vezir Hanı.[43] Various guilds were confined again and again to the European quarters in order to prevent violation of the traditional character of the life in the Oriental quarters of the town. Thus instructions of the year 1221/1806 included the prohibition to establish in Istanbul proper shops of European physicians and chemists, shops for the sale of European garments and other shops in the European style; all these shops were confined to Galata.[44] Similarly, shops of the guild of sellers of punch and candied fruit were confined to Galata, Pera and the European shore of the Bosporus.[45] Even in the first decades of the nineteenth century shops selling articles of European stationery were confined to Galata and Pera and not allowed to establish themselves in Istanbul.[46] At about the same time (1250/1834–5) each of the guilds of Seres was confined to the specific market bearing its name (*hallaçlar çarşısı, demirciler çarşısı*, etc.) – except those guilds who had a particular permission to work all over the town.[47]

The concentration of all the sellers or craftsmen of a particular trade in one location was a characteristic feature of the Muslim Bazaar. Regimes preceding the Ottomans had also made efforts to maintain this feature intact. The Mamluks, for instance, often required traders to gather in one place. The purpose of this practice, called *taḥkīr* was to prevent tax evasion, to assure the regime a more effective exploitation of the markets, and to benefit the emirs as property owners by enabling them to raise rents to the highest possible levels.[48] There are no indications that the Ottoman instructions attempted at achieving the same objects.[49] It would rather seem that their purpose was to prevent violation of traditions by keeping European style trades to the European quarters Galata and Pera and to secure efficient administrative control of the town-population by a guild system in which members of each guild worked as close to each other as possible.

However, it was in the nature of a number of trades and occupations that they should be dispersed over various parts of the town. In these cases the purpose of efficient administrative control was often achieved by establishing a separate guild in each of the different concentrations of the trade. Thus the *dellallar* (criers, brokers, auctioneers) of the different markets of Istanbul had separate guilds in each of these markets,[50] and there were separate guilds of butchers in each of the neighbourhoods in which they were established.[51] However, some occupations which were dispersed all over the town were united nevertheless in one guild; this was the case, for instance, with the bow-makers, the cutlers, the Armenian joiners, the tailors, etc.[52]

Crafts and trades were not only confined to specific places, but often to certain groups of people as well. Evliya relates that vacant positions as watchmen of the Bezestan were given to the porters of the Bezestan.[53] Some crafts were the exclusive occupation of the same families for generations, for instance, an Armenian family of cymbal-makers.[54] Similarly, the trade of the Istanbul booksellers remained for generations in the same families.[55] 'Both Moslem and Armenian porters consider the profession as an heirloom, and generally rear up their sons to the same occupation, much in the manner that the Bosphorus Greeks monopolize the craft of watermen'.[56] However, while a large proportion of the apprentices were the masters' sons, a considerable number of them were not. As we shall see, all the documents dealing with the transfer of rights to shops and tools after the master's death provide for their transfer to the master's son only if he had acquired the skill of the craft; they all make provision for the opposite case, in which the rights are transferred to other journeymen or to the guild.[57]

But if the occupation or the business may have passed occasionally from one family to another, its confinement to members of the same religious or ethnic community seems to have been quite a decisive characteristic of Turkish trades and guilds. Gibb and Bowen have maintained that after the Ottoman conquest the Christian guilds already existing in Constantinople were merged in those of the victors and Muslims and non-Muslims were united in common guilds. 'From about the middle of the seventeenth century relations between the two sections grew less amicable' and the two classes then took to meeting in separate lodges; later the non-Muslims acquired the right of having their own non-Muslim officers.[58] Unfortunately, this sweeping theory is not based on any factual evidence, except one document reproduced by Nuri, according to which the Christian dealers in velvet and brocade applied, in the year 1182/1768 (not the middle of the seventeenth century), for their separation from the Muslims occupied in the same trade.[59] But, first of all, Nuri has also examples of an opposite trend: the wholesale merchants dealing in Morocco leather and those dealing in oil were at first all Muslims, but later non-Muslims entered this business and conducted it together with the Muslims.[60] Moreover, an even more important argument against the thesis of Gibb and Bowen is the large number of concrete examples of guilds confined to one community to be found in the sources. To judge by these examples, such guilds outnumbered mixed guilds not only in the eighteenth and nineteenth centuries but also, at least to the same extent, in the sixteenth and early seventeenth centuries.

Our principal sources for the history of Istanbul guilds in the early period are Refik's collection of documents and Evliya Çelebi's narrative. Unfortunately, the documents reproduced by Refik do not contain much information on the religious or ethnic composition of the guilds. Evliya, too, does not state explicitly that the members of this or that guild were Muslims – except in very few instances (wax-merchants, merchants of dried salted beef).[61] Apparently this was too obvious for him to be stated in most cases. On the other hand he mentions the religious or ethnic composition of many non-Muslim and non-Turkish guilds. Thus the liver-merchants, the sellers of sausages made of chopped liver, the mustard-merchants, and the diggers of aqueducts were all Albanians;[62] the sellers of tripe, the salad-makers and the fish-cooks were all Greeks;[63] the tin-melters, the pearl-merchants, the refiners and the parchment-makers were all Jews;[64] the brick-makers, the stone-draggers, and the miners were all Armenians.[65] There were both Muslim and Jewish druggists, but they had their separate guilds.[66] As against this, we have found only two explicit references to religiously or ethnically mixed guilds in the seventeenth century – the makers or sellers of linen skull caps and the charcoal-men.[67] About a few other guilds Evliya says that 'most' of their members were Armenians (nail smiths) Lazes (kettle-merchants), Greeks (manufacturers of caps called *kellepuşu*), Jews (satin-merchants), or Albanians (paving men).[68] This may perhaps imply that these were mixed guilds, but definite proof is lacking. In any case, in the early seventeenth century, mixed guilds were far from being more evident than guilds confined to a specific community.

The same may be said about the eighteenth and nineteenth centuries, except perhaps for the fact that for this period we have found evidence of quite a number of mixed guilds – contrary to what one would expect if Gibb and Bowen had been right. For the eighteenth and nineteenth century we have Nuri's evidence that until 1826–7 Muslim decorators had a monopoly of painting stucco with oil colours and Christians were not allowed to perform this craft; similarly groceries were confined to Muslims until 1839–40 in Istanbul and until 1845 outside Istanbul (including Ankara).[69] Many similar examples have been recorded by White in his description of Istanbul. Thus he says: 'Yâghlik Tcharshy [Handkerchief Market] is occupied exclusively by Turks, who are privileged to deal in embroidered articles though latterly some few Greeks and Armenians have obtained permits from the elders of the guild'.[70] Other exclusively Muslim guilds mentioned by White were the carpet-merchants, the turners, the booksellers, the stationers, the tent-makers, the engravers and the Eyüp barbers.[71] In addition he remarks: 'It is worthy of remark that all active trades of Constantinople are with few exceptions in the hands of Turks. It will suffice to enumerate blacksmiths, carpenters, stone-hewers, sawyers, armourers, shoemakers, saddlers, braziers, nail-makers, and boat-builders.[72] On the other hand, the tenants of the Sandal Bezestan were exclusively Armenians who formed a numerous and wealthy guild and other exclusively Armenian guilds were the furriers, the Istanbul barbers, and the timber merchants.[73] The retail fishmongers were principally Greeks, the basket or panniermakers gipsies, most of the poulterers were Bulgarians and the horse-dealers were mostly Albanians.[74] The latter examples may imply that these were mixed guilds, but there is also explicit evidence for the existence of such guilds. Eighteenth century documents show that the guilds of printers, greengrocers, silk spinners, and saddlers were mixed guilds of Muslims and non-Muslims.[75] White, who describes early nineteenth century Istanbul, says that the boatmen were mainly Turks and Greeks, with some few Jews and Armenians;[76] the water-carriers' corporation consisted of Armenians and Turks; the drapers were Greeks and Armenians; the butchers' corporation was composed of Muslims and Christians; and the porters were Armenians and Muslims from East Anatolia.[77] The dealers in fez tassels 'form a numerous and wealthy company. They are almost all Armenians, Greeks and Hebrews'.[78] To sum up, although there were also mixed guilds, in general guilds were confined to people of a specific community.

Most of the restrictions mentioned so far were controlled by a particular and remarkable institution, the *gedik* system. *Gedik* literally means 'breach', and hence acquired the meaning of privilege.[79] Thus a *gedik* was the right to exercise a craft or a trade, either in general or, more frequently, at a specific place or shop. Accordingly there were two kinds of *gedik*, *havaî*, i.e. the personal right of somebody to pursue his calling anywhere, and *müstakar*, a *gedik* attached to a specific place. Young has defined this difference as follows: 'Le guédik peut être représenté comme le matériel d'un atelier ou aménagement d'une boutique ou encore comme le droit d'occuper un immeuble ou un site pour y exercer un métier contre payement d'un loyer (mustekirr); mais le droit peut aussi exister dans le vide, sans se rapporter à une bâtisse (guédik non fixe, ou servitude sur l'air)'.[80] The *havaî* kind of the *gedik* was originally called *ustalık* and represented nothing more than the right (*salâhiyet*) to exercise a trade or a craft; it was thus the equivalent of the *tezkere* of the *esnaf* which later took its place.[81] Later, however, most *gediks* included the right to the tools of a workshop or a business, a right which sometimes was also called simply *destgâh*, i.e. 'work-bench', 'workshop', 'machine-tool'.[82] Thus a document of the transfer of a miller's *gedik* included the horses which moved the mill, or a grocer's *gedik* document included scales, weights, jars, and barrels.[83]

Mantran maintains that itinerant merchants had no *gediks*: 'Il est en tout cas à peu près certain que les marchands ambulants n'ont pas de *gedik* et que ce métier est ouvert à quiconque ne peut pénétrer, faute d'argent ou de moyens, dans une corporation organisée'.[84] This seems to be too sweeping a generalization. Nuri explicitly mentions a special kind of *gediks* called *tabla gedikleri*, i.e. a right of itinerant vendors to establish themselves with their *tabla*, the circular tray for their goods which they carried on their heads, at a certain place.[85]

According to Gibb and Bowen, the use of the term *gedik* in the general sense of the right to exercise a trade originated only about the year 1140/1727–8, when it replaced the term *ustalık*. Until then it had been used, so they claim, to denote the custom by which trade implements were handed over without payment to purchasers or inheritors of *ustalık* rights.[86] This too seems to be inexact. The *gedik* of water-carriers mentioned in a document dated 1040/1630, the *gedik* of the criers of the inner Bedestan mentioned by Evliya, as well as the *gedik* of the *Dıvan-ı hümayun kâtibleri ve şakirdleri* mentioned in a document dated 1125/1714, most probably were of the general kind meaning only the right to exercise a trade and were not connected with the implements of a craft.[87]

In the course of the nineteenth century the *gedik* system gradually disappeared. Selim III had already introduced some reforms: according to instructions of 10 July 1805 no *gedik* could be issued except by firman and the *havaî gedikleri* were no longer recognized.[88] The most important official orders connected with the decline and disappearance of this system was an *irade* of 22 May 1860 and a *nizamname* of 17 June 1861.[89] Although these orders did not officially abolish the *gedik*, the system gradually disappeared from then onwards as a result of the administrative and economic transformation during the nineteenth century. The first of these two regulations ordered that from the date of its implementation onwards no new *gediks* were to be issued by government institutions and the *evkaf* and that *havaî gediks* which had become vacant were no longer to be sold to new owners. The second of these regulations laid down in detail the procedure of disposing of *gediks* according to the *irade* of 1860. In addition a variety of *gediks* were abolished, such as the *tabla gedikleri*, *sarraf gedikleri* (issued on the basis of documents of the mint), and *gediks* based on *temessük* (title-deeds) documents issued by the guilds' *kethüdas*. Nevertheless, many *gediks* remained intact, especially those of the last-mentioned variety; the *temessük* documents of the *kethüdas* were just replaced by official *seneds*.

As we have said above, it was the function of the *gediks* to control the restrictions forming the framework of the Turkish guild system. Since most of the *gediks* were of the *müstakar* variety, i.e., attached to a specific place, their first and most important natural function was of course to limit and control the location of the craft or trade and to prevent its dispersion.

A second important kind of restrictions which were controlled by the *gediks* was the limitation of the number of guild members. Nuri says that he has seen hundreds or thousands of firmans limiting the number of masters of a craft by fixing the number of *gediks* and ordering that nobody was allowed to become a master and open a shop without owning one of these *gediks*. Therefore a *gedik* had to become vacant (generally by the death of one of the masters of the guild) before a new master could be accepted into the guild.[90] For instance, a firman issued to the guild of printers dated zilhicce 1138/July 1726 stated that there were only 27 *gediks* in this guild and that a candidate for membership in the guild (i.e., for becoming a master of the craft) would have to wait until one of these *gediks* had become vacant and could be transferred to him – with the consent of the guild.[91] Similarly, according to a firman dated 1200/1785–6 issued to the guild of weavers of crape or gauze (*bürüncük*) the number of their *destgâhs* was limited to 182. A new master could be accepted into the guild only if one of the owners of these *destgâhs* died.[92] Even early in the nineteenth century, youths destined for the trade of engravers worked at fixed wages after finishing their apprenticeship, 'until they are enabled to purchase the good-will of a shop, and are admitted master members of the corporation, which is limited to fifty'.[93]

The number of *gediks* in each trade was not very flexible. Thus we have a firman from the year 1142/1730 explicitly prohibiting to make any changes in the number of *gediks* of physicians.[94] Nevertheless, in periods of prosperity the number grew and in periods of recession it decreased; *gediks* could even be transferred from one trade to another according to the relative situation of different trades. Thus the number of *gediks* of the sellers of snuff in Istanbul and vicinity was increased, at a certain time, from 47 to 94; however, nobody was allowed to sell snuff without being the owner of such a *gedik*.[95]

The *gedik* system attempted at controlling not only the number of guild members but also their nature. In order to keep the craft as long as possible in the same families, the son of the owner of a *gedik* had priority to inherit the *gedik* on his father's death, but only if he fulfilled all the other conditions required for becoming a master in the craft.[96] Thus the *gediks* of the sellers of snuff usually were transferred to the sons of deceased masters, and the above-mentioned firman to the weavers of *bürüncük* provided for the transfer of the *gedik* either to the sons of deceased guild members or to one of their veteran and skilled journeymen (*kalfa*).[97] About the booksellers of Istanbul, early in the nineteenth century, White says the following: 'Their numbers are limited to some forty, and it is impossible for any person not brought up to the business to purchase the goodwill of a shop, unless he be son or next of kin to a member of the company'.[98]

But even if, for some reason, the *gedik* could not be transferred to the son of its owner, the system was supposed to ensure that the business passed to somebody as close to the master's social, ethnic, or religious group as possible. Nuri says that hundreds of firmans he has seen all state that vacant *gediks* should be given to the *çıraks* (apprentices) and *kalfas* (journeymen) of the guild, and never to anybody outside the guild. As an example he quotes the firman issued to the guild of masters of punch and candied fruit in Istanbul ordering that vacant *gediks* should be sold only to a suitable member of the guild. The firman prohibits the transfer of *gediks* to foreign subjects.[99] Similarly, the above-cited firman to the guild of physicians prohibits the transfer of their *gediks* to foreigners, and the orders concerning the *tabla gedikleri* prohibit their transfer to non-Muslims.[100] In any case, the guild reserved to itself the decision who the new master would be. Thus vacant *gediks* of the guild of sellers of snuff were sold by the guild; and in the firman of 1726 to the printers' guild as well as in the firman of 1778 to the weavers of ribbons of the fire brigade it is said that a *gedik* should be given to a new master by general consent of the guild.[101]

This does not mean, however, that the guilds independently controlled the whole *gedik* system. Although there were *gediks* based on *temessük* documents issued by the guilds' *kethüdas*, as we have seen above, quite a large number of *gediks* were based on *seneds* of the *evkaf*. To give only one example: at a certain period of recession the sellers of tripe in Istanbul left their shops and returned the *gediks* to the *haramayn hazinesi*, the *vakıf* for the benefit of Mecca and Medina, to whom the *gediks* belonged.[102] *Gediks* were issued by a large variety of government institutions, and many were based on *hüccets* (title-deeds) of the *Şeriat* Courts.[103] It was the *kadı* who increased the number of *gediks* if necessary or abolished *gediks* if they had become redundant, and it was he who registered the transfer of *gediks* or changed their purpose or conditions attached to them.[104] As we have seen above, the reforms carried out in the *gedik* system in the years 1805 and 1860–1 aimed at strengthening even more the government's control over this system.[105]

This leads us to our final remark on the relation between the government and the monopolies and restrictive practices of Istanbul guilds in general. Not only the *gedik* system, but almost all the restrictions dealt with in this article were not only sanctioned by the government but explicitly decreed as government orders: the need for the agreement of the guild's officer for exercising a craft or trade, the restriction of the number of people or shops in every branch, the prevention of 'wild' competition, the limitation of each guild to producing or selling specific goods only, and the confinement of trades or guilds to specified places. The fact that the members of each craft and trade were generally of the same social, ethnic or religious group was not the result of a government order, but it was surely in the interest of the government because it facilitated tremendously the administrative control of the guilds. Thus the monopolies and restrictions were part of a system in which the government was interested for administrative or economic reasons. Restrictive practices which were contrary to the interest of the government, such as the enforcement of minimum prices by agreement among the guild's members, for instance, did not prevail; in any case, no sign of their existence is shown in our sources.[106]

NOTES

1. Our analysis is based primarily on the following collections of documents: Osman Nuri, *Mecelle-i umur-u belediye*, vol. 1, Istanbul, 1922 (Nuri in later references); Ahmet Refik, *Onuncu asr-ı hicrîde Istanbul hayatı*, Istanbul, 1333 (Refik X in later references); Id., *Hicrî on birinci asırda Istanbul hayatı*, Istanbul, 1931 (Refik XI in later references); Id., *Hicrî on ikinci asırda Istanbul hayatı*, Istanbul, 1930 (Refik XII in later references). Another major source is Ch. White, *Three years in Constantinople*, London, 1845, 3 vols.
2. Cf. Nuri, pp. 644, 647–8.
3. Nuri, p. 619; Refik X, p. 169; etc.
4. Nuri, p. 559. For these functionaries of the guilds, as well as the guilds' structure in general, see below, Chapter 3.
5. Nuri, p. 558.

6. Nuri, p. 559.
7. F. Taeschner, 'Das Zunftwesen in der Türkei', *Leipziger Vierteljahrsschrift für Südosteuropa*, 5 (1941), p. 183.
8. White, vol. 1, p. 310; vol. 3, p. 325.
9. Nuri, p. 572. For similar practices in Egyptian guilds of the nineteenth century see G. Baer, *Egyptian guilds in modern times*, Jerusalem, 1964, pp. 105–6. In some cases, however, it was an official who issued the *tezkere*; for instance, the *arzuhalcı başı* (officer in charge of the *arzuhalcıs*, the writers of petitions) granted the licences of the *arzuhalcıs* (firman of the year 1178/end of 1764). Refik XII, p. 207.
10. Refik X, p. 170. The supply of a guarantee for the good character of the guild members was an important function of the guilds. See above, Chapter 1.
11. Refik XI, pp. 47–8.
12. Refik XII, pp. 179–80.
13. Nuri, p. 673.
14. Nuri, p. 680 (*berat* dating from the year 1225/1810).
15. Nuri, p. 341.
16. White, vol. 1, p. 98.
17. White, vol. 1, p. 310; vol. 2, pp. 17, 154; vol. 3, pp. 148, 325.
18. White, vol. 1, p. 310. For 16th century Bursa see H. Inalcik, 'Capital formation in the Ottoman Empire', *The Journal of Economic History*, vol. 29, no. 1, March 1969, pp. 116–17.
19. Refik X, pp. 171–2.
20. Nuri, pp. 668–9.
21. Refik XI, pp. 42–3, cf. also Refik X, pp. 178–9.
22. Refik XII, pp. 34–5.
23. White, vol. 2, p. 210.
24. On the *Levends* see M. Z. Pakalın, *Osmanlı tarih deyimleri veterimleri sozlüğü*, Istanbul, 1946 et seq., vol. 2, pp. 358–9; H. A. R. Gibb and H. Bowen, *Islamic Society and the West*, vol. 1, pt. I, London, 1950, pp. 99, 193n.
25. Refik XII, p. 34.
26. Refik XII, pp. 9–10.
27. R. Mantran, *Istanbul dans la seconde moitié du XVIIe siècle*, Paris, 1962, p. 386; Refik XII, pp. 36–7.
28. In contrast with European guilds, this was a characteristic feature of Middle Eastern guilds in general. See G. Baer, 'Guilds in Middle Eastern history', in M. A. Cook (ed.), *Studies in the economic history of the Middle East*, London, 1970, pp. 11–30. Cf. also Inalcik, p. 117.
29. Refik XI, p. 45.
30. Nuri, p. 646.
31. Mantran, p. 387.
32. Nuri, p. 646.
33. Refik XII, p. 37.
34. Nuri, pp. 650–51; cf. Gibb and Bowen, pp. 282–3.
35. Refik XII, pp. 103–4.
36. Nuri, p. 502.

37. Refik XII, pp. 230–32.
38. Gibb and Bowen, p. 283. For Egypt cf. Baer, *Egyptian guilds*, p. 28.
39. Evliya Çelebi, *Seyahatname*, vol. 1, Istanbul 1314, pp. 512–669 (Evliya in later references); and the English translation of another, often much better manuscript – J. von Hammer, *Narrative of Travels in Europe, Asia, and Africa in the seventeenth century, by Evliya Efendi*, vol. 1, part 2, London, 1846, pp. 104–205 (Hammer in later references). For comparative notes about these two editions see above, Chapter 1, note 12.
40. Hammer, pp. 183–4 (the first two examples are missing from the Turkish edition); Evliya, pp. 571, 574, 599, 612, 628; Hammer, pp. 189, 192, 211, 220, 231.
41. White, vol. 2, p. 154.
42. Refik XII, p. 41.
43. Nuri, p. 558.
44. Nuri, pp. 649–50.
45. Nuri, pp. 657–8.
46. White, vol. 2, p. 210.
47. Nuri, p. 692. The Macedonian town of Seres was burnt down and the old city was completely destroyed as a result of its changing hands frequently during the Balkan wars. A detailed description of the guilds of Seres by a native of that town who had moved to Istanbul is included in Nuri's work.
48. I. M. Lapidus, *Muslim cities in the later Middle Ages*, Cambridge, Mass., 1967, p. 100.
49. The nearest example is the above-mentioned order to supply hides to the Yedikule tanneries only (see above). But in this case too the aim was not to raise rents for the benefit of individual property owners but to prevent loss of income to the *evkaf*. As against this, some of the documents connected with the *gediks* (see below) state explicitly that property owners are not allowed to intervene in the *gedik* system of restrictions by raising rents. See, for instance, documents concerning the sellers of snuff and the makers of punch and candied fruit, Nuri, pp. 656, 658.
50. Evliya, pp. 614–7; Hammer, pp. 221–4. The same was the case in Egypt – see Baer, *Egyptian guilds*, p. 27.
51. Refik XII, pp. 132–3, 141; cf. Baer, *Egyptian guilds*, p. 23.
52. Evliya, p. 580; Hammer, p. 195; Nuri, pp. 559, 576–7; White, vol. 1, p. 9. Cf. Baer, *Egyptian guilds*, pp. 28–9.
53. Evliya, p. 614; Hammer, p. 221.
54. Nuri, pp. 610–11.
55. White, vol. 2, p. 154.
56. White, vol. 3, p. 324. Cf. also, for examples from Egypt, Baer, *Egyptian guilds*, p. 109.
57. For these rights see below, discussion of the *gedik* system. Apprenticeship is analysed in Chapter 3 below.
58. Gibb and Bowen, p. 289.
59. Nuri, p. 577. Nuri was the first to draw general conclusions from this document (p. 570), though without fixing the date of the alleged transformation.
60. Nuri, p. 671.

61. Evliya, p. 559; Hammer, pp. 143, 175 (the second guild is missing from the Turkish published text).
62. Evliya, p. 631; Hammer, pp. 149, 152 (only the last-mentioned guild is found in the Turkish published text).
63. Hammer, pp. 149, 153, 161 (all missing from the Turkish edition).
64. Evliya, pp. 565, 571, 573, 595; Hammer, pp. 165, 189, 191, 207.
65. Evliya, pp. 629, 632; Hammer, pp. 231, 232, 233.
66. Evliya, pp. 600, 602–3; Hammer, pp. 212, 214.
67. Refik XI, p. 55; Hammer, p. 184.
68. Hammer, pp. 183, 187, 202, 222, 232; Evliya, pp. 590, 615, 629 (the first two are missing from the Turkish edition).
69. Nuri, pp. 645, 648.
70. White, vol. 2, p. 101.
71. White, vol. 2, pp. 117, 123, 154, 210; vol. 3, pp. 38, 147.
72. White, vol. 2, p. 123.
73. White, vol. 2, p. 252, 267; vol. 3, pp. 229, 326.
74. White, vol. 1, p. 98, 290; vol. 3, pp. 120, 277.
75. Refik XII, p. 104; Nuri, pp. 568, 584–5, 633–4.
76. White, vol. 1, pp. 51–2; however, they may have formed separate guilds.
77. White, vol. 2, pp. 17, 50; vol. 3, pp. 108, 324.
78. White, vol. 3, p. 186.
79. Nuri, p. 652; Gibb and Bowen, p. 282, n. 1.
80. G. Young, *Corps de droit ottoman*, Oxford, 1906, vol. 6, p. 114, n. 7. Cf Nuri, pp. 659–60; Gibb and Bowen, p. 282.
81. Nuri, pp. 652, 656, 658, 665.
82. Nuri, pp. 558, 652, 657.
83. Nuri, p. 655, n. 1. Cf. also *gedik* document reproduced in Baer, *Egyptian guilds*, pp. 157–8, showing that the *gedik* of a dyer included the shop with the implements necessary to exercise the craft.
84. Mantran, p. 368, n. 3; also p. 438.
85. Nuri, p. 663.
86. Gibb and Bowen, p. 282, n. 1.
87. Mantran, p. 369, n. 1; Evliya, p. 614 and Hammer, p. 222; Refik XII pp. 44–5.
88. Nuri, pp. 655–6.
89. Nuri, pp. 662 ff.; *Düstur*, vol. 1, Istanbul, 1289, pp. 258–62.
90. Nuri, pp. 559, 656, 658.
91. Nuri, p. 558.
92. Nuri, p. 657.
93. White, vol. 3, p. 148. The 'goodwill' is White's translation of *gedik*.
94. Refik XII, pp. 106–7.
95. Nuri, pp. 660, 656–7.
96. Nuri, p. 559.
97. Nuri, pp. 656, 657.
98. White, vol. 2, p. 154.
99. Nuri, pp. 657–8.
100. Refik XII, p. 107; Nuri, p. 664.
101. Nuri, pp. 656–7; 558.

102. Nuri, pp. 664, 660–61.
103. Cf. Nuri, pp. 662–3, 664.
104. Nuri, pp. 302, 661.
105. Cf. Nuri, pp. 654–5, 662–5.
106. Cf. also Baer, *Egyptian guilds*, p. 105.

3

THE STRUCTURE OF TURKISH GUILDS AND ITS SIGNIFICANCE FOR OTTOMAN SOCIAL HISTORY

Research in the field of Ottoman guild history suffered for a long time from the lack of a clear definition of the term 'guild'.[1] There were authors who used it to denote urban craftsmen in general, even when they found no sign of any organization; there were others who applied it to such organizations as the *fütüvvet* associations and the *ahi* societies in Anatolia, even though it is now evident that these associations and societies were not organized along professional lines. One of the results of this absence of a precise definition is that, for more than two generations, orientalists dealt primarily with concepts and ideas supposedly pertinent to the 'guilds', and dealt hardly at all with the economic, social and political reality. This approach distorted research of guild structure in particular, since no differentiation was made between the ideal, theoretical hierarchy that is found in the *fütüvvet* books and the ranks and positions that in fact obtained in the professional guilds.[2] In this study the opposite approach will be taken, and the actual structure of the guilds will be examined on the basis of firmans and documents from everyday life. We propose first to study the ranks through which a craftsman, merchant or transportation or service worker passed until he reached the rank of *usta* (master), and then to analyse the character and significance of the several positions and institutions of the guild.

I. APPRENTICES

The apprentice, lowest rank among the craftsmen, was usually called *çırak* or, in a term derived from Persian, *şagird*. A person who had learned his trade but had not served as an apprentice was not allowed to be a master. Many documents enunciate this principle – an indication that it was not always followed. One task of the guild was to make sure that the rule was obeyed; the head of each guild, its notables and office-holders were required to certify that a certain person had passed this stage of his schooling before he had licence to open an independent business.[3]

Guild supervision of apprentices had another aspect. The apprentice was not tied to one *usta*, but was not permitted to quit an *usta* without the guild's consent. If he did try to quit without it, the guild made sure that no other *usta* would accept him.[4]

Learning his trade was, of course, the main part of the apprentice's instruction; in certain periods, however, guilds also concerned themselves with his general education. For example, the apprentices of the saddlers' guild studied the Koran in the *medrese* of the Mehmed Fatih mosque; and there was a similar school in the Grand Bazaar for apprentices of the guilds in the area. Nevertheless, it appears that the guilds did not, as a matter of course, undertake to teach their members Koran and cultivate good qualities in them; this was the task of the religious institutions and orders.[5] Nuri, who claims that there were links between the guilds and religious orders (although his evidence is not convincing), explains that the breaking of these links in the passage of time brought about a decline in learning among the guilds, and as a result the Grand Bazaar school was empty for long spells.[6]

Even though certain guilds continued to provide a general syllabus to their apprentices during the nineteenth century, the State did not consider this enough. Many children had not learnt to read and write before they began work as apprentices, and many others were taken out of the Koran schools at an early age by their parents and apprenticed, to help in supporting the family. As a counter-measure, Mahmud II issued an *irade* in 1824/5 forbidding members of guilds to accept as apprentices any children who had not finished their schooling. Every apprentice had to have a *tezkere* certifying his elementary education. The certificates were issued by the local kadi and approved by the head of the guild.[7]

II. JOURNEYMEN

The customary word for the rank above apprentice was *kalfa*, a Turkish corruption of Arabic *khalīfa*, which, in its original form, also designated the intermediary rank of craftsman, between *çırak* and *usta*.[8] This guild structure was termed 'a rigid hierarchy' by Gibb and Bowen.[9] It seems to me that the facts do not justify the term. First of all, there were places where there were four ranks, and not the three mentioned. For instance, the apprentice in the Macedonian city of Seres began his work as a *yamak* (assistant), and only after two years of regular work, and with a guarantee from his guardian or father, was he ceremonially promoted to the rank of *çırak.*[10] In the printers' guild, there seems to have been, in the eighteenth century, a fourth rank between *kalfa* and *usta*, called *şerik.*[11] Moreover, whereas in most guilds the lowest rank was *şagird* or *çırak*, the intermediate level *kalfa*, and the highest grade *usta* or *üstad*, among the builders there appears to have been a different terminology. In two salary lists for construction work – one from 1741/2 and one from 1814 – *kalfa* is the highest wage-earner, and the *üstad*, or *usta*, occupied the second or third place. *Şagird* is the lowest wage-earner in the builders' guild as well.[12] Also, a number of documents indicate that in some guilds, during certain periods, it was not necessary for the *çırak* to pass through the grade of *kalfa* to become an *usta*. These documents – among them a firman of the eighteenth century to silk spinners – tell of *başka çıkmak*, the opening of an independent business, by an apprentice, a *şagird* or a *çırak.*[13] This explains why Nuri lists the *çıraklar* and *kalfalar* of the guild among those with priority to gain the right of occupying an empty store (*gedik*).[14] A similar situation prevailed in Egypt, where, in certain guilds, the apprentice could rise directly to the rank of *usta* without passing through the intermediate grades. Therefore, with regard to Egypt likewise, it would not be appropriate to term the guild hierarchy 'rigid'.[15] The structure of the guilds in the Middle East was fairly flexible compared to their European counterparts, and the border-line between ranks was not tightly drawn. This is probably the main reason for the absence of information on organizations or uprisings of apprentices or craftsmen in Turkey and Egypt, unlike the *compagnons* and the *Gesellen* in Europe,[16] a conclusion that seems to have wider significance in view of the fact that the Ottoman feudal system, too, did not have a hierarchy as solid as that in most European countries.

All the same, in most guilds there undoubtedly was an actual differentiation between *çırak* and *kalfa*. For instance, Nuri provides information on payments made by the *usta* of the Grand Bazaar of Istanbul to the guild treasury when his *çırak* was raised to the rank of *kalfa.*[17] Moreover, some of the guilds observed the ceremony of promoting the *çırak* to the rank of *kalfa* – called *şed bağlamak* (the binding of the waist-belt) or *peştamal bağlamak* (the binding of the towel) – which was based on *fütüvvet* traditions.[18] The ceremony was performed by those guilds that, in other matters, too, held to tradition and maintained their social uniqueness. The tanners' guild, for instance, which was headed by the *şeyhs* called *Ahi Baba*, performed it.[19] According to the *Great Fütüvvet Book*, dating from the beginning of the sixteenth century, the ceremony was performed at that time by the butchers and helva and candy merchants, but not by the smiths, locksmiths, used-clothing-and-shoes merchants (*eskiciler*), or, amazingly enough, by the shoemakers.[20] The only detailed description of the ceremony available to us concerns the guilds of Seres.[21] When an apprentice in that city completed three years of training, the *üstadlar* of the appropriate guild were invited to a special session of the guild council. On that occasion, the candidate for the first time wore the peculiar garments of his guild. After the boy's *üstad* had given evidence of his character and his piety in prayer, and his guardian had expressed his agreement, the *Fātiḥa* was recited in memory of members of the guild who had passed away. Then all assembled stood up, and the head of the guild girded the candidate with a special towel, while giving him advice on the profession. At the end, the new *kalfa* kissed the hands of all the *üstadlar* present, and his guardian presented the guild's *vakıf* with a tray or bowl.[22] It is interesting to note the similarity between this ceremony in the Macedonian town of Seres and the same ceremony in Cairo at the beginning of the nineteenth century as described by Lane.[23] The main difference was that no gifts were made to the guild, since the Egyptian guilds, except for the shoemakers, had no mutual aid funds.

III. MASTERS

The highest rank of craftsman or merchant in the Turkish guilds was the *üstad* or *usta*. Graduation to this rank was called *başka çıkmak* (to become independent), and the status of *usta* was termed *üstadlık*.[24] To become an *usta*, a member of the profession had to belong to the familial, religious or social group of which the guild was composed, and be affluent enough to purchase a *gedik*, that is, the right to practise his profession. Purchase of this right and the rank of *usta* were so closely conjoined that one type of *gedik* was originally called *ustalık*.[25] But, in the guilds that clung to tradition, the candidate for *üstadlık* was required, as well, to have served as a *kalfa* for three years without any complaints being lodged against him; to have shown dedication to the tasks assigned to him, particularly the education of apprentices; to have maintained good relations with his fellow *kalfalar*; to have treated his customers fairly; and to have displayed the ability to manage a business independently. Only after the candidate's *usta* had testified that these conditions had been fulfilled would the guild council accept him as an *usta*.[26] Of course, proficiency in his vocation was also required,[27] but the requirement was not formally defined. Aside from information about the physicians and surgeons, who were examined during the sixteenth century by the *hekim başı*,[28] no evidence has been found indicating that the candidate had to pass a professional examination. Nor is there evidence that he was called upon to produce a masterpiece, such as the *Meisterstück* or chef d'oeuvre of the European guilds. On the contrary, it has been explicitly stated that this custom did not pertain in Turkey.[29]

The reason of this is undoubtedly the fact that – in contrast to their European counterparts – the Turkish guilds played only a limited role in supervising the quality of their members' products and upholding the professional level. Regulations concerning the quality of products were issued by the Government, and the heads of the guilds merely saw to compliance with them, and, if a counterfeiter or transgressor of the regulations was discovered, the guilds did not punish him themselves, but reported the infraction to the Government, which took whatever measures it thought necessary. As a result, the competence of the *usta* was determined more by his relations with the Government than with the guild. The guild decided whether to accept a candidate or not mainly on the strength of his financial standing, his religious and family ties with the members of the guild and his record as an apprentice.[30]

Just as graduation from *çırak* to *kalfa* was marked in several guilds by a special ceremony, there were guilds that celebrated the transition from *kalfa* (or *çırak*) to *usta*. It appears, however, that only very few traditional guilds did so. Of two descriptions of this type of ceremony, one found in the *Fütüvvetname* and quoted in Nuri[31] should be considered a theoretical regulation rather than an account of what actually took place. Perhaps this fact is another expression of the lack of a stringent hierarchy in the guilds. In any case, it supports the contention that the guilds and the *fütüvvet* societies were two different types of organization, and that the rise of the professional guilds was connected with the decline of the free *fütüvvet* and *ahi* societies.[32]

Among the few guilds that kept up the *fütüvvet* tradition and conducted the ceremony of accepting a new *usta* were those of Seres.[33] When the head of a guild in that city was informed that a candidate for the rank of *usta* in his guild had purchased a business, he would invite all the *ustalar* of the guild, the heads of the other guilds and religious dignitaries to a ceremony. First, there would be the ceremonial entrance of the candidate, his *usta* and the head of his guild. After the appropriate greetings, the *mufti* would give a sign, and the *imam* would read verses from the Koran and prayers, and explain *ḥadīths*. Then the head of the candidate's guild would deliver a sermon in which he told of the guild's patrons and advised the candidate to be honest in his business, to obey the Sultan, to honour the *ulema* and his masters, to treat his apprentices and workers as though they were his children, and so on. Next, the candidate's *usta* would testify to his education and achievements, and the new master would make a vow as to his honourable intentions. At this point, his journeyman's towel (*kalfalık peştamalı*) was removed, and he was girded with the master's towel (*üstadlık peştamalı*). All present then rose to their feet and exclaimed *allahu ekber*, and additional prayers were said by the religious dignitaries. After the new *usta* had kissed the hands of the notables, everyone went outside, and there the *ulema* and the several ranks of the guild extended their salutations in prescribed order. Coffee and cold drinks were served, there was an evening prayer and the reading of the *Fātiḥa* for the dead of the guild. The ceremony culminated in a gala dinner for guests and the town poor.

IV. THE GUILD *Élite*

Upon becoming an *usta*, the guild member had entered the highest professional rank of his trade. Within the guild, however, there was a differentiation between the regular *usta* and an *élite* of the *ustalar*, which apparently was composed of the veterans of the guild. It is of interest that the usual name for this group was *ihtiyarlar*, a word connected, like the word *élite*, with the meaning 'chosen'. But since Middle Eastern society links prestige to age, the Arabic word *ikhtiyār* came to mean 'old' both in Turkish and in modern Arabic.[34] An indication of the informal character of this *élite* group is the fact that, besides *ihtiyarlar*, it was designated by a number of terms, such as *ihtiyar ustaları*, *müsin ve ihtiyar iş erleri*, *müsin ve ihtiyar söz sahibleri*, *ileri gelenler* and *esnafın muteberanı*.[35] The sources for this study indicate no rules, laws or customs determining when and under what conditions an *usta* became a member of the group – further evidence of the lack of a 'rigid hierarchy'.

The informal character of the *élite* group is reflected in its functions as well as its composition. Documents that mention the activities of the *ihtiyarlar* show that they did not have any well-defined task. Their principal function was to support the head of the guild, especially in his relations with the authorities, and thus demonstrate that he was acting in the guild's name. They also served as a channel through which public opinion in the guild was transmitted to its head and to the authorities. The following examples of the group's activities are taken from documents in Nuri's collection: the *ihtiyarlar* of one guild, together with its head, submitted to the Government a list of *üstadlar* to be appointed as members of the guild council; the *ihtiyarlar* and head of a guild went to the kadi to complain about a member of another guild who broke their monopoly by establishing a business which only theirs was allowed to conduct or by selling a product in which only theirs was allowed to trade; the *ihtiyarlar* and head of a guild reported to the kadi that certain individuals were using counterfeit or defective weights and measures. If the Government wanted to enforce certain standards of quality, the *ihtiyarlar*, along with the head of the guild, were authorized to supervise their application.[36] In short, the *ihtiyarlar* were a kind of unofficial advisory and executive committee, composed of the veteran guild members, whose size and composition were not fixed by any rules. One gets the impression from the documents that a group of this type existed in practically every guild.

V. OFFICERS OF THE GUILD

As well as the informal *élite* group, there were certain guild officers who had specific functions. Their names may be divided into two classes: those taken from the *fütüvvet* vocabulary and those created by the professional guilds. The *fütüvvet* tradition is mirrored in a small number of special guilds, such as those of Seres and the barbers, and also in Evliya's description dating from the end of the seventeenth century. The most important officer mentioned by Evliya alone is the *nakib*, who, according to him, marched in the procession which he describes.[37] But it is doubtful whether, in fact, the professional guilds in Turkey at that time still had an officer called *nakib*, since the term does not appear in documents dealing with these.[38] Nuri explains that the ceremonial function fulfilled by the *nakib* of the *fütüvvet* societies gradually disappeared, and, as a result, the *yiğit başı* took his place.[39] This would seem to show that the *nakib* vanished from the Turkish much sooner than from the Egyptian guilds, in which the deputy head of the guild was called *naqīb* until the beginning of the nineteenth century.[40] This, by itself, however, is insufficient proof of an earlier change in the character of the Turkish guilds. There are at least two other plausible explanations: first, as will be seen, the functions of the *nakib* were carried out in some Turkish guilds by a person with the title of *şeyh*, who was not the head of the guild; and second, it is possible that in Turkey the Turkish term *yiğit başı* was preferred to the Arabic *nakib*, while in Arabic-speaking Egypt the Arabic term was kept on, even though, in the later period, the two offices were identical.

Two other traditional posts which existed in the early period of the development of Turkish guilds, and were retained by a few tradition-minded guilds, were the *duacı* and the *davetci*. The *duacı*, whose original function seems to have been the recitation of prayers, is mentioned by Evliya as having taken part in the processions.[41] The barbers' guild had an officer so styled as late as the end of the eighteenth century, but his function had changed: in ceremonies on the occasion of graduation from one rank to another, the *duacı* was shaved in public.[42] It is not surprising to find that traditions were preserved by the barbers, since, in Egypt as well as the other Middle Eastern countries, barbers had a special place in the guild system and its ideology.[43] As we saw, the same is true of the guilds of the Macedonian city of Seres, and, in fact, there too we find a post entitled *duacı*; the holder of that office discharged the original task of reciter of prayers.[44] The second office as well, the *davetci*, existed only in Seres, where this was the title of the chief assistant to the head of the guild. Although this title has been explained by that assistant's duty of calling people to prayer and to appear before the head of the guild, it is possible that, here again, we have a remnant of tradition. The same office is mentioned in reference to the barbers' and physicians' guild in the Egyptian manuscript *kitāb al-dhakhā'ir wa'l-tuḥaf fī bīr al-ṣanā'i' wa'l-ḥiraf* (apparently from the seventeenth century), which is strongly influenced by the *fütüvvet* literature.[45]

Another term which dropped out of the Turkish guilds in a subsequent period is *çavuş*. This title appears occasionally in the writings of Evliya, usually along with the *nakib*.[46] Nuri says, on the one hand, that it is not clear what the functions of the *çavuş* were, but, on the other, that they were later transferred to the *yiğit başı*.[47] White, writing at the beginning of the nineteenth century, claims that every guild has a *çavuş*, a messenger; but this is mentioned in the theoretical part of his work, which undoubtedly is based on Evliya, whereas in the sections describing the actual activities of the guilds the *çavuş* is not mentioned at all.[48] The Egyptian guilds did not have a *çavuş*,[49] but, in nineteenth-century Damascus, the *shāwīsh* was the chief assistant to the head of the guild.[50]

In Turkey, that chief assistant was called *yiğit başı* during the entire period for which we have documentation of the existence of guilds. *Yiğit* is the Turkish equivalent of the Arabic *fatā*, which means a brave and generous young man. The term is thus a vestige of the *fütüvvet* associations,[51] although in the professional guilds it was totally emptied of its primal meaning and content. The assistant to the head of the guild was, in fact, called *yiğit başı*, but the members of the guild were no longer called *yiğitler*.[52] Among the *yiğit başı*'s tasks were helping the head of the guild in all matters concerning the guild and acting as a channel of communication between him and its members. The *yiğit başı* was chosen from among the notables of the guild, and apparently by them, but their choice had to be confirmed by the authorities. Evidence to support this is found, among other sources, in a document from the Istanbul *sicil* of 1664, dealing with the candle-makers' guild, and in the money-changers' regulations of 1864.[53]. This is another reflection of the lack of autonomy of the Turkish guilds and their marked dependence on the authorities, an important characteristic whose social significance will be discussed later.

The *yiğit başı* always belonged to the same religious or ethnic community as the other members of the guild, and even when the head of a Christian craft or merchant guild was a Muslim, as was customary in several guilds during certain periods, the *yiğit başı* would still be a Christian of the same denomination as the craftsmen and merchants.[54] Also, a guild frequently had more than one *yiğit başı*.[55]

During the nineteenth century, the assistants to the heads of the guilds were called *vekil* rather than *yiğit başı*. The reason for this may have been that, even earlier, the head of the guild acted through a representative or agent who was appointed by the kadi – *kethüdasının ba hüccet-i şer'îye vekili olan . . .* – in addition to the *yiğit başı*.[56] In any case, at the beginning of the nineteenth century, the guild of boatmen in Istanbul had two *vekils*, one for the city and one for the suburbs. The merchant guilds of the markets and the seal-engravers had *vekils*, and the city's porters registered at regular stations, of which each was supervised by a *vekil*.[57] In certain merchant guilds the head of the guild was called *şehbender*, and his assistant *muhtar*.[58]

VI. *Lonca* AND GUILD COUNCIL

The meeting-place of a guild was called *lonca*, a word derived from Italian or Spanish;[59] the term is not found in documents prior to the eighteenth century. Nuri as well as Gibb and Bowen claim that in earlier periods the meeting-place was designated by Sufi terms, such as *zaviye*, and they all try to explain the change in terminology by intricate justifications, none of which carries conviction.[60] It is hardly necessary to refute these explanations, since there are no indications that the meeting-place of the professional guilds was ever called *zaviye*. Nuri bases his contention on the *Fütüvvetname*, while Gibb and Bowen quote Thorning, whose book is also based entirely on the *fütüvvet* literature. The fundamental error which underlies their argument and their involved explanations is the failure to differentiate between the *fütüvvet* associations and the professional guilds, and the widespread belief that there was a close link between the guilds and the Sufi orders. On several occasions, I have endeavoured to show that the *fütüvvet* associations were not professional guilds, that the rise and development of the guilds occurred at a time when the *fütüvvet* associations were in decline, and that there is no substantial evidence proving the existence of strong ties between the guilds and the Sufi orders. On the contrary, a study of Egyptian guilds has led to the conclusion that, as a result of their differing functions, the guilds and the orders existed side by side with a certain degree of contact but no regular nexus. Nuri's attempt to prove that there was a powerful connection between the guilds and the Melâmî order is not at all convincing, and actually proves the opposite of what he set out to demonstrate.[61] To sum up, the source of the *lonca* should not be sought in the *zaviye*, and the simple reason why the *lonca* is not mentioned before the eighteenth century is perhaps that there was no institution of this type at that time and that it was only created later, when the professional guilds had developed into a widespread network.

Just as in other languages the term 'lodge' was expanded as time went on beyond the idea of a place of meeting, so, too, the term *lonca* came to mean the body that met in the place. *Lonca*, therefore, was the term used for the guild council. However, a distinction was sometimes made between *lonca dairesi* or *lonca odası* to designate the meeting-place, *lonca heyeti* referring to the council itself and *lonca ustası* to a council member.[62] We only have information about the composition of these councils from the nineteenth century. The number of members evidently differed from guild to guild. In the 1840s for example, the Muslim and Armenian merchant guilds in the bazaar of Istanbul were each adminstered by a guild head, his deputy and six notables. The money-changers' guild council in 1864 was composed of four members; the Seres guild councils had five; and the Ankara tanners' guild council, at the beginning of the twentieth century, numbered ten or eleven of the veteran members.[63]

Similarly, there seem to have been considerable differences in the way in which the councils were elected. According to a document of 1806, the heads and notables of the Armenian carpenters' guild appeared before the kadi of Istanbul and explained to him that its members were scattered over divers parts of Istanbul and on that account it was difficult to assemble them. They therefore asked that seventeen persons listed by name be appointed as *lonca ustası*, that is, members of the guild council. The kadi complied and the seventeen were appointed.[64] On the other hand, in a description of the election of the *lonca heyeti* of Seres, whose guilds were generally more autonomous, no mention is made of the need for appointment by the kadi. In Seres, the councils were elected by the guild's *ustalar* from among members with at least five years' seniority who had never been found guilty of a transgression and were known as upright and trustworthy men. The election took place simultaneously with the election of the guild head and had to be approved by him. If he declared that he was unwilling to cooperate with the newly elected council, his own election or that of the council, or both, was repeated until a headman and a council were selected that were willing to work together. The council met every first and third Friday of the Muslim month at the *lonca dairesi*. At the council meetings, the head of the guild reported on the events of the past two weeks and on the performance of previous decisions, and a discussion was held.[65]

The following functions of the guild council are mentioned in the sources: discussing complaints of one guild member against another; arbitration of disputes among guild members 'before the Government takes notice of them'; the temporary exclusion of a member from the guild, that is, forbidding a member from plying his trade because he has contravened the traditional orders and customs of the guild; control and supervision of the guild's finances in general, and inspection of the guild fund's accounts in particular, as well as decisions on loans to be granted from this fund.[66] Thus, the guild council dealt with all matters concerning the internal organization of the guild and relations among its members; it did not deal with matters concerning the relation of the guild with outside bodies. Wherever the firmans and *şeriat* court documents note that a delegation from a guild appeared before the kadi, the head of the guild, the *yiğit başı* and the *ihtiyarlar* are mentioned as representing the guild, never the *lonca* or the *lonca heyeti*. Similarly, in Egypt, contact with the authorities and decisive economic and fiscal matters were handled by the *'umad* (plural of *'umda*), an informal group of the guild's notables and wealthier members, and a formal council rarely existed, or, if it did, its powers were negligible.[67] This phenomenon has a double significance. It is a further expression of the lack of formal rigidity in the ranks, functions and institutions of Ottoman society in recent centuries. But, beyond this, it shows that the members of the guild with determining power were those who merited it by the criteria of their society, and foremost among them – age. The authorities recognized this fact and therefore regarded the *ihtiyarlar* as the true representatives of the guild. Formal elections were foreign to this society. They appear only in the nineteenth century, apparently under European influence, and information of the existence of formal councils refers primarily to the Armenians and the guilds in Macedonian Seres.

VII. THE HEAD OF THE GUILD

In contrast with Egypt, where the head of the guild was always called *shaykh*, sources on the history of the Turkish guilds mention two terms for the office: *şeyh* and *kethüda* or *kâhya*. According to Nuri, the *şeyh* fulfilled ceremonial functions in the main, while the *kethüda* dealt with the material and administrative aspects of guild life. Therefore, as the *fütüvvet* traditions were forgotten and the guilds undertook primarily economic and administrative tasks, it was no longer necessary to elect a *şeyh*, and the office gradually disappeared. Instead, the *kethüda*, who acted as intermediary between Government and guild, rose to a dominant position.[68] Thus, again according to Nuri, the relation between the two offices in Turkey was similar to that between the *shaykh* and the *naqīb* in the Egyptian guilds.[69] This may have become the reason why the *nakib* vanished from the Turkish earlier than from the Egyptian guilds. In any case, it explains the existence of a *şeyh* and a *kethüda* at the same time in Turkish guilds.

It would seem that, generally speaking, published documents confirm Nuri's interpretation. Most guild documents in which both a *şeyh* and a *kethüda* are mentioned are early ones from the sixteenth century, such as a firman of 1581 concerning the tanners' guild and a firman of 1582 concerning the manufacturers and retailers of needles and pins.[70] The only later document mentioning the two, and the only one cited by Nuri, is a firman of 1795/6 dealing with the barbers' guild,[71] which may be connected with the fact that barbers all over the Middle East were known for their particularly close affinity to traditional ceremonies. Nevertheless, in nineteenth-century Turkey as well, the secular head of the booksellers' guild was called *şeyh*;[72] but in this case, too, it may be significant that the traditional title was maintained by this particular guild.

There were certain guilds in Turkey whose heads were designated by other terms. First of all, the head of the tanners' guild in each city was called *Ahi Baba*.[73] This was the title of the *şeyh* of the *tekke* (dervish convent) of Ahi Evran in Kırşehir, who was the patron of the tanners' guilds in the Ottoman Empire; consequently, the heads of all the tanners' guilds took this title (more precisely, it was *Ahi Baba vekili*, and *Ahi Baba* for short). This guild and its heads had a prestigious place among the Turkish guilds, and it is not surprising that even in later periods they kept a name which betokened their uniqueness.[74] Secondly, the heads of the Seres guilds were eventually given the title of *mütevelli*.[75] This may have originated in old guild traditions which, as we have shown, were well preserved. According to the Egyptian *Kitāb al-dhakhā'ir* of the seventeenth century, the acting *shaykh* of a guild was called *al-shaykh al-mutawallī* (in contrast to a person who had reached the rank of *shaykh* but was not the acting head of the guild).[76] There may, however, be a simpler explanation: one of the functions of the *mütevelli* of a Seres guild was to administer its *vakıf*,[77] and the manager of a *vakıf* is generally called *mütevelli*.

The *kethüda* was usually chosen by the guild members without formal elections, and his appointment then confirmed by the kadi.[78] Nuri reproduces many documents illustrating this procedure. For instance, a document of 1726 records that the *Ahi Baba* of the Istanbul tanners was appointed by the kadi on the recommendation of the guild notables. Similarly, in March 1778, the veteran members of the ink-case-makers' guild (*devılar*) asked the kadi to confirm the acting *kethüda*, despite the intriguing of some malicious persons.[79] Article 8 of the money-changers' regulations of 1864 lays down that the *kâhya* is appointed by the Government, but, if there are complaints by the members of the guild, they will be investigated.[80] This was apparently the custom in other guilds as well, as is attested by a document concerning the dismissal of the *kethüda* of the Istanbul greengrocers as a result of complaints to the kadi.[81] The *kethüda* was also dismissed if he failed to carry out the Government's regulations.[82] Newly established guilds would ask the Government to appoint a *kethüda*, as did the tobacconists when their guild was established in September 1725.[83] In some cases, the appointment was accompanied by the grant of an official certificate, a *berat*, or a letter of appointment by the kadi, *mürasele-i şer'iye*.[84]

The method of appointing a *kethüda* as described here is identical with the method of appointment of the *shaykh* in the Egyptian guilds. In

Egypt, too, the *shaykh* was appointed by the Government on the recommendation of the guild notables, and in certain cases received a certificate of appointment.[85] In other Arab countries for which information on their guilds is available, the usage was the same. The only exception is Damascus, which preserved its autonomy in all matters, guild affairs included. The office of guild *shaykh* in Damascus was hereditary; if there was no fit heir, the new *shaykh* was freely elected by the guild notables. This election had to be approved by the *shaykh al-mashāyikh* of the guilds, a special office in Damascus, which will be discussed below. The election of the *shaykh* did not, however, require the approval of the Ottoman authorities.[86] In all other cities of the Empire the choice of heads of guilds did require that approval, which reflects the fact that the guilds in the Muslim Middle East developed under official auspices and as an integral part of the Government's administrative system. Associations that were organized from below, without connection with the Government or even in opposition to it, were not guilds, that is, were not organized along professional lines. The guilds were maintained from above, and their principal purpose was to oversee the townspeople.[87] We need not wonder, therefore, that the Government reserved the right to approve the appointments of their heads.

Since the *kethüda* was appointed on the recommendation of the guild notables, he was usually one of the prominent members among them. Such a person was acceptable to both notables and Government, for the Government was interested in the incumbency of a *kethüda* with as much influence as possible, so that he could effectively discharge his official duties. Quite frequently, however, individuals who were not members of the guild were appointed *kethüda*, for various reasons. Some were retired civil servants who agreed to renounce their pension in exchange for the appointment. During the reign of Abdülhamid II, favoured courtiers were appointed by the Sultan – often at the instance of the guild, whose members hoped to use a courtier's connections to further their own concern. An interesting case is that of the French proselyte who founded the Istanbul fire brigade and, as a reward, was appointed *kethüda* of the newly-formed build of weavers of ribbons for the brigade; moreover, his son inherited the post.[88]

Nuri maintains that there were at first only Muslim *kethüda*s, even in guilds with Christian members; but the Christians gradually began to elect their own *yiğit başı*s, and, afterwards, Christian *kethüda*s as well. Gibb and Bowen write that 'until much later [than the middle of the seventeenth century?] *kâhyâ*s continued in all cases to be Moslem; but eventually this office as well was granted in some instances to non-Moslems'.[89] Hitherto published documents do not seem to bear out this theory. On the one hand, as early as the sixteenth and seventeenth centuries, there were non-Muslim *kethüdas*, such as the Jewish *kethüda* of the woollen drapers (*çuhacılar*), who is mentioned in two firmans of 1584, or the non-Muslim *kethüda* of the manufacturers and retailers of linen skull-caps (*takyeciler*), named in a firman of 1657.[90] On the other hand, Nuri himself includes documents from the second half of the eighteenth century in which Muslim *kethüdas* of non-Muslim or mixed guilds are mentioned, such as the non-Muslim tailors (1764), the mixed guild of greengrocers (an undated document, but probably quite late), the non-Muslim velvet merchants (1768) and the Greek and Armenian silk-spinners (1759 and 1762).[91] Heading the section of the market called Sandal Bedesteni, which was occupied by Armenians exclusively, there was a Muslim *kâhya* until the nineteenth century.[92] By contrast, Nuri has only one earlier document noting a Muslim *kethüda* of a non-Muslim guild – the Christian candle-makers (1664) – and none at all mentioning non-Muslim *kethüdas* for any period.[93] It would appear, therefore, that there is no factual basis for determining the trends in religious affiliation of guild heads, and nothing to support dates of any development in this regard. Above I have sought to show that the second part of the theory of Nuri and of Gibb and Bowen is also unfounded, namely, their contention that, at first, the Muslims and the Christians were organized in mixed guilds and that, in the middle of the seventeenth century, they split and organized separate ones.[94] If there were trends in the religious composition of the guilds and the affiliation of guild heads, we certainly do not have enough information at the present time to establish their nature or dates. All that can be postulated at this point is that, apparently in all periods, there were more separate guilds than mixed ones, and that there were more cases of members and heads being of the same religious and ethnic community than cases of their provenance from different communities. Nevertheless, there were many instances in which a non-Muslim guild had a Muslim *kethüda*.

Like Cairo, Istanbul had no common head of all the guilds either. The organization of all urban guilds under a chief *shaykh* or *kethüda* was a sign of a measure of autonomy not possessed by guilds in towns which were the seat of the central Government. Such autonomy existed only in certain provincial centres, such as Damascus, where the position of the *shaykh al-mashāyikh* of the guilds was strongly rooted in the city's social fabric and he had important functions to carry out.[95] It is not surprising, then, that in Macedonian Seres, with its powerful guild organization, there was an institution similar to the Damascus *shaykh al-mashāyikh*. The twenty-four *mütevellis* of the guilds formed a council called *kâhyalar meclisi*, which met on the last Friday of every Muslim month. One of the *mütevellis* was elected *kâhyalar başı*, or chief *mütevelli* of all the guilds for life. His responsibilities were: surveillance of the activities of the *loncas* and *mütevellis*; arbitration in disputes between guilds; execution of punishments pronounced by the *lonca*s and *mütevelli*s; mediation between Government and guilds; inspection of the *mütevelli*s' accounts; and hearing complaints against *mütevelli*s and deciding whether to confirm their continued tenure of office or recommend their replacement.[96] These responsibilities were more or less the same as those discharged by the *shaykh al-mashāyikh* of Damascus. The difference of greatest moment was that in Damascus the office was hereditary and held by the 'Ajlānī family of *ashrāf*, whereas the Seres *kâhyalar başı* was elected by the heads of the guilds. That the institution existed in Seres constitutes still further evidence of the wider autonomy of its guilds.

SUMMARY

The autonomy of the Seres guilds is the exception that proves the rule – of the great degree of the Turkish guilds' attachment to, and dependence on, the Government which we found in all the guilds outside of Seres, and particularly in Istanbul. We have discovered close links between most of the offices and councils of the guilds and the Government: the selection of the *yiğ-it başı* required the Government's approval, and the authorities appointed the *lonca* as well as the *kethüda*. This feature undoubtedly goes beyond the guilds, since Ottoman urban society was noticeably wanting in autonomous nuclei of local and independent governance and administration, a lack which delayed its development and impeded its modernization.

A second feature that is reflected in the fabric of the Turkish guilds and has larger significance for Ottoman social history is the absence of a rigid hierarchy. There are parallels to this in other areas of Ottoman society. In the guilds, it was manifested in the fluidity and fluctuation of the number of ranks in all guilds and during all periods; in the possibility of moving from one rank to another without examination, without preparing a masterpiece, and, in most guilds, without special ceremonies; and in the *élite* which was paramount in guild relations with the Government as well as in other important matters, being an informal group, free from stern limitations, composed of notables and elders of the guild. One of the social consequences of this state of things was the absence of organization along class lines within the guild and of a class struggle between guild strata and ranks.

There was additional significance in the fact that graduation from one rank to the next did not involve an examination requiring certain professional achievements. We saw that the role of the guild in vocational training, in elementary education and in cultivating good character was marginal. Its functions were, first and foremost, administrative and economic, and its social and cultural part was secondary. This situation is assuredly bound up with the strong connection of the guilds with the Government and the fewness of their ties with primarily social, educational and ideological organizations, such as the Sufi orders. There were certain guilds which fostered the social and ideological aspect. The tanners, the barbers and the Seres guilds preserved such *fütüvvet* traditions as the ceremonies of transition from one rank to another, the titles of guild heads and the maintenance of supplementary offices reminscent of the descriptions in the *fütüvvet* books. But these guilds were the minority, and for most of the guilds the ideological-traditional framework had no consequence. The reason for this, it would seem, is that the all-embracing system of the guilds developed after the decline of the *fütüvvet* assocations, under the aegis of the Government and in a close nexus with it.

NOTES

1. For our definition see above, Chapter 1.
2. Descriptions of such hierarchies were based mainly on H. Thorning, *Beiträge zur Kenntnis des islamischen Vereinswesens*, Berlin, 1913.
3. See the firman to the carpenters of 1726/7 and the summary of firmans to other guilds in: Osman Nuri, *Mecelle-i umur-u belediye*, I, Istanbul 1922, p. 559. For a firman to the lead-workers of 1703 see Ahmet Refik, *Hicrî on ikinci asırda Istanbul hayatı*, Istanbul 1930, pp. 36–7 (Refik, XII in later references).
4. C. White, *Three Years in Constantinople*, I–III, London 1845, III, p. 148; Nuri, p. 613.
5. See above, Chapter 1, pp. 166–7.
6. Nuri, pp. 613–614.
7. Ibid., pp. 614–616.
8. Ibid., p. 558.
9. H. A. R. Gibb & H. Bowen, *Islamic Society and the West*, Vol. I, Part 1, London 1959, pp. 281–282.
10. Nuri, pp. 707–708.
11. Ibid., p. 558.
12. Refik, XII, p. 155; Ahmet Refik, *Hicrî on üçüncü asırda Istanbul hayatı*, Istanbul 1932, pp. 232–234 (Refik, XIII in later references).
13. Nuri, pp. 519, 582, 584.
14. Ibid., p. 658: '. . . ve mühnal olan gedikler esnaftin çırak ve kalfalarına verilmesi . . .' Cf. above, Chapter 2, pp. 183–5.
15. G. Baer, *Egyptian Guilds in Modern Times*, Jerusalem 1964, pp. 58–62.
16. Although the bronze and brass workers' guild complained to the kadi in 996 (1588) that soldiers were intervening in guild affairs and inciting the apprentices to revolt (Nuri, pp. 622–623), this appears to have been an isolated incident in Turkey. In Damascus, on the other hand, the *ṣunnāʿ* appear to have organized and rebelled fairly often. See E. Qoudsî, 'Notice

sur les corporations de Damas', *Actes du sixième Congrès International des Orientalistes*, Vol. II, Sect. 1, Sémitique, Leiden 1885, p. 15.
17. Nuri, p. 580.
18. For details on this ceremony according to the *fütüvvet* books see Nuri, pp. 524, 526–529; cf., Baer, *Egyptian Guilds*, pp. 50–52; H. Thorning, *Beiträge zur Kenntnis des islamischen Vereinswesens, passim*.
19. Nuri, p. 537; F. Taeschner, 'Das Zunftwesen in der Türkei', *Leipziger Vierteljahrsschrift für Südosteuropa*, V (1941), pp. 183–184.
20. *Fütüvvetname-i kebir*, by Sayyid Mehmed b. Sayyid 'Alā' al-Dīn al-Hüseynī al-Raḍawī, of 931 (1524), cited by Nuri, pp. 528–529. In some of the guilds it was customary to present the new *kalfa* with the tools of his trade; for example, the carpenters were presented with a saw, hammer and drill, and the weavers given a shuttle.
21. Nuri, p. 708. On the uniqueness of the functions of the tanners' guild and the Seres guilds see above, Chapter 1, pp. 164–7.
22. These dishes were hired out by the guilds for parties, and the fees for their hire were an important source of income for a guild's mutual aid funds. See above, p. 163.
23. E. W. Lane, *The Manners and Customs of the Modern Egyptians*, London 1944, Everyman's Library, pp. 515–516.
24. Nuri, pp. 557–558, 582, 584, 708–709, etc.
25. Ibid., pp. 559, 656, 658; for details, see above, p. 184.
26. Cf., with regard to Seres, Nuri, pp. 708–709; and with regard to the tanners, Taeschner, 'Zunftwesen', p. 183.
27. Nuri, pp. 558–559, 657.
28. See the firman of 981 (1573/4) cited in: Ahmet Refik, *Onuncu asr-ı hicrîde Istanbul hayatı*, Istanbul 1333, pp. 89–90 (Refik, X in later references).
29. H. Schurtz, 'Turkische Basare und Zünfte', *Zeitschrift für Social-wissenschaft*, VI (1903), pp. 704–705. In Egypt, this custom existed in several craft guilds which required special expertise; see Baer, *Egyptian Guilds*, pp. 64–65.
30. For details on these matters see above, Chapter 1.
31. Nuri, pp. 529–530; Evliya Çelebi, *Seyahatname*, I, Istanbul 1314, pp. 495–497, and in the English translation: Evliya Efendi, *Narrative of Travels in Europe, Asia and Africa in the Seventeenth Century*, transl. J. von Hammer, Vol. I, Part 2, London 1846, pp. 94–95. Evliya claims that he is describing a ceremony in which he himself took part.
32. A detailed discussion of this problem can be found in G. Baer, 'Guilds in Middle Eastern History', in M. A. Cook, *Studies in the Economic History of the Middle East*, London 1970, particularly pp. 28–29.
33. Nuri, pp. 709–711.
34. Ibid., p. 578; cf. Gibb & Bowen, p. 284, n. 6.
35. Nuri, pp. 558, 576, 559, 578, 302, 574. For the different Arabic terms for this group in Egypt, see Baer, *Egyptian Guilds*, pp. 53, 65–66.
36. Nuri, pp. 302–303, 559, 576–577.
37. Evliya, pp. 526, 545, 579, 592, 598, 607, 617; in von Hammer's translation pp. 114, 128, 194, 204, 209, 217, 223.
38. The term does not appear in the firmans reproduced by Nuri, and Mantran,

who perused the archives dealing with the seventeenth century, states clearly that he did not find it. See R. Mantran, *Istanbul dans la seconde moitié du XVIIe siècle*, Paris 1962, p. 372, n. 1.

39. Nuri, pp. 525, 575. The *yiğit başı*, and not the *kâhya*, as erroneously claimed by Gibb and Bowen, p. 284, n. 7.
40. Baer, *Egyptian Guilds*, p. 68.
41. Evliya, pp. 617, 632; in von Hammer's translation pp. 223, 233.
42. A document of 1210 (1795/6); Nuri, p. 563.
43. Cf. Baer, *Egyptian Guilds*, pp. 3, 49 ff., 63 and note.
44. Nuri, p. 693. The term is used here in its Persian form, *du'āgū*.
45. Cf. Baer, *Egyptian Guilds*, p. 57. On the manuscript see ibid., pp. 2–3.
46. Evliya, pp. 527, 545, 563, 579, 592, 598, 607, 632; in von Hammer's translation pp. 114, 128, 163, 194, 204, 217, 233.
47. Nuri, pp. 563–564, 574. Mantran is not exact in claiming (p. 372, n. 2) that Nuri does not provide the sources of his information about the *çavuş*; he mentions the *Fütüvvetname*, Evliya, and the document about the barbers' guild cited above, n. 42.
48. White, I, p. 202.
49. Evliya notes the existence of a *çavuş* in Egyptian guilds in the tenth volume of his travel journal, but it is possible that he brought this term with him from Turkey. Cf. Baer, *Egyptian Guilds*, p. 156.
50. Qoudsî, pp. 14–15.
51. Nuri, p. 574.
52. I have not found any substantiation of Gibb and Bowen's contention to the contrary (p. 285).
53. Nuri, p. 574; G. Young, *Corps de droit ottoman*, Oxford 1905–1906, IV, p. 32.
54. Nuri, pp. 574, 585; on the question of the religious community of the guild heads and members see above, Chapter 2.
55. Mantran, p. 376, n. 2.
56. Nuri, p. 563.
57. White, I, p. 52; II, pp. 228, 254; III, pp. 148–149, 324–325.
58. Nuri, p. 681. *Mukhtār* and *wakīl* were also the terms used to denote the assistant to the head of the guild in nineteenth-century Egypt. See Baer, *Egyptian Guilds*, pp. 67–68.
59. Nuri, pp. 576–577. On the etymology of the term see Gibb and Bowen, p. 285. In some merchant guilds the meeting-place was called *tacirhane*. See Nuri, pp. 669–670.
60. Nuri, p. 575; Gibb & Bowen, p. 285.
61. Nuri, pp. 552–556, 613–614; Gibb & Bowen, p. 286; cf. Baer, *Egyptian Guilds*, pp. 125–126; and above, Chapter 1, pp. 166–7.
62. Nuri, pp. 576–577, 692, 694–696, 708; Taeschner, 'Zunftwesen', p. 184.
63. White, II, pp. 228, 254; Young, IV, p. 32; Nuri, pp. 694–695; Schurtz, pp. 704–705.
64. Nuri, pp. 576–577.
65. Ibid., pp. 694–696.
66. Ibid., pp. 576, 638, 694, 696–697; Young, V, p. 288.
67. Baer, *Egyptian Guilds*, pp. 65–66, 68–69.

68. Nuri, pp. 560, 561, 575.
69. Cf. Baer, *Egyptian Guilds*, p. 14.
70. Refik, X, pp. 168–169, 170–171.
71. Nuri, p. 563.
72. White, II, p. 158.
73. Refik, XII, p. 9 (document of 1692); Nuri, p. 549 (document of 1726).
74. See F. Taeschner, 'Akhī Baba', *Encyclopaedia of Islam*², I, pp. 323–324.
75. Nuri, p. 692.
76. Cf. Baer, *Egyptian Guilds*, pp. 2–3, 55.
77. Nuri, p. 694.
78. Ibid., pp. 564–565, 692; for details on the election procedure in Seres in the nineteenth century, see pp. 694–695.
79. Ibid., pp. 549, 565–566.
80. Young, IV, p. 32.
81. Nuri, pp. 568–569.
82. See, for example, the firman to the *kaymakam* and the kadi of Istanbul, dated 1716: Refik, XII, pp. 54–56.
83. Nuri, pp. 569–570.
84. Ibid., pp. 566–567, 568–569, 692; Young, V, pp. 288–289, § 1.
85. Cf. Baer, *Egyptian Guilds*, pp. 12, 69–72.
86. Qoudsî, pp. 13–14; cf. Baer, *Egyptian Guilds*, p. 72, n. 102.
87. A detailed discussion on this subject can be found in Baer, 'Guilds in Middle Eastern History'.
88. Nuri, pp. 564, 573, 594; Young, V, p. 288.
89. Nuri, p. 570; Gibb & Bowen, p. 289.
90. Ṛefik, X, pp. 178–179, 180–181; Ahmet Refik, *Hicrî on birinci asırda Istanbul hayatı*, Istanbul 1931, p. 55; Mantran, p. 374.
91. Nuri, pp. 567, 568, 577–578, 584–586.
92. White, II, p. 254.
93. Nuri, p. 574. The religious affiliation of the *kethüda* mentioned in the *sicil* of the Istanbul kadi of 1806 is not completely clear (p. 576).
94. See Chapter 2, pp. 181–2.
95. Qoudsî, pp. 10 ff; cf. Baer, *Egyptian Guilds*, p. 11, n. 44; pp. 22–23.
96. Nuri, pp. 697–698.

4

OTTOMAN GUILDS – A REASSESSMENT

Since the time I published a book on Egyptian guilds, three articles on Turkish guilds and two studies on guilds in Middle Eastern history in general,[1] a number of new studies on Ottoman guilds have been written. Among those, one should mention in particular Professor Inalcik's writings based on the study of fifteenth century Bursa, the dissertation of my student, Haim Gerber on Bursa in the seventeenth century, André Raymond's monumental work on the merchants and artisans of Cairo in the eighteenth century, and an article by Abdul Karim Rafeq on the Damascus guilds in the early eighteenth century. In addition, I have had regard to material published in two recent Turkish studies, by Neşet Çağatay and Özer Ergenç.[2] In the following, I shall try to examine the results of a comparison of all these writings and to reassess the characteristic traits of Turkish guilds and my own conclusions in view of subsequent research.

Before going into details, it seems to be necessary to define again what a guild is. Our discussion becomes meaningless if 'guild' is taken to be just another name for merchants and artisans, or if it is considered to be any organisation in which artisans or merchants participate, whatever its character, social, religious, or political. As a separate category, the term 'guild' is justified only if it is used for a body organized according to professional criteria, and not any other ones, fulfilling economic, social and administrative functions by means of specific officers or a hierarchy of functionaries. Unfortunately, we still do not know where and when merchants or craftsmen of the Ottoman Empire began to organize in professional groups. Franz Taeschner has shown that though the young men of the *Akhi* movement were recruited mainly among the craftsmen, the association as such was non-professional.[3] At some time, the *akhi* movement fused with the beginnings of a guild system in which *akhi* and *futuwwa* traditions survived. As Inalcik has put it: 'In the cities, each group of craftsmen was organized, according to futuwwa principles, under the leadership of an *akhi* whom they chose from their own ranks.'[4] But where the professional organization originated is not yet clear. In Egypt and Syria, in any case, it did not exist prior to the Ottoman conquest, in Mamluk times, as I. Lapidus has shown in his study of late medieval cities in this area.[5] Therefore, I would not interpret the polemic in the Egyptian guild literature against the Ottomans as showing a decline in the guild system or 'an unfavourable attitude of the Ottomans towards the guild system'.[6] The opposite may be nearer the truth. What the authors of the seventeenth century treatise of the Egyptian guild of barbers deplored was not a deterioration of the guild system, but of the conceptual framework, the *futuwwa* ideology. They also resented Ottoman control of the guilds.

The guild system itself must, in fact, have developed in the opposite direction, since by the seventeenth century it encompassed, in Istanbul and Cairo, the entire gainfully employed urban population except the military and the *'ulamā'*. Recent research, however, has shown that this was not necessarily the situation in all other towns. For eighteenth century Damascus Rafeq has found a rather widespread ramification of the system, including as it did, in addition to artisans, all kinds of merchants as well as people engaged in services.[7] In early seventeenth century Ankara, the guild system was not as comprehensive as that, though it included, in addition to artisans and merchants, a guild of pedlars and about five guilds of people engaged in services, among them mule drivers.[8] But in fifteenth century Bursa guilds apparently existed only in a restricted number of traditional crafts, and even in seventeenth century Bursa, labourers did not belong to the guilds, and there were neither guilds of itinerant pedlars nor of merchants engaged in international commerce (such merchants had a guild-like organization in Cairo with functions like those of a guild but headed by a *shahbandar*, not a shaykh, who had much more authority than regular guild shaykhs).[9] Moreover, there were industries without guild organizations, such as domestic industries or some industries regularly supplying the state with materials in bulk,[10] and there were also a number of towns in which scholars who studied them have not found any traces of a guild organization.[11] It would seem, therefore, that considerable differences existed between Ottoman guild systems in different periods and different areas and towns, and one should not make the mistake of generalizing on the basis of findings for a specific town or a specific period. By and large, the system was more comprehensive in the big centres of government, Istanbul and Cairo, than in smaller towns, apparently for administrative and fiscal rather than economic reasons.

A similar distinction must be made in answering the question whether the performance of a profession and membership in a guild was free or restricted. In contrast with other places of the Ottoman Empire, Gerber found a rather free system in seventeenth century Bursa. He found a large number of shop transactions recorded in the *sicill*, where no mention is made that such transactions were subject to a guild's acquiescence. The term *gedik* was not in use in Bursa at that time, and *gedik*-like arrangements were very rare. Gerber found only two examples of limitation of the number of shops that could be opened in a specific branch of business. Moreover, artisans were very often accepted as members of a guild if they just proved that they were practising the craft.[12] Nevertheless, even in the freer system of Bursa, nobody could open a shop without having served for a number of years with a master craftsman.[13] And for other places, the principle of a closed shop as an integral part of the guild system has been reconfirmed: Raymond found that *gediks* were common and usual items in the estates left by Cairo merchants and artisans at their death,[14] and in Damascus, apprenticeship within a guild was a necessary condition for anybody who wanted to practise the craft, and he was allowed to do so only in places prescribed by the guild.[15]

Professor Inalcik is perfectly right in asserting that it is an exaggeration to say that the state created the Ottoman guilds.[16] The question whether the state controlled the Ottoman guilds is more complicated, and it is worth our while to examine it in short in view of both old and new material. It would seem that the autonomy *vis à vis* the government of the Bursa guilds, which served as the basis of Inalcik's study, was greater than anywhere else. This indeed is Gerber's conclusion, who also studied Bursa: 'The finding of this study is that this measure of autonomy in Bursa was much larger than in other places, as detected in former guild studies.'[17] This is reflected in guild agreements and regulations, which were of the nature of free contracts recorded in the *sicill* for notarial purposes only. Witnesses were summoned as evidence that these agreements were old usages, which shows not only that the regulations did not emanate from the government but that they were not even known to it. The *qāḍī* would confirm every regulation acceptable to the guild. Thus guild agreements were not given legality by the court, but merely ratified in a notarial fashion.[18]

So far, so good. But even in such an autonomous guild system as that which existed in Bursa, the *qāḍī* had more to say in guild affairs than just register their agreements. First, a guild would bring to court cases of infringement of its monopoly, and the *qāḍī* would pronounce judgement in such cases.[19] Exactly the same was the situation in another town at least as famous for its guilds' autonomy as Bursa, namely Damascus. There the *qāḍī* sometimes had recourse to *fatwā*s to support his view if he did not favour the monopolization of a craft by a certain guild.[20] Similarly, 'if a group working in a specialized branch of a craft became sufficiently large, they chose a kethüdâ and appeared before the kâdî to inform him that they wished to become a guild. The main guilds often opposed this, refusing to recognize the elected kethüdâ and claiming the new guild's master to be unqualified. In such a case, the government's approval was essential for the establishment of the guild'.[21] In other words, even in Bursa, the guild's autonomy depended on whether there was agreement among its members, and it was infringed when they disagreed. Moreover, offenders against guild regulations were generally punished by the state authorities.[22] Several of the Bursa guild regulations specified this explicitly, and even those quoted by Gerber as examples of the opposite do not really say that the guild itself was to punish the offenders but only that they be punished according to the guild's usage or view, which does not mean that the punishment might not be meted out by official authorities.[23] It was only in Damascus and Seres, as well as among guilds with long traditions and privileges, that guild shaykhs, *kethüda*s or *Ahi Baba*s punished offenders or criminals, for instance the Istanbul and Cairo shoemakers or the Kırşehir tanners.[24]

The free election of a guild's *kethüda*, the right of the guild's members to remove a *kethüda* and their resistance to government interference in the election of a new one has been adduced as another proof of the guilds' autonomy *vis à vis* the government.[25] The appointment was made in court, but in seventeenth century Bursa always on the initiative of guild members; in many cases the *qāḍī* did not even know that a guild was temporarily without a *kethüda*. Therefore Gerber considers the nomination by the *qāḍī* to have been a mere formality.[26] Though in the course of time, *kethüda*s usually received a diploma from the governor or the sultan on their election, the mode of election did not change.[27] The same was true for Damascus, though in view of Rafeq's study of the Damascus *sicill*, one has to correct slightly Qudsī's account stating that the election of a guild's shaykh had to be approved by the *shaykh al-mashaykh*, but did not require the approval of the Ottoman authorities.[28] Rafeq now tells us that a shaykh had to be confirmed by the Grand Ḥanafī *qāḍī*.[29] Moreover, if there were more than one candidate for the post, not only the *qāḍīs'* confirmation, but even the decision of the governor of Damascus would become important.[30] In Egypt, too, throughout the centuries, the shaykh of a guild was elected by the guild's members and then officially appointed by the *qāḍī* or other representatives of the authorities. But there as elsewhere the measure of decisiveness of the authorities' nomination differed from one situation to another.[31] As long as members of the guild agreed among themselves, did not engage in subversive activities, and the guild performed the functions in which the government was interested, the authorities did not mind who was elected as the guild's head. After all, only a shaykh or *kethüda* acknowledged by the guild could guarantee the satisfactory performance of these functions. But even for Bursa, it has been stated that, in the last analysis, the guilds enjoyed whatever authority the central government allowed them, either through lack of interest or inefficiency, and in Ankara, in the early seventeenth century, the guilds, according to Ergenç, were under the tight control of the state.[32]

Another aspect of the relation between the guilds and the authorities was the control of the quality of products, the supervision of weights and measures and the fixing of prices. Most of the new studies confirm our earlier conclusion that instructions in these spheres were issued by the government. No new material on the guilds' task to supervise the implementation of quality control in Turkey and Syria has been published, but as in Istanbul and Cairo, prices in Ankara too were fixed after consultation with the guilds' notables.[33] Of particular interest in this respect are the detailed instructions issued early in the seventeenth century and reproduced in Cağatay's book on the Akhīs and the guilds.[34] However, the study of the Bursa *sicill* of the seventeenth century yielded completely different results. They showed that in seventeenth century Bursa, production standards were not handed down by the government, but were set by the guilds to prevent too much competition. For the same purpose, some guilds tried to enforce minimum prices for their products. All this is connected with the economic *raison d'être* of the Bursa guilds, to which we shall return later on.

The most important link, however, between the guilds and government was the guilds' fiscal function. Recent studies not only confirm our earlier findings on this link, but even accentuate them. Inalcik says that the state intervened in the guild organization mainly to guarantee tax revenues from this source, and goes on to illustrate this statement.[35] Gerber even tries to show that, in seventeenth century Bursa, guild membership was attained by paying a certain tax and that the tax problem was crucial for the whole system.[36] Moreover, our earlier impression that the fiscal function of the Syrian guilds was secondary must be corrected in view of the material from the Damascus *sicill*, which abundantly shows the important role the guilds played in collecting the taxes and distributing them among their members.[37]

The important place taxation occupied in the functioning of the guild system is also shown by the fact that for this purpose all guilds in Bursa were grouped around some twenty or thirty guilds, referred to as main guilds, while each of the smaller guilds, referred to as *yamak* (helper)-guilds, contributed their share to the sum imposed as a tax on the main one. *Yamak* relations were based on various principles and considerably influenced the structure and working of the guild system in seventeenth century Bursa.[38] In some cases, such as the early Bursa silk industry, *yamak*-relations seem to have originated in the position of entrepreneurship of certain guilds which were able to reduce others to a dependent status.[40] But in seventeenth century Bursa, this kind of relation was not any longer the predominant basis for *yamak*-connections. In addition to *yamak*-connections, some of the Damascus guilds were also grouped under official heads of certain categories of professions, such as the *qaṣṣāb-bāshi* or the *mi'mār-bāshi*,[41] not unlike the Cairo structure where no *yamak*-relations existed.[42]

Though most of the recent studies mention the problem of guild and religious or ethnic community, the picture has not become more decided than it was before. According to one author, the early guilds of Istanbul, Bursa and Edirne were separated according to religious community, Christian and Jewish guilds having their own *kethüda*s and *yiğitbaşı*s.[43] But guilds of seventeenth century Bursa were not, on the whole, separated according to religious community, with the exception of three exclusively Jewish guilds.[44] In Damascus of the early eighteenth century, there were both mixed guilds and guilds whose members belonged predominantly to one community. Shaykhs, however, were all Muslim.[45] Concerning Cairo, Raymond disagrees with an earlier conclusion of mine, namely that with few exceptions, members of a guild belonged to the same religious or ethnic community. He found that most guilds were mixed, with Muslim shaykhs. This he explains by the basically administrative character of the guilds, which had lost their ideological superstructure. Only in the nineteenth century, when the position of Christians improved under Mehmed 'Alī, did the number of separate guilds grow. However, non-Egyptian Muslim ethnic groups, such as Turks, Nubians, or Mahgribis, had their own guilds.[46] Since it is totally impossible to arrive at any quantitative estimate, let alone exact calculation, the differences seem to be mainly a question of emphasis.

An important contribution to our knowledge of guild history is comprised in H. Inalcik's account of social differentiation in the guilds of fifteenth century Bursa. At that time in many of the guilds of large Ottoman cities, such as Istanbul, Bursa, Salonika, or Edirne, there was a growing social and economic distinction between guild members who became capitalist entrepreneurs and those whom they employed. However, the Ottoman government's strong support of the traditional guild structure prevented the development of separate organizations for workers and foremen, and for capitalist masters, as in Europe.[47] Whether this was the reason, or other trends of economic development, the result was that from the seventeenth century onwards, Ottoman guilds lacked a rigid hierarchy; it was relatively easy to move from one rank to another; the élite of the guild was an informal group and any organization along class lines within the guild and of a class struggle between guild strata and ranks was absent.[48] One aspect of this lack of class differentiation within the Ottoman guilds has been reconfirmed in one of the recent studies. Writing about the Egyptian guilds 13 years ago, I said the following: 'There were of course differences among the shaykhs of guilds in the different occupations: while the shaykh of cloth-merchants or slave-dealers was probably a rich man, the shaykh of the donkey-drivers or porters was not. But the economic position of the shaykh was determined rather by that of the occupation of his guild members than by the fact that he was a shaykh. Generally speaking, the mercantile guilds and their shaykhs were probably the richest.'[49] This has now been statistically proved by Raymond's analysis of the documents of inheritance in Cairo's *sharīʿa* court. He not only found that artisans were poorer than merchants, but also that the average inheritance of a guild shaykh was not higher than that of other members of the guild.[50]

An appropriate conclusion of this short reassessment may be a discussion of the *raison d'être* of Ottoman guilds. In particular, the two studies which are based on material concerning Bursa include important ideas about the basic economic function of the early guild system. First, guild representatives bought raw material at a fixed wholesale price and distributed it to the masters, because this material was available only in limited quantities. The aim was to prevent it from falling into the hands of other parties or profiteers, and to distribute it in a way which left none of the guild masters unemployed. Studies based on Bursa agree that this was the main function of the guilds, so much so that a *kethüda* was often appointed specifically for this purpose.[51] Secondly, since there was a similar shortage of workmen, especially of highly skilled craftsmen, the guild officers also controlled the distribution of manpower. Finally, the market also was limited, and with only a limited amount of raw material available and a limited market, it was necessary to restrict the number of shops and workshops and to protect the market from outsiders. The state, therefore, granted each guild a monopoly within a clearly defined area, and the guilds prevented competition by fixing well-defined standards.[52] In Gerber's view, these monopolistic and restrictive practices were aimed primarily at ensuring equality among members and thereby their economic independence. Inequality would have deprived some members of their property and turned them into wage labourers. Thus guild regulations were intended to serve the interests of the less efficient majority.[53]

There seems to have been an essential difference between this system of industrial and commercial Bursa and the guild systems which became prevalent in the great administrative centres of the Ottoman Empire, such as Istanbul and Cairo. The buying of raw material is not mentioned at all among the functions of Egyptian guilds, and only very rarely in Damascus.[54] Instructions concerning the quality of products, weights and measures and fixing of prices were issued by the government, not by the guilds, according to all studies except those concerning Bursa. Moreover, a considerable proportion of guilds and their members consisted of people engaged in transport and services, or in branches for which the economic functions of the Bursa guild system would not have been relevant. Finally, studies of the *sicill*s of Cairo, Damascus, and Istanbul, as well as other sources, show that the principal functions of the guilds in these towns were to serve the government as an administrative link, to collect taxes (except in Istanbul prior to the nineteenth century), and to supply labour and services to the government. To keep order and stability and to secure the payment of taxes or supply of manpower, the government had to rely on existing units of the society headed by leaders to whom their followers would be loyal.[55] It may well be that for this purpose the Ottoman state used early loose, free and spontaneous beginnings of guild organizations and moulded them later into an all-embracing elaborate system.

NOTES

1. G. Baer, *Egyptian Guilds in Modern Times*. Jerusalem, 1964; 'The structure of Turkish guilds and its significance for Ottoman social history', *Proceedings of the Israel Academy of Sciences and Humanities*, vol. 4, 1970, pp. 176–196; in Turkish in *Tarih Araştırmaları Dergisi*, Cilt VIII–XII, 1970–1974, pp. 99–119 (see Ch. 3 above); 'Monopolies and restrictive practices of Turkish guilds', *Journal of the Economic and Social History of the Orient*, vol. 13, 1970, pp. 145–165 (see Ch. 2 above); 'The administrative, economic and social functions of Turkish guilds', *International Journal of Middle East Studies*, vol. 1, January 1970, pp. 28–50 (see Ch. 1 above); 'Guilds in Middle Eastern History', in M. A. Cook (ed.), *Studies in the Economic History of the Middle East*. London, 1970, pp. 11–30; 'The organization of labour', in *Handbuch der Orientalistik: Wirtschaftsgeschichte* (in press).
2. H. Inalcik, *The Ottoman Empire: the classical age 1300–1600*. London, 1973, pp. 151–162; H. Gerber, *The Anatolian City of Bursa in the Seventeenth Century: Economy and Society*. Unpublished Ph.D. thesis, Hebrew University of Jerusalem, 1976 (in Hebrew), Ch. 3: The guilds. Published in English as 'Guilds in Seventeenth-Century Anatolian Bursa', *Asian and African Studies*, vol. 11, Summer 1976, pp. 59–86; N. Çağatay, *Bir Türk kurumu olan Ahilik*. Ankara, 1974, pp. 111–156. Özer Ergenç, '1600–1615 yılları arasında Ankara iktisadi tarihine ait araştırmalar', in Osman Okyar (ed.), *Türkiye iktisat Tarihi Semineri* (1973), Hacettepe Universitesi, Ankara, 1975, pp. 145–168; A. Raymond, *Artisans et commerçants au Caire au XVIIIe siècle*, vol. 2, Damascus, 1974; A-K. Rafeq, 'The Law Court Registers of Damascus, with special reference to craft corporations during the first half of the eighteenth century', in J.

Berque et D. Chevallier (ed.), *Les Arabes par leurs archives (XVIe–XXe siècles)*, Paris, 1976, pp. 141–159.
3. Fr. Taeschner, 'Akhi', *EI*^{2}, vol. 1, pp. 321–3.
4. Inalcik, pp. 151–2.
5. I. M. Lapidus, *Muslim Cities in the Later Middle Ages*, Cambridge, Mass., 1967, pp. 96, 98, 101.
6. Raymond, p. 543.
7. Rafeq, p. 147.
8. Ergenç, p. 151.
9. Gerber, p. 63; Raymond, pp. 578–82.
10. Inalcik, pp. 159–60.
11. For instance, Prof. A. Cohen's Studies of Jerusalem in the 16th Century, or Professor R. Jennings' studies of Kayseri in the 17th century.
12. Gerber, pp. 63–4, 78.
13. Ibid., p. 67.
14. Raymond, pp. 549–50.
15. Rafeq, p. 153.
16. Inalcik, p. 152. Though I am given as reference for such a statement, I do not recollect ever having made it. Anyway, it is not included in the quoted article.
17. Gerber, p. 86.
18. Ibid., pp. 69–71.
19. Ibid., p. 75.
20. Rafeq, p. 155.
21. Inalcik, p. 159.
22. Ibid., p. 155.
23. Gerber, pp. 82–3.
24. For Damascus, see Ilyās Qudsī, 'Nubdha ta'rīkhiyya fī'l-ḥiraf al-dimashqiyya' ('Notice sur les corporations de Damas'), *Actes du sixième Congrès International des Orientalistes*, Deuxième partie, Section I: *Sémitique*, Leiden, 1885, p. 13. For Seres, the shoemakers and tanners, see sources quoted above, Ch. 1, p. 162.
25. Inalcik, p. 152.
26. Gerber, pp. 66–7. See also p. 75.
27. Inalcik, p. 155.
28. Cf. above, ch. 3, pp. 204–5.
29. Rafeq, p. 150.
30. Ibid., p. 149.
31. See Baer, *Egyptian Guilds*, pp. 12, 13, 56, 69–71.
32. Gerber, p. 86; Ergenç, p. 151.
33. Inalcik, p. 154; Rafeq, p. 148; Raymond, pp. 565, 566–7; Ergenç, pp. 151, 155.
34. Çağatay, pp. 113–19.
35. Inalcik, pp. 153–5.
36. Gerber, pp. 61–3; 71 ff.
37. Rafeq, pp. 153–5; cf. Baer, 'Guilds in Middle Eastern History', pp. 21–2.
38. Gerber, pp. 61–2, 71–3.
40. Inalcik, p. 159.

41. Rafeq, pp. 154; 150–1.
42. This has now been confirmed by Raymond's study of the Cairo *sicill* (pp. 519–20). Cf. Baer, *Egyptian Guilds*, pp. 42–4.
43. M. Akdağ, *Türkiye'nin iktisadî ve ictimaî tarihi*, cilt 2, 1453–1559, Istanbul, 1974, p. 31.
44. Gerber, pp. 83–4.
45. Rafeq, p. 148.
46. Raymond, pp. 523–6.
47. Inalcik, pp. 157–8.
48. Cf. above, ch. 3, especially pp. 207–8.
49. Baer, *Egyptian Guilds*, p. 74. I never said, of course, that Ottoman guilds formed a socially undifferentiated community (Inalcik, p. 152).
50. Raymond, pp. 237, 556.
51. Inalcik, p. 156; Gerber, pp. 74–7. See also Ergenç, pp. 151–2, 154, for early 17th century Ankara.
52. Inalcik, pp. 156–7.
53. Gerber, pp. 84–5.
54. Rafeq, p. 154.
55. Cf. Inalcik, p. 155.

Part Four

URBAN AND RURAL REVOLT

1

POPULAR REVOLT IN OTTOMAN CAIRO

Popular unrest was a rather frequent occurrence in Ottoman Cairo, and various aspects of it have been discussed in studies on Ottoman Egypt published in recent years.[1] In this study it is our aim to analyse this phenomenon systematically and to re-examine some conclusions of former studies.

The first question to be asked is of course: who are the 'popular' elements of Ottoman Cairo whose unrest or revolt we are studying? Evidently, one must exclude the political and economic elite of that time against whom revolt was directed: not only the Ottoman and Mamluk bureaucratic and military establishment, but also indigenous rich merchants (*tujjār*) who had established family ties and other relations with the Ottomans and Mamluks. This elite was no strictly defined class but rather an informal and amorphous group, designated in the sources by such terms as *akābir* (grandees), *a'yān* (notables) etc. In addition, one must exclude the retainers of these grandees and the military, both Ottoman and Mamluk, as long as the soldiers did not mix with the Cairo artisan and merchant class.

Apart from the elite and the military establishment, Cairo's population was composed of three major groups. First, there were the artisans and small merchants, the owners of shops, workshops or stores, called by Jabartī *arbāb al-ḥiraf wa'l-ṣanā'i'* or *ahl al-aswāq*. Secondly, there were people without capital (except, perhaps, beasts of burden) engaged in occupations yielding low incomes or involving dirty or immoral work. According to various lists, this group of people of low social status included street vendors and hawkers of all kinds; cooks and sellers of various dishes in the streets; scavengers, blacksmiths and water-carriers; donkey-drivers, camel-drivers, porters and ferrymen; servants and runners of various kinds; entertainers of all sorts; beggars, dervishes and soothsayers; prostitutes and panders; and finally vagabonds, rogues and pickpockets.[2] These people were called by contemporary authors *al-'āmma* or *al-sūqa*, but frequently terms used to designate them explicitly define their low social status, as e.g. *ahl-al-ḥiraf al-sāfila, arbāb al-ḥiraf al-danī'a, al-nās al-dūn* etc.,[3] or imply their moral inferiority.[4] Jabartī also makes it clear, that most of them live in the suburbs, *al-ḥārāt al-barrāniyya*, specifically in al-'Uṭūf, al-Ḥusayniyya, Kafr al-Zaghārī, al-Ṭammā'īn, al-Qarāfa, al-Rumayla, and al-Ḥaṭṭāba.[5]

The third 'popular' group, the group of dark-skinned slaves, is mentioned only very rarely in contemporary sources. They may be classified into Abyssinians and black slaves from different parts of Africa, male and female. Abyssinian (primarily Galla) girls were preferred to black concubines by Mamluk Amīrs, and the black female slaves were used mainly as servants of upper class women. Black male slaves too were primarily domestic servants and used for coarse work, and only sporadically as soldiers. Some were castrated and served as guards for the harems and their inmates. Before the nineteenth century apparently black slaves were not used in Egypt in any significant number in agriculture and industry.[6]

A category apart, but an important element of Cairo's population in the Ottoman period, were the *'ulamā'* – persons engaged in teaching, implementing the *sharī'a* or performing the ritual of Islam. However, from the point of view of social status and position they must be divided at least into two different groups. On the one hand there were the leading *shaykhs* of al-Azhar as well as *'ulamā'* of the Bakrī and Sādāt families, who had acquired towards the end of the eighteenth century enormous wealth originating in *waqf* income, control of *awqāf*, rural *iltizām*s, connections with rich merchants and the Mamluk elite, and finally the tremendous support they received from the French occupation.[7] On the other hand, there were the lower religious functionaries, such as *imāms* and *khaṭībs* in the small mosques of various town-quarters, clerks of *sharī'a* courts, *ma'dhūns* (marriage notaries), teachers in *maktabs* (Qur'ān schools) as well as students at al-Azhar. When Jabartī throws together *'al-muta'ammimīn wa'l-'āmma wa'l-aṭfāl'*[8] ('the turbaned, the rabble and the children') he certainly means the lower layers of the *'ulamā'*. Similarly, there existed a sharp contrast between the Naqīb al-Ashrāf, who controlled extensive *waqfs*, and those 'popular' *sharīfs* who in February 1712 rioted in Cairo because one of them had been killed in an affray.[9]

All these distinctions are highly relevant for the discussion of our subject, since these groups did not participate in popular revolt to the same extent and in the same way. To begin with, as far as we know there were no revolts of black slaves in Ottoman Egypt. This was due, in the first place, to the wide dispersion of black slaves among various elements of the local populations. Since they did not work in large conglomerations, such as industrial or other economic enterprises, but each of them was secluded in the family to which he belonged, they had practically no way to organize. Moreover, they considered themselves as part of these families and most of them were much better off than the lower layers of Cairo's 'free' society. Finally, slavery was only transitional, and before long slaves used to be freed. Slave girls married into their masters' families, and freedmen often acquired adequate positions, income and even wealth.

Another group of people who generally did not take part in Cairo's popular revolts were fellāḥīn who had come to town. In the context of these revolts they are mentioned thrice. First, Jabartī says that during the famine riots of 1695 *ahālī al-qurā wa'l-aryāf* had come to Cairo in great numbers, but he does not enumerate them together with the active participants in these riots.[10] Throughout the eighteenth century rural elements were not connected in any way with the numerous revolts in Cairo. They reappeared in October 1798, in the first revolt against the French – but mainly in the form of a rumour. When the revolt was about to collapse, the common people began to

> behave heedlessly. They did and said all kinds of unheard-of things. They fabricated all sorts of lies. It happened that someone would start a lie or invent a falsehood in which they would rejoice without any proof of its validity . . . The one who would relate what he had heard would swear to its truthfulness with all kinds of oaths and people would pass the story on at the top of their voices and the women would utter shrill and quavering cries of joy (*zaghratna*) from the windows. Among these lies were that the Muslims had taken the citadel . . . One of them would exclaim 'The French have perished and died', while another would shout 'they have been killed and have passed away'. A third would exclaim 'The bedouin have arrived with thousands of horsemen'. A fourth would state 'The fallaḥīn have come from the villages and have gathered outside the town from all directions and have killed all the French who were at the garbage dump (*kīmān*) so that not even one miserable specimen remained of them', and other such inventions were spread, people swearing to their truth even to the extent of swearing divorce if they were lying.[11]

Apparently the incitement to *jihād* and the prospect of plunder had brought in fact a few thousand bedouins and fellahs to the outskirts of Cairo, and some may even have penetrated the town, but very soon the French prevented them from joining the rebels. Similarly, there were reports in 1800 that fellahs had come to join the revolt, but no such threats materialized.[12] Finally, when in Ṣafar A. H. 1220 (May 1805) the popular masses of Cairo (*al-'āmma*) assembled and demanded to depose the Ottoman Paşa and appoint Muḥammad 'Alī in his stead, the Turkish Paşa declared that he would not quit his office 'by order of the fellāḥīn' (*bi-amr al-fallāḥīn*).[13] This has led some authors to the erroneous assumption that 'forty thousand fellahin converged upon the Cairo courts in 1805 . . .'[14] However, these people almost certainly were no peasants, but lower-class urban Egyptians called fellāḥīn by the Ottoman Paşa in a derogatory way: Lane says that 'the Turks often apply this term (El-Fellaḥeen) to the Egyptians in general in an abusive sense'.[15] Since contact between Cairo and the countryside seems to have been rather loose and urbanization non-existent in the seventeenth and eighteenth centuries, it is not astonishing to find that fellahs did not participate in Cairo's popular revolts.[16]

As we said, the Ottoman military units were part of the Ottoman establishment in Cairo rather than of the popular masses. In two instances, however, they participated in revolts of Cairo's population. First, in March 1800, when the people of Cairo revolted against the French, both the Turks living in Khān al-Khalīlī and the Janissary soldiers took part in the fighting.[17] This was of course so because the revolt was part of the regular Ottoman military campaign against the French. The second revolt in which Ottoman soldiers (*al-ajnād wa'l-ujaqliyya*) took part was the unrest leading to the rise to power of Muḥammad 'Alī in 1805 – this time because the unrest involved fighting among the different military units.[18] Since most of the members of the *ocaks* had established connections or mixed with the merchants or artisans of Cairo, their position in times of popular unrest must be considered together with these groups.

Artisans and merchants, however, played a passive role rather than an active one in almost all popular revolts which occurred in Ottoman Cairo. As soon as agitation grew, they closed their shops and the markets. In many cases they were required to do so by the rabble. In the riots of 1715–1716, the revolting people roamed through the markets *'wa-kull man ra'ūhu wa-dukkānuhu maftūḥa yaqfilūhā'*. In 1733 the blind Azhar students raided the markets *wa-kull mā marrū bi-dukkān maftūḥ ḍarabū ṣāḥibahu waqafalūhā'*.[19] Jabartī says that in 1786 and 1790 the *'āmma 'intasharū bi'l-aswāq fī ḥāla munkara wa-aghlaqū al-hawānīt'*,[20] or *'mashū ṭawā'if ya'murūn bi-ghalq al-dakākīn'*.[21] In 1795 the Azhar shaykhs *'amarū al-nās bi-ghalq al-aswāq wa'l-ḥawānīt'*.[22] But in another case it is just said that the merchants whose market was near the Azhar mosque closed their shops.[23] When this was the only form of their participation in the revolt, and in most cases it was, it probably resulted from their fear that the shops might be looted and harm be done to their property. Only in one instance, as a reaction against the forced loan which Ismāʿīl Bey intended to levy from Cairo's merchants in Muḥarram 1202 (October 1787), the merchants closed their shops and assembled in the Azhar mosque to induce the shaykhs to defend their cause. However, the active participants in the violent activities of this revolt too were other elements of the population.[24] And even in the 1798 revolt against the French these layers of Egyptian society did not take an active part. 'Si la lie du peuple, quelques grands, et la secte des dévots, avaient signalé leur présence dans la révolte par de lâches atrocités, la classe moyenne s'était montrée à la fois plus prudente et plus humaine . . . Presque tous les Français qui se réfugièrent dans les maisons turques y trouvèrent sécurité complète et franche hospitalité.'[25]

One important element among the active and violent participants in Cairo's revolts were the Azhar students. It is not astonishing that in 1777 the Maghribi students rioted to claim *waqf* income which was denied them by a Mamluk Bey.[26] Again in 1785, poor Azhar students, as well as the blind ones, revolted because they did not receive their rations and their payments.[27] But it was not only the Maghribi and poor students who rioted, nor was their own income and rations the only issue which stirred them. *ʿImyān al-Azhar*, the blind students, conducted the riots of 1733, and *mujāwirū al-Azhar*, Azhar students in general, were active in revolts of the 1780s even when their cause concerned other groups or Cairo's population in general.[28] Later, in 1798 and 1805, the active religious element in the revolts is called by Jabartī *al-mutaʿammimīn*,[29] which may include other 'turbaned' people in addition to the Azhar students, but probably they continued to form the nucleus of this group. After all, revolts of *medrese* students were a widespread phenomenon in other parts of the Ottoman Empire, and, for that matter, have remained – *mutatis mutandis* – an important feature of the Middle East scene to this day.

However, the bulk of the rioters in Ottoman Cairo was made up of the second group, according to the above-mentioned classification, i.e. people without capital and with low incomes, and those engaged in activities with low social status. Again and again the following categories are involved, according to Jabartī's nomenclature: *al-ʿāmma, al-ʿawāmm, al-ghawghāʾ, al-jaʿīdiyya, arādhil al-sūqa, al-awbāsh, al-ḥasharāt, al-ḥarāfīsh.*[30] These general categories included, *inter alia*, three specific groups. The first group consisted of beggars and destitute persons, who were prominent in the famine riots of 1695.[31] The second group were people from the suburbs. Among these the most prominent in Cairo's riots were the inhabitants of the north-eastern Ḥusayniyya quarter who participated actively in many of the revolts, and often instigated them.[32] Apparently they had developed a strong *esprit de corps* created by the leadership of the shaykh of the Bayyūmiyya *ṭarīqa*, whose centre of activity was in the Ḥusayniyya quarter. However, Ḥusayniyya was not the only one of the suburbs which supplied rioters to Cairo, and others mentioned in this context were al-'Uṭūf, al-Qarāfa, al-Rumayla, al-Ḥaṭṭāba, and al-Ṣalība.[33] The following description from Jabartī's original and detailed account of the 1798 revolt is worth quoting:

> The riff-raff gathered, forming discussion circles, and talk and their rancour was stirred up and their hidden fanaticism came to light. They were joined by great crowds of rabble, ruffians, inhabitants of al-'Uṭūf and al-Ḥusayniyya, as well as Maghribīs of al-Faḥḥāmīn and Kafr al-Zaghārī and al-Ṭammā'īn; inhabitants of lodgings and quarters and the like . . . Sayyid Badr al-Maqdisī came accompanied by those mentioned above and those we forgot to mention such as the scoundrels (*ḥasharāt*) of al-Ḥusayniyya and the crooks (*zu'ar*) of the outlying quarters, the inhabitants of the 'Uṭūf quarter as well as others distinguished by their roguery and depravity.[34]

It may well be that people of the suburbs were more rebellious than those of Cairo's centre because the police were weaker in the outskirts of the town. Another reason may have been that they needed to defend themselves against bedouin attacks and therefore armed bands of youth, the *zu'ar*, organized particularly in these quarters. For similar peculiarities of the outlying quarters of Damascus we have evidence in the histories of that town in the Mamluk and Ottoman period.

Finally a specific group of the mob often mentioned in connection with Cairo's revolts were children: *al-sighār, al-awlād, al-aṭfāl.* This too has been a persistent feature of the Middle Eastern political landscape. Their principal activity was to make noise, to cry out slogans and to induce people to close their shops and assemble in the Azhar. They often performed these activities by climbing the minarets of the mosques.[35]

Popular revolt in Ottoman Cairo was stirred up by various motives. Famine, as the result of bad harvest of grain crops, was rather rare as the reason of unrest in eighteenth century Cairo, but it caused at least three consecutive revolts at the end of the seventeenth century: in 1678, 1687 and 1695.[36] However, a considerable increase in food prices resulting from bad harvests or from monetary measures taken by the government was a frequent reason for the people to rise against the authorities in the first half of the eighteenth century. This happened in 1714, 1715–16, 1722, 1723, 1724, 1731 and 1733.[37] After quite a long period of relative prosperity from 1736 to the 1770s, new popular revolts broke out during the last quarter of the eighteenth century. The main cause of these later revolts was the growing oppressive exactions of money from the urban population by the Mamluk Beys who had come to power.[38] Thus the revolt of 1787 resulted from Ismā'il Bey's attempt to levy a forced loan from Cairo's merchants.[39] Similarly, the first revolt against the French, in October 1798, started as the result of the new property taxes imposed by the French,[40] and in the uprising which brought Muḥammad 'Alī to power in May 1805 the people complained about the arbitrary and excessive imposts, such as *al-maẓālim, al-firad, qabḍ al-māl al-mīrī al-mu'ajjal, ḥaqq ṭuruq al-mubāshirīn, muṣādarat al-nās* etc.[41] Together with their attempts to extract more and more money from the population of Cairo in the form of taxes and imposts, the Mamluk Beys also tried to deprive the beneficiaries of *waqfs* of their allocations. Among the victims of this policy were the Azhar students, who for this reason started the riots of 1777 and 1785.[42] In addition, the renewed rise to power of the Mamluk Beys in the second half of the eighteenth century and the increasing use of mercenary soldiers in their service sharpened the conflict between the military and the urban population. From time to time the people of Cairo were harassed by the soldiers, and their reaction was riot and revolt. The riots of 1786 were the result of the violent attacks of Ḥusayn Bey Shaft, a follower of Murād Bey, against Aḥmad Sālim, the Shaykh of the Bayyūmiyya in the Ḥusayniyya quarter, and four years later the *wālī* (head of police) Aḥmad Agha intruded in the same way into the Ḥusayniyya quarter and brought about similar results.[43] The demolition of the gates between the quarters of Cairo by the French army was considered by Napoleon Bonaparte, in his memoirs, as one of the important reasons for the Cairo revolt of 1798.[44] And one of the aims of the popular rising which brought Muḥammad 'Alī to power in 1805 was to get rid of the Dālātiyya[45] about whose arbitrary violence and oppression the people of Old Cairo complained.[46] Finally, in the revolts against the French, in 1798 and 1800, a strong religious motive was involved: the Muslim masses of Cairo resented the loss of their privileged position and the self assertion of the 'infidel' Christians.[47] The March 1800 revolt was closely connected with the Ottoman military campaign against the French, and the religious zeal of Cairo's populace was consciously stimulated by the Ottomans, whose representatives incited them to 'kill the Christians and wage a *jihād* against them'.[48] Thus, one may discern two gradual changes which occurred in the motives of Cairo's revolts in the course of the eighteenth century: first dearth and exorbitant prices of food were replaced by taxation and excessive imposts as the principal economic reason, and secondly, political motives were added to the economic reasons, which however persisted throughout the whole period.

These changes found their expression in the demands and slogans voiced by the revolting people of Cairo. We know very little about slogans raised in the early revolts, but as far as we know they were concerned primarily with the supply of food, the prices of consumer goods and the value of the money. Towards the end of the century

Cairo's rioters raised more and more political issues. When the Azhar students terminated their revolt in 1777 which started because they were deprived of their *waqf* income, they demanded that from then on the police and market inspectors (*al-āghā, al-wālī, al-muḥtasib*) should not be allowed to pass through the Azhar quarter. Similarly, in 1790 the revolting people of the Ḥusayniyya quarter demanded the deposition of the head of police (*al-wālī*).[49] The slogan of the first revolt against the French, which broke out in October 1798 because of the imposition of the new property taxes, was 'May God give victory to the Muslim' and 'May God grant victory to Islam' (*naṣar-Allāh al-muslimīn*, and *Allāh yanṣur al-Islām*), and a druggist disguised as a *faqīh* incited the people and exclaimed: ' "God is most great, O Muslims. The 'ulamā' have commanded you to kill the infidels. Make ready, O stalwarts, and strike them everywhere" '.[50] In March 1800 the revolting people of Cairo shouted *'Allāh yanṣur al-Sulṭān wa-yuhlik Farṭ al-Rummān'* (May God give victory to the Sultan and destroy 'Pomegranate Seeds' – the nickname of Barthelemy).[51] In 1805, on the other hand, the Ottoman Paşa became discredited to such an extent that the people of Cairo, who revolted against oppression, demanded his deposition and even exclaimed: *'Yā rabb ya mitgallī ahlik al-'uthmallī'* (O Lord, O Thou who hast revealed Thyself to man, May Thou destroy the 'Uthmanli).[52]

The principal social 'crises' of Cairo, as Raymond calls them, proceeded according to a rather invariable scenario, presented by him as follows:[53]

> The mob hurries towards the Great Mosque (al-Azhar), occupies the minarets from where inflammatory appeals for resistance are sent down, in a rhythm given by the rolling of drums; the mob causes the markets and shops to be closed, assembles in the large court and in front of the gates, calls for the shaykhs and demands vigorously their intercession with the authorities so that the wrong of which they complain be redressed; a procession is formed and the *'ulamā'*, sometimes more dead than alive, are placed at its head; one turns towards the Citadel to set forth the situation to the authorities.

Thus, indeed, began almost all the revolts of Cairo's population in the eighteenth century, as well as the unrest of May–June 1805 which brought Muḥammad 'Alī to power. However, most of them did not end therewith, but involved some sort or other of violence. In many cases the people who marched in the procession began to pelt their opponents with stones: in 1695 they stoned the Divan of the Paşa at the citadel, in 1722 – the beys who were on the way to the Divan, in 1731 – the Head of Police, in 1733 – the new Paşa on entering Cairo, in 1777 – the Agha of the Bayt al-Māl, in October 1798 – the Qāḍī al-'Askar, in 1805 – the Ketkhudā of the Paşa.[54] In 1790 they clashed with Aḥmad Agha, the head of the police and his men, and the result was two dead and many wounded.[55]

Another sort of violence was prevalent in the famine-riots of the end of the seventeenth century, which proceeded according to a somewhat different scenario. When food became excessively rare and dear, the people assembled below the Citadel to protest. But soon the demonstrations became unruly and the mob stormed the grain stores of Rumayla. Together with the stores the neighbouring shops were plundered as well. This at last led to severe suppression of the revolts.[56]

Rumayla was the scene of these events because the grain stores and grain markets were concentrated there, and because of its vicinity to the Citadel; the plundering of stores and shops was only natural in periods of famine. However, this violent aspect of popular revolt in Cairo was not confined to Rumayla nor to periods of famine. In 1724 the revolting people of Cairo looted the markets because of rising prices of food.[57] When in 1785 the poor Azhar students were deprived of their rations, they raided the markets and plundered whatever they found, and they were joined in this venture by the mob (*'yarmaḥūna bi'l-aswāq wa-yakhṭafūna mā yajidūnahu min al-khubz wa-ghayrihi wa-tabi'ahum fī dhālika al-ja'īdiyya wa-arādhil al-sūqa'*).[58] A year later, in 1786, Shaykh Dardīr incited the revolting people of Ḥusayniyya quarter to plunder the houses of the beys, but apparently this was not carried out.[59] However, in the first revolt against the French, in October 1798, looting reappeared on a grand scale. This is how Jabartī describes it:

> Meanwhile the situation among the gathering crowds became more and more serious and their impudence increased so much that bounds were exceeded in every respect. They began to steal, plunder, and loot and then attacked the Juwwānīyya quarter in the district of al-Jamāliyya, completely looting the houses of the Syrian Christians as well as Muslim houses in the vicinity. They looted property held as deposits and trusts, raped the women and girls, and also plundered the Khān al-Milāyāt (store for women's outer garments) looting all its merchandise and whatever else was to be found.'[60])

Similarly, the second revolt against the French, in March 1800, started with the looting of wood and copper from French army quarters in Cairo, continued with the plundering of French and Christian houses in the town, including the garments and jewellery of the women who were found there, and ended in Būlāq with the looting of tents and other goods from the French army camp, the storming of grain stores and other magazines of the French, and the plundering of the houses of Copts and Syrian Christians.[61]

Though looters generally did not discriminate between victims of different religious communities, in 1798 and 1800 Copts and other

Christians in particular were hard hit. Especially the second revolt against the French turned into a general massacre of Christians and other minorities. At a certain stage of the revolt the mob moved to the Christian quarters (*ḥārāt al-naṣārā wa-buyūtihim*), attacked the houses and slaughtered indiscriminately men, women and children (*faṣārū yakbisūna al-dūr wa-yaqtulūna ma yuṣādifūnahu min al-rijāl wa'l-nisā' wa'l-ṣibyān*).[62] Anybody who captured a Christian, a Jew or a Frenchman and brought him to the Ottoman representatives, received a baksheesh; but many just killed their victims and presented their heads to get the baksheesh.[63] This violent aspect of the 1800 revolt has been explained by Raymond as follows: 'Le pillage de nombreuses maisons chrétiennes, lors de la révolte du Caire de 1800 contre les Français, s'explique moins par une animosité traditionelle des musulmans que par les relations qui s'étaient établies entre les chrétiens et les occupants . . . Sans doute les *dhimmī* avaient-ils un statut diminué; du moins eurent-ils rarement à souffrir de mouvements populaires d'hostilité . . .'[64] There can be no doubt that the co-operation of the local Christians with the French Expedition aggravated their situation during the revolt. However, the Muslim religious elite too had co-operated with the French but did not suffer from popular wrath in any way comparable with the massacre of the Christians. Moreover, there was not only a traditional animosity between the Muslim popular masses and non-Muslims, but from time to time this animosity erupted into violent attacks. In 1749 the Copts decided to organize a pilgrimage to Jerusalem and even received a *fatwā* confirming their plan. However, they staged the whole enterprise in a pompous manner and thus aroused the anger of the Muslims, who would not tolerate that the Christians had their *ḥajj* too. The result was that the Muslim *'āmma* and Azhar students attacked the camp which the Copts had established, pillaged them, stoned and beat them, looted a neighbouring church and caused them a considerable number of killed and wounded.[65] During the popular unrest resulting from the Ottoman military re-occupation of Egypt in July–August 1786, the *'āmma* had terrorized the Christians and caused them harm.[66] And in 1798, *before* the French had arrived in Cairo, the people attempted to massacre the Christians and Jews, and would have implemented their design had they not been prevented from doing so by those in power (*'wa'l-'āmma lā tarḍā illā an yaqtulū al-naṣārā wa'l-yahūd fa-yamna'uhum al-ḥukkām 'anhum wa-lawlā dhālika al-man' laqatalathum al-'āmma waqt al-fitna'*).[67]

In addition to spontaneous violence – the characteristic aspect of popular unrest in Cairo up to the end of the eighteenth century – the two revolts against the French, especially the second in March 1800, showed some features of somewhat organized civil war. One of these features was the building of barricades. In 1798, the Muslims 'destroyed the stone benches of the stores, using them for barricades with which to fortify themselves and to hinder the enemy's attack at the time of the battle. Before each barricade stood a great number of people'.[68] However, in 1798 even such faint traces of some kind of organization soon disappeared. 'Cependant la canaille de la ville . . . songeaient, comme de coutume, à exploiter le désordre. Grâce à son intervention, la révolte changea bientôt de caractère: ce ne fut plus une lutte, mais un pillage'.[69] In March 1800, people slept behind the barricades they had built in Cairo, and the people of Bulāq erected barricades and fortifications by using the material they had pillaged from the French army camp.[70] In 1805 too the people of Cairo used the barriers erected by army units around the Citadel as their own barricades.[71] This was of course the result of the longer duration of these revolts and the involvement of army units which conferred on them the character of civil war rather than an eruption of riots. In 1800 this character was stressed by additional features. First, the people of the different quarters of Cairo formed a kind of popular militia, each territorial group joining the Ottoman military unit stationed in its area. Thus patrols in the streets and posts behind the barricades were manned day and night. With the help of the Ottomans a gun factory was established, in which local artisans were employed. The rich merchants generously paid for supplies and everybody donated his belongings, people helping each other.[72] This is how the French saw this development:

> Ainsi nulles rumeurs, nulles nouvelles défavorables ne pouvaient attiédir le zèle de cette population qui croyait à l'impunité. Ne doutant pas du succès définitif, elle eut de beaux élans de fanatisme et de persévérance. Plus de vingt canons enfouis jusqu'alors dans des maisons particulières furent déterrés et mis en batterie, une poudrerie fut installée en vingt-quatre heures dans la maison de Qayd-Agha; un atelier de serrurerie, une forge à boulets où venaient se foudre, le fer des mosquées, les marteaux, les outils des ouvriers qui les offraient volontairement; d'autres ateliers de charrons et d'artificiers; enfin une fonderie, industrie extraordinaire et nouvelle pour l'Egypte, une fonderie où l'on coula des mortiers et des canons: tout cela fut organisé en trois jours avec un ordre merveilleux et un dévouement admirable. On alla recueillir, dans les maisons des particuliers, les provisions qui y abondaient pour en former des réserves et des magasins publics; on établit un système de distributions journalières, des quelles étaient exceptés tous les hommes qui ne jouaient pas un rôle actif dans l'insurrection. Ainsi les spectateurs oisifs devaient périr de faim, s'ils n'étaient passés par les armes. Manquant de munitions, les rebelles épiaient la chute des projectiles que lançaient nos forts, et ils nous renvoyaient ainsi des boulets encore chauds de notre feu.[73]

In addition, the two camps had crystallized: on the one hand, the revolting Cairenes persecuted alleged collaborators with the French, such as Shaykh Khalīl al-Bakrī, who had been appointed Naqīb al-Ashrāf by Bonaparte, or Muslim domestic servants who were suspected of having served the French (the house of the former was looted, and the latter were massacred);[74] on the other hand, the Copts organized as well and defended themselves against assaults of the Muslim rebels.[75] Thus, revolt at the end of the eighteenth century against the French differed from earlier popular unrest not only in its motives, demands, and slogans, but also in its actions and organization. One should not forget, however, that the organized character of the civil war of March 1800 was primarily the result of the involvement of Ottoman forces and the presence in Cairo of Ottoman officers, who directed the revolt as far as they could.

This leads us to the question: who headed these revolts, or who were the instigators, agitators and leaders? In this context we intend to re-examine the somewhat simplistic thesis about the popular leadership of the *'ulamā'* in the revolts against the French and in the 1805 revolt which brought Muḥammad 'Alī to power, and to ask such questions as: can one speak about the *'ulamā'* as one group in the context of these revolts, or did different elements among them perform different functions? What kind of relations existed between these different groups of *'ulamā'* on the one hand and the masses and their leaders on the other? And finally, had these revolts a popular leadership independent of the *'ulamā'* and what was its character?

Quoting Raymond's characterization of the 'social crises' of Cairo, we left the scenario presented by him at the moment when the *'ulamā'* were placed at the head of a procession turning towards the Citadel. He continues saying that, if a favourable answer was given by the authorities, the shaykhs became the guarantors for the implementation of whatever promises were made, and on the other hand, undertook to calm the demonstrators and convince them to disperse. On various occasions (1703, 1786, 1788, 1790) the shaykhs agreed to present the demands of the people of Cairo to the paşas or the beys; on other occasions they refused (1725, 1787, 1790). The *'ulamā'* always found themselves twixt the devil and the deep blue sea: they risked being accused either by the people of betraying their interests or by the Ottomans or Mamluks of instigating popular unrest.[76] But even when they agreed to head the procession to the Citadel, they often did so under duress. In January 1716, for instance, the rioters, on their way through the market, encountered Shaykh Muḥammad Shanan, Shaykh al-Azhar and one of the richest men of his time, riding on his mule. They seized him by force (*akhadhūhu bi'l-qahr*) and ascended the Citadel with him to meet the Paşa.[77] Generally speaking, when riots broke out the *'ulamā'* were rather helpless. When in 1731 the Head of Police was pelted with stones and the newly arrived Paşa wounded, he assembled, on the next day, the *'ulamā'*, the Bakrī and Sādāt families and the Naqīb al-Ashrāf and rebuked them for looking on indifferently, whereupon they replied that they were waiting for his arrival (*muntaẓirīn qudūm mawlānā al-wazīr*).[78] A few years prior to this event, in 1724, when the rioters stormed the Azhar, the *'ulamā'* fled to their homes and locked themselves in.[79] Thus, the *'ulamā'* of al-Azhar could hardly be called the leaders of Cairo's popular revolts prior to the French occupation. In some cases they acted as mediators, often under duress, but they certainly preferred to be let alone.

There were, however, two exceptional cases which need an explanation. One was the case of Shaykh Aḥmad al-Dardīr, the Mālikī *muftī* and Shaykh of the Ṣa'īdīs in the Azhar, who twice actively intervened and supported popular revolt. In June 1777 he supported the rioting Maghribī Azhar students who protested against the usurpation of waqf property endowed for their *riwāq*. As the result of a clash with the usurper, Shaykh Dardīr had al-Azhar closed and all prayers and studies in the mosque suspended, until his case was won.[80] A few years later, in January 1786, the people of al-Ḥusayniyya quarter rioted as the result of the attacks of Ḥusayn Bey Shaft, a follower of Murād Bey, against Aḥmad Sālim, the Shaykh of the Bayyūmiyya in the Ḥusayniyya quarter. They invaded al-Azhar and pleaded their case before Shaykh Dardīr. 'He comforted and supported them and told them: "I am with you". After more riotous behaviour Dardīr told them: "Tomorrow we will assemble the inhabitants of the suburbs, the quarters, Bulāq, and Old Cairo and I shall ride with you and we will loot their houses as they have looted ours. Either we shall gain victory or die as martyrs".' As a result a list of goods looted from Aḥmad Sālim was made and the Mamluks promised to return them.[81] In addition to Dardīr's strong personality and independent position (he controlled the *waqf* of the Ṣa'āyida in the Azhar), religious considerations probably played a part in both cases: as Mālikī *muftī* he had strong ties with the Maghribīs, and 'Alī al-Bayyūmī, the founder of the Bayyūmiyya, was his contemporary and a former Khalwatī Ṣūfī, the order whose shaykh and *khalīfa* Dardīr was for a long time.[82]

The second case is not really a case of popular revolt, although it has sometimes been considered as such. In the summer of 1795 the inhabitants of a village in Sharqiyya which was the *iltizām* of Shaykh 'Abdallāh al-Sharqāwī, the Shaykh al-Azhar, came to Cairo to complain of oppression by certain Mamluks. Thereupon al-Sharqāwī assembled the Azhar Shaykhs, and when they did not receive satisfaction from Murād and Ibrāhīm they closed the al-Azhar, ordered the merchants to close the markets and shops and organized a demonstration. They were joined by large numbers of the *'āmma*, and later more people from the suburbs assembled in the Azhār. Thereupon the Paşa and the Mamluks in power, Murād and Ibrāhīm, sent for a limited number of shaykhs to negotiate. They went 'and prevented the *'āmma* from following them'. Thus the matter was settled (although in the long run none of the promises was kept).[83] In this case al-Sharqāwī and the Azhar shaykhs initiated the protest movement, for the simple reason that the issues materially affected the shaykhs: negotiations concerned agricultural taxes, income from *waqf* and pensions. The Cairo mob, eager for the fray, took advantage of the opportunity to join, but quite soon was sent home by the shaykhs themselves.

In October 1798, when the first revolt against the French broke out, the Cairo mob assembled 'without a chief to rule them or a leader to guide them' (*fatajamma'a al-kathīr min al-ghawghā' min ghayr ra'īs yasūsuhum walā qā'id yaqūduhum*).[84] The great *'ulamā'*, the Azhar shaykhs, tried to prevent the revolt, and when they did not succeed, they made efforts to keep out of the conflict. Their attitude has been very well described in two authentic accounts. This is what Jabartī says in his detailed work on the French occupation:

> Shaykh al-Bakrī warned the residents of the Azbakiyya areas not to revolt and discouraged their uprising completely. Shaykh al-Fayyūmī did the same in the 'Ābdīn and Qūṣūn quarters . . . Thus they prevented rioting, warning them of the bad consequences . . . As for the Shaykhs, there were those who fled from their homes and sat hidden in their neighbours' houses; others feared their enemies and bolted their gates, sitting with their women folk. Others left their homes, setting out for the building of Qāyitbāy in the desert and living there. Shaykh al-Bakrī took both al-Sirsī and al-Mahdī [two leading *'ulamā'*] and went to the *kātib al-ruznāma* . . . They then asked him to send guards to take them to the Ṣārī 'Askar [Napoleon Bonaparte] . . . Upon entering into the presence of the Ṣārī 'Askar . . . he asked them what were these evil events . . . They answered him: 'These are the deeds of the foolish among the subjects and those who do not consider the consequences of their actions'. The Ṣārī 'Askar asked them: 'Where are the Shaykhs of the Dīwān and those who see to the affairs of the people and are entrusted with the management of the government; those whom we have raised, chosen, and distinguished from others?' So they told him that they had a good excuse since their arrival was blocked.[85]

The second account is that of Bonaparte himself. He says that 'the Great Shaykhs had tried to explain to the people the inevitable consequences of their behaviour; but they were unable to achieve anything and therefore were compelled to keep silence and join the irresistible movement . . .

They hid in their harems . . . sixty shaykhs and *imāms* of al-Azhar had remained faithful, but had been unable to resist the rage of the people'.[86] Thus, in 1798 the leading *'ulamā'* were very far indeed from being the leaders of the revolt, let alone having roused the population to action.

This does not mean that people engaged in religious functions did not play an active part in the 1798 revolt against the French. First, those who stirred up the mob and incited the people to revolt were, according to Jabartī, the *muta'ammimīn*, the 'turbaned'. As we have shown above, when using this term he must have had in mind the lower layer of religious functionaries, such as minor *imāms, mu'adhdhins, maktab*-teachers, as well as Azhar students. Some of these *muta'ammimīn* 'applied themselves to stirring up rebellion with those people and set out to influence the masses, summoning them to slaughter the French who had conquered them. Indeed, they preached to them a clear sermon, exclaiming "O Muslims, the *jihād* is incumbent upon you. How can you free men agree to pay the poll tax (*jizya*) to the unbelievers? Have you no pride? Has not the call reached you?" '[87] Moreover, Bonaparte even claimed that the rebels had formed a divan, consisting of about one hundred *imāms, mu'azzins*, and Maghribīs, 'tous gens de la basse classe'.[88] There can be no doubt, therefore, that the lower layers of religious functionaries, the minor *imāms, mu'azzins*, *maktab*-teachers and Azhar students, acted as instigators, and perhaps also as conspirators, although one can hardly call them the leaders of the revolt: they did not organize it, nor did they lead it in a clear direction or towards a definite aim.

However, among the religious functionaries there were three prominent persons, whose position as *'ulamā'*, in society, and as popular leaders needs a more detailed investigation. The first was Sayyid Badr al-Maqdisī, who arrived in Cairo as soon as the revolt broke out, 'accompanied by . . . the scoundrels of al-Ḥusayniyya and the crooks of the outlying quarters . . . He preceded them, mounted on a well-equipped horse surrounded by these innumerable groups all yelling and clamouring with a great uproar and tumult.'[89] Sayyid Badr al-Dīn (as his real name was) belonged to a famous family of *ashrāf*, who for some time occupied the position of *nuqabā' al-ashrāf* in Jerusalem. His brother, Ibn al-Naqīb, who was a famous scholar and a generous donor, moved to al-Ḥusayniyya quarter where he died in November 1772. Badr al-Dīn succeeded his brother as teacher in the al-Mashhad al-Ḥusaynī mosque as well as in his prominent social position. In particular he established close ties with the al-Ḥusayniyya quarter and its inhabitants. There, in 1790–1, he built a new house, into which he moved, and a spacious mosque, well endowed with a *waqf* by him. His noble descent, his learning and his wealth, in addition to his character and personality, made him the natural chief of al-Ḥusaynīyya quarter. He cared for the needs of its inhabitants, judged them and arbitrated their disputes, and defended them against those who encroached upon their rights, even if they were *amīrs* and rulers. Thus he became their patron (*marjā' wa-malja' lahum*), he achieved great esteem and prestige among them (*ṣāra lahu wajāha wa-manzila fī qulūbihim*) and they feared his authority (*yakhshawna jānibahu wa-ṣawlatahu 'alayhim*).[90] When the French occupied Egypt and the first revolt broke out, his 'zeal was kindled' as Jabartī says (*taḥarrakat fīhi al-ḥamiyya*), he assembled his people from al-Ḥusayniyya and other outskirts of Cairo and fought the Ifranj.[91]

After the revolt, Badr al-Maqdisī managed to escape to Syria, and thus he evaded the fate of the five shaykhs who were executed as leaders of the revolt.[92] Among these five three are unimportant and minor shaykhs. One of the other two was Shaykh Aḥmad al-Sharqāwī, a teacher at al-Azhar who succeeded his father in this position.[93] Sharqāwī, too, had established close ties with a particular group of the population – the fellahs of the neighbourhood of 'his villages'. Jabartī does not explain what he means by that, but we may perhaps assume that he had an *iltizām* in Sharqiyya province – like his namesake 'Abdallāh al-Sharqāwī.[94] However that may be, these fellahs used to come to him and submit to him their legal cases, their disputes and their marriage arrangements. He would judge them and write for them opinions (*fatāwā*) for their legal actions at the *qāḍī*'s court. He treated them quite harshly, even cursing and beating them, but they used to obey him and honour his judgements. Sometimes they brought him gifts and money. His fame and their reverence for him was great, and it is at least possible that he made use of this influence during the revolt.

The third was Shaykh Sulaymān al-Jawsaqī, the shaykh of the blind (Zāwiyat al-'Imyān) at al-Azhar. According to some of the French accounts, he was the main conspirator who directed the revolt.[95] He certainly was an extraordinary and impressive figure.[96] After he had become the shaykh of the blind he assumed their leadership with vigour and terror to further his aims. For their sake, as it were, he collected enormous sums of money, acquired real estate and manipulated complicated commercial and financial transactions connected with *waqf* income. Reluctant debtors were sent a commando of blind students to make them pay. His agents brought loads of grain, clarified butter, honey, sugar, oil etc. from the Upper-Egyptian *multazims* in his own boats, and he would hoard all this to sell it in times of dearth at exorbitant prices. The grain was ground in his own mills – the flour to be sold and the bran to be used to make bread for the poor blind – as an addition to what they collected as alms. Whenever one of the blind died the shaykh inherited everything he had collected. Thus his wealth became so large that he was able to lend great sums of money to the rulers of Egypt. He became one of the foremost notables in Cairo whose word was obeyed and whose power was feared. Conspicuous consumption was not neglected by him either: he wore furs, rode mules, was accompanied by a great number of followers, married many rich wives, and acquired numerous concubines – white, Abyssinian and black. His arrogance led him to instigate the revolt which brought about his end.

Thus the 1798 revolt against the French witnessed a basic pattern of leadership, elements of which existed in former revolts as well. The great *'ulamā'* of the Azhar were rather passive, reluctant to do anything, here and there even trying to prevent the rising, mainly evading involvement as far as they could, but sometimes dragged along against their will. The new element was the activity of the lower strata, the *muta'ammimīn*, as conspirators and instigators. However, the most interesting feature emerging from the somewhat confused picture was the leadership of certain persons who had established a patron-client relationship with a particular group of the population. In this Sayyid Badr al-Dīn, Aḥmad al-Sharqāwī, and Shaykh al-'Imyān resembled earlier leaders, such as Shaykh Dardīr and 'Abdallāh al-Sharqāwī. The fact that it was particularly such patrons who headed their clientele in the revolts may be explained, at least partly, by their fear of losing the clientship, either through the interference of the authorities, or through the establishment of a new order, or by ignoring spontaneous movements of their clientele.

In the second revolt against the French, in March–April 1800, the *'ulamā'* of Cairo played only a secondary role, and certainly not a leading one. In fact the revolt was to a large extent a by-product of the struggle between the French, the Mamluks and the Ottomans. According to the Convention of al-'Arīsh (24 January 1800) the French were given the right to evacuate their troops to France, and the Cairo garrison was preparing to leave: they began to abandon the fortifications, sold their belongings and weapons, and money was collected to make the evacuation possible. Meanwhile an Ottoman army had occupied Lower Egypt and Ottoman soldiers, Mamluks and Egyptians who had left Cairo because of the French occupation returned to the town. Ottoman emissaries arrived with firmans from the Sultan and the Cairo notables visited the camp of Mustafa Paşa in Bilbays; the Mamluks too, who camped near the town, had established close ties with its inhabitants and the Chief of the Merchants, Aḥmad al-Maḥrūqī, catered for them.[97]

Under these circumstances French power and authority deteriorated considerably and Cairo's population openly showed the French their malicious pleasure in this situation. Moreover, the *maktab*-teachers arranged processions of their pupils shouting anti-French slogans and cursing the Christians.[98] At the beginning of March sporadic clashes occurred between Ottoman soldiers and the French, and barricades were erected.[99] Meanwhile, however, the French had learnt that the

Convention was disavowed by the British, who required the surrender of the French. Kléber decided to resist, and on 20 March the battle of Heliopolis ('Ayn Shams) outside Cairo was fought and ended in Ottoman defeat.

When the people of Cairo heard the cannonade of Heliopolis, they did not know what was happening, and for a long time they were not aware of the outcome of the battle. Thus the riots and the civil war began, which is known as the second revolt against the French and which lasted for thirty-seven days. The organizers and leaders of this civil war were the Ottoman representatives in Cairo, particularly Naṣūḥ (or Nāṣīf) Paşa and 'Uthmān Ketkhudā, as well as a number of Mamluk beys.[100] Among the latter one of the most prominent was Ḥasan Bey al-Jaddāwī, a *mamlūk* of 'Alī Bey with a long career of exploits and adventures.[101] In his account of the revolt, only two local notables are mentioned by Jabartī in any leading capacity, Aḥmad al-Maḥrūqī and 'Umar Makram, but in all three instances in which they were mentioned they appear together with leading Ottoman officials and Mamluks.[102] Thus it certainly cannot be said that Maḥrūqī and 'Umar Makram were the leaders of the revolt. Moreover, the circumstances in which they are mentioned are not particularly indicative of a position of popular leadership, except perhaps the last instance in which they incited the population to continue the *jihād*. Aḥmad Maḥrūqī, the son of a devout silk merchant of Cairo had an illustrious career in the course of which he became the richest merchant of Egypt at that time. He joined the anti-French forces probably because of his strong personal ties with Murād and Ibrāhīm. Although he had had personal contact with Napoleon and had even accepted his appointment to his divan, after Bonaparte's departure he apparently considered French rule to be nearing its end and he re-joined his old patrons.[103]

The fact that 'Umar Makram's name is connected with the revolt has been considered by some authors as another instance of *'ulamā'*-leadership of popular rebellion in Cairo. However, 'Umar Makram cannot really be seen as an *'ālim*. He was a *sharīf* born in Asyūṭ where the *ashrāf* formed an influential and important faction of the town's society. He never taught at al-Azhar or elsewhere, nor did he compose *fatāwā*, commentaries or other works of religious learning, which is the reason why he is never called *shaykh* but always *sayyid*. His career began in 1791 as an emissary of Murād and Ibrāhīm, who were at that time in their Upper-Egyptian exile, to negotiate their case in Cairo. The success of his mission considerably contributed to their return to Cairo in July of that year, and as a reward they appointed him in November 1793 Naqīb al-Ashrāf of Cairo. In this capacity he acquired great prestige and influence, since he controlled the large income of the *awqāf* endowed for the *sharīfs*. When the French invaded Egypt, 'Umar

Makram supported his Mamluk patrons and followed the defeated Ibrāhīm to Gaza. He was dismissed from his post as Naqīb al-Ashrāf by Napoleon and his property was confiscated. When Napoleon invaded Palestine, 'Umar Makram was apprehended in Jaffa, brought back to Damietta, and in the course of time allowed to return to Cairo.[104] His active part in the civil war against the French was therefore the natural sequence of his former career, and it has nothing to do with any 'popular leadership of the *'ulamā'*.'[105]

To be sure, at a certain juncture the *'ulamā'* joined with the Ottomans, Maḥrūqī, 'Umar Makram and others to call for the *jihād*,[106] but otherwise they were inconspicuous throughout the rebellion. Only at the end the French demanded from the Ottoman paşa and *ketkhudā* to send the shaykhs to negotiate a ceasefire to end the civil war. In their parleys with the French they accused the Ottomans of having instigated the rebellion. It is an interesting reflection on their influence at that time that they were unable to implement the agreement which they had concluded with the French; this was left to the Mamluks some time later.[107]

In fact, if Cairo's *'ulamā'* or other notables had had any authority over Cairo's popular masses, they had lost it in the course of the March 1800 rebellion. The situation has been very well defined by Jabartī as *mughālabat al-juhalā' 'alā al-'uqalā' watatāwul al-sufahā' 'alā al-ru'asā*[108] (the ignorant gained mastery over the intelligent and the fools treated the chiefs with arrogance). When the shaykhs announced the agreement they had concluded with the French, the Janissaries and the population not only opposed them but cursed them, beat them and threw down their turbans and finally accused them of having become French or taken bribes.[109] On the other hand, a popular leader had emerged from the lower layers of the population. Jabartī does not mention his name, but only says that he was a Maghribī, who had no family, no abode and no property in Egypt. At the beginning of the revolt he headed groups of *'awāmm* and soldiers engaged in looting and killing of French and Christians, and when at the end the shaykhs announced their agreement with the French, he declared the peace agreement null and void (*'al-ṣulḥ manqūḍ'*) and demanded the continuation of the *jihād*; whoever disobeyed him was decapitated.[111] When the second peace agreement with the French was concluded by the Mamluks, he again headed the resistant crowds which he now recruited from al-Ḥusayniyya quarter – the everlasting reservoir of effervescent masses. But this time the army dispersed the rebels and suppressed the revolt.[112] Jabartī draws an interesting portrait of this Maghribī, and Jabartī's indignation is excited in particular by his arrogance and pretensions: by collecting the rabble around him he posed as an amīr (*al-taṣawwur bisūrat al-imāra bi-ijtimā' al-awghād 'alayhi*) – but the people supported him. However, Jabartī concludes: 'He interfered in things which do not concern him, since he appeared in town like the paşa and the *ketkhudā* and the Mamluks. What is this fool worth that he declares an agreement null and void or confirms it? What is he that he appoints himself without having been appointed by anybody? It is civil strife which turns any ignoble bird into a vulture, especially when the rabble riots and the mob and riff-raff rises. This is what suits their aims.'[113]

If the second revolt against the French was a by-product of the struggle between the French, the Mamluks and the Ottomans, the 1805 riots were the result of the struggle for power between Muḥammad 'Alī and the Ottoman Paşa of Egypt, Ahmed Hurşid, in which also Mamluks and various kinds of military units and individual soldiers were involved – Janissaries, Albanians and Dālātiyya.[114] The local population of Cairo entered the stage on 1 May 1805 when the inhabitants of Old Cairo appeared at the Azhar Mosque and complained about cruel excesses perpetrated by the Dālātiyya in their part of the town. As usual, the Azhar shaykhs rode to the Paşa, who issued a firman to the Dālātiyya, but neither this nor a second appeal to them had any effect. Next day the shaykhs assembled in the Azhar and ceased teaching, but when unrest continued they reacted as they had often before: when the Paşa sent his *ketkhudā* to the Azhar in the afternoon, nobody was there, because the shaykhs had gone home, as Jabartī says *'li'aghrād nafsāniyya wafashal mustamirr fīhim'* (for carnal [or selfish] purposes and because of continuous cowardice [or torpidity] inherent in them). There they remained for over a week and although the town was boiling they appeared neither at al-Azhar nor at the Citadel.[115] They reappeared on 12 May at the Qāḍī's house, where the *'āmma* had assembled and where Janissary officers, the Defterdar and other officials met. A petition to the Paşa including the popular demands was composed. Next day the Paşa sent his reply, demanding their appearance at the Citadel for consultation, but they refrained from going for fear of being murdered.[116] As a result the shaykhs, army officers and officials assembled again at the same place the following day, but this time they prevented the *'āmma* from entering. All of them together rode to Muḥammad 'Alī and declared that they wanted him to become Paşa. 'Umar Makram and Shaykh al-Sharqāwī robed him and his investiture was announced in town.[117] After that the main task of the shaykhs was to write announcements and *fatwās* confirming the investiture of Muḥammad 'Alī by the local dignitaries of Cairo.[118] To sum up this first stage of the 1805 popular unrest, it is again inexact to claim that the *'ulamā'* acted as the leaders of Cairo's popular masses. After a very short repetition of the traditional pattern of conveying popular demands to the Paşa, they disappeared from the scene during a crucial week, to reappear in close co-operation with Janissary officers and other dignitaries, who all joined Muḥammad 'Alī in the struggle for power – probably because they considered him to have become stronger than his opponents. Far from leading the popular revolt, they supported the power which was able to reestablish order.[119] In any case, at the end of the riots two months later, the common people were cursing the *'ulamā'* for having forsaken them (*wa'akhadhū yasubbūna al-mashāyikh wayashtumūnahum li-takhdhīlihim iyāhum*).[120]

The Ottoman Paşa, Ahmed Hurşid, did not acquiesce in Muḥammad 'Alī's investiture and thus a regular civil war broke out, in which the army was split (most of the Janissaries supporting Muḥammad 'Alī, while most of the Albanian troops supported Aḥmed Hurşid) and in which Cairo's population fought against the deposed Ottoman Paşa. Jabartī does not mention any active role of the *'ulamā'* in this civil war, which lasted for almost two months, except that from time to time they are reported to have ridden to Muḥammad 'Alī or gone here and there, or that their sanction was used as a legitimation for fighting the Paşa.[121] During the second stage of this revolt or civil war, which lasted from about mid-May to about mid-June, the leader of Cairo's population and of its resistance to the Paṣa was 'Umar Makram. As we have shown above, 'Umar Makram definitely cannot be considered an *'ālim*, and therefore it is totally misleading to attribute his activity to the role played by 'the *'ulamā'*' in the revolt. But there can be no doubt that it was he who organized the military activity of the resistance, such as the siege of the Citadel or the supply of workers and manpower wherever necessary as well as its financial support. It was 'Umar Makram who headed, on 27 May, a large demonstration of soldiers and armed citizens in support of Muḥammad 'Alī.[122] Early in June the French representative in Cairo wrote: 'On fait monter le nombre des armés à quarante mille, qui tous exécutent aveuglement les ordres du cheikh Said Omar devenu leur général, et que l'on regarde comme le chef de la ville.'[123]

However, during the last stage of the revolt 'Umar Makram's authority over the popular masses seems to have waned, and by July he had apparently lost his leadership. When the messenger from Istanbul who brought Muḥammad 'Alī's official charter of investiture arrived in Cairo, 'Umar Makram's cortège consisted of local soldiers, Maghribīs, Ṣa'īdīs and Turks only, but not of the indigenous popular masses of Cairo, who formed another enormous demonstration headed by different leaders (see below).[124] Moreover, when in July the clashes between soldiers and Cairo's civilian population grew more and more vehement, the shaykhs tried to settle quarrels by prohibiting civilians to carry arms and making Muḥammad 'Alī the arbitrator of any offence perpetrated by the army, while 'Umar Makram would be appointed judge of offences committed by civilians (*ra'iyya*). The people rejected this arrangement, and 'Umar Makram was forced to disavow it.[125]

Finally, 'Umar Makram had lost the reins completely and was unable any longer to control the rioting masses: *'waṣāḥa al-Sayyid 'Umar 'alā al-nās min al-shubbāk ya'muruhum bi'l-sukūn wa'l-hujū' falam yasma'ū lahu wanazala ilā asfal wawaqafa bibāb dārihi yaṣīḥ bi'l-nās falā yazdādūna illā khubāṭan . . .'*[126]

In fact, since the second week of June assaults of soldiers against Cairo's civilian population had increased from day to day, and gradually the revolt or civil war deteriorated to anarchy. According to Jabartī, it became a free and indiscriminate fight: *'falā ya'rifu kilā al-farīqayn al-ṣāḥiba min al-'aduww'*.[127] No wonder that in these circumstances the traditional dignitaries suffered discredit and loss of authority, and that new popular leaders sprouted as they had done in 1800. Moreover, this time they are even known by name. Relating the events of 6 June, Jabartī mentions for the first time that the people of Rumayla were headed by Ḥajjāj al-Khuḍarī and Ismā'īl Jawda.[128] The former was the shaykh of the greengrocers' guild, a popular leader with great authority and influence in Rumayla quarter and elsewhere.[129] On 15 and 16 June the people of Rumayla, under the leadership of Ḥajjāj, foiled the efforts of parts of the army to convey supplies to the Paşa who was besieged in the Citadel.[130] In the narrative of events of 29 June Ḥajjāj is again mentioned as the leader of the fighting population.[131] The climax, however, was his appearance on 9 July at the head of a huge demonstration to welcome the Sultan's messenger who brought Muḥammad 'Alī's charter of investiture – this time together with another popular leader, Ibn Sham'a, the shaykh of the butchers' guild. This demonstration (in contrast to the cortège of 'Umar Makram) consisted of Cairo's popular masses, *al-ghawghā' min al-'āmma, al-fuqahā' al-'āmilīn ru's al-'uṣab* (religious functionaries heading bands), inhabitants of the suburbs and the popular quarters of Cairo, as well as soldiers from the *ocaks* – a long procession 'whose passing took about three hours'. As a symbol of his power, Ḥajjāj held in his hand a sword drawn from its sheath.[132] Thus in 1805, as in 1800, the protraction of popular unrest led in the end to the supplanting of the traditional leadership by new leaders who emerged from the popular masses.

To sum up: the attitude of the 'high *'ulamā'*' towards popular revolt in Ottoman Cairo was rather passive. Their principal function was to convey popular demands to the authorities, often under duress. If they could not prevent the revolt (which they sometimes tried, e.g. in 1798), they made all efforts to evade involvement, often by hiding or locking themselves in their homes. When called to the rulers, they attempted to prevent the *'āmma* from following or joining them. At the end they always joined the winning side.

Nevertheless, there were two types of *'ulamā'* who participated more actively in popular revolts. First, the lower layers of religious functionaries, such as *imāms*, Azhar students, *maktab*-teachers, etc., who frequently instigated unrest and revolt, albeit without giving it leadership or direction. Secondly, individual prominent *'ālims*, who had relations of patronage with specific groups, such as the Ṣa'āyida and Maghribīs (Dardīr), the inhabitants of the Ḥusayniyya quarter (Badr al-Dīn al-Maqdisī), the blind at al-Azhar (al-Jawsaqī), or fellahs of the shaykh's *iltizāms* (the Sharqāwīs). This patron-client relationship, which was the basis of their influence, was both the motive and the means of their leadership of the revolts.

The most powerful leader of all, no doubt, was 'Umar Makram, whose case certainly was *sui generis*. One must bear in mind, however, that he was no *'ālim*, and his influence was based on his material and moral power as Naqīb al-Ashrāf and the support of the Mamluk chiefs Murād and Ibrāhīm. Material wealth and Mamluk support was also the basis of Maḥrūqī's leadership. In addition, one cannot ignore the important role played by army commanders and Mamluks as leaders in the popular revolts of the years 1798 to 1805, which formed part of the struggle among the different political forces of that time.

Finally, an interesting feature of the revolts of 1800 and 1805 was the emergence of popular leaders: the Maghribī in 1800, and the chiefs of some guilds in 1805. This phenomenon, a rather rare one in Ottoman and modern Egyptian history,[133] was the result of the anarchical circumstances which developed in these years and the prolonged and fierce struggles between the different dominant powers. It should be pointed out that this popular leadership acted in contrast with the traditional one, not in co-operation with it – as has been frequently assumed.

NOTES

1. The most serious and comprehensive study of the social history of Ottoman Cairo including copious references to our subject is André Raymond, *Artisans et commerçants au Caire au XVIIIe siècle*, Damas, 1973–4. We have used Raymond's excellent work extensively in some parts of this paper.
2. Cf. G. Baer, *Egyptian guilds in modern times*, Jerusalem, 1964, pp. 33–7. See also 'Abd al-Raḥmān al-Jabartī, *'Ajā'ib al-āthār fī'l-tarājim wa'l-akhbār*, Cairo-Bulāq, 1297/1870–1, vol. 3, p. 43 and *passim*; Nicolas Turc, *Chronique d'Egypte 1798–1804*, ed. G. Wiet, Cairo, 1950, p. 45 (translation), p. 31 (Arabic text).
3. Jabartī, *'Ajā'ib*, vol. 3, p. 40 (where he explains that they live from hand to mouth – *lā yamlik qūt laylatihi*); p. 191; Turc, ibid.; etc.
4. Such derogatory terms are numerous; Jabartī uses the following: *ajlāf, awbāsh, awlād al-ḥarām, arādhil al-sūqa, akhlāṭ al-nās, al-ghawghā',*

asāfil al-'ālam, ra'ā', ḥarāfīsh, hamaj al-nās, ḥasharāt – see *'Ajā'ib*, vol. 1, pp. 344, 374; vol. 2, pp. 93, 103, 116; vol. 3, pp. 83, 10, 11, 13, 25, 48, 88, 91, 99, 151, 240, 248, 250, 254; vol. 4, p. 207; etc.

5. Jabartī, *'Ajā'ib*, vol. 3, pp. 25, 331; 'Abd al-Raḥmān al-Jabartī, *Tārīkh muddat al-fransīs bi-miṣr*, ed. by S. Moreh, Leiden, 1975, f. 18a. Cf. also A. Raymond, 'Quartiers et mouvements populaires au Caire au xviiieme siècle', in P. M. Holt (ed.), *Political and social change in modern Egypt*, London, 1968, pp. 104–16.
6. See G. Baer, *Studies in the social history of modern Egypt*, Chicago, 1969, ch. 10.
7. This development has been discussed in various studies. See G. Baer, *A history of landownership in modern Egypt 1800–1950*, London, 1962, pp. 60–1; D. N. Crecelius, *The ulama and the state in modern Egypt*, Ph.D. dissertation, Princeton University, 1967, University Microfilms, Ann Arbor, Michigan, pp. 48–84; Afaf Lutfi al-Sayyid Marsot, 'The political and economic functions of the 'Ulamā' in the eighteenth century', *JESHO*, vol. xvi (1973) pt. 2–3, pp. 130–153 and discussion ibid., vol. xviii, pt. 1, pp. 115–119; Raymond, *Artisans*, pp. 424–9.
8. Jabartī, *'Ajā'ib*, vol. 3, p. 329.
9. Ibid., vol. 1, p. 50.
10. Ibid., vol. 1, p. 26. Cf. Raymond, *Artisans*, p. 87.
11. Jabartī, *Tārīkh*, f. 19b (pp. 97–8 of S. Moreh's translation – the original is in amusing *saj'*). This penetrating description of the hysterical mood of the rioters was omitted by Jabartī from his narrative of the revolt in his *Maẓhar al-taqdīs bi-dhahāb dawlat al-fransīs* (cf. ed. A. M. Jawhar and 'U. al-Dasūqī, Cairo, 1969, p. 80) as well as in his *'Ajā'ib* (cf. vol. 3, p. 26).
12. *Histoire scientifique et militaire de l'expédition française en Egypte*, Paris, 1831, vol. 4, pp. 170–2; vol. 7, p. 399.
13. Jabartī, *'Ajā'ib*, vol. 3, p. 330.
14. See J. B. Mayfield, *Rural politics in Nasser's Egypt*, Austin and London, 1971, p. 25. See also our discussion of Mayfield's assumption in *Asian and African Studies* (Jerusalem), vol. 9, no. 1, 1973, p. 99.
15. E. W. Lane, *The manners and customs of the modern Egyptians*, London, Everyman's Library, 1944, p. 27. See also Jabartī, *'Ajā'ib*, vol. 3, p. 333: *'waminhum man yughrī al-'askar 'alā awlād al-balad wa-yaqūlūna lahum bilisānihim wa-bi'l-'arabī iḍribū al-fallāḥīn wa-naḥw dhālika'*. For another example of the same use of the term *fallāḥīn* see Raymond, *Artisans*, p. 787.
16. For rural-urban relations in Ottoman Egypt see above, Part One, Ch. 2.
17. Jabartī, *'Ajā'ib*, vol. 3, pp. 91, 93.
18. Ibid., p. 331. There were of course frequent fights among the different *ocaks* throughout the Ottoman period, but these can hardly be considered as popular revolt or unrest by any definition.
19. Aḥmad Çelebi b. 'Abd al-Ghanī al-Ḥanafī al-Miṣrī, *Awdaḥ al-ishārāt fīman tawallā Miṣr al-Qāhira min al-wuzarā wa'l-bāshāt*. Yale University Library, Landberg MS. No. 3, ff. 79b–80a; 240a.
20. Jabartī, *'Ajā'ib*, vol. 2, p. 103 (Jumādā al-Ūlā 1200/March 1786).
21. Ibid., p. 189 (Muḥarram 1205/September 1790).

22. Ibid., p. 258 (Dhū'l-Ḥijja 1209/June–July 1795).
23. Ibid., p. 9 (Jumādā al-Ūla 1191/June 1777).
24. Ibid., p. 152; Raymond, *Artisans*, pp. 802–3.
25. *Histoire scientifique*, vol. 4, p. 183.
26. Jabartī, *'Ajā'ib*, vol. 2, pp. 8–9; Raymond, *Artisans*, p. 794.
27. Jabartī, *'Ajā'ib*, vol. 2, p. 93.
28. Aḥmad Çelebi, f. 240a; Jabartī, *'Ajā'ib*, vol. 2, pp. 102 (1786), 152 (1787), etc.
29. Ibid., vol. 3, pp. 25, 329; Jabartī, *Tārīkh*, ff. 18a, 21b.
30. Jabartī, *'Ajā'ib*, vol. 2, pp. 9 (1777), 93 (1785), 103 (1786), 152 (1787), 189 (1790); vol. 3, pp. 25 (1798), 91, 93 (1800), 329, 331 (1805). In Aḥmad Çelebi's account of earlier years the revolting element is designated by the more general term *al-ra'iyya* – see ff. 111b, 155a, 235b, 240a, 241b etc.
31. Ibid., vol. 1, p. 26; Raymond, *Artisans*, p. 87.
32. Jabartī, *'Ajā'ib*, vol. 2, p. 103 (1786); p. 189 (1790); vol. 3, p. 25 (1798); p. 93 (1800); p. 331 (1805).
33. Ibid., vol. 3, pp. 93, 331.
34. Jabartī, *Tārīkh*, f. 18a (pp. 93–4 of S. Moreh's translation).
35. Jabartī, *'Ajā'ib*, vol. 1, p. 26; vol. 2, p. 9; vol. 3, pp. 93, 328–9; etc.
36. Raymond, 'Quartiers', p. 113; Raymond, *Artisans*, p. 818.
37. Raymond, *Artisans*, pp. 91–7, 761; Raymond, 'Quartiers', pp. 113–4.
38. For a detailed description of this process see Raymond, *Artisans*, pp. 790 ff.
39. Ibid., pp. 802–3; Jabartī, *'Ajā'ib*, vol. 2, pp. 151–2.
40. Jabartī, *Tārīkh*, f. 17b; Jabartī, *'Ajā'ib*, vol. 3, p. 25; *Histoire scientifique*, vol. 4, p. 153.
41. Jabartī, *'Ajā'ib*, vol. 3, p. 329.
42. See above, notes 26 and 27.
43. Jabartī, *'Ajā'ib*, vol. 2, pp. 103, 189; Raymond, *Artisans*, pp. 794, 805; Raymond, 'Quartiers', p. 115.
44. Napoléon, *Campagnes d'Italie, d'Egypte et de Syrie*. Bibliothèque de l'Armée Française, Paris, 1872, vol. 2, pp. 247–8.
45. A mercenary unit of Kurdish and Turkoman cavalry.
46. Jabartī, *'Ajā'ib*, vol. 3, p. 328.
47. Cf. *Histoire scientifique*, vol. 4, pp. 138–9; and see also note 87 below.
48. Jabartī, *'Ajā'ib*, vol. 3, p. 91. For religious slogans of the revolts see further on.
49. Ibid., vol. 2, pp. 9, 189.
50. Jabartī, *Tārīkh*, ff. 18a–b.
51. Jabartī, *'Ajā'ib*, vol. 3, p. 93. For Barthélemy, a Christian soldier who rose to power, see ibid., p. 11 ff.
52. Ibid., pp. 329–30.
53. Raymond, *Artisans*, p. 432.
54. Jabartī, *'Ajā'ib*, vol. 1, p. 26; vol. 2, p. 9; vol. 3, pp. 25, 328; Raymond, 'Quartiers', p. 113; Aḥmad Çelebi, ff. 111b, 235b, 241b.
55. Jabartī, *'Ajā'ib*, vol. 2, p. 189.
56. Raymond, 'Quartiers', p. 113.
57. Aḥmad Çelebi, f. 155a (read 1137 for 1138, which is written once erroneously).

58. Jabartī, *'Ajā'ib*, vol. 2, pp. 93.
59. Ibid., p. 103.
60. Ibid., vol. 3, pp. 25–6; Jabartī, *Tārīkh*, f. 19a (S. Moreh's translation with small changes).
61. Jabartī, *'Ajā'ib*, vol. 3, pp. 91, 94, 95–6. Additional details, as well as reports of looting in other quarters of the town and the house of Khalīl al-Bakrī, are included in the account of Nicolas Turc, pp. 82–4 and 86 of the Arabic text. Būlāq was pillaged a second time shortly afterwards by the French soldiers – see ibid., p. 87. Cf. also *Histoire scientifique*, vol. 7, p. 402 ff.
62. Jabartī, *'Ajā'ib*, vol. 3, p. 92.
63. Ibid., p. 93. For a detailed account see also Nicolas Turc, pp. 82–3.
64. Raymond, *Artisans*, p. 455.
65. Jabartī, *'Ajā'ib*, vol. 1, p. 188. Raymond, ibid., gives references to additional sources for this incident. He puts the blame on the Coptic notables and their imprudent provocative behaviour. But even if one accepted this judgement, this would not change the fact that the Copts suffered in this instance from a 'mouvement populaire d'hostilité'.
66. Jabartī, *'Ajā'ib*, vol. 2, p. 116.
67. Ibid., vol. 3, p. 7.
68. Ibid., p. 25; Jabartī, *Tārīkh*, f. 18b (our quotation is of S. Moreh's translation); cf. *Histoire scientifique*, vol. 4, p. 165–6.
69. *Histoire scientifique*, vol. 4, p. 166.
70. Jabartī, *'Ajā'ib*, vol. 3, pp. 92, 96.
71. Ibid., p. 332.
72. Ibid., pp. 93–4; 96.
73. *Histoire scientifique*, vol. 7, pp. 412–13.
74. Jabartī, *'Ajā'ib*, vol. 3, p. 94; Nicolas Turc, p. 86.
75. Jabartī, *'Ajā'ib*, vol. 3, pp. 92, 96; Nicolas Turc, p. 84.
76. Raymond, *Artisans*, pp. 432–3.
77. Aḥmad Çelebi, ff. 79b–80a.
78. Ibid., f. 235b.
79. Ibid., f. 155a. The students who had remained in the Azhar fought the rioters with guns and sticks.
80. Jabartī, *'Ajā'ib*, vol. 2, pp. 8–9. For Aḥmad al-Dardīr's biography see ibid., pp. 147–8.
81. Ibid., p. 103.
82. Ibid., pp. 147–8, and 'Bayyūmiyya', *EI*[2].
83. Jabartī, *'Ajā'ib*, vol. 2, pp. 258–9.
84. Ibid., vol. 3, p. 25. Also Jabartī, *Tārīkh*, f. 18a.
85. Jabartī, *Tārīkh*, ff. 18b–19a (S. Moreh's translation).
86. Napoléon, *Campagnes*, vol. 2, pp. 252, 255, 256.
87. Jabartī, *Tārīkh*, f. 18a. In his *'Ajā'ib*, written years later, Jabartī added: 'some of the *muta'ammimīn*, who did not think about the consequences' (*lam yanẓur fī 'awāqib al-umūr*).
88. Napoléon, *Campagnes*, vol. 2, p. 252. According to the *Histoire scientifique*, vol. 4, p. 154, this assembly, which was held in the night between 20 and 21 October, consisted of thirty people only.

89. Jabartī, *Tārīkh*, f. 18a (S. Moreh's translation).
90. Jabartī, *'Ajā'ib*, vol. 1, p. 373. For the biography of Ibn al-Naqīb and the story of Badr al-Dīn up to the year 1805 see ibid., pp. 371–4.
91. Ibid., p. 374.
92. Ibid., vol. 3, pp. 27–8; Jabartī, *Tārīkh*, f. 21b.
93. For his biography see Jabartī, *'Ajā'ib*, vol. 3, p. 61.
94. See above, note 83.
95. See, e.g., *Histoire scientifique*, vol. 4, pp. 153–4. However, later on the same source says that he was arrested as the result of calumny by other shaykhs – see ibid., p. 190.
96. The following account is based on Jabartī, *'Ajā'ib*, vol. 3, pp. 61–2.
97. Ibid., p. 88–9.
98. Ibid.
99. Ibid., p. 90.
100. For their predominant part in the civil war see Nicolas Turc, p. 80 ff.; and Jabartī, *'Ajā'ib*, vol. 3, pp. 91–5.
101. See Jabartī, ibid., p. 98. For his biography see ibid., pp. 171–2.
102. Ibid., pp. 91 (twice) and 98.
103. See ibid., pp. 323–6, for Aḥmad Maḥrūqī's biography.
104. Jabartī has no biography of 'Umar Makram because his chronicle ends shortly before 'Umar Makram's death (1822). There are many modern panegyrics of the hero 'Umar Makram. One of the most recent fairly scholarly ones is by Dr. 'Abd al-'Azīz Muḥammad al-Shanāwī, Professor of Modern and Contemporary History at al-Azhar University: *'Umar Makram, baṭal al-muqāwama al-sha'biyya*, Cairo, 1967.
105. In Jabartī's list of those who incited the people to join the *jihād*, 'al-Sayyid 'Umar al-Naqīb' is listed separately from *'al-mashāyikh wa'l fuqahā'* – *'Ajā'ib*, vol. 3, p. 98.
106. Ibid.
107. Ibid., pp. 99, 102–3.
108. Ibid., pp. 98–9.
109. Ibid., pp. 99–100.
110. Ibid., pp. 94, 100.
111. Ibid., pp. 94, 99.
112. Ibid., p. 103.
113. Ibid., p. 100.
114. The fullest description of the background and details of this struggle is of course Jabartī's – ibid., pp. 228 ff. A good modern analysis is Shafik Ghorbal, *The beginnings of the Egyptian question and the rise of Mehemet Ali*, London, 1928, pp. 207–32.
115. Jabartī, ibid., p. 328.
116. Ibid., p. 329. For the list of demands see also G. Douin, *Mohamed Aly, Pacha du Caire (1805–1807)*, Cairo, 1926, pp. 26–7.
117. Jabartī, vol. 3, pp. 329–30; cf. also vol. 4, pp. 32–5.
118. Ibid., vol. 3, p. 330.
119. Moreover, it would seem that their importance in bringing about Muḥammad 'Alī's victory has been considerably overestimated, partly, perhaps, as the result of the evaluation of contemporary French observers,

such as Drovetti, the French representative in Alexandria (see, e.g. Douin, pp. 36–7). This may have been a Napoleonic heritage, or wishful thinking, as a counterpoise to Alfī Bey's Mamluks, Britain's clients. The legitimation of the newly established order by the *'ulamā'* was of course important as a moral prop, but Western observers tend to attribute to it an operational and decisive influence which it has not had.

120. Jabartī, *'Ajā'ib*, vol. 3, p. 338.
121. Ibid., p. 331. See especially the discussion between 'Umar Makram and Hurşid's messenger, which has often been adduced by modern writers as an illustration for the role played by the *'ulamā'* in these events (see note 119 above). Cf. A. Rifaat Bey, *The awakening of modern Egypt*, London, 1947, p. 19; A. Loutfi el-Sayed, 'The role of the *'ulamā'* in Egypt during the early nineteenth century', in P. M. Holt (ed.), *Political and social change in modern Egypt*, London, 1968, p. 273 f.
122. Jabartī, *'Ajā'ib*, vol. 3, pp. 330, 332, 334; Douin, p. 35.
123. Douin, p. 45.
124. Tuesday, 10 July 1805, Jabartī, ibid., p. 336.
125. Thursday, 12 July 1805, ibid., p. 337.
126. Friday, 13 July 1805, ibid., p. 338.
127. Ibid., p. 333.
128. Ibid., p. 332.
129. See Jabartī, *'Ajā'ib*, vol. 4, p. 279. He was executed by the *muḥtasib* on 31 July 1817. For a detailed biography of this popular leader see A. Raymond, 'Deux leaders populaires au Caire à la fin du xviie et au début du xixe siècle,' *La Nouvelle Revue du Caire*, vol. 1, 1975, pp. 281–98.
130. Ibid., vol. 3, pp. 333–4.
131. Ibid., p. 335.
132. Ibid., p. 336.
133. For the lack of political functions performed by the shaykhs of the guilds in Ottoman Egypt, and the temporary change in this respect which occurred as the result of the French occupation, see Baer, *Egyptian guilds*, p. 75.

2

FELLAH REBELLION IN EGYPT AND THE FERTILE CRESCENT

Introduction

In this chapter 'fellah rebellion' is considered to be a movement of resistance against the ruling authority whose participants are predominantly fellahs, i.e. settled peasants. Accordingly, we have excluded from our discussion rebellions of semi-sedentary and tribal populations, such as the Kurdish revolts and the insurrection of 1920 in Iraq. Similarly, we do not intend to deal with wars between different groups of peasants, such as the feud between the Qays and Yaman factions or the communal clashes in nineteenth century Lebanon.[1]

We shall begin our discussion with a fellah rebellion which occurred exactly 200 years ago. This does not mean that such rebellions did not take place in this area prior to the end of the eighteenth century. On the contrary, there are indications that they did. In his treatise on the Egyptian fellah Shirbīnī mentions as one of the functions of the *kāshif* the suppression of riots or revolts of fellahs against their *multazim* or the *qā'immaqām*.[2] Similarly, in a collection of Ottoman documents on Palestine, some armed rebellions of fellahs are mentioned.[3] However, so far too little is known on the rural history of Egypt and the Fertile Crescent prior to the eighteenth century to include this information in a meaningful analysis of fellah rebellions.

Throughout the last 200 years there was no generation which did not witness a fellah rebellion in at least one of the areas of Egypt or the Fertile Crescent. The first about which some documentation exists was the insurrection in Ṭahṭa, Upper Egypt, recorded by the French naval officer Sonnini in 1778. In 1795 villagers of Sharqiyya marched to Cairo to present their claims.[4] Meanwhile Lebanese fellahs had rebelled against the ruling authorities in 1784 and 1790.[5] A wave of peasant rebellions swept Egypt in 1798 when fellahs in various areas of the northern Delta as well as in Upper Egypt resisted the French. Fellah insurrections did not stop, but rather multiplied during the reign of Muḥammad ʻAlī. After isolated instances of fellah protest near Benhā in August 1807 and against Muʻallim Ghālī, Muḥammad ʻAlī's chief agent for taxation and land registration, in the spring of 1812,[6] a considerable number of fellah revolts succeeded each other in the 1820s. In 1236/1820–1 fellahs revolted in the northern part of Qenā province, in 1822–3 in its southern part near Luxor, less than a year later in Minūfiyya, near Cairo, and at the beginning of 1824 a new large insurrection erupted in the Farshūṭ area, again the northern part of Qenā province. In 1826 the focus of revolt again moved to Sharqiyya.[7]

For the following twenty years Muhammad ʻAlī apparently was not troubled by rebellions of Egyptian fellahs. However, the fellahs of the empire he had created were not quiet at all. In 1834 his son Ibrāhīm had great difficulties in quelling an uprising in Palestine known by the name of the 'peasants' revolt', and in 1837–8 the Druze peasants of the Ḥawrān revolted and defeated several Egyptian military expeditions. Similarly, in the Nuṣayriyya Mountains the Egyptians established control only after suppressing two successive insurrections of the ʻAlawī peasants, in the autumn of 1834 and in spring 1835.[8] Finally, in 1840, the Lebanese peasants revolted against Ibrāhīm Pasha and Bashīr II in the so-called *ʻāmmiyya*. Before this, a smaller revolt against Bashīr had occurred already in 1820.[9]

After the end of Egyptian rule in the Fertile Crescent, peasant revolt reappeared in Egypt, and towards the end of Muḥammad ʻAlī's rule, in 1846, several rebellions of Egyptian peasants were recorded by his Armenian engineer Hekekyan, both in the rice-growing areas of the Delta (Sharqiyya province) and in Middle Egypt (Minyā).[10]

Muḥammad ʻAlī's successors were not saved from peasant unrest either. Several villages in Gīza district revolted in 1854; in the years 1863–5 there was a great deal of unrest among fellahs of Upper Egypt in general and the district of Abū Tīg (Asyūṭ) in particular, and in the years 1877–9 uprisings broke out mainly in the district between Sūhāg and Girgā. In 1880 unrest moved to the rice-growing region of the Delta, as it had done in 1846. Finally, in 1882, a strike broke out among the tenants of the Khedive's estates in Zankalūn (Sharqiyya).[11] After this the British occupation of Egypt in 1882 put an end to fellah rebellions for more than a generation.

Meanwhile, however, the Lebanon had been the arena of a peasant revolt which resulted in the expulsion of the feudal Khāzin lords and the establishment of a peasant republic in Kisrawān in the years 1858–61. This revolution is certainly the best documented of all the rebellions in the Middle East and it differed in many of its features from most of the others. Moreover, it has been studied in recent years by a number of scholars, whose works will be used in the following analysis.[12] At the same time the ʿAlawī peasants continued to harass the Ottoman government which had been re-established after the withdrawal of the Egyptians from the Fertile Crescent,[13] and towards the end of the century, the Druze fellahs of the Ḥawrān rose against their shaykhs in 1890 and against the Ottomans in 1877–9 and 1895–6.[14]

Between the two World Wars fellah rebellions broke out in three countries in some connection or another with the national movement against foreign rule. In Egypt, in 1919, fellahs not only participated conspicuously in the anti-British nationalist revolt, but also attacked, in Upper Egypt, large landowners;[15] in Syria the Druze peasants started the revolt of 1925 and continued to constitute its main element until it was suppressed; and in the years 1936–8 the Palestine Arab revolt was carried out mainly by Muslim villagers of the lower strata.[16] We shall try to find out what these revolts had in common with other fellah revolts in the Middle East and elsewhere, and to what extent they differed from them and from each other. In the late 1930s there was also rural unrest in the Kurdish mountains of northern Syria.[16a]

Finally, clashes between Egyptian fellahs and officials who executed foreclosures during the depression of the 1930s[17] were the first signs of a much wider movement which gained momentum after World War Two. Insurrections of fellahs against their landlords had occurred apparently in the Mosul area as early as 1946, and in ʿArbat, a Kurdish village southeast of Sulaymāniyya, in 1947.[18] Five years later, in 1951, widespread agrarian unrest occurred in Egypt as well as in Syria. During that year armed clashes between Egyptian fellahs and their landlords or the official security forces happened in Buhūt (Gharbiyya), Kufūr Nijm (Sharqiyya) and Dikirnis (Daqahliyya). In al-Sirū (Daqahliyya) peasants carried out a sitdown strike.[19] In Syria peasant rebellions against landowners spread during that year to Ḥoms, Ḥamāh, Māʿarrat al-Nuʿmān, Ḥawrān, and Lādhiqiyya.[20] From 1952 onwards fellah insurrection became endemic in Iraq: in 1952 in ʿAmāra, 1953 in Arbīl and Diyālā, 1954 in al-Shāmiyya (Dīwāniyya), 1955 in Rumaytha, 1958 again in Kūt, ʿAmāra, and Dīwāniyya, and 1959 again in Mosul.[21] Unrest continued in Iraq in the 1960s, while in Egypt and Syria no fellah insurrections have occurred (or have become known?) since the establishment of military regimes and the implementation of agrarian reforms in each of these countries.

Background and motives

Under what conditions did fellah rebellions happen in Egypt and the

Fertile Crescent during the last 200 years? Obviously, revolt was easier for those peasants who were located out of the reach of the ruling authority. This has been observed as a basic condition of peasant revolt all over the world. 'There were thus some geographical features that were common to the areas where revolts occurred most often: distance from the capital ...; a certain degree of isolation and difficult communications which result in an area which is relatively backward from the economic standpoint, in the feeling that it is at a disadvantage in relation to other areas and exploited by "outsiders", ... the demands of the state, not balanced by a firm hand on its own agents, on the lords, or on the mere entrepreneurs and landowners, because its control over these areas was feebler than elsewhere, and the strong could oppress the humble people with impunity.'[22] And another author adds that the tactical effectiveness of rebellions in peripheral areas 'is "tripled" if they contain also defensible mountainous redoubts'.[23] Generally speaking peasant rebellions in Egypt and the Fertile Crescent during the last 200 years fitted into this geographical pattern. The total number of peasant rebellions mentioned above amounts to about forty. More than a quarter of these rebellions occurred in the mountainous areas of Syria and Palestine: Judea and Samaria, Jabal al-Durūz in the Ḥawrān, the Nuṣayriyya mountains, the Kurdish mountains of northern Syria, and Lebanon. Almost one fifth took place in Upper Egypt, far away from the centre of government in Egypt, Cairo. Another fifth occurred in the more distant areas of the Egyptian Delta, in which the government was weaker than near the capital: the northern Delta, Sharqiyya, and Daqahliyya. Similarly, most of the Iraqi peasant uprisings took place in areas bordering on the desert, such as Dīwāniyya or the northern border districts, such as Sulaymāniyya, Mosul or Arbīl. Only three Egyptian fellah insurrections were recorded in provinces near to Cairo (Minūfiyya, Qalyūbiyya and Gīza) and two in areas not very distant from it (Gharbīyya and Minyā).

The record of the last two hundred years does not confirm two prevalent assumptions concerning the geographical distribution of peasant unrest in the Middle East. First, the 'submissive' Egyptian fellah has often been compared to the 'rebellious' Syrian one. Elsewhere I have tried at length to refute this theory;[24] the preceding list of fellah rebellions further shows that it is completely unfounded: more than half of all instances of which we found any trace in sources known to us occurred in Egypt. Nevertheless, it is true that the 'tactical effectiveness of rebellions', as Wolf put it, had been considerably strengthened when they occurred in mountainous areas, which exist in Syria but not in Egypt. Thus none of the Egyptian fellah insurrections lasted continuously three years, like the Kisrawān revolt, or even two years, like the Druze revolt of 1925 – to give only two examples. Moreover, it was always much easier to suppress Egyptian fellah insurrections, even in far away Upper Egypt, than to fight Druze guerillas who used to retreat into the rough and forbidding lava area of al-Laj'a ('refuge', generally rendered: Leja) northwest of the Jabal, where 'groups of 3–5 would lay ambushes behind these rocks and shoot at the soldiers and hit them while the fire of the soldiers would rarely hit the bandits'.[25] Similarly mistaken is the assumption that most Egyptian peasant revolts occurred in Upper Egypt. This is how an otherwise excellent observer of Egyptian society put it about the middle of the nineteenth century: 'In the Saïd these people, fellâhs by birth and position, are distinguished from the serfs of the Delta, and other low provinces by many peculiarities . . . one which, no doubt, depends principally on their distance from the seat of government. This is their love of arms and their independent disposition. In spite of the attempt, made frequently, to disarm them, warlike weapons are constantly to be seen in their hands – spears, swords, and even guns. . . . The few formidable insurrections that have taken place among the Egyptian peasants have been about Siout'.[26] This is not exact even if we count only the rebellions which occurred prior to the time when Bayle St. John wrote his book; among the twenty-two Egyptian rebellions listed above for the whole period covered by this essay, only eight took place in Upper Egypt. Bayle St. John certainly was under the impression of the wave of insurrections in Upper Egypt, which occurred in the 1820s under Muḥammad 'Alī. But some areas in the Northern Delta and Sharqiyya were even less accessible to the central authorities than Upper Egypt, which consisted of a narrow strip of cultivated land along the Nile.

Favourable geographical conditions were not the only factor contributing to the outbreak of fellah rebellion – political conditions played an important role as well. They manifested themselves in three major patterns. First, just as the Hundred Years' War served as a background for the French Jacquerie in 1357 and the rural insurrection in England in 1381, many Middle Eastern fellah rebellions too broke out after the central government had been weakened by wars or otherwise. The insurrection in Upper Egypt in 1778 came in the wake of the civil war between Ismā'īl Bey on one hand and Murād and Ibrāhīm on the other, and the Lebanese fellahs rebelled in 1784 and 1790 when the rule of the Shihābī Amīr Yūsuf was weakened by civil war instigated or supported by Jazzār Pasha. Fellah resistance against the French in 1798 followed the destruction of the traditional power structure of the Mamluks and the Ottoman army. The 1846 rebellions occurred during the last years of Muḥammad 'Alī's rule when his vigour had weakened considerably, and the 1854 rebellion took place in the period between the death of 'Abbās and Sa'īd's ascension to the throne. The years 1877–82 were years of a general political upheaval and disintegration of government which led to the deposition of Ismā'īl, the 'Urābī rebellion and the British occupation. In addition, these were also years of natural calamities, such as drought, livestock epidemics and others,[27] which had often served as a background to peasant uprisings in European countries as well.[28] On the other hand, the establishment of a strong central government in the wake of the British occupation introduced a period of almost forty years without peasant rebellions in Egypt. This period was terminated by World War I which brought with it the termination of Egypt's Ottoman connection, the insecurity of Egypt's political future, the exhaustion of the British army and the undermining of the British-inspired Egyptian conservative government by the upsurge of the national movement. This was the background of Egypt's rural unrest in 1919. Conditions after World War II had again considerably unbalanced the political system of Egypt. The defeat in the war with Israel, the deterioration of the prestige of the ruling monarch, the unsolved conflict with Britain as well as economic hardship of wide sections of the population caused by the war had all weakened the power of the government to rule and served as a fertile ground for the eruption of social conflicts in 1951 and 1952. In Syria the post-war political upheaval had even been greater: in the wake of the Palestine debacle there had occurred, by 1951, a number of successive *coups d'état* and more were to follow; in addition, Syrian politics had been permeated by inter-Arab rivalries which made them extremely unstable. Moreover, in both Egypt and Syria central figures of the tottering political establishments were themselves large landowners, against whom the rebellions were directed: e.g., Fārūq and the Muḥammad 'Alī family in Egypt, or the Barāzī family in Syria. In Iraq, in the late 1940s and the 1950s, the political regime had been undermined by urban unrest of workers and students unleashed by the conflict with Britain which needed, from time to time, military intervention; after 1952, Nasserist propaganda had exacerbated the situation and in 1959 fellah unrest was connected with the Shawwāf revolt in Mosul. Finally, in Palestine in 1936–8 government in the Arab sector had collapsed as the result of the nationalist rebellion against British policy of support for the establishment of the Jewish National Home. But here peasant bands came to the fore as the result of the suppression of disorder in the towns, the elimination of the traditional urban leadership of the national movement by rigorous measures taken by the Mandatory Government, and the discontinuation of non-Palestinian Arab military intervention in the struggle.

The second and third pattern of political conditions contributing to fellah rebellions in the Middle East involved not the weakening of the central government but rather the opposite – the imposition of central rule or control upon intermediate, local or autonomous forces. This contributed to fellah insurrections in two different ways: either the imposition of central control weakened local lords or intermediate tax-farmers to such an extent that the fellahs were able to exploit the situation and revolt against them; or the local lords were strong enough and influential enough among their peasant dependants to be able to react against the attempt of the central government by revolting against it at the head of their fellahs. The first case (our second pattern) is represented by two important instances of fellah rebellion: the rural unrest in the early years of Muḥammad 'Alī's rule and the peasant revolt of 1858 in Kisrawān. The power of the *multazims* – the tax-farmers and traditional absentee lords of the Egyptian countryside – was thoroughly undermined by Muḥammad 'Alī soon after he had come to power: in 1811 he staged the great massacre of the Mamluks (the most important *multazims*), then he set up a special *dīwān* to hear fellah grievances, then he confiscated the *iltizāms* in Upper Egypt, and finally, in 1814, those of Lower Egypt. Thus the traditional agrarian structure had been shaken by the attempt to impose direct rule of the central government. When former *multazims* tried to make fellahs work on their private *ūsiyya* land which they had retained in Lower Egypt, – as they were used to do in former times – their answer was: 'Find someone else, I'm busy. What remains to you in this land? Your days are past, now we are the Pasha's fellahs!'[29] In Kisrawān the curtailment of the power of the *muqāṭa'ajīs*, the local lords, dated back to the rule of Bashīr II who, among other measures, had taken away from them judicial authority and, like Muḥammad 'Alī, encouraged the peasants to voice complaints against the shaykhs. After the restoration of Ottoman rule, Shakīb Effendi's scheme for the reorganization of Lebanon's administration subordinated the shaykhs of the *muqāṭa'āt* to the *qā'imaqāms*, the Ottoman governors, to councils that were to advise the *qā'imaqāms*, and to *wakīls* – representatives of the population – which considerably strengthened the emancipatory trends among the peasantry. Finally, the Ottoman authorities did nothing to prevent the peasants from organizing against the growing oppression by their lords, the Khāzins: they welcomed all unrest that might serve as a pretext for restricting Lebanon's autonomy.[30]

The third pattern, revolt of local lords at the head of their fellahs against imposition of centralized government, was peculiar to the mountain areas, the hills of Judea and Samaria in Palestine, Jabal Durūz in the Ḥawrān, Jabal Nuṣayriyya near Lādhiqiyya and Lebanon. In 1834 the local rural notables of the hilly areas in Palestine resisted conscription decreed by the Egyptian government because this would have undermined the patron-client relation between them and their fellahs. The same happened in Jabal Durūz four years later. In 1840 Lebanese peasants followed their notables in the revolt against Bashīr II and the Egyptians, who had attempted to impose various measures of direct rule such as taxation, conscription, and forced labour. The 'Alawī chiefs rebelled for similar reasons, at the head of the rural population of Jabal Nuṣayriyya in the 1850s against the Ottomans who attempted to re-establish central government after the Egyptians had withdrawn in 1840.[31] Agrarian unrest in the Druze area of Ḥawrān towards the end of the nineteenth century was closely connected with the administrative reform of Midhat Pasha, *Vali* of Damascus in 1878–80, who had appointed an Ottoman *qā'imaqām* in Suwaydā, divided the Jabal into eight *mudīriyya*s, and established official law-courts and military posts.[32] And in 1925, Captain Carbillet again attempted to establish direct rule of the central French Mandatory government and thus stirred up the Druze lords to revolt at the head of their peasants.

> Until then the population had thronged the audience halls where the Druze lords entertain their guests at the expense of the village. These guest houses of the nobles became less frequented. The peasants began to question the utility of the contributions demanded from them for the upkeep of this hospitality when they saw petitioners and plaintiffs repairing more and more to the French officers. There is no doubt that this produced a certain resentment among the chiefs . . . To destroy the prestige of the lords . . . was his [Carbillet's] deliberate aim; but his fatal mistake was to embark on this formidable enterprise without first having made sure of the peasantry's good will. So far from this, he had contrived to exasperate all classes of the population alike.[33]

However, in addition to general geographical and political conditions contributing to the occurrence of fellah rebellions, concrete immediate causes were necessary to bring about this eruption. Up to the end of the nineteenth century the most important of such causes was the aggravation of the tax-burden. Rulers of Egypt and the Fertile Crescent felt the need to increase their revenue for various reasons. During the later part of the eighteenth century the Mamluk Beys of Egypt recovered their predominance over the *ocak*s, the Ottoman military units, and began to exact more and more taxes from the population – *inter alia* in order to expand their mercenary troops which they needed to fight each other. 'Ce "brigandage général de la part des Beys, de leurs gens et des officiers les plus subalternes", comme écrivait Mure [French consul], ne put naturellement que s'aggraver lorsque le conflit entre Murād Bey et Ismā'īl Bey menaça de tourner à la guerre civile'.[34] This, according to the French naval officer Sonnini, was the motive of the peasant insurrection in Upper Egypt at that time.[35] When Muḥammad 'Alī had come to power, he needed an ever increasing amount of revenue for the establishment of his new army (the *niẓām-i cedid*), the building up of a powerful fleet, the wars in Arabia, Sudan, and Greece, the erection of numerous factories and workshops and the building of a network of irrigation canals and regulators, as well as the Maḥmūdiyya Canal. For this purpose taxation was increased more than tenfold. Up to the 1820s, land tax continued to amount to more than half the total revenue. Thus fellahs had to bear the brunt of the additional burden, and this was the immediate cause of most of the insurrections in the early years of his reign and in the 1820s – Luxor in 1822–3, Minūfiyya in 1823, and Sharqiyya in 1826.[36] A similar situation arose in the 1870s. The Khedive Ismā'īl needed ever increasing amounts of money for his public works, the Abyssinian War of 1815, successive payments to the Sultan to increase gradually his autonomous privileges and titles, for acquiring landed estates from his relatives and, last not least, for the building of palaces and other means of ostentation. The iniquitous conditions of the loans he contracted to cover his needs only submerged him in ever swelling financial obligations. As a result, he tried to squeeze his fellahs to the utmost limits. After he had already raised the liability on medium and low quality land from one-third of the harvest to almost one-half, he introduced additional taxes in the late 1860s and early 1870s. After the end of the cotton boom, fellahs could definitely no longer pay these taxes. In 1877, the authorities in Upper Egypt tried to collect the taxes by selling the fellahs' property or confiscating their live-stock. Many fellahs left their villages and lost their land, but others resorted to revolt. The result was the violent resistance and rebellion of fellahs between Sūhāg and Girgā in the years 1877–9.[37]

But it was not only in Egypt that increased taxation led to peasant unrest. Additional taxes caused, in Lebanon, the revolts against Amīr Yūsuf in 1784 and against Bashīr II and Jazzār in 1790.[38] In 1820 Amīr Bashīr doubled the tax imposed on Lebanon's peasants in order to be able to satisfy the Ottoman Pasha's additional demands and to pay for the building of his palace and for his mercenaries.[39] And the revolt against Ibrāhīm Pasha in 1840 was the result, *inter alia*, of the introduction of an oppressive system of taxation by the Egyptian government. By now taxes were collected several times every year, often in advance. The main use of this additional revenue was the maintenance of the Egyptian army and the wars waged by Ibrāhīm Pasha. According to the Russian Consul General in Beirut early in the nineteenth century, the Lebanese *jizya* amounted to 150,000 piastres in the 1770s and to 600,000 at the end of the century; French diplomatic sources mention a sum of 2.5 million piastres for taxes collected in Lebanon in the 1820s, and 8.75 million for the time of the Egyptian occupation.[40] This meant an enormous increase in taxation, even if we take into account that the currency was depreciated by half in the eighteenth century and again, up to the 1830s, to about one-fifth of its value at the beginning of the nineteenth century.

Taxation also was an important cause for the revolt of the 'Alawī peasants against Egyptian rule in the 1830s,[41] as well as for the Druze rebellion in the Ḥawrān in 1895. In both cases it was the concomitant of the centralization of government. And even in mid-nineteenth century Lebanon, the Khāzins' attempt to boost tax collections among the peasants in an endeavour to increase their declining revenue was one of the causes of the revolt, though not the most important one.[43]

From this point of view fellah rebellions in Egypt and the Fertile Crescent up to the end of the nineteenth century resembled peasant uprisings in many other countries of the world in various periods. 'Where the royal authority has increased and intensified the burden on the peasantry in order to meet the costs of an expanding military establishment and administrative bureaucracy, as well as an expensive policy of courtly magnificence, the growth of royal absolutism may contribute heavily to peasant explosions.'[44] In the seventeenth century,

> the immediate and proclaimed motive of the revolts was, in the majority of cases, in France, the burden of taxation imposed by the state. Increased taxes, new taxes, taxes collected more strictly – those provide the acknowledged reason for rebellion . . . in Russia state taxation was also a heavy burden and was certainly one of the underlying causes of the revolts . . . In China too, increased tax burdens were a cause of revolt . . . There seem to have been two main reasons for this increase in the pressure of taxation. The first, and by far the most important, was the frequency of national wars . . . The second reason was the development of the organs of the state itself, which was becoming more and more centralized and administrative in character – the increase in the number of its agents, through whom alone it could be effective.[45]

Similarly, in Japan of the Tokugawa period, 'the rate of taxation was high, and there was a natural tendency for it to get higher as the standard of living of the tax-receiving *samurai* class rose . . . Taxes amounting to 60 per cent of the crop were by no means uncommon and special levies and advance collections were frequent. The recurrence of peasant revolts . . . showed how near these exactions brought the peasants to desperation'. Similar troubles accompanied the reform of the tax system in the early Meiji period.[46] And in Southern India too 'peasants revolted several times from the beginning of the 19th century to protest against the exorbitant land revenue exactions, the neglect of irrigation facilities and the extortionate method of tax collection'.[47]

However, in the Middle East, unlike most other countries in the world, resentment against the increased tax burden was frequently accompanied, prior to the twentieth century, by resistance against conscription to the army as a major cause of fellah rebellion. This was the case in particular in the revolts against Ibrāhīm Pasha and the revolts of Druze peasants, but not exclusively so. This is how the Monk Neophytos of Cyprus described the causes of the insurrection of the 'fellaheen' in his entry for April 28, 1834, in the manuscript from the Mar Saba collection:

> 'In those days there was a great uprising in all Arabia, and in all the villages around Jerusalem, in Judea and Samaria, for the people revolted against Ibrahim Pasha, the Egyptian overlord.
>
> These were the causes of rebellion. On the 4th day of *Diakainesimos* (Easter Wednesday) April 25, Ibrahim Pasha convoked all the leading men and notables of the districts of Samaria and Judea and put to them the following questions: "As we, Moslems, have as perpetual enemies the Nazarene nations, is it or is it not necessary for us to have a big standing army?" They replied: "Yes, undoubtedly it is necessary".
>
> The Pasha continued: "If so, from whom shall we take men for this army, from the Christians or from the Moslems?"
>
> They replied: "From the Moslems, assuredly."
>
> He said: "You have answered aright. Therefore, it is necessary for you, if you are true Moslems and with the welfare of the nation, to send in your young men from every city and from every village, so that they may learn from their youth the art of war and be trained in it, and so be ready in case of need."
>
> Silence fell upon the meeting and for long they thought of the reply: "Your order be upon our heads, but there is no need for us to give our boys and young men for war. When the enemy of our religion enters our country, all of us, young and old, will go out and fight and willingly shed our blood for our faith and our fatherland.'

Thus, the leader of the revolt, Qāsim al-Aḥmad, wrote the following to the leaders of the Jerusalem and Hebron districts: . . . 'Fight bravely for your homes and your honour, for your rights and especially for your beloved children of whom he is thinking to deprive you for military service . . .'[48]

Conscription of Lebanese peasants into the army by Ibrāhīm Pasha, in violation of early promises to abstain from such measures, was one of the major reasons for the 1840 insurrection in Lebanon as well. First one male out of three was recruited in each family, and in 1840 one out of two. The immediate impulse of the revolt was the order to disarm the population of Mount Lebanon. But the Lebanese peasants rightly perceived that this measure was nothing but a preparation for recruiting them into the army, and thus decided to revolt.[49] Resistance to conscription also played an important part as a motive for the revolt of Druze fellahs in the Ḥawrān against Ibrāhīm in 1838 and against the

Ottoman administration in 1895.[50] Some of the insurrections of Egyptian fellahs in the 1820s were also the result of the refusal of fellahs to serve in the newly formed *nizām-i cedid* of Muḥammad ʻAlī. This is what happened in Minūfiyya in 1823 and in the Farshūṭ district of Qenā province early in 1824; and in April 1838 an uprising in the area of Manfalūṭ in Upper Egypt occurred when the population refused to furnish the contingent claimed from it.[51] In a somewhat different and rather indirect form the same theme recurred as late as in the period of World War I, when the conscription of peasants into labour battalions during the War was among the important factors which had incited them and which led in 1919 to their participation in the revolt.[52] The reason why conscription constituted an important cause for fellah rebellions in the Middle East but not in other parts of the world was the fact that Arabs of the Middle East considered the army as being composed of Turks and slaves, and that the centralized administration was imposed in the nineteenth century quite suddenly and from above while local forces were still strong and no national consciousness had yet developed from below – certainly not among the illiterate fellahs.

Conscription to the army was a novelty for Arab fellahs in the nineteenth century, against which they rebelled when conditions were suitable for rebellion. On the other hand, forced labour (*corvée*) for public needs, such as building dams to prevent inundations or to till the private plot of the *multazim*, was common and considered legitimate. There were, however, certain groups of the population who were exempted from this duty, or whose obligations in this matter or similar matters were limited. When attempts were made to encroach on their privileges, such groups tended to resist violently. Thus Lebanese peasants were used to *corvée* duties for their shaykhs, the *muqāṭaʻajī*s, but under the Egyptian occupation they were forced to supply labour for completely uncommon services, such as the transportation of munitions and provisions to army camps, the working of coal mines in Qurnāyil and Salīma under terrible conditions, as well as the conveyance of the coal from these mines to the ports of Acre, Beirut and Jūnya. There can be no doubt that this was one of the causes for revolt in 1840.[53] A parallel and connected case was the billeting of soldiers with the peasants in order to secure the payment of taxes (*ḥawwāla* in Lebanon). This was the privilege of the Amīr and the *muqāṭaʻajī*s, but when Ibrāhīm Pasha resorted to the same measure in 1840 the Lebanese peasants resisted.[54] In Egypt, as Consul Borg explained in one of his excellent reports, 'Rice growers, from time immemorial, have been exempted from sending men to Corvées, and have enjoyed the privilege of obtaining men from neighbouring moudiriahs to assist them in the harvest season'. But, as we learn from an entry in the diary of Muḥammad ʻAlī's Armenian engineer Hekekyan, in 1846, 'the Pasha orders such a large quantity of land to be cultivated in rice that the disposable lands in the villages are not sufficient and as efforts might be made to press men from the private cultivators of rice we see entire villages armed night and day defying the officers of the Government.... Of 180 men taken from Coreyn [Qurayn, Sharqiyya] for works of the rice mill, 70 ran away to work in their own fields.' And Borg continues his report, written in May 1880, as follows: 'The Minister of Public Works insisted, this year, that those privileges should not be continued ... The consequence of this was that the Chiefs made a stand against the measure – the Behera province has no sufficient hands to spare ...'.[55] Similarly, in 1925 Captain Carbillet's public works were executed by compulsory and unpaid labour so that the forced levies among the Druzes became heavier in the Jabal than in the State of Damascus, although the Druzes had been less accustomed than the Damascenes to bear the yoke of *corvées*. The peasantry evidently considered the burden of the *corvées* to outweigh the benefits that accrued to them from Captain Carbillet's agrarian policy, and therefore they joined the revolt.[56] Elsewhere, the revival of the *corvée* or the introduction of additional *corvées* had contributed to the English peasant revolt of 1381, the French rebellions of the 1660s and the German peasant war of 1525.[57]

From the middle of the nineteenth century onwards, peasant revolts in Egypt and Lebanon were no longer caused by fiscal pressure alone or by political coercion of fellahs to render unpaid services as soldiers or labourers, but rather by economic processes which brought about the deterioration of the fellah's position, such as rising rents, growing indebtedness, or loss of land tenure rights. In other parts of the Fertile Crescent a similar change occurred only much later, about the middle of the twentieth century. This change was the result of two related developments. First, the transition of Middle Eastern agriculture from a subsistence economy to cash crops. It should be stressed, however, that it was not this transition which brought about fellah rebellions, and even less the fiscal pressure which caused fellah rebellions. Both of these phenomena existed in the Middle East prior to the transformation of agriculture, as we have seen clearly by means of many examples above. The transformation of agriculture only changed the causes of fellah rebellion. The second development which brought about this change was the decline and disappearance of tax farming (*iltizām*) and the emergence of private landownership. Both of these developments happened in Egypt between fifty and a hundred years earlier than in the Fertile Crescent[58] – except for Lebanon. Lebanon was a special case with regard to land tenure and relations between landlord and peasant, but like Egypt it had been drawn into the orbit of the world economy by the middle of the nineteenth century.[59]

This, indeed, was the background for the immediate causes of the

1858 peasant revolt in Kisrawān.[60] The French Revolution had disrupted France's silk trade with Lebanon, severely affecting the position of the Khāzins, the lords of Kisrawān, as suppliers of the raw silk to the French spinneries. By the middle of the nineteenth century the silk trade with Europe had revived, but in a modified manner: the European traders now re-exported the silk to Lebanon in processed form, competing ruinously with the local cottage silk manufacturers of Lebanon which had employed the peasant women and constituted an important source of revenue for the shaykhs. The situation deteriorated further when the French set up modern spinning mills in the Shūf and Matn Districts, located closer to the port of Beirut than Kisrawān. Their economic decline forced the Khāzin shaykhs to sell land to their tenants, but they endeavoured to keep the peasants dependent on them by incorporating in the deeds of sale various provisions designed to stress this dependence, such as the obligation to deliver to them annual duties in kind or in cash. In addition, in order to increase their declining revenue, the Khāzins attempted to exact greater payments from their peasants, in taxes or otherwise. Moreover, the Khāzins redoubled their oppression of the peasantry by increasingly cruel and arbitrary treatment. A contemporary eye-witness put this as follows: '. . . Terror was instilled by the Khāzin family into the people of Kisrawān. For they no longer took any account of their subjects, not even of the leading persons among them. They would say that the fellah and his possessions belonged to them, showing not the slightest regard for him. The most insignificant of the Khāzins would insult the most eminent of the people . . .'[61] Finally, the economic position of the Kisrawān shaykhs and their peasants was hit acutely by the 1857 crisis in the silk trade in the wake of the Crimean War, as well as by a number of natural calamities.[62]

The new economic and social trends of the late nineteenth and twentieth century contributed to the outbreak of peasant rebellions in other parts of the Middle East as well. In 1865 a rebellion occurred among the fellahs working on the estates of the Khedive Ismā'īl in Upper Egypt south of Abū Tīg. After the cotton boom of the early 1860s, which was the result of the American Civil War, prices collapsed from the second half of 1864 onwards.[63] As a result, the following happened in a village which must have been in the area afflicted by the rebellion – as described in one of the best accounts of Egypt's social developments at that time:[64]

> The prices of cotton being low, and the taxes higher than they had ever been before, the commune fell grievously into arrears; and one day an official came down from Cairo . . . he declared that the Khedive . . . would take over the debt with a portion of the land . . . the result was that three fourths of the land belonging to members of

the commune were detached from the remaining fourth and incorporated into a large Khedivial estate which was then being created in the vicinity. This estate was used as a sugar-plantation and on it was built a large sugar-factory . . . As the peasants had no longer sufficient land of their own, they willingly worked on the estate and in the factory, but the pay which they received was very small and paid very irregularly . . . At the same time, a great deal of gratis forced work had to be done.

The ensuing revolt, which was headed by Aḥmad 'al-Ṭayyib' who claimed to be a *mahdī*, has been described in detail in many sources, and we shall return to discuss various aspects of it. Here we are concerned with its causes, which have been summarized as follows by Hekekyan: 'Men dispossessed of their lands, and forced to remain on them, and made to work for daily wages 25 per cent of the daily wages freely given to other labourers on other lands, will of course begin to plunder and to massacre when they think they can do so with impunity.'[65]

As we have seen above, the agrarian unrest between Sūhāg and Girgā in Upper Egypt in the years 1877–9 was caused primarily by the swelling burden of taxation. One must add, however, that these were the years in which the problem of peasant indebtedness had become acute. As the result of the shift to a market economy, many of the fellahs now needed to buy the foodstuffs they had replaced by cash crops. Whereas they would formerly have had to abandon their plots or starve, in the event of drought or some other calamity, they could now borrow from a money-lender. Often, however, they were unable to redeem these debts. Moreover, since the middle of the nineteenth century fellahs owned their land so that they could now be granted credit on its security. The result was that, after an enormous growth in money-lenders' credit, much fellah land was foreclosed. One of the reasons for the increase in loans and foreclosures was the legal sanction given to the acquisition of land by foreigners in 1867–8 and the establishment of Mixed Courts in 1875, which brought about the introduction of mortgages as known in the West. Drought (1877–8) and floods (1878) aggravated the situation. Between 1876 and 1882 legal mortgages rose from £0.5 to £7.0 million, of which some £5.0 million were village mortgages. To this an estimated £3–4 million worth of debts to money-lenders should be added. In Upper Egypt, as in the Delta, land was often sold to pay the villagers' debts.[66] This was very similar to what happened in Southern India at exactly the same time.

During the boom years of the American Civil War, cotton and railway building brought new prosperity to the Deccan districts. Using as collateral the legal right acquired under raiyatwari, the peasant contracted heavy debts, and the end of the boom in the late

1860s, a series of bad harvests and a new and higher revenue assessment all combined to drag him down. When the money-lender hurriedly called in loans which the peasant had no hope of repaying, his land was put into jeopardy. He expressed his resentment in the Deccan Riots of 1875.[67]

Expropriation of land as the result of indebtedness became again the cause of agrarian unrest in Egypt in the 1930s, this time in a somewhat different way. As the result of the world economic crisis Egyptian landowners were severely hit, and their mortgaged land was frequently seized because they could not pay their debts. Those who suffered most were their tenants, who in many cases were evicted from the land. For instance, the following incident happened on 23 April, 1936. A great bank foreclosed the estate of a notable of Shubrā Rīs in Kafr al-Zayyāt District, which was rented to fellahs. When the officials arrived to execute the order, they met with the opposition of the villagers. The police intervened and sent an armed force, which was attacked by the tenants of the estate. Order was restored only after some fierce fights with the armed forces. 'Voilà une histoire qui n'est pas extraordinaire,' concludes Father Ayrout, who relates this event in his book on the Egyptian fellah.[68]

One of the greatest problems of Egypt's agrarian structure throughout the twentieth century was the rise of rents. Owing to the rapid population increase in relation to the available land rents rose considerably while real wages of agricultural workers remained constant or declined. After World War II, this problem was aggravated, like so many other social problems of Egypt. While the average rent per feddan amounted to £E7.2 in 1935–9, it had risen to £E16.5 in 1948, £E20.2 in 1950 and almost £E25 in 1951. This rise was partly the result of the cotton boom, and it brought about a number of peasant rebellions in 1951. The sharpest conflict took place on the estates of the Badrāwī-'Āshūr family in the village of Buhūt (Gharbiyya) in June of that year. Clashes between the villagers and security forces resulted in many casualties. Similar events took place in the course of the same year in Kufūr Nijm (Sharqiyya) on the estates of Prince Muḥammad 'Alī Tawfīq, then Crown Prince, and the Averoff estate near Dikirnis (Daqahliyya).[69]

In Syria, especially in Ḥamāh, a different development led to the relative, or even absolute, deterioration in the fellah's situation. In central Syria a prevalent share of division between the landowner and the cultivator was 50:50. But if the landowner provided seed, working livestock and water, he took 75 per cent of the gross produce. After World War II, cotton cultivation in the Ḥoms-Ḥamāh plain expanded considerably, which meant the increase in the proportion of share-croppers working for 25 per cent of the crop. Though in the Ḥoms region this may not have reduced their total income, in Ḥamāh it probably did, because of the increase of population in a densely settled area. This, as well as serious damage to the cotton crop done by worms, was the background for peasant unrest in the early 1950s, whose centre was Ḥamāh.[70]

Fellah rebellions in Iraq in the late 1940s and in the 1950s were the result of changes in land tenure or land tenure legislation. In 'Arbat, southeast of Sulaymāniyya, lands had been held by the peasants in the Ottoman period. But after World War I Shaykh Maḥmūd of the powerful Barzinja family gradually succeeded in taking possession of the entire village. His heir, Shaykh Laṭīf, imposed on the peasants a variety of additional dues, such as marriage fees, grazing charges, and a water tax, and he exacted from them forced and unpaid labour. This was the background of the 1947 rebellion.[70a] In 'Amāra, a southeastern province of Iraq, most of the land was up to the middle of the century *mīrī-ṣirf* land, i.e. full property of the state. It was in actual possession of powerful shaykhs, who formally were *multazim*s, tax farmers of the government. In other parts of the Middle East, tax farming had been abolished in the course of the nineteenth and the first half of the twentieth century, and the land, which formerly had belonged to the state, had become private property. But in Iraq, because of its tribal structure, a large proportion of the land had remained state domain, *mīrī ṣirf*. In the course of this transformation, large estates had been created or had emerged all over the Middle East, but since this was in general a gradual process it did not bring about violent upheavals. Iraq, however, attempted to perform such a transformation suddenly on a large scale, and at a time when Egypt had already decreed a law of land reform aiming at distributing the large estates among the peasants. According to the 1952 'Amāra law *lazma* (limited property) rights were to be granted as follows: the primary *multazim* – one-half of the area for which he had paid taxes plus 200 dunums (120 acres); the secondary *multazim* – one-quarter of the area which he had leased but not more than 90 acres; the fellahs – up to 15 dunums (9 acres) per family. Thus the shaykh and his family would have been able to secure most of the land, since the law considered a secondary *multazim* who was a relative of the shaykh as a primary *multazim*. This brought about violent resistance of the fellahs, first in 'Amāra in October 1952, and then in Arbīl in March 1953.[71] Like the 1951 fellah rebellions in Egypt, the rebellions in Iraq were the prelude to an agrarian reform which, together with military rule, was designed to prevent the recurrence of such events. But when the shaykhs and landlords attempted, in the Mosul revolt of 1959, to prevent the implementation of agrarian reform, the fellahs of that area rebelled again.[71a]

Demands and aims

Information about the demands made by rebelling fellahs is much scarcer than accounts of the background and causes of these rebellions. Obviously, in most cases one central demand was put forward by the rebels which resulted from their main grievance. Thus, when the Lebanese peasants of the Matn and of Kisrawān met in 1820 in Anṭalyās they demanded that taxes should only be levied from them once a year, '*māl wāḥid wa-jizya wāḥida*'.[72] The tenants of government land in al-Sirū (Daqahliyya) who carried out a sitdown strike in October 1951 demanded that the government keep its promise to sell them the land instead of offering it at a public auction, because 'public auctions inevitably benefit the capitalists . . . and the government cannot ignore the rights of those struggling for their piece of bread'.[73] Iraqi fellahs in the 1950s demanded either a more favourable distribution of *mīrī ṣirf* lands or of yields between them and the shaykhs.[74] In some cases a small number of demands were made by the insurgents covering two or three major issues of the revolt. Thus the leader of the fellahs of the Hebron area, 'Īsā 'Amr, wrote to Ibrāhīm Pasha in June 1834 and demanded the following: (a) a general amnesty and pardon should be granted to the rebels; (b) the levy of young men should be discontinued; (c) taxes higher than those paid to former Pashas should not be demanded.[75] When the fellah rebellion was connected with a nationalist movement, the aims of the nationalists usually determined the slogans and demands of the insurrections (Egypt 1919, Syria 1925, Palestine 1936–8), though in 1919 the demand for bread began to rise above nationalist slogans among the fellahs of Asyūṭ Province.[76]

Only two insurrections are known to us in which fellah rebels in the Middle East formulated a whole programme of about a dozen demands. Both took place in Lebanon, within one generation. The first was the *'āmmiyya* of 1840 in which the rebellious peasants demanded the abolition or revocation of a whole set of decrees and regulations introduced during the period of the Egyptian occupation. We have three divergent but overlapping lists of these demands; a five-point one from Shidyāq's chronicle, a ten-point one from the Egyptian archives published by Rustum and a nine-point one recorded by Ismail which is based on French archives and the *Revue Patriarcale*.[77] The following demands are included in at least two of these lists: taxes should be paid once a year only; orders to disarm the population of Mount Lebanon and to deliver muskets to Ibrāhīm Pasha should be revoked (all three lists); the inhabitants of Mount Lebanon should not be recruited into the army, and decrees to this effect should be repealed; forced labour in the mines, as well as other forced labour for the government, should be abolished (all three lists). In addition, two lists include demands concerning the *ḥawwāla* (billeting of soldiers in the population); according to Ismail's list, this should not be done at the expense of the population and in Rustum's list only the control of such an operation is being dealt with. Shidyāq's list has two additional political demands: the dismissal of Butrus Karāma from the Amīr's Dīwān and the appointment of two people from each community. Ismail alone mentions the abolition of the *firda* (poll tax) and of the responsibility of relatives for tax liability of an insolvent debtor. The list from the Egyptian archives includes the most detailed fiscal and economic demands: reductions of the *i'āna* tax,[78] abolition of the tax on mills and on silk called *ḥārithat al-ḥarīr*; abolition of wholesale purchase of grain or cattle by the government (*mubāya'a*)[79] and of compulsory regulations concerning peasants in the Ba'lbek and Biqā' area. In addition, the rebels who presented this list demanded that booty taken in the course of the insurrection (by either side) should not be returned, and that Amīr Khanjar al-Ḥarfūsh (one of the leaders of the insurrection) should retain his income. This Amīr Ḥarfūsh is one of the signatories of this list of demands and he had joined the rebellion because the Ḥarfūshs, the Shī'ī lords of the Biqā' centred in Ba'lbek, had been constrained by Bashīr II, like other *muqāṭa'ajī*s. This explains the special demands concerning Ba'lbek and the Biqā'.

The programme of Lebanon's rebellious fellahs eighteen years later was completely different. This was of course primarily the result of the fact that this time they revolted not against a foreign government but against the local feudal lords, some of whom had been their leaders in the 1840 rebellion. Therefore they demanded, first and foremost, the repeal of the oppressive customs and payments recently introduced by the Khāzin Shaykhs.[80] These included oppressive deeds, extortionate practices and irregular payments, as well as the innovation of *rusūmāt al-mu'āyadāt*, i.e. payments and duties imposed on fellahs whenever the shaykhs sold land to villagers. However, in 1858 the Kisrawān peasants were no longer satisfied with the repeal of innovations. Their strong position *vis à vis* their opponents emboldened them to demand changes in the traditional relations between lord and peasant, in particular the abolition of any indication of serfdom-like customs. Thus they demanded the abolition of billeting of the shaykhs' men on the peasants at the latter's expense (*ḥawwāla*), and even the repayment of such expenditure to the fellahs, the abolition of traditional holiday and wedding gifts to the lords, and of the right of the shaykhs to administer flogging and jail sentences. Moreover, they went so far as to demand complete equality between peasants and members of the shaykh families, an equality, so they said, which was established by the Tanzimat edicts of the Ottoman government. Shaykhs and peasants should pay the same rates of poll tax and other taxes, they should be equally punished by law, conflicts between shaykhs and peasants should be settled by two arbitrators, each side electing one of them, and nobody should be distinguished or humiliated by any ceremony or custom. Finally, they demanded that one or two *wakīl*s should be appointed in each village, and while the northwestern moderates were satisfied with the selection of a *ma'mūr* (an administrator of the area) by the Patriarch, the southern villagers insisted upon his election from among the common people.

The Kisrawān peasant revolt of 1858 was therefore almost unique in that the rebels demanded to make changes in the traditional relations between lord and peasant. There may have been a small number of other fellah rebellions in the Middle East in which similar demands were made. Thus in the Druze peasant movement of the Jabal of the year 1890 the rebels demanded to abolish the old custom according to which the Shaykhs received one-third of the crop.[81] We know too little about the demands of fellah rebellions to say whether other fellah rebels too demanded such changes. However there can be no doubt that in the overwhelming majority of cases they only demanded the return to traditional usage and the repeal of oppressive innovations, such as the aggravation of the tax burden, conscription to the army, the introduction of the *corvée* for groups formerly exempted, registration of state-domain in the name of shaykhs or large landowners, raising of rents or shares of crops to be delivered by tenants to landlords, and so forth. In this respect the majority of fellah rebellions in the Middle East resembled peasant insurrections in many European countries for long periods. 'What infuriates peasants (and not just peasants) is a new and sudden imposition or demand that strikes many people at once and that is a break with accepted rules and customs'.[82] Thus the first stirrings of peasant discontent in Germany, prior to the *Bauernkrieg*, took the form of efforts to retain or return to 'das alte Recht'.[83] In 17th century France rebellious peasants demanded 'respect for the traditional customs, privileges, and liberties of the provinces and districts, a return to the old taxes . . .' They cried out 'against the tyranny of the Parisians, against the excessive centralization of the state, the increase in taxes, the "innovations" '. 'The program of the Russian peasants in the Time of Troubles seems also to have been rather a return to a customary condition of things, somewhat idealized'.[84] The programme of the Kisrawān peasants, on the other hand, was much more like the twelve *Artikel* of the German *Bauernkrieg* in 1525, with due regard, of course, to the different conditions. In addition to the abolition of oppressive innovations, such as the restitution of woods and pastures appropriated by the lords to the commune and the abolition of newly introduced duties and *corvées*, the *Artikel* included such changes as the abolition of the tithe on fruit and cattle, of the *Todfall*, i.e. right of the lord to receive part of the inheritance of his peasant and of the exclusive hunting and fishing privileges of the lords. Moreover they demanded the freedom of peasants and the abolition of serfdom ('dass man uns für Eigenleute gehalten hat').[85] The reason why the Kisrawān peasants went beyond the traditional demands to abolish innovations was the extreme weakness of their opponents, the Kisrawān shaykhs, and the political constellation which enabled the revolt to persist for three years without serious resistance or intervention. Thus their demands gradually became more and more radical[86] and reached a stage at which the peasants were no longer satisfied with the return to the situation prior to the newly introduced oppressions.

It should be stressed, however, that at no stage did the Kisrawān peasants include in their programme a demand to expropriate the estates of the Khāzin shaykhs or of any shaykh at all. When they expelled the Khāzins and took over their property they did so not because this had been one of the aims of their revolt but as the result of the inability to come to terms with the Khāzins.[87] Neither did any of the other fellah rebellions in the Middle East go as far as that. Even the demand to implement a land reform programme, i.e. to expropriate large estates and distribute the land among small and landless peasants, was voiced about the middle of the twentieth century by groups of intellectuals, not by rebellious peasants. Only in one case, that of Akram Ḥawrānī's party in Syria, was there any connection between the intellectual land-reformers and rebellious peasants.[88]

Indeed, fellah rebellions in the Middle East lacked not only clear demands for change of property relations but any well formulated ideology of social change. As we have seen, the demands of the Kisrawān peasants in 1858 to establish equality between the peasants and the shaykhs was not based on any social or religious principles but on the Tanzimat edicts of the Ottoman Empire.[89] According to a report of a village *'ālim* to Lady Duff Gordon, the leader of the fellah rebellion in Upper Egypt in 1865, Aḥmad al-Ṭayyib, wanted 'to divide all property equally. "He would break up your pretty clock", said Yussuf, "and give every man a broken wheel out of it, and so with all things".' Thus the image of Aḥmad al-Ṭayyib among some of his contemporaries was that of 'a mad fanatic and a communist';[90] unfortunately we do not know more about his ideas, if he had any. Even the ideas of Akram Ḥawrānī and his party, the leaders of peasant rebellion in northern Syria in 1951, were not more than a rather vague 'anti-feudalism', which meant in fact antagonism to the families of large landowners in northern Syria, not any well-defined social principle. This is about all we know about social ideas of rebellious fellahs or their leaders in the Middle East – a very meagre crop indeed. We find in Lebanese, Egyptian and Syrian fellah rebellions rudiments of egalitarianism, millenarianism (mahdism) or anti-feudalist ideas which constitute the main ideological elements of peasant rebellion elsewhere as well. But we have not found anything even remotely as elaborate as the ideas of John Ball and the Lollards in England of the 1380s, the Bundschuh and related social and religious movements in Germany of the 1520s, or the anarchism of the Mexican or Russian peasant insurrections of the twentieth century. As we shall see, this was partly due to the absence of a movement like the Reformation in Islam. In addition, Islam was so deeply rooted and fellahs so ignorant that social ideologies could neither grow indigenously nor be acquired by them from outside sources. In fact such ideologies were adopted by a small layer of urban intellectuals in the last few generations only, but different belief systems caused an almost complete lack of communication between them and the fellahs; among contemporary groupings only the Muslim Brotherhood succeeded in penetrating the countryside, and even this not very deeply.

Like their social aims, the political aims of most fellah rebellions in Egypt and the Fertile Crescent were rather limited. The overwhelming majority of rebellions aimed at changing government policy only, not the government or the ruler. As far as we know, prior to World War One, only once did such a rebellion endeavour to overthrow the ruler: Aḥmad al-Mahdī, the leader of the insurrections near Luxor in 1822–3, declared 'that he had an order from God and the Grand Signor to dethrone Mohammed Ali Pasha'.[91] All the other fellah rebellions against Muḥammad 'Alī and his successors strove to redress this or that grievance but not to replace the ruler. The same is true for the revolts against Ibrāhīm Pasha's policy in Palestine and Syria, none of which declared its aim to be the liquidation of the Egyptian occupation. Even in 1840, when Ibrāhīm's rule in Syria began to totter, the rebels declared that if oppression were removed they would return to obedience, because 'we do not aim at establishing a[nother] rule'.[92] Nor did any of the fellah rebellions in the Jabal aim at overthrowing the Ottoman government. Since all these rebellions were led by rural notables, their aims were determined by the political outlook of this social group. At that time, rural notables did not aspire to replace the established central authorities but only to enjoy their traditional autonomy and power within the framework of the government of the Sultan or his Viceroy.

Things changed to some extent with the establishment of European rule in the Middle East. In 1919 in Egypt and in 1925 in Syria fellah rebellions became an important part – in Syria even the main part – of a movement for independence from foreign rule. The revolt in Palestine, on the other hand, demanded only a change in the British policy of support for the Jewish National Home. However, in these cases the political object of the revolt was set by urban politicians, although the active rebels were mainly peasants.

Beyond the principle of independence and self-determination, very few political ideas were expressed in the course of these revolts. An exception was the proclamation of the Druze leader Sulṭān al-Aṭrash in 1925 in which he summoned all Syrians to fight for (*inter alia*) 'the application of the principles of the French Revolution and the Rights of Man'.[93] This, however, was no doubt the product of the inspiration of the Westernized nationalist intellectual, Dr. 'Abd al-Raḥmān al-Shāhbander, who had escaped from the French to Jabal al-Durūz and tried from there to integrate the Druze peasant rebellion into an all-Syrian nationalist movement.

Only one of the Middle Eastern peasant rebellions, the Kisrawān revolt of 1858, adopted principles of democratic government. We have mentioned before that the rebellious villagers had demanded that the *ma'mūr*, the administrative official of the area, should be elected from among the common people, not the shaykhs.[94] Moreover, after they had elected Ṭānyūs Shāhīn as their leader and he had set up a machinery of government, he stressed that he functioned by virtue of 'the authority of the people' (*al-jumhūr*) or 'the authority of the republican government' (*bi-quwwat al-ḥukūma al-jumhūriyya*).[95] It may well be, as Porath suggests, that Shāhīn had heard about ideas of the French revolution from Lazarist monks who operated a school in his village Rayfūn. But, on the other hand, this unique democratic trend was probably at least partly the result of the fact that nowhere in the Middle East had fellahs achieved in the middle of the nineteenth century an educational level comparable to that of the Lebanese peasants, and only in Lebanon some organizations of peasants from below had preceded the fellah rebellion. We shall return to the discussion of this organization further on.

Peasants and other groups

Some early German peasant revolts of the fifteenth century, especially one near Worms in 1431 and a rebellion of the peasants of Alsace in 1493, directed their main thrust against the Jews.[96] Similarly, peasant uprisings in the wake of the revolt of the Ukrainian cossacks under the leadership of Bogdan Khmelnitsky in the middle of the seventeenth century were instrumental in the infamous pogroms against the Jews. Communal conflict which often led to violent excesses against Christians or Jews was a very frequent concomitant of Middle Eastern peasant insurrections as well, perhaps even more persistently than in other parts of the world. As we shall see, usually rebellious peasants were unable to cope with their principal opponent, the central government, and therefore they often vented their ire on a weak group of the population. In addition, the minorities were associated with the central or foreign government because of their function as agents of the government or because of their common religion or their common interests and policy. Thus Copts were the agents of Muḥammad 'Alī's government in financial and agrarian affairs as well as his tax collectors; Ibrāhīm Pasha's rule in Palestine represented the policy of toleration and equality for minorities introduced by Muḥammad 'Alī in Egypt; the French Mandate was implemented by Christians who favoured the Christians in Syria and Lebanon; and the British in Palestine, on top of being Christians, supported the establishment of a national home for the Jews. Attacks on Jews and Christians by Muslim popular masses has been a recurrent feature of Middle Eastern history, and peasant rebellions often served as an occasion for such attacks. When the fellahs of the northern Delta revolted in 1798 against the French occupation, the Christians of Damietta feared for their lives because they dwelled in the *wakāla*s (caravanserais) near the sea near to the French quarters. The fellahs began to shout: 'Allah is against you, Oh Christians, and against the French. This night we shall slaughter all of you and take your belongings and your wives as booty'. This time, however, they were unable to carry out their threats.[97] During the insurrection near Luxor in 1822–3, 'some of the Prophet's more zealous followers handed in a requisition to be allowed to decapitate all the Copts'.[98] In this case it was the leader of the rebellion who apparently succeeded in restraining his followers from implementing their intention. On other occasions the peasant leaders were less successful. In the 1834 rebellion against Ibrāhīm Pasha, when the Damascus Gate of the Old City of Jerusalem had been opened, thousands of fellahs rushed in, captured the city, and 'the following night began to loot the shops of the Jews, the Christians, the Franks and then the Moslems . . . During the following days they began to strip and loot the houses of the Orthodox, the Franks and the Armenians, but the leaders of the fellaheen and the sheiks prevented them by telling them that if they harmed the Rayas, they would incur the displeasure of the Royal Powers. In spite of this, they continued to loot the uninhabited houses every night . . .'.[99] During the same rebellion the fellahs robbed the Jews of Tiberias and Safed 'of immense property, as is reported, for there was no one to offer any opposition'.[100] An eyewitness has vividly described the pogrom-like attack of the villagers of Upper Galilee on the Jews of Safed on 15 June 1834. The Jews were stripped of their clothes and driven out of the town, the remaining women and youths were violated, the belongings of the Jews were looted and their holy articles were desecrated.[101]

In 1894, 'in order to escape the oppressive rule of their shaykhs, a considerable portion of the Druze turned against the Moslem and Christian villages in the vicinity of Jabal al-Durūz and wrought havoc in the area'.[102] When the Druze insurgents entered Damascus on 18 October 1925, one of their first activities was to commit atrocities in the

Armenian refugee camp to the south of the city and in the Armenian quarter. This was in reprisal for excesses previously committed by the irregulars in the French service, who were chiefly recruited from among the Armenians and the Circassians. Later the revolt spread to the western slopes of Mount Hermon and on 11 November 1925, the Christian village of Kawkaba was occupied. Fighting broke out between Druzes and Christians and was followed by looting and arson. As a result, the Christian population of the invaded districts took to flight and many Christians joined the French army. Again the leaders condemned these outrages and Zayd al-Aṭrash, the military commander of the revolt, declared that the revolution was not a religious movement. He restored looted Christian property to its owners and punished his followers when they committed robbery and murder.[103]

Finally, in the 1936–8 revolt in Palestine, which had assumed the character of a movement carried by peasants, gradually slogans of a Muslim *jihād* gained the upper hand and antagonism to non-Muslim minorities developed. Tension between Muslims and Christians grew and anti-Christian leaflets were distributed. Moreover, attempts were made to boycott Christians in the same way as Jews were boycotted, and in some cases even violent acts against minorities (not only Jews) were perpetrated.[104]

A special case was the 1858 peasant revolt in Kisrawān, for two reasons: first, the revolting peasants were themselves Christians, and second, the rulers against whom they revolted were also Christians and not a foreign government or a central government using or protecting religious minorities. Moreover, these Christian lords were so weak that the peasants were able to defeat them and had no need to look for scapegoats. Nevertheless, even there inter-communal tension merged with the peasant revolt, whose dominant trait was that of class conflict, more than any of the other fellah insurrections in the nineteenth century. As Porath put it, in three ways the Kisrawān revolt was an important factor leading to the outbreak of the armed inter-communal conflict and the massacre of Christians. First the existence of a Christian force in northern Lebanon, connected with the Maronite clergy, strengthened the fanatic fervour of some of the leaders of the clergy particularly the Maronite Bishop of Beirut, Ṭūbīyā 'Awn; second, the Kisrawān revolt exacerbated the social tension, which in central and southern Lebanon turned into communal conflict because there the peasants belonged to other religious groups than their lords; and finally, the appearance of Ṭānyūs Shāhīn's peasants in al-Matn and south of Beirut in the summer of 1860 provoked the Druzes into action and helped to set alight the great inter-communal conflagration of that year.[105]

Thus inter-communal conflict or, more often, outrages against religious minorities, which were apparent in some of the European peasant insurrections, occurred even more frequently and persistently in Middle Eastern fellah rebellions. As against this, the latter lacked completely another, major feature of European peasant uprisings, namely their anti-clerical flavour and their attacks on institutions and property of the church. Comparing demands of Middle Eastern rebellious peasants with their European counterparts, we have pointed out the similarity between the programme of the Kisrawān revolt in 1858 and the twelve *Artikel* of the German *Bauernkrieg.* There was however one important difference: in their first *Artikel* the German peasants demanded the right of every village commune to elect their priests and to dismiss them. Nothing remotely similar was demanded by any group of rebelling Middle Eastern peasants. Moreover, nowhere in the Middle East did any attacks on the religious establishment occur comparable, for instance, to the expulsion of the priests and the refusal to pay the tithe by the peasants of Flanders in 1323–8, the looting and burning of monasteries by the German peasants in 1525 and their demand to expropriate church property, or the sale of church property in the French Revolution.[106] The principal reason for this difference is the fact that in the Middle East there was no 'church' functioning independently as a major landlord whose direct oppression was felt by the peasants and to whom they owed the payment of tithes. Up to the beginning of the nineteenth century in Egypt and up to the end of the nineteenth or even the first half of the twentieth century in Syria, Palestine and Iraq, the land belonged to the state and the fellahs were oppressed by tax-farmers, the bureaucracy, or local lords serving in both capacities. The religious establishment received its income from endowments (*waqf*) which were either urban property leased to merchants or craftsmen or allocations from rural income by the state. Thus fellahs in general did not clash directly with the Muslim 'clergy', the *'ulamā'*, except for a short period in eighteenth century Egypt when individual *'ulamā'* served as *multazim*s. Even in Syria, and later also in Palestine, where control of rural income (mainly in the form of tax farming) was in the hand of powerful urban notables among whom *'ulamā'* played a prominent role, they confronted the fellahs not independently as a church establishment but only as an integral part of the class of urban notable families. It was only after the development of private property of land in the nineteenth and twentieth centuries that new 'true' *waqf*s could be established on rural property and the religious establishment became able to control such trusts independently. But even in Egypt, where this process had taken place earlier and more profoundly than elsewhere in the Middle East, at mid-century, out of about 600,000 feddans (acres) of *waqf* land (ca. 10 per cent of all properties except state-domain) only 100,000–150,000 feddans were *khayrī waqf*s (i.e. for religious or charitable purposes). Thus, in addition to its different character, the extent of control of rural property by the religious establishment in the Middle East was very small indeed.

Conditions in Lebanon differed considerably from this pattern. First, because of the limited control of the Ottoman state over this area, landed property in Lebanon was considered not to be of the *mīrī* (state owned) category but *mulk*, the property of its holders. Secondly, and as a result, *waqf* land constituted a larger proportion of Lebanon's agricultural landed property than anywhere else in the Middle East; thirdly, since we are dealing with an area in which a large proportion of the population was Christian, an important factor during the agrarian unrest of the nineteenth century was the Maronite Catholic Church, which was much less connected with the Muslim state than the Muslim *'ulamā'*; and finally, as a result of the preceding features, the Maronite clergy and orders of monks were one of the largest landowners (or *waqf* beneficiaries) in Lebanon: according to various estimates, they owned (or occupied) between one-fifth and one-fourth of the land in the Mountain (and the plains).[107]

If nevertheless no antagonism emerged between peasants and church in Lebanon, this was the result of two main causes. First, the lower clergy of the Maronite Church were poor for the most part. They had to engage in manual work and their way of life was very similar to that of other peasants. Moreover, the Maronite Church retained the ancient practice of choosing its bishops by all members of the clergy. Therefore, out of eleven bishops who served at the end of the 1850s and the beginning of the 1860s ten were of humble origin, and even the Patriarch was of peasant stock. Secondly, Bashīr II had weakened the position of the shaykhs and amīrs and thus the Maronite Church succeeded in freeing itself of their influence. It aimed at gaining the predominant position in the administration of Lebanon by excluding the *muqāṭa'ajīs* – if necessary with the help of the peasants' leaders.[108] Therefore the Maronite clergy not only supported the rebellion of 1840 against Ibrāhīm Pasha,[109] but also offered some assistance to the rebellious peasants during the Kisrawān revolt and, in particular, attempted to mediate between the two sides. In the course of the revolt the Patriarch's proposals of a compromise gradually drew closer to the peasants' demands, until the church finally accepted the rule of the rebel peasants in Kisrawān. The clergy thus gave a stamp of legitimacy to the peasants' authority.[110] Support of peasant rebellion by a clerus of peasant origin was not uncommon in Europe as well, e.g. in England in 1381, in Normandy in 1639, in Brittany in 1675, or in the Ile de France during the French Revolution.[111] But the sympathetic neutrality of the top of the church establishment towards peasant revolt, as in Lebanon in 1858–61, was quite a unique phenomenon.

Peasant movements in Flanders and England in the fourteenth

century and in Germany in the sixteenth century were strongly encouraged in their attacks against the established church by early evangelical and protestant ideas and movements such as John Wyclif's Lollards, and by the Reformation. In the Middle East, and in Islam in general, there was no Reformation, which may have contributed to the lack of anti-clerical trends among rebellious peasants in this area. As we shall see, some of the Egyptian fellah insurrections were led by Mahdist pretenders, and one of them has even been reported to have wanted 'to kill all the Ulama and destroy all theological teaching by learned men and to preach a sort of revelation or interpretation of the Koran of his own'.[112] But the source of this rather vague information is an English lady, and even she did not talk to Aḥmad al-Ṭayyib directly but only reported what she heard from others. Moreover, such messianic ideas may have been likely to contribute to a clash with the secular authorities but scarcely with the religious establishment, with whom the fellahs had very little direct contact.

So far we have discussed the relation between rebellious fellahs and two other groups in Middle Eastern society, religious minorities and the religious establishment. However, the character and fate of these rebellions were influenced at least as decisively by their relation to the urban population as such. Summarizing his study of peasant uprisings in seventeenth century France, Mousnier stressed the fact that 'the periods of revolt nearly always began in the towns.'[113] This was not at all the case in Egypt and the Fertile Crescent during the last 200 years. In Egypt there were no revolts of the urban population between 1806 and 1918, though a fair number of fellah rebellions occurred in this period. This is remarkable, because during that time the economic, religious and administrative ties between town and country in Egypt grew considerably.[114] Among the probable reasons one may mention that fellah rebellions broke out in distant regions, the slow pace of urbanization during that period, and the strengthening of the central government, specifically in the towns. However that may be, in the overwhelming majority of cases in which fellah rebellions in the Middle East had some relation with the urban population, the initiative was that of villagers. Often the townsmen remained passive, and in some cases the urban population or part of it even opposed the rebellious villagers. On the other hand, under certain circumstances, which we shall try to elucidate, the urban population cooperated with the rebellious fellahs, and in a few instances even initiated the revolt.

In 1798, when the French had occupied Egypt, the villagers in the vicinity of the port of Dimyāṭ (Damietta) revolted under the leadership of Shaykh Ḥasan Ṭūbār. About 8,000 fellahs of this area made an attack on the town in order to exterminate the French garrison. In the course of the attack they attempted to incite the inhabitants of the town to support them. The townspeople, however, did not raise a finger but waited to see whether the fellahs would accomplish anything. When they realized that the fellahs had lost the battle, they remained in their houses.[115] It should be noted that the only town which revolted against the French was Cairo, but there was no connection between the popular revolt of Cairo and rebellious fellahs, as we have shown elsewhere.[116] The rebellion of the villages of the Damietta area preceded the Cairo rebellion by one month. In 1838 the rebellious Druzes of the Ḥawrān tried to incite the leaders of the people of Damascus to join the revolt against Ibrāhīm Pasha by sending them written messages to this effect. The messages were intercepted by Ibrāhīm Pasha's agents. Anyway, the Damascenes did not join the insurrection.[117] The most remarkable instance of urban aloofness *vis-à-vis* rural revolt was the 1925 insurrection of the Druzes in Syria. The case is remarkable because a great effort was made by nationalist leaders to merge the Druze revolt in the Syrian national movement, and the 1925 insurrection is called variously by some authors *al-thawra al-sūriyya al-kubrā* ('The Great Syrian revolt') or 'the nationalist crusade in Syria'.[118] This is what we are told by the author of the *'Nationalist Crusade'*:

> Aleppo, left almost defenceless by the sending of reinforcements to Hama, was imperilled by a threat of combined action on the part of its disaffected Muslim citizens and wandering Bedouin tribes outside the city. These two groups had agreed to join in an uprising on October 6. The tribesmen, thirsting for loot, gathered in around the city; but their collaborators within the city failed to carry out their part of the bargain . . . With 1,000 French troops and 200 Syrian gendarmes the task was assumed of keeping the turbulent elements of the population from joining forces with their Bedouin allies. In this attempt the French authorities succeeded. But outside the city banditry increased at an alarming rate, and soon became indistinguishable from guerilla warfare throughout the region between Aleppo and Hama.[119]

A similar situation existed in the other towns, and by mid-November 1925 the French held the cities while the countryside was in the hands of rebels.[120] Of particular interest is the account of the revolt in Ḥamāh by its instigator, Fawzī al-Qā'uqjī, a captain in the Syrian army established by the French. He writes that on 4 October 1925, he set out from Ḥamāh with a mounted unit to the Bedouins. He recruited some Bedouin shaykhs for the revolt and allocated each of them a salary and a task. After some preparations they attacked the garrison of Ḥamāh, seized its weapons and conquered the government building. When the French sent reinforcements, Qā'uqjī and his Bedouin were compelled to retreat. 'Leaders of Ḥamāh broke their promise and refrained from joining the revolt; they behaved cowardly and fearful.'[121] Even Damascus, the centre of the nationalist movement, did not really participate in the revolt. Dr. Shāhbandar, several of his associates and other nationalist leaders escaped to the Jabal al-Durūz, and when the Druze insurgents entered, on 18 October, the Maydān and Shāghūr quarters of Damascus, the majority of the population shut themselves up in their houses, and only a small number made common cause with the invaders.[122] This remained the prevalent pattern of the revolt, which was conducted by the Druze fellah rebels who penetrated from time to time into the outer quarters of Damascus.[123]

The passivity of the urban population in these revolts may have had two related reasons. First, the military power of the government was much stronger in the towns and was able to prevent an insurrection of their population. Secondly, the traditional urban notables of Syria and Palestine were better situated than the Druze shaykhs to adapt themselves to the respective new rulers, and not as strong as the Druzes to resist the change. It was indeed the urban notables who in many cases remained loyal to the rulers and resisted the rural rebels, and without their leadership the lower strata of urban society could not move easily. In 1834, the ‘Abd al-Hādīs and al-Nimrs remained loyal or neutral towards Ibrāhīm Pasha's rule and thus prevented the population of Nāblus from joining the revolt.[124] Similarly, Safed's notables tried to make peace with Egyptian rule, but in this case they did not succeed in preventing the popular groups of the town from joining the villagers in the outrages against the Jews.[125] About ninety years later, ‘the majority of Damascene notables preferred peace and were not yet ready to follow the leaders of the People's Party into active conflict with the French authorities. They sent messages to Sultan Pasha [the Druze leader] requesting him not to enter the city . . .’ Similarly, the Aleppo notables supported the French regime.[126] The fact that the people of Bethlehem refused to join the fellahs who had revolted against Ibrāhīm Pasha in June 1834 was clearly the result of their being Christians. They took refuge in the nearby monasteries. ‘Often the fellaheen told them to come out and fight with them against the Pasha, but they replied that being Christians and *Rayah*s they must not fight. The fellaheen, therefore, decided on Sunday, June 3, to attack the monasteries and rob the people of Bethlehem.’[127]

However, when the central government weakened and townspeople had the same grievances as the fellahs, the urban population wavered or even cooperated with the rebels. This is what happened in Cairo in 1795 when fellahs from an *iltizām* in Sharqiyya came and complained about oppression by Mamluks, and were joined in their action by the Azhar shaykhs and the Cairo mob.[128] This is also what happened in the towns of Palestine in 1834, with the exception of Nablus and Bethlehem. The story of the events in Jerusalem, as related in the manuscript of Monk

Neophytos, is most illuminating in this respect.[129] Shortly after Easter 1834 Ibrāhīm Pasha left Jerusalem, allegedly because he feared the plague which had broken out in the vicinity.

> 'As soon as the Jerusalemites and the fellaheen heard of the departure of the Pasha, they gathered together from all parts and held council secretly as to whether they should obey the order of the Pasha or revolt. Despite their party feuds, they unanimously decided to revolt . . . At the beginning, some of the Jerusalemites showed themselves on the side of the Pasha, others said they were indifferent, but secretly, all of them, as time proved, were on the side of the fellaheen . . . The *Bimbashi* [*binbaşı*, the military commander with the rank of major] asked the notables of the city to come to him and he explained the situation to them. They replied that it was not a wise policy for them to fight against the fellaheen and they pleaded all kinds of excuses, but especially the lack of arms . . .' The commander said to them: ' "I want to know if you are on the side of the Pasha or with the fellaheen". They replied: "May it never come to pass that we should be on the side of the fellaheen, we are the force of our Effendi, the Pasha etc . . ." The *Bimbashi*, therefore, said to them: "If you will be faithful to the Pasha, I will make you the promise that the Pasha will not ask one man from the city of Jerusalem for the army". They gave him so many promises and assurances that he went to the Court and wrote with his own hand promising that he would remain and defend Jerusalem to the end, and that he would not demand one man for the army. This he signed, and the *Mullah* was witness and surety.'

However, about a week later the locks of the Dung Gate were broken and the fellaheen poured into the city.

> 'Then the people of Jerusalem, who said that they did not have any arms, appeared fully armed and joined the fellaheen . . . The *Bimbashi* and the *Miralais* [colonels], now certain that the citizens were in league with the fellaheen, called the elders of the city, Omar Effendi, the *Bashkatib*, [chief clerk] the *Mufti* and the rest, to the Law Courts and said to them: "You are in league with the fellaheen against the Pasha." They replied: "A few of the more undisciplined youths joined the fellaheen, and others joined them in order to save their homes and shops from being looted by the fellaheen." '

When, on the same day, about 2,000 villagers from the Nablus area arrived to join the rebels near Jerusalem, 'the people of Jerusalem hurried and broke the locks of the Damascus Gate and opened it. Thousands of fellaheen rushed in and captured the city surrounding the citadel.' However, at the end of May Ibrāhīm Pasha decided to return to Jerusalem, and when he approached the city 'he was apprehensive lest he should have to engage the thousands of fellaheen from outside and the citizens from within. The latter, however, who were cowardly, fled when they heard of his arrival. Some hid themselves in the cellars of their houses, while others rushed to get out of the city by the Gethsemane Gate . . .' And Neophytos concludes with the remark: 'Those who once ran about Jerusalem like flying eagles, with swords in their hands, now tried to run to Mount Olivet [*sic*] and escape with their wives and children, and some of them collapsed by the way from sheer fear.'

On 24 July, 1834, in Hebron, too, townspeople fought alongside of fellahs against Ibrāhīm's soldiers.[130] When Muḥammad 'Alī came to Jaffa, during the rebellion, he beheaded the shaykhs of the villages around Jaffa who had been in league with the rebellious fellahs. 'He would have executed some of the notables of Jaffa also, because they had joined the fellaheen in an attempt to kill the soldiers and capture the fortress, but they escaped to Cyprus'.[131]

Outside Palestine, similar events occurred in the town of Lādhiqiyya. When the fellahs of Jabal Nuṣayriyya, Jabal al-Akrād and the village of Lādhiqiyya district had conquered the town in September 1839, the inhabitants took the opportunity to loot the government granaries and stores, to seize 482 horses belonging to the authorities and to besiege the *mutasallim* [acting governor] at his residence.[132]

Lebanese fellah insurrections of the mid-nineteenth century found support among the inhabitants of some small Lebanese towns. This was the result of the emergence of a prosperous independent bourgeoisie in these places. One of these towns was Dayr al-Qamar, which grew tremendously during the third and fourth decade of the century and became famous for its silk manufactures. Its merchants became rich, built luxurious houses, acquired landed property, established a municipality of their own, and 'assumed an air of independence and superiority'.[133] Another was Zūq Mikhāyil, south of Jūnya, whose prosperity also derived largely from the silk trade and silk processing. This had made them independent of the shaykhs. Moreover, a certain antagonism seems to have prevailed between them and the Khāzins.[134] In 1840 it was the people of Dayr al-Qamar who initiated the revolt in Lebanon against Ibrāhīm Pasha. When Lebanon's population was required to deliver all arms in their possession, the people of Dayr al-Qamar sent messages to the inhabitants of all districts inciting them not to deliver the arms.[135] Later they established a military unit composed of merchants, craftsmen and peasants living in the town to support the revolt whose main combatants were peasants recruited by their shaykhs.[136] In 1858 the people of Zūq Mikhāyil declared their support for the peasant cause and joined the revolt, and by January 1859 two citizens of Zūq Mikhāyil were in key posts in the leadership of the revolt.

Moreover, Zūq Mikhāyil became the seat of the council of the rebel government.[137]

In 1919 Egyptian fellahs participated in fact in two insurrections which were different from each other in their character. The first was the general nationalist revolt in which the whole population took part. This revolt began on 9 March in Cairo with demonstrations of students and on 10 and 11 March Cairo's workers and government employees went on strike, the merchants closed their shops and huge demonstrations were held throughout the town. Only a few days later the revolt spread to the provinces and the fellahs began their insurrection which consisted mainly in acts of sabotage of railway and telegraph lines.[138] Though these activities were not always coordinated with the urban nationalist revolt, the two complemented and supported each other. As against this, the second rebellion which took place in Asyūṭ was directed against the owners of large estates in that province and did not enjoy the support of any urban group.[139] Its connection with the activity of townspeople was confined to the fact that it erupted in the wake of the first revolt which started in Cairo.

Another nationalist rebellion in the Middle East also started in the towns, but gradually the rural element became predominant and the revolt ended up with conflict and clashes between fellahs and the rebels. This was the rebellion in Palestine in 1936–8.[140] The revolt began in April 1936 with a general strike which was initiated in two meetings held in Nablus and Jerusalem and with violence committed by the Arab inhabitants of Jaffa. The strike spread to the main Arab towns in Palestine. Peasants hardly joined the strike at all, since their losses would have been severe had they stopped harvesting their spring crop. When violent acts against Jews and Jewish property became a permanent feature of the revolt, villagers near the towns began to participate, but at first not as the main force. When armed bands were formed in May and attacks began to be directed against government installations, railways, the police, and the army, the initiative still was in the hands of urban leaders. However, when the government succeeded in bringing the urban centres under control, the rural areas were gradually integrated into the revolt. Instrumental in this process were natives of villages or rural towns who had graduated from secondary schools, entered into government service and returned to rural areas as teachers, clerks, health officers etc. Moreover, those who had been banished by the government to rural areas were very active in spreading the spirit of revolt. At first, the reaction of the peasants to this propaganda was rather lukewarm, but gradually more and more villagers showed readiness to bear arms. From the middle of May onwards the rural sector became the centre of gravity of the revolt. In the beginning of June armed bands, almost completely manned by peasants, were operating all over the country. In its second stage too, the revolt was carried out mainly by Muslim villagers of the lower strata, the participation of urban, educated or notable families being rather slight. This found its expression in the change of headgear among the Arab population at that time. Since the rebels with their rural dress were conspicuous in the towns they ordered the townsmen to replace the Ottoman *ṭarbūsh* (fez) with the rural and bedouin *kafiyya* and *'iqāl*. The wearing of the *kafiyya* and the *'iqāl* by the townsmen was meant 'to encourage the peasant and to demonstrate that he serves as the true symbol of Arabism'. It should be added, however, that gradually the villagers became tired and a rift opened between them and the armed rebel bands. When the revolt was resumed in the fall of 1937, the rural population was reluctant to support the rebels, and even formed counter-bands to defend themselves against their demands and extortions.

Participants and leaders

It is not always possible to arrive at an exact assessment of the extent of the fellah rebellions discussed in this essay. Estimates of the number of participants do not help very much. First, for many of the important rebellions we have not even an estimate. This is the case, for instance, with regard to most of the Egyptian insurrections in the 1820s, the Egyptian revolt of 1919, or the agrarian unrest all over the Middle East in the 1950s. Secondly, statistics and exact numbers are not the strong suit of Middle Eastern historical documentation, especially if we go back to periods prior to the twentieth century. Thus Mubārak's remark that the followers of Aḥmad al-Ṣalāḥ of Salīmiyya in the 1820–1 revolt numbered 'about forty thousand, as has been reported' (*'alā mā qīla*) is rather dubious, among other reasons because the number forty is used in Middle Eastern parlance to denote 'many'.[141] Available estimates tend to fall into two categories – a few thousands, generally between five and ten thousand, and 20–30,000 for some of the larger revolts. However, not all these numbers are comparable, because some of them relate to the inhabitants of rebellious villages, some to the number of fellahs meeting in a rebellious gathering or demonstration, and some to the number of active combatants. Thus, concerning Lebanon, Shidyāq tells us that about 6,000 peasants attended the famous Anṭalyās meeting in 1820, the number of fighters in the early stages of the 1890 rebellion against Ibrāhīm has been estimated at about 5,000, and the number of inhabitants of rebellious villages in the 1858 revolt in Kisrawān amounted to about 11,000.[142] Perhaps somewhat more reliable (and comparable) are two other figures, Oppenheim's estimate of 6–7,000 Druze combatants against the Ottoman government in 1896, and Porath's estimate of 9–10,000 members of rebel bands in the Palestine insurrection in 1936–8.[143] Even the figures given by an English eye-witness of the 1822–3 insurrection in Luxor are rather vague. According to his account, the nucleus of the insurrection in Ba'īrāt consisted of 300–400 men, but soon he heard 'rumours . . . of the increase of the insurgents to the number of three thousand', and some time later the leader of the rebellion appeared before Qenā 'with from ten to fifteen thousand men'.[144] Estimates of a participation of 20–30,000 we find only for some of the insurrections which extended over larger areas, such as the revolts against Ibrāhīm. Thus the number of Lebanese insurgents in the later stages of the revolt of 1840 was estimated by French diplomatic sources at 15–20,000, the number of fellahs who took part in the attack on Jerusalem in May 1834 is put by Monk Neophytos at 20,000, and the army collected by Qāsim al-Aḥmad in June of the same year at 30,000.[145]

Perhaps more meaningful and comparable are the data concerning the geographical extent of the various rebellions. By this criterion we may divide Middle Eastern fellah rebellions into three categories: those which were confined to one estate or village or comprised a small group of villages, those which extended over a district or a certain limited geographical area which was often identical with a social unit, and finally rebellions which spread more or less to a whole Ottoman province or later a country or a state. An analysis of the result of such a division shows that all the rebellions of the first category occurred in Egypt. In 1795 it was the fellahs of Sharqāwī's *iltizām* near Bilbays who appeared in Cairo, in 1826 rebellion broke out in six villages in Sharqiyya, in 1854 two or three villages in Gīza were 'in open rebellion against the government authorities', in 1865 the insurrection led by Aḥmad al-Ṭayyib comprised four villages – al-Rayāyina, Qāw, al-Natra, and al-Shaykh Jābir, in 1882 the people of another four villages on the Khedive's estate in the area of Zankalūn (Sharqiyya) went on strike; in 1951 clashes between peasants on one hand and landowners and armed forces of the government on the other hand occurred in the village of Buhūt (Gharbiyya) on the estates of the Badrāwī-'Āshūr family, in the village Kufūr Nijm (Sharqiyya) on the estates of Prince Muḥammad 'Alī Tawfīq, and on the Averoff estates near Dikirnis (Daqahliyya); and in October of the same year peasants who rented government land in al-Sirū (Daqahliyya) staged a sit down strike on these lands.[146] It is not impossible that similar limited eruptions happened in the Fertile Crescent as well, but they have not become known. Apparently better communications in Egypt than in the Fertile Crescent and the lack of mountains or swamps worked in favour of the authorities rather than the fellahs and enabled the rulers to confine many rebellions to a small area and suppress them before they spread.

The large majority of fellah rebellions in the Middle East belonged to the second category. A rebellion of this size affected a dozen to about thirty villages situated in one area. In Syria and Lebanon such an area was defined by common social attributes. Thus two of these rebellions, in 1837–8 and 1895–6, took place in Jabal Druze, the former overflowing to the Druze population of Rāshayyā and Ḥāṣbayyā in Wādī Taym.[147] Similarly, the 1834–5 rebellion occurred within the area inhabited by ʻAlawī peasants, and the 1937–9 unrest in the Kurdish mountains.[148] In these cases the rebelling peasants belonged to a common sect as well as a common social system. The social bond of the Kisrawān peasants consisted of a common *muqāṭaʻajī*, i.e. a lord, or a family of shaykhs with functions and privileges many of which resembled feudal systems. The two areas of the Kisrawān revolt together comprised 20–30 villages.[149] According to various reports the 'spirit' or 'mood' of revolt spread to other *muqāṭaʻāt*, but there are no concrete accounts of acts of rebellion outside Kisrawān.[150]

In Egypt there were no such common social characteristics of the rebellious peasants which distinguished them from the fellahs of other calm areas. At least we have not been able to find such bonds, except the fact that the 1846 and 1880 rebellions occurred in the rice growing regions.[151] In all other cases our sources just mention the geographical extent: in 1778 it was the 'district' of Ṭahṭā, but apparently no specific administrative unit was affected since several *kāshifs* (Mamluk district officers) fought the insurgents;[152] in 1798 the insurrection in the north-eastern Delta comprised villagers of the Manzala, Fāriskūr, Shaʻrā and Buḥayrat Ṭanāḥ districts;[153] in 1807 Shaykh Sulaymān gathered the fellahs of villages in the neighbourhood of Benhā al-ʻAsal (Qalyūbiyya) including a number of *nāḥiyas*;[154] Aḥmad al-Mahdī's insurrection in 1822–3 extended over the plain of Thebes, from Armant in the south to the Qenā area in the north;[155] and in 1877–9 peasant resistance to the government and battles with armed bands of peasants haunted the whole area between Sūhāg and Girgā.[156] All these areas included not more than three dozen villages, which apparently was the maximum extent a peasant rebellion could achieve in Egypt before the central government was able to localize and then suppress it – unless it had strong allies in the town.

This happened in Egypt only once, in 1919, when the sabotage of communications carried out by fellahs all over the country[157] was part of a general revolt initiated by the basically urban national movement. It should be mentioned here, by the way, that the 'second' fellah rebellion of that year, the one against large landowners, remained confined to a small area in Asyūṭ, since it had no allies in the town or in a political movement. Anyway, all the other fellah rebellions of the third category, i.e. those which spread over a whole country, occurred in Syria, Palestine, and Lebanon, which again reflects the greater stability of the central government in Egypt than in the Fertile Crescent. Among these rebellions two occurred in Lebanon, the revolt of 1820 in which peasants 'from all the *muqāṭa'āt* except the Shūf and the four *aqālīm*' took part,[158] and the 1840 revolt against Ibrāhīm which spread over the whole of Lebanon (and other areas as well).[159] Two of the country-wide rebellions took place in Palestine, the revolt of 1834 in which fellahs fought Ibrāhīm's soldiers in Samaria, Hebron, Judea, Jerusalem, Ramleh, Lydda, Jaffa, Tiberias, Safed, Salt, the Haifa area and Acre,[160] and the revolt of 1936–8, whose centre was the Triangle (Nablus–Jenin–Tulkarm), but which comprised most areas of Mandatory Palestine.[161] Finally, two of these rebellions happened in Syria. In 1925, in addition to the Druze insurgents whose activity extended over a wide area, Sunni bands operated in the Nabk and Jabal Qalamūn area and Shī'ī bands in the Biqā'.[162] And in 1951 the 'anti-feudal' fellah unrest in Syria spread from the Ḥamāh and Ḥoms areas to the Ḥawrān and the Lādhiqiyya coastal area.[163] The large extent of these rebellions had various reasons. Some were part of a national movement or in league with such a movement, and the insurrections against Ibrāhīm had the support of foreign powers (in 1834 the Ottomans, and in 1840 the Ottomans and Britain). Finally, 1951 was a year of culmination of the post-war social tension in many countries of the Middle East and of the disintegration of the traditional ruling class in the wake of the Palestine war. But Syria was the only country in the Middle East in which urban politicians made an attempt to organize and direct the social unrest in the countryside. This particular character of the Syrian peasant leadership was an important reason for the large extent of the 1951 unrest.

So far our discussion of participation in fellah rebellions has been concerned with their quantitative extent. As we have seen, this discussion leads to a related question: what kind of peasants participated in these rebellions and who were their leaders? Recent studies on peasant rebellions in the world have stressed the important role played by landowning 'middle peasants' or a class of wealthy peasants in many of these revolts, because 'possession of their own resources provide their holders with the minimal tactical freedom required to challenge their overlord'.[164] It was this class on which, for instance, peasant revolt was based in Flanders and England in the fourteenth century, in various areas of Germany in the early sixteenth century, or in Mexico early in the twentieth century.[165] For most of the period covered by this essay, and in most of the areas discussed, no such class of landowning wealthy 'middle peasants' existed. The rural population consisted of the great rather undifferentiated mass of ordinary fellahs and a very small group of wealthy notables, generally one family per village or group of villages. The land belonged to the state, and taxes were farmed out to *multazim*s (tax farmers), mainly urban residents but in some areas, especially the hills of Lebanon and Palestine, to the rural notables. In Egypt rural notables were the agents of the *multazim*s, and after the abolition of *iltizām*, of the government. Gradually, in the course of the nineteenth century, a process of social differentiation took place as the result of the introduction of cash crops and the development of private property of land. One of the results of this process was the emergence of owners of medium-sized landed property. The same process took place in Syria and Palestine much later – up to World War I the *iltizām* persisted and more than 70 per cent of the land in Palestine was commonly held by the village (*mushā'*) – and in Iraq still later, about the mid-twentieth century. Lebanon was a special case, to which we shall return further on.[166] Throughout most of the period under discussion, fellahs in the Fertile Crescent (and to some extent in Egypt too) were dependent on the rural notables, who served as intermediaries between them and the government. As a result they held enormous economic, administrative, political and military power. Rebellions of fellahs against them was practically impossible. On the other hand, when conflicts arose between them and the government, they were able to recruit the fellahs to fight for them. This does not mean that the fellahs were not interested in these struggles – on the contrary, since the issues were taxation, conscription, *corvée* for the state, etc., the fellahs' and the notables' interests coincided. In many areas the fellahs considered the notables as their customary protectors and traditional leaders. As a result, most fellah rebellions in the Fertile Crescent, and some in Egypt, were led by these rural notables.

Peasant rebellions under the leadership of their local lords was not a peculiarity of the Middle East. In England, for instance, the Pilgrimage of Grace (1536–7) was an antiroyal movement in which peasants rose with their lords.[167] In Languedoc, in the seventeenth century, 'well-to-do peasants followed their lords in defence of the liberties of their province against the central government'.[168] Barrington Moore's generalization of such situations fits very well many of the Middle Eastern peasant rebellions of the nineteenth century:

> . . . to the extent that it takes over the protective and judicial functions of the locally residing overlord, royal absolutism weakens the crucial link that binds the peasants to the upper classes. Or if it takes over these functions only partly and haphazardly it is likely to find itself in competition with local elites in extracting resources from the peasants. In such circumstances there is a temptation for the local notables to side with the peasants.[169]

This is precisely what happened in Palestine, Lebanon and Syria under the Egyptian occupation in the 1830s, and the result was a series of peasant rebellions under the leadership of the notables. According to one document, the initiative to resist Ibrāhīm Pasha's order concerning conscription in Palestine was taken by the fellahs themselves, but this may have been an excuse made by the notables to Ibrāhīm.[170] However that may be, the leaders of the revolt in the Hebron district were shaykhs of the most powerful family of notables of the area, the 'Amr family centred in Dūrā,[171] and in Jabal Nāblus the rebellion was led by Qāsim al-Aḥmad of the important Qāsim family, of east Jammā'īn, with their centre and castle in Bayt Wuzin.[172] In 1820, the Lebanese rebels elected as their leader Shaykh Faḍl al-Badawī al-Khāzin, a member of the ruling family of Kisrawān.[173] The Beirut branch of the 1840 revolt against Ibrāhīm in Lebanon was led at the beginning by two common persons, but soon another member of the Khāzin family was put at its head, Fransīs Abū Nādir al-Ghusṭāwī. Other units of the rebels were headed by amīrs from the Shihāb and Abu al-Lam' families and other notables. Appropriately these leaders were known as *wujūh al-'āmmiyya* – 'the notables of the popular movement'.[174] In the Biqā' the leader of the rebels was the *amīr* Khanjar al-Ḥarfūsh of the Shī'ī family centred in Ba'lbek which ruled the Biqā'.[175] Among the leaders of the 'Alawī rebellion against the Egyptians in the summer of 1834 who were caught and executed by the Egyptian commanders, two bore the title of *amīr*.[176] Finally, the 1837–8 insurrection in the Ḥawrān was conducted by Yaḥyā al-Ḥamdān, 'Shaykh Mashāyikh Durūz Ḥawrān', i.e. the head of the Ḥamdān family, the ruling family of the Ḥawrān Druzes at that time.[177]

After the Ḥamdāns had been replaced by the Aṭrashs as the leading family of the Jabal during the second half of the nineteenth century, subsequent revolts of the Druze peasants were headed by shaykhs of this family. Even when the Druze peasants revolted in 1888–90 against the shaykhs and refused to deliver them the traditional third of the crop, they put at the head of their movement (*'āmmiyya*), according to some accounts, one of the Aṭrash notables, Shiblī al-Aṭrash.[178] Sulṭān al-Aṭrash was the well known leader of the revolt against the French in 1925–7, and the council of the revolt elected in July 1926 included four more 'Ṭurshān' (pl. of Aṭrash), three representatives of the 'Āmir family, three of the Hinaydī family, two Rizqs, two 'Izz al-Dīns, two Ghānims, and other notables. In the resolution which established this council it was explicitly stated that every hundred conscripts would be headed by a *ra'īs* from among the well known families.[179]

Egyptian rural notables never became as powerful in the nineteenth century as their counterparts in the Fertile Crescent. As the result of topographical conditions, the central government never depended on the cooperation of rural notables, and even in the eighteenth century the *multazim*s were absentees living in Cairo, not provincial lords as in the Fertile Crescent. Therefore fellahs were not as dependent on them as in

Palestine, Lebanon, or Jabal Druze, and they were not the natural leaders of fellah rebellion. An exception were some distant areas of the northern and eastern Delta, where connection with the government was weak and powerful local notables ruled the peasants. In these areas peasant rebellions were headed by local shaykhs. Thus the rebellion against the French in 1798 in the Damietta area was headed by Shaykh Ḥasan Ṭūbār, 'Shaykh Iqlīm al-Manzala'.[180] Similar conditions existed in the rice growing areas of Buḥayra and Sharqiyya. In 1846 it was the village shaykhs of the Qurayn district in Sharqiyya who refused to pay the customary taxes and send men to the *corvée*, and it was these shaykhs who were captured by Khurshīd Pasha in order to suppress the violent revolt which they had instigated among their peasants.[181] And again in 1880, in the rice-growing districts of Buḥayra province, the shaykhs and chiefs of the villages led the resistance to the *'amaliyya*, i.e. the forced labour for the government.[182]

As we have said, late in the nineteenth and early in the twentieth century a new class of wealthy landowning peasants had emerged in the Egyptian countryside and created a new group of notables, *a'yān*, with quite a large extent of economic freedom and independence and rather strong economic and political ties with the towns. It was from this class that a number of nationalist politicians and leaders emerged – for instance Sa'd Zaghlūl, the leader of the Wafd. Having suffered losses and hardship during World War I, this class of new rural notables supported the nationalists and conducted the rural uprising against British rule in 1919.[183]

However, most Egyptian peasant revolts in the nineteenth century were not led by rural notables, but consisted of violent eruptions of the mass of poor fellahs. These were mostly fellahs in villages without wealthy notable families formerly exploited directly by absentee *multazim*s. When *iltizām* was abolished, order often collapsed. Some of the peasants had become tenants or labourers of the newly established estates of the Muḥammad 'Alī family. Generally their situation was desperate, its worsening unbearable, and the chances to change it almost nil. They had no independent economic basis and no connection with towns or any other social group. Even in order to establish some connection with neighbouring villages in the area some external factor was needed. Such a situation was ideal for the appearance of mystic shaykhs, holy men, prophets and *mahdī*s to lead the fellahs in their desperation. This indeed was the prevalent pattern in Egypt in the nineteenth century. In 1798 a *sharīf* from Mecca called Shaykh Muḥammad al-Jaylānī appeared in Upper Egypt at the head of a great number of followers, claimed *wilāya* (saintship, to be under the protection of God) and thus raised a large army of rebels against the French, until he was defeated by General Desaix and killed.[184] In 1807 another saint appeared near Benhā (Qalyūbiyya) called Shaykh Sulaymān. Again the villagers believed that he possessed *wilāya* and assembled to support and worship him. He called on the fellahs to refuse to make payments to the government and to resist the government agents whenever they came to collect taxes and duties.[185] Shaykh Aḥmad, called al-Ṣalāḥ, who revolted in 1820–1 at the head of thousands of fellahs in the area of Ḥijāza (south of Qūṣ), seems also to have been considered a holy man – to judge by his sobriquet. When the revolt was suppressed, he fled to the Ḥijāz.[186] Two years later, in 1822–3, the much larger revolt which broke out not far from there, near Luxor, was headed again by a leader named Aḥmad, this time called al-Mahdī (or al-Wazīr). In the eye-witness account of the English traveller J. A. St. John he is invariably called 'the Prophet'. He too fled to the Ḥijāz.[187] In 1824 a Maghribī called Aḥmad b. Drīs (Idrīs), who had become involved with the customs at Quṣayr on his way back from Mecca, declared that he had been sent by God ('se disait inspiré' according to Clot Bey) and headed a rebellious movement of fellahs over quite a large area, between Isnā and Farshūṭ.[188] And finally, under Ismā'īl's reign, the large outbreak of fellah rebellion in the Abū Tīg region was once again headed by a man named Aḥmad and called al-Ṭayyib. He claimed to be a descendent of the Prophet Muḥammad through 'Alī and the *imām*s, to have *'ilm* and *wilāya* or, according to some reports, to be the *mahdī*. Many fellahs believed in his supernatural powers and swore allegiance to him.[189] It is interesting to note that the rich neighbouring village al-'Uqāl did not participate in the rebellion as the result of the efforts of its rich *'umda* (village shaykh) 'Abd al-'Āl al-'Uqālī, 'the owner of great wealth and extensive agricultural lands'. Moreover, he and his villagers helped the Khedive's army to suppress the revolt.[190]

Most Egyptian fellah rebellions of the twentieth century were not led by wealthy peasants or rural notables either. This seems to be quite clear, though we have very little information on the leadership of these uprisings. But they also lacked holy men and *mahdī*s. This may have been one reason for the geographical limitation and the short duration of these outbreaks, which were generally confined to the tenants of one estate – that of Maḥmūd Sulaymān in 1919 (the 'second' revolt), and of the Badrāwī 'Ashūrs, Prince Muḥammad 'Alī Tawfīq, the Averoff estates and the government estate in al-Sirū in 1951.

Like the Egyptian rebellions of 1951, the Syrian fellah uprisings of the same year were also revolts of tenants or share-croppers who tilled the land of large estate owners. The rebellions occurred primarily in the Ḥamāh, Ḥoms and Aleppo provinces which had the highest percentage in Syria of large estates of more than 1,000 dunums – 56, 48 and 45 respectively.[191] The issue of the rebellions clearly was the percentage of the crop which the share-croppers were required to deliver to the landlord.[192] Like their Egyptian contemporaries, Syrian fellahs were neither led by wealthy peasants, nor by rural notables, nor by holy men and *mahdīs*. But unlike them their rebellion did not manifest itself in isolated eruptions here and there but in a mass movement which extended over a number of provinces. The principal reason for this difference was the fact that they enjoyed the advantage of a strong leadership in the shape of Akram Ḥawrānī and his Arab Socialist Party. Ḥawrānī was born in Ḥamāh and he studied in Aleppo and in the Law School of Damascus University. His father had been a landlord but the family's wealth had been dissipated by an uncle. Thus his family was at a disadvantage in the local political relations with the great landowning families of Ḥamāh – al-'Azm, Barāzī, Kaylānī, and Bārūdī. To fight these families, Ḥawrānī organized the youth of the town in a band called Jam'iyyat al-Shabāb which later became Ḥizb al-Shabāb and in 1950 the Arab Socialist Party. But he also tried to undermine their power by supporting and inciting the fellahs of Ḥamāh (and later of other provinces) against the owners of the land they were tilling, and by declaring 'war against feudalism'. The climax of his campaign was an 'anti-feudalist' rally in Aleppo which started on 16 September 1951. Attended by thousands of fellahs from all parts of Syria, the demonstration opened with a great parade of peasants through the streets carrying banners reading: 'The fellahs' hoes will remove feudalism'; 'No more feudalism, exploitation and imperialism'; etc.[193] Peasant uprisings in Iraq in the 1950s seem to have resembled the Syrian pattern in most of its elements. As we have seen, the rebellious Iraqi fellahs were also landless tillers of *mīrī ṣirf* land and they demanded a more favourable distribution of the land and the crops between them and the shaykhs. And at least in some cases they were led by lawyers, and in others by Communist activists directed from urban centres.[194] But apparently unlike Syria no coinciding country-wide movement developed. Unfortunately, we have too little information to draw definite conclusions with regard to Iraq. However, it is clear that while rebellious poor peasants in the Middle East were led in the nineteenth (and sometimes even in the twentieth) century by rural notables or by men with religious pretensions, in twentieth century Syria (and perhaps Iraq) a new kind of leadership for this class of fellahs had emerged – urban lawyers and a political party.

Only once in Middle Eastern history did poor and wealthy peasants revolt together against a feudal-like aristocracy, and the common participation in the revolt found its expression in its leadership. This was in the peasant revolt of 1858–61 in Kisrawān. Lebanon was the only place in the Middle East where such a layer of wealthy peasants emerged as early as the first half of the nineteenth century, at a time when the class of powerful notables, the lords of the *muqāṭa'as*, was still the dominant economic and political power. No doubt, the great majority of the peasants were poor share-croppers owning tiny parcels of land or no land at all. According to one estimate, they amounted to three-fifths of the population.[195] But there are clear indications that by the time of the revolt a class of rich peasants had come into being who employed wage-labour, not share-croppers (*shurakā'*) as did the *muqāṭa'ajīs*. According to the French Consul Henri Guys, 'Cette classe de propriétaires, qui est celle des paysans aisés, ne s'associe à personne. Elle se sert, à l'époque de la récolte de la soie, de malheureux journaliers qui vivent, les trois quarts du temps en attendant cette époque où leurs bras sont utilisés'.[196] As we have seen, land in Lebanon was *mulk*, full private property of its owners, and thus could be transferred to peasants and become their property. This seems to have happened in various ways. For once, plantations were often cultivated by *mughārasa* contracts, according to which one-quarter to one-half of the trees and the land on which they are planted become full property of the tenant who supplied the work.[197] It was through this method that, e.g., peasants of the coastal plain south of Beirut had become landowners.[198] But in many cases the lords just sold land to the peasants. This is what the Khāzins did, when their economic position deteriorated, and we have seen that they endeavoured to keep the peasants dependent on them by incorporating in the deeds of sale an obligation of the peasant who bought the land to pay them certain annual duties. The abolition of these *rusūmāt al-mu'āyadāt* was one of the main demands of the revolt and may have been an important aim of rich peasants in joining the rebellion.

The general commander of the Kisrawān revolt was Ṭānyūs Shāhīn, a mule-driver and blacksmith from Rayfūn village. Because of his occupation he had wide connections with fellahs of different villages and was economically independent of the Khāzin lords.[199] This social background may have been an important reason for his election as leader. But there can be no doubt that he belonged to the lower layers of Kisrawān society. However, other layers of this society were represented in the leadership of the revolt as well. This has been shown by Porath in his excellent analysis of the revolt.[200] The rebel government of Kisrawān rested on the village *wakīls* chosen by the villagers. Among 116 individuals who exercised this function, nine or ten were priests[201] and 28 belonged to families two, or even three, of whose members were *wakīls*. In some cases the *wakīl*'s signature of documents is followed by the words 'and his family', and various members of certain families served as *wakīls* at different times. In one source it is clearly implied that a *wakīl* was a man of means. A poor family could hardly have afforded more than one *wakīl*, and the words 'and his family' show that the family had some influence. Thus Porath concludes that at least some of the *wakīls* were wealthy villagers or notables. This may have been the reason why the Kisrawān rebels did not demand any changes in property rights.

This does not mean, however, that the lack of active participation of wealthy peasants in other fellah rebellions in the Middle East has led inevitably to a revolutionary programme of social change. In fact the last rebellion to be discussed in this context shows that this did not happen. The Palestine rebellion of 1936–8 began as a national movement led by urban nationalists in which all classes of Palestinian Arab society participated. However, gradually the armed revolt was carried out mainly by Muslim villagers of the lower strata, the participation of urban, educated or notable families being rather slight – though townsmen contributed to the revolt as advisers, intelligence agents, etc. In the course of the revolt townspeople and members of notable rural families gradually deserted the fight – according to one interpretation because they could not bear a situation in which they were often subject to the command of fellahs from the lower classes. Most of them went home to their ordinary life, and the armed bands and their commanders were now composed almost exclusively of poor fellahs from the lower classes. For instance, among the commanders there was only one *mukhtār* (village headman), while the *mukhtārs* were copiously represented among the victims of the revolt. Nevertheless, the rebels did not put forward any social demands of their own, even in an inarticulate way, let alone elaborated any social ideology. This is the more remarkable as the urban national leaders of the upper classes had left the country or had been expelled and had lost control of the rebellion.[202]

Action and organization

According to Bakunin, peasant revolutions are anarchic by their very nature.[203] Spontaneous outbursts of wanton violence have indeed accompanied a large number of fellah rebellions in the Middle East and sometimes been their main feature. After describing the rebellion of 1778 in Upper Egypt, Sonnini sums it up in the words 'arbitrary violence'.[204] This expression or similar ones used by various authors comprise, however, two somewhat different kinds of violence. On the one hand we have eruptions of anger and acts of vengeance for the wretched conditions in which the fellahs found themselves. The most frequent manifestation of these feelings was the burning of buildings and property belonging to the fellahs' enemies. In 1919, fellahs in the central and eastern Delta set fire to the houses of employees of the State Domains and buildings of the large land companies,[205] and in June 1951 fellahs burnt the dwellings and farm houses of the Badrāwī-'Āshūr family in Buhūt.[206] Sometimes property was destroyed by other means as well. Thus in 1919 fellahs of Daqahliyya and Buḥayra province 'attacked irrigation canals and cuts, removing the baulks which are used to regulate the water supply. A canal bridge between Mansura and Simbellawein was destroyed, blocking the canal and causing the flooding of a large tract of country'.[207] Another manifestation of anger and vengeance was the murder of village dignitaries or functionaries, a frequent occurrence in the Egyptian countryside. In April 1846 Hekekyan recorded in his diary, that several village shaykhs had been murdered recently by fellahs in Minyā province.[208] In 1944, a writer complained in *al-Ahrām* about the recent tremendous increase in the incidents of murder of owners of estates, their agents or superintendents, village shaykhs and guards.[209] The Palestine revolt of 1936–8 too abounded in assassinations, but these were rather political than manifestations of peasant wrath. However, in addition to anger and vengeance fellah violence has been impelled by another important motive, the free gain of material benefit, mainly of basic necessities of consumption. Thus looting has been among the most prominent activities of rebellious fellahs. For instance, when in May 1834 thousands of fellahs rushed into Jerusalem after the Damascus gate had been opened, 'young and old fell to looting, beginning with the houses of the *Miralais*, whence they removed the heavy articles which had been left behind, such as pillows, blankets and wooden tables. Then they looted the Jewish houses in the same way. The following night, the fellaheen, with some low-class bandits of Jerusalem, began to loot the shops of the Jews, the Christians, the Franks and then the Moslems. The grocers, the shoemakers and every other dealer suffered alike. Within two or three days there was not one shop intact in the market, for they smashed the locks and the doors and seized everything of value . . . On Thursday morning they looted the stores, that is, the places where the government kept provisions (rice, lentils, beans, etc.) and divided the spoils. Next, they opened the government granary and each one took wheat and barley whenever he wished, and as much as he wished.'[210] Similar events took place in 1919. 'On the 15th [of March] the disorders extended to Upper Egypt. At Reqqa, the morning express from Cairo was attacked and pillaged, all passengers' baggage being looted, while the station was sacked and burnt. . . .' The daily bulletin issued at General Headquarters on 21 March has the following: 'In the central Delta and east thereof disorderly mobs are continuing the campaign of destruction and loot. The peasants have helped themselves to crops of the State Domains . . .'[211] It is significant that the assembly of Druze leaders at Shaqqa on 1 July 1926, specifically prohibited pillage and looting in the resolutions issued on that occasion.[212] Similar outbursts accompanied the fellah movement in Iraq in the 1950s. 'Thus, in the late summer of 1958, the peasants stormed, looted and burned down the residences of big landlords in the provinces of Kūt and 'Amāra.'[212a]

In the course of some fellah rebellions violent actions with the aim of free gain of material benefit were perpetrated not only by individuals or amorphous masses but also by groups of peasants banded together for this purpose. Brigandage, however, was not a very typical feature of Middle Eastern fellah rebellions. Many of the conditions enumerated by Mousnier to explain that banditry did not develop in France on the Russian and Chinese scale[213] obtained in the Middle East as well. In the Fertile Crescent, in particular, the existence of autonomous communities with their notables who served as leaders of the peasantry on one hand, and the domination of the fringes of the settled area by beduin tribes, another socially defined formation, on the other, considerably hampered the emergence of fellah brigands. In Lebanon the density of settlement constituted a further impediment. It was only in the slightly elevated desert margin of the Nile valley in Upper Egypt that brigand bands were sometimes formed in the wake of fellah rebellions. This is what happened in 1778, when Sonnini wrote about the Ṭahṭā district (between Sūhāg and Asyūṭ): 'The fields were abandoned or laid waste; the husbandman forsook his plough to fly to arms; the flocks were carried off, or destroyed, and every sort of provision became the prey of the enemy or of robbers. The highways, lined with banditti were shut against communications and intelligence of every kind.'[214] Exactly one hundred years later, the area a little more to the south, between Girgā and Sūhāg, was again the scene of widespread brigandage. The recurrent demands of taxes induced the fellahs to become robbers and attack the boats navigating the Nile. A rich Copt was kidnapped and his family forced to pay ransom of £1,000. Furthermore, near Luxor, robbery was prevalent too. From Isnā and Aswān it was reported that fellahs were seizing cattle from others in order to be able to pay their taxes. The Egyptian authorities explained the brigandage of the Girgā-Sūhāg area as the result of the drought. The fellahs who had fled to the hills had formed bands of 50–60 men, and whoever was required to pay taxes joined them.[215]

Theoretically, the area around Damascus should not have been a fertile ground for brigandage, neither from the geographical nor from the social point of view. If nevertheless serious brigandage occurred there it was because of the specific conditions of the 1925 revolt, in which Druze bands had used the area of the Ghūṭa plantations as a basis for attacking Damascus, eliminated regular government and exasperated the fellahs. Late in October 1925 the special correspondent of *The Times* reported from Damascus: 'The brigands are becoming more numerous almost every day. This is due to the French practice of burning any village where brigands are reported to have been harboured or victualled. The destruction of every such village, which is accompanied by the confiscation of all movable property, naturally adds to the number of people without homes or means of livelihood at large in the country and converts these villagers into brigands, as their only means of subsistence is to take what they want. Lawlessness is thus steadily growing.'[216] The national revolt in Palestine in 1936–8 was also progressively accompanied by more and more instances of extortion and robberies for the private ends of bands and their leaders.[217]

Finally, another area in which brigandage spread for a while was the Ḥawrān. Generally the leadership of the Druze notables, first the Ḥamdāns and later the Aṭrashs, was strong enough to dominate the fellah movements of the Jabal. But towards the end of the century internal conflict brought about the disintegration of Druze society. In 1894, Druzes together with beduins formed armed bands of robbers called *kassāra* ('breakers') who roamed over the plain. Later even Christians and settled Muslims joined them. Other Druze bands, called *zaghghāba* (?) based on Salkhad, were reported to have aimed at eliminating injustice and helping the oppressed.[218] Similarly, the disintegration of Kurdish society in northern Syria in the late 1930s had undermined the authority of the notables, the *aghas*, who according to the rebels had usurped the land which belonged to the peasants. There too the peasant movement was accompanied by brigandage.[218a]

However, fellahs did not only revolt in order to give vent to their anger or to enjoy free gain. To achieve their common aims they had to use different means. First of all, they banded together and arranged a demonstration. Middle Eastern peasant demonstrations differed both in scale and in character from the great peasant marches which had taken place in India since 1855.[219] In general, they were a local affair, such as the gathering of fellahs in front of Mu'allim Ghālī's house in April 1812, or the march of the villagers of Buhūt on the residence of the Badrāwī-'Āshūrs, their landlords, in 1951.[220] Fellah unrest in Iraq in 1954 often started with similar local demonstrations, such as that on the estates of the then Senator Rāyiḥ al-'Aṭiyya in Dīwāniyya, and in 1955 the fellahs of Banī Lurayiq in Rumaytha staged a strike.[221] Only once in Middle Eastern history did fellahs muster a demonstration exceeding local dimensions – the Aleppo rally of thousands of fellahs from all parts of Syria in mid-September 1951. Sure enough, such demonstrations frequently provoked violent clashes and led to other forms of insubordination.

Next to demonstrations come strikes. Strikes too were local incidents, sometimes resorted to by tenants who opposed decisions of the landlord concerning the lease or sale of the land they were tilling. In the spring of 1882 the tenants of the Khedive's estates in Zankalūn (Sharqiyya) struck because the manager of the estates leased part of the lands to a large renter, while the peasants claimed they had priority in exchange for cultivating the private lands of the Khedive. They declared that they would not work for the new landlord and would oppose him and the government by force. As a result, the renter eventually gave up his lease.[222] About seventy years later, in October 1951, peasants who rented government land in al-Sirū (Daqahliyya) staged a sit-down strike on the lands they had formerly rented and demanded that the government should sell them the land instead of offering it at a public auction. In their public statement they declared that 'public auctions inevitably benefit the capitalists and despite all the government's need for money it cannot ignore the rights of those struggling for their piece of bread'.[223]

Demonstrations and strikes aimed at forcing the opponent of the peasants to grant them their demands. In various cases, however, peasants implemented their demands themselves. As we have seen, the most frequent of such implementations were the refusal to pay newly imposed taxes, or resistance to conscription for the army and forced labour. We have dealt with this in detail and need not repeat it here. When tenants considered the situation unstable enough and themselves strong enough they ceased to pay the rent which they owed the shaykhs or landlords. This is what happened in Kisrawān in 1858, in the Ḥoms-Ḥamāh area in 1951, or in 'Amāra in 1952.[224] In Palestine the rebels declared that an indefinite moratorium on debts would be effective from 1 September 1938, and that all court actions concerning debts would be stopped.[225]

When they were able to do so, fellahs went one step further and expelled the landlords from the area of their estates. Only once did fellahs succeed in performing such an action systematically and in bringing about the expulsion of landlords for some years – in Kisrawān in 1859. But the Khāzin shaykhs were so powerless that a bloodless attack of a rather small force of peasants on an assembly they were holding was enough to achieve this aim.[226] During the Druze *'āmmiyya* of 1888–90 the Ḥawrān fellahs too expelled their shaykhs from the Jabal for some time, and the Kurdish *aghas* of northern Syria had to leave their villages in the late 1930s.[227] Pamphlets distributed in the Ḥawrān in 1951 threatening large landowners with death and signed the 'Black Glove' apparently were less successful, but in the same year farm workers and tenants in other areas of Syria were reported to have driven off both landlords and their agents on various occasions.[228] And in 1958 the fellahs of Kūt and 'Amāra chased away the agents and supervisors of the landlords, took over the agricultural equipment and settled down as owners.[228a] However, only in Kisrawān did the expulsion of the landlords last long enough to be accompanied by their expropriation – *de facto* though not *de jure*. First the rebels confiscated the crops from the Khāzins' land; then they took horses and work animals belonging to them. Later the peasants compiled lists of property which they claimed had been taken away from them by the shaykhs. The bands that confiscated Khāzin property were headed by *wakīls*, which means that these were organized operations rather than pillage and looting. Mulberry plots which the shaykhs had not leased to peasants were divided up among them. Finally, in order to prevent the shaykhs from returning, the rebels chopped down their trees in woods and olive groves.[229]

All these actions involved insubordination of fellahs to the ruling authorities and therefore led before long to violent clashes. Armed hostilities between rebellious fellahs and the ruling authorities fall into two main categories – guerilla warfare and frontal battles of armed masses of peasants. Often both kinds of warfare occurred in the same rebellion. It has been said that guerilla warfare is the most suitable form for the expression of armed peasant action, because of 'the ability of the amorphous guerilla "army" to dissolve itself in times of need into the sympathetic peasant mass and vanish into the expanses of the countryside . . ., its ability to survive without outside supplies and the adequacy for this type of warfare of primitive weapons'.[230] One may add the advantage the peasants have over their enemies by being well acquainted with the natural features of the battleground. Because of the nature of these advantages, it is not surprising that all peasant rebellions in Egypt and the Fertile Crescent during the last 200 years in which guerilla warfare was predominant were rebellions against a foreign ruler. In Egypt guerilla tactics manifested themselves mainly in the sabotage of communications which accompanied the rebellions against the French in 1798 and against the British in 1919. In 1798 the insurgents attacked the Nile boats of the French[231] and in 1919 the fellah destroyed or damaged railway, telegraph, and telephone communications and sacked railway stations and trains.[232] In Palestine the mountains of Judea and Samaria enabled the peasants in 1834 to harass Ibrāhīm Pasha's army by using typical guerilla tactics: they lay in ambush at the places most difficult to pass on the way to Jerusalem and rolled down huge boulders blocking the road and then peppering the army with shots; they used rocks and trees as barricades near Bethlehem, hid in caves, and then lured Ibrāhīm to the Pools of Salomon where they surprised him when he was in a powerless position; and the fellahs of Samaria used similar devices to fight him there. Generally the fellahs would stand behind a tree or a stone, fire a shot, and then on the approach of the enemy run for the mountains.[233] In Lebanon, in 1840, Egyptian convoys transporting supplies and ammunition to Beirut were ambushed and attacked by peasant rebels.[234] In the Druze revolt against Ibrāhīm in 1838 villagers from Ḥāṣbayyā attacked the ammunition convoy from Acre at Sa'sa'a,[235] and eighty-seven years later, a supply train of munitions and provisions on the Ḥijāz Railway 'was suddenly charged by a swarm of Druze horsemen . . . and the entire convoy, including several field guns, fell into the Druses' hands . . . Commandant Aujac committed suicide . . .'.[236] As we have seen, in 1838 the rough lava area of the Laj'a served as an ideal ground for Druze guerilla warfare against the Egyptians, and in 1925 the Damascus Ghūṭa fulfilled a similar function: 'With its dense groves of fruit-trees which broke the field of vision, and its innumerable water-courses and irrigation channels which impeded the transport of artillery, the Ghūtah lent itself admirably to the tactics of guerilla warfare; and under the cover which it afforded, the insurgents hovered at the gates of Damascus waiting for their next opportunity to push their way in.'[237] One student of the Druze revolt who paid particular attention to its military aspect has observed that the victories of the Druzes were won in guerilla warfare, and whenever they fought battles of a regular army they lost and were utterly defeated.[238] Basically this is true as well for the 1936–8 Palestine revolt against the British Mandate. Members of the guerilla bands operated near their villages, and since their equipment was primitive they moved much lighter than the British military units. They easily dispersed among the population, hid their arms and became 'innocent' fellahs. They enjoyed the service of an excellent intelligence network and usually were not surprised by the British army. Among their activities were the destruction of all the railway stations between Jerusalem and Lydda and most of the stations between Lydda and the Egyptian border. In many towns police stations, post offices, bank branches and town halls were attacked and robbed, and arms and ammunition were seized. The Nablus–Jerusalem telephone lines were cut.[239] Only in this way could the rebels score any points in their struggle. Finally, the Kurdish peasant bands of northern Syria also had recourse to guerilla tactics in their fight against the French army which had come to support the local *aghas* early in 1939.[239a]

This does not mean that in insurrections against foreign rulers frontal attacks of armed masses did not occur. As we shall see presently, such attacks sometimes took place in addition to guerilla warfare. But in none of the rebellions against native landlords or even against an indigenous government did guerilla warfare prevail. In one of its publications of the early 1950s, the Iraqi Communist party explained 'that the fallāhīn were not ready for such actions . . . successful guerilla warfare necessitated the developing of an incipient military force and the creation of a zone of operation within an area which government forces could not easily reach . . . [which] was impossible to find in southern Iraq'.[239b]

Masses of villagers were recruited for a battle against an enemy by an institution called *faz'a*. This is an alarm calling all the villagers to assemble immediately with their arms in face of an external danger. Apparently the institution was adopted from the beduins,[240] and generally villagers had recourse to *faz'a* in the feuds between villages and factions. In the context of peasant rebellions we have found references to the *faz'a* in the account of the resistance of fellahs near Benhā to Muḥammad 'Alī's soldiers in 1807,[241] and in the 1936–8 revolt in Palestine: when a rebel band was surrounded by British soldiers, fellahs from nearby villages would gather by means of the *faz'a* to impede the fighting and to enable the band to escape.[242]

Frontal clashes of masses of armed fellahs with an army occurred, for instance, near Farshūṭ in Upper Egypt in the rebellion of 1824, or in the Judean mountains in 1834.[243] In various cases masses of armed fellahs attacked single specific objects, such as the estate or the houses of a landlord (as we have seen repeatedly in this essay – for instance in connection with fellah rebellion in Iraq in the 1950s). In the 1919 revolt in Egypt the large sugar factory at Ḥawāmidiyya was attacked by villagers, and at Mīnat al-Qamḥ fellahs from the surrounding villages raided the government buildings and released all the prisoners.[244] Frequently fellah armies set out to attack the towns which served as the centre of government and the fortified bastion of the authorities, the enemies of the fellahs. Thus in 1834 a large army of fellahs first besieged and then conquered Jerusalem; masses of fellahs laid siege to Jaffa and Acre and attacked al-Salṭ; the fellahs of the 'Atlīt coastal plain invested Haifa; and the fellahs of the Nuṣayriyya mountains, the Lādhiqiyya plain and Jabal al-Akrād penetrated into the town of Lādhiqiyya, killed the soldiers, looted the officers' houses and besieged the governor.[245] Similarly, in the 1822–3 insurrection of Aḥmad al-Mahdī near Luxor, he collected about a thousand of his followers, marched on Qamūla, attacked it and drove out its garrison. Then he mobilized several thousand additional villagers and managed to threaten the gates of the city of Qenā.[246]

Unfortunately, we have very little information on the military organization of Middle Eastern peasant rebellions. Even for the best documented of these rebellions, the 1858–61 Kisrawān revolt, almost no data exist on military organization.[247] As against this, an abundance of details concerning this aspect of the 1936–8 revolt in Palestine are available and have been admirably published by Arnon and Porath. However, because of the lack of data for other rebellions and the numerous unique features of this revolt most of these details cannot be analysed in accordance with the framework of this essay.

Generally speaking, many of the fellah rebellions in Egypt and the Fertile Crescent were limited and short events in which the necessity of an elaborate military organization did not arise. On Aḥmad al-Ṭayyib, the leader of the rebellion in the Abū Tīg area against the Khedive Ismā'īl, Mubārak just says: *'waja'ala min jamā'atihi ser 'askar waḍubbāṭ katartīb al-jihādiyya'* (he appointed from among his fellows a commander-in-chief and officers, like the organization of the army).[248]

But once the rebellion had lasted for more than a few months and comprised more than a few dozen villages the problem of co-ordination of guerilla or other military activity arose. If we take the rebellions of our third category[249] we must start by stating that we do not know to what extent the military activities of the rebels in the 1820 and 1840 rebellions in Lebanon were directed from a centre, from regional commands or from any other point. All we know is that the 1840 rebellion had two principal foci (*foyers*), Shūf and Kisrawān, and five main areas of concentration (*rassemblement*), but not how they functioned.[250] Concerning the 1919 revolt in Egypt, the question whether the violent actions of the fellahs all over Egypt were directed, and if so, by whom, is the subject of a controversy which has not yet been decided and probably will remain unsolved at least for many years to come.[251] Finally, the Syrian peasant unrest of 1951 did not involve any military campaigns. There remain one Syrian and two Palestinian rebellions, and in all these three movements the problem of military co-ordination played a prominent role, though in a different way in each. In 1834, Ibrāhīm Pasha succeeded in beating the different fellah conglomerations one by one because there was no military co-ordination whatever among them.[252] In the Druze revolt of 1925 there was an acknowledged central commander-in-chief, Sulṭān al-Aṭrash, but on the lower level apparently not everything went smoothly. From the beginning of the revolt the creation of some organization for the various bands in the Ghūṭa had posed a problem, but only in February 1926 did the commanders of the bands meet and decide to establish a unified command which would distribute the forces according to military needs. Though this was stated explicitly in Article 1 of the published resolution, Article 3 said that each band would conduct its military operations in its own area according to the opinion of its military adviser. Only general operations would be decided upon by a National Council. Moreover, the resolution deemed it necessary expressly to forbid members of bands to leave the band in which they were enrolled and join another band (Art. 5).[253] The activity of rebel bands in the Palestine revolt had begun in May 1936, and at the end of July the first attempts were made to achieve some co-ordination among them. In August Fakhrī 'Abd al-Hādī was recognized as Commander-in-Chief of all bands in the Jenīn-Ṭulkarm area, but in the south 'Abd al-Qādir al-Ḥusaynī and other commanders acted separately. When Qā'uqjī arrived, at the end of August, six commanders of large bands (not including the southern commanders) recognized him as Commander-in-Chief and he divided his forces into three foreign and one Palestinian unit under Fakhrī 'Abd al-Hādī. However, quite soon the Palestinians divided again into various bands, each under its own commander. Moreover, since Qā'uqjī inclined towards the Nashāshībī faction, rebels in the southern regions, who were under Ḥusaynī influence, did not establish any connection with him, and even those Samaria band commanders who were pro-Ḥusaynī hesitated to accept Qā'uqjī's orders. At the second stage of the revolt, in 1938, there were again a few regional commanders each operating in a specific region. For the sake of co-ordination and contact with the political Central Committee, a 'Bureau of the Arab Revolt in Palestine' was formed towards the end of 1938, but again the bands of the Jerusalem–Hebron area were not represented in it, and although it had decided that all the bands would be under its control, it authorized every chief commander to conduct the operations of the bands in his region. Moreover, each of the regional commanders had direct contacts with the political leadership in Damascus. As a result, each commander acted in his area regardless of what was going on elsewhere.[254]

If information on the military organization of Middle Eastern peasant rebellions is scarce, information on their political organization is even scarcer. But in this respect the reason most probably is that there existed no political organization of peasants almost anywhere in the Middle East. At least in one case, the 1919 revolt in Egypt, we have more direct proof for such a conclusion than the lack of information. Not only does Dr. Rifā'ī not mention any peasant organization in a special chapter of his book dealing with the revolutionary organizations in 1919,[255] but Rāfi'ī explicitly says that there were none, in so many words: 'The movement comprehended the whole countryside without any arrangement or organization; there was no propaganda for it nor any body or committee or group directing it or issuing instructions or controlling it.'[256] Even in Syria of the 1950s, peasant organizations were set up by Ḥawrānī only more than two years after the unrest of 1951.[257] This concurs with what has been observed in other parts of the world as well. Peasants everywhere are generally incapable of institutionalizing political participation since they possess relatively little of the resources, such as expertise and education, associated with organization-building.[258]

Lebanon was a conspicuous exception to this rule. Lebanese peasant rebellions of the nineteenth century were accompanied by the political organization of the peasants, who elected their representatives, *wakīl*s, and whose young men grouped themselves around chiefs, *shuyūkh al-shabāb*, for political action. The general background for this difference between Lebanon and other areas in the Middle East was the higher educational level of Lebanese peasants because of the activity of the Maronite Church, which had established an early connection with Europe, as well as their higher economic standard and greater economic independence. But there were also a number of specific social and political conditions which facilitated this development. It would seem that *wakīl*s, a *wakīl* for every village, were appointed for the first time in the 1820 rebellion at the Anṭalyās meeting of the Christians from Matn and Kisrawān, and that it was Bishop Yūsuf Isṭifān, the principal of 'Ayn Waraqa College, who initiated this arrangement.[259] This was the result of the conflict which arose at that time between the Maronite clergy and Bashīr II. In 1840 again, elected *wakīl*s were summoned by the leaders of the movement, this time five from each village, to form a central committee, the *dīwān*, and take charge of the rebellion.[260] The communal clashes of the years 1841–5 further strengthened this institution of *wakīl*s, mainly as an instrument of the Maronite Church to enhance its influence.[261] It was these communal clashes which gave to another organized political institution of the Lebanese peasantry, the *shuyūkh al-shabāb*.[262] The *wakīl* system was then incorporated in Shakīb Effendi's Regulations of 1845 as one of the means to weaken the *muqāṭa'ajīs*, and thus the Ottoman authorities made their contribution to the political organization of the Lebanese peasant class.[263] Finally, in 1858 the Khāzin lords of Kisrawān themselves tried to enlist the peasants in their struggle against the Christian *qā'imaqām*, Bashīr Aḥmad, and for this purpose appointed *wakīl*s in the villages of Southern Kisrawān.[264] Thus, when they revolted in 1858, the peasants of Kisrawān very soon used their by now traditional political institutions as organizations for conducting their rebellion against the *muqāṭa'ajīs*. In each of the rebellious villages a *shaykh shabāb* was appointed,[265] and the village *wakīl*s constituted the political framework of the whole Kisrawān revolt.[266] Even in this case peasant organization apparently originated from outside (the clergy, Shakīb's Regulations, the Khāzins) but in other peasant rebellions of the Middle East there was not even a peasant organization initiated by non-peasants, and in the crucial stage of the 1858 Kisrawān revolt the peasants themselves set up their political framework which was formed, it is true, according to a familiar pattern.

When a fellah rebellion persisted longer than a few months and succeeded in evicting the established authority from a certain territory, it became necessary to set up administrative arrangements. True, there are hints that rudiments of government were created by insurgents in some of the shorter Egyptian revolts as well. Thus Aḥmad al-Ṣalāḥ, who led the revolt in Qenā province in 1820–1, is said to have appointed governors from among his followers and imposed taxes on the district under his control, though his revolt held out for two months only.[267] Some British authors claim that in 1919 villages set up their own 'soviets' (in addition to independent governments in some towns), but this seems to be rather doubtful.[268] However, serious administrative arrangements were set up only in three rebellions each of which lasted longer than two years – Kisrawān in 1858–61, Jabal Druze in 1925–7 and Palestine in 1936–8. There was however, a decisive difference between Kisrawān and Jabal Druze on one hand and Palestine on the other; the first two rebellions enjoyed the leadership of an acknowledged chief, established councils to govern the newly created independent community, and enabled local units to elect or appoint their representatives to these bodies, while nothing of this kind existed or was successfully created in Palestine.[269] This was the result of the smaller size and relative geographical and social compactness of Kisrawān and Jabal Druze, as against conflict-ridden Arab Palestine: the separation between North and South, the incompatibility between notables and upstarts, the animosity between families and clans and between fellahs and townsmen, the clashes between the Palestinians and the foreign volunteers and military commanders, the deep political split between the Ḥusaynī and the Nashāshībī factions, and, finally, the violent collisions between the rebel bands and the fellahs themselves and between rebel bands and 'peace bands'. From the administrative point of view the Palestinian rebellion excelled only in one field, the judiciary. As early as 1936 a special 'Court of the Revolt' was established to judge traitors and spies, and to enforce 'justice, security and order'. In addition to spies it tried thieves and other petty criminals. It was revived in the second stage of the revolt, in 1938 and operated successfully. It dealt with ali criminal, civil, and personal matters, officially according to Islamic law. However, as a result of its initial success so many claims were brought before this Court that lower courts had to be established in the various regions, and the system gradually became corrupt. Moreover, the central Court of Appeal depended upon the regional band commanders for the execution of its sentences.[270]

Results and conclusion

It has been stated that 'peasant revolts have been repressed far more often than they have succeeded. For them to succeed requires a somewhat unusual combination of circumstances that has occurred only in modern times'.[271] The attempt to examine whether this rule holds true for Middle Eastern history has led us to the conclusion that it is not always easy to divide fellah rebellions into successes and failures. In fact we have found that their results may rather be grouped into four categories: first, clear-cut failures, i.e. rebellions which were speedily crushed and which left no results; secondly, rebellions which succeeded only for a relatively short time, a few weeks, and were then suppressed without gains to the rebellious peasants; thirdly, rebellions which achieved their limited aims, totally or partly; and finally, rebellions which ended without having an immediate impact, but which led, after some time, to deeper social changes. Moreover, the results of a small number of the more important rebellions of Middle Eastern peasants were a combination of two or three of these categories.

It is true that among fellah rebellions discussed in this essay the earlier ones tended to be failures while among the later ones partial, complete, or delayed successes prevailed. Before the last quarter of the nineteenth century all fellah rebellions in Egypt and the Fertile Crescent, with four or five exceptions, were either immediately crushed or held out for a few weeks. Those which succeeded temporarily were the following: the 1795 movement of the Sharqiyya peasants who came to Cairo and succeeded, with the help of the Azhar shaykhs and the Cairo mob, in bringing about the abolition of certain taxes – for 'about one month after which everything returned to be as mentioned before, and even worse';[272] the Qenā revolt in 1820–1 of Aḥmad al-Ṣalāḥ, whose 'government' held out for about two months;[273] the Luxor revolt in 1822–3 of Aḥmad al-Mahdī who ruled for a few weeks;[274] the Farshūṭ revolt in 1824, which lasted about six weeks;[275] and the Lebanese revolt in 1820 which brought about the exile of Bashīr II and later the deposition of his successors – and the return of Bashīr.[276]

It is also true that the reason why late rebellions were more successful has to be sought in the combination of circumstances under which each of these rebellions occurred. Three of the totally or partially successful rebellions took place in the Jabal Druze. In 1837–8 the Druze rebellion against Ibrāhīm Pasha was the most successful of the various insurrections against Egyptian rule before 1840;[277] in 1888–90 Druze peasants scored important partial successes against the shaykhs by reducing the proportion of the demesne land and acquiring the right to own the land they tilled and the houses they inhabited;[278] and in 1925 the Druzes succeeded in maintaining their autonomy, though the Syrian national movement did not succeed in achieving its goals.[279] Most of these achievements of the Druzes of the Ḥawrān were due, no doubt, primarily to the rugged topography of their territory, the compact structure of their community, and the martial traditions of their society. To a lesser extent somewhat similar conditions brought about the success of some of the 'Alawī rebellions against the Ottomans in the 1850s, though not of all of them.[280]

Before the second half of the twentieth century only two Egyptian peasant rebellions were partially or totally successful: in 1880 the peasants in the rice-growing region of Buḥayra forced the government to revoke the order by which they should have been conscripted for the *corvée*, and in 1882 the tenants on the Khedive's estates in Zankalūn forced the manager to refrain from leasing part of the lands to a large renter.[281] These were years in which government in Egypt was extremely weak and unstable and local forces in areas on the border of settlement were able to evade the control of the central authorities.

In addition to the Druze victories over Ibrāhīm Pasha, the Lebanese revolt against Egyptian rule in 1840 also achieved its aims. This time foreign intervention played the decisive role in bringing about this result. British and Ottoman agents had fomented the rebellion, British, Austrian and Ottoman warships bombarded Beirut, and Ottoman troops landed in Lebanon. Thus internal and external pressure together toppled the regime of Ibrāhīm and Bashīr and put an end to the Egyptian occupation.[282]

The only other successful peasant rebellion in the nineteenth century took place in Lebanon as well. Though ostensibly the Kisrawān peasants were compelled in 1860 to agree to the return of the shaykhs to their homes and the recovery of their property, their surrender remained on paper only. According to Art. 6 of the Regulation for the Administration of Lebanon of 9 June 1861 all feudal privileges, especially those appertaining to the *muqāṭa'ajīs*, were abolished, and the equality of all before the law was proclaimed.[283] It is not clear how much of the Khāzins' land was restored to them in the end, but apparently they lost quite a substantial proportion of it to the peasants who had seized it. Thus the peasants had achieved almost all their aims. This was the result of the declining power of the ruling shaykhs, the struggle between them and the *qā'imaqām* and between them and the Maronite Church and clergy, the attempt of the Ottomans to undermine the autonomy of the Lebanon by exploiting the rebellion for this purpose, and, finally, the French military expedition which, for political reasons, supported Ṭānyūs Shāhīn.[284]

Peasant rebellions in the first half of the twentieth century were in most cases connected with the national movement against foreign rule. Consequently, it is not easy to assess their results. In 1919, Egyptian peasants rioted for about a fortnight only, after which they were suppressed. Their rebellion may have contributed to the release of Zaghlūl a fortnight later, but even if this was the case it was a very limited success indeed, and to claim that it contributed to the unilateral abolition of the Protectorate three years later would stretch a point too far. In 1925, as we have seen, Druze aims were achieved by the Druze peasants to a large extent, but not those of the Syrian national movement, which made its first progress towards independence only ten years after the revolt. Even more complex were the results of the 1936–8 rebellion in Palestine. Up to October 1938, for more than two years, the rebels held large parts of the mountainous regions of the country. Then the British army, assisted by the Jewish *Haganah*, crushed the revolt, which had been weakened by the internal split. At the same time, Britain decided to grant the Arabs important political concessions, such as a drastic restriction of Jewish immigration and land purchases, as well as the withdrawal from the Partition plan. However, World War II and its repercussions deprived the Palestine Arabs of most of the gains they had achieved in 1939 as the indirect result of the revolt.[285] Thus in each of these three rebellions political conditions had different effects, but in general it can be said that insofar as they succeeded at all their achievements were rather partial and limited.

All peasant rebellions of the 1950s, in Egypt, Syria and Iraq, were of the fourth category, i.e. they ended without immediate achievements but led after some time to deeper social changes. Like most peasant insurrections, they were too scattered and isolated to overcome the political and military power of the central government. Even in Syria, where unrest spread over a relatively large area and where the peasants enjoyed some urban political support, their ally was a political group which in 1951 was not yet sufficiently organized and powerful to constitute a match for the political and social establishment. Nevertheless, agrarian unrest in the early 1950s doubtless contributed in various ways to the implementation of agrarian reform in all of these three countries during that decade. In Egypt, it was this agrarian unrest which apparently convinced the newly established military régime that land reform was necessary if communism was to be avoided. This is the gist of an article written in 1954 in *al-Ahrām* by Sayyid Mar'ī, former Minister of Land Reform and a central figure of the Egyptian régime until this very day.[286] In Iraq, agrarian unrest in 'Amāra province resulted in 1954 in a decree which cancelled the law of 1952 and provided for a distribution of *mīrī ṣirf* land in a way which was much more advantageous for the peasants;[287] and the rebellions in other provinces in the years 1953–8 probably had an effect on the implementation of land reform in 1958 similar to that which agrarian unrest had in Egypt. The same may be said of the peasant movement of 1951 in Syria, which certainly was the main cause for the decree of 23 October 1952 on the distribution of state domain among landless peasants, and probably had a delayed effect on later agrarian legislation.[288] Moreover, in Syria the peasant movement was a much more important component of the political group which later implemented land reform than in other Middle Eastern countries.

In conclusion we may say that peasant rebellions in Egypt and the Fertile Crescent during the last 200 years occurred in four major groups, one major single revolt and a few scattered minor eruptions. To the first group belong almost all Egyptian peasant insurrections of the first two-thirds of the nineteenth century. Many, though not all of them, took place in Upper Egypt, and they were fought against excessive taxation or against conscription for the army or forced labour. Many of them were led by persons claiming *wilāya*, mystic shaykhs, *sharīf*s, *mahdī*s, etc. Such a leadership, as well as topographical conditions, precluded the use of guerilla tactics, and therefore in these uprisings frontal battles were fought by masses of armed fellahs. All of these rebellions were crushed either immediately or after short initial military successes lasting not more than a few weeks.

The second group includes the revolts of peasants in the Fertile Crescent against 'foreign' governments (Egyptian, Ottoman, French) in the 1830s, the 1850s, the 1890s and 1925. These revolts broke out in mountainous areas – Judea and Samaria, Lebanon, Jabal Druze, Jabal Nuṣayriyya – and the participants belonged in most cases to communities with a large measure of social cohesion or a tradition of political autonomy. The reason for these rebellions was the attempt to centralize government, especially by introducing conscription of the peasants by the central authorities. They were led by local notables, the traditional leaders and protectors of the peasants, and fought by means of guerilla warfare which suited well the fact that the opponents were 'foreign', the leaders local notables, and the battlefield rugged and hilly lands. Therefore the proportion of successful revolts in this group was relatively high.

One of the rebellions in this second group, the Druze revolt of 1925, belongs to the third group as well – rebellions between the two World Wars which constituted part of national movements against foreign rule. The common characteristics of the three rebellions in this group – Egypt 1919, Syria 1925 and Palestine 1936–8 – were their country-wide range, their connection with urban politicians, their use of guerilla tactics and their partial and limited achievements. Otherwise they differed from each other considerably. In centralistic Egypt the towns, especially Cairo, initiated the revolt and the urban population continued to form its principal force, while in Syria the towns remained more or less aloof, and in Palestine the centre of gravity gradually moved from the towns to the peasants. In addition Egyptian peasants apparently were led by the new class of well-to-do peasants and medium local notables, the Syrian ones by prominent notables from traditional families, and the Palestinian peasant bands by leaders of all kinds but more and more by peasants of the lower strata and by fugitives from the law.

The fourth group consists of peasant violence in Egypt, Syria, and Iraq in the 1950s. In contrast with all the rebellions mentioned so far, peasant violence of the 1950s was directed against landlords, not against the central government, though the armed forces of the state generally came to the rescue of the landlords and clashed with the peasants. This change in the peasants' opponents was the result of the development of private property of land and of large private estates in the course of the late nineteenth and the twentieth centuries. Therefore the issue was no longer taxation and forced labour but rents and the division of the product between landlord and peasant, and in some cases the distribution between them of newly registered state domain. In their struggle against the landlords the peasants had recourse to demonstrations, strikes, seizure of crops and land, and sometimes armed attacks on the mansion of the landlord. The leadership of the fellahs apparently differed considerably from one country to another: in Egypt eruptions were spontaneous and the leaders, if any, came from among the rebellious peasants; in Iraq, in some cases at least, urban lawyers and Communist activists seem to have led the insubordination; and only in Syria was the movement organized by the party of an energetic and extremist politician. Though none of these eruptions ended with the immediate victory of the peasants, all of them resulted in delayed success, because they induced the new régimes which were established in these countries in the 1950s to implement land reform.

A unique phenomenon in Middle Eastern history was the revolt of the Kisrawān peasants in 1858–61, which differed in most of its features from any other peasant rebellion in the Middle East. It was the longest of all, having established a peasant republic which lasted for about three years. It was the only one directed against local lords whose rule had many feudal-like features. In fact it was these features which the peasants set out to change. They adopted principles of equality and democratic government – the only incidence of such an ideology found among revolting Middle Eastern peasants. Moreover, the revolt was conducted by an organization established by the peasants themselves – a leader from among the lower strata of the villagers and a council of representatives, *wakīls*. Among these we find wealthy peasants who played an important part in the revolt. Another unique factor in this revolt was the Maronite Church and clergy, whose position considerably facilitated the achievement of the peasants' aims. Finally, the direct result of the Kisrawān revolt was a profound redistribution of property between the lords and the peasants. Such a unique revolt could occur only in a country whose social features differed from those of all other areas in the Middle East: an agrarian system with feudal features and private property of land; a relatively high level of education and standard of living of the peasants; and a régime of political autonomy. Favourable conditions for revolt were created by the economic decline of the Khāzin shaykhs, Ottoman politics aiming at undermining Lebanese autonomy, the rivalry between the Maronite Church and the shaykhs and finally, the French military expedition.

NOTES

1. These communal clashes have been dealt with by Smilianskaya together with the 1858 peasant revolt in Kisrawān under the common heading of 'fellah movements' or even 'the fellah movement' (see I. Smilianskaya

al-Ḥarakāt al-fallāḥiyya fī Lubnān, Beirut and Damascus, 1972, *passim*, especially pp. 236, 247). It would seem to us that such an approach is methodologically unjustified and misleading, since in the communal clashes peasants belonging to different religions fought each other.

2. Yūsuf al-Shirbīnī, *Hazz al-quḥūf*, Cairo, al-Maktaba al-Maḥmūdiyya, n.d., p. 122, ll. 20–3 (see above, p. 15).
3. Uriel Heyd, *Ottoman Documents on Palestine 1552–1615*, Oxford, 1960, Part Two, III, pp. 79–89, especially doc. no. 42, p. 88.
4. Cf. G. Baer, *Studies in the social history of modern Egypt*, Chicago, 1969 (Baer, *Studies*, in later references) pp. 95–6, and pp. 237–8 above.
5. Smilianskaya, p. 68.
6. 'Abd al-Raḥmān al-Jabartī, *'Ajā'ib al-Āthār*, Bulāq 1297/1880, vol. 4, pp. 63–5, 142.
7. For details see Baer, *Studies*, pp. 96–8, and analysis below.
8. Cf. Moshe Ma'oz, *Ottoman reform in Syria and Palestine, 1840–1861*, Oxford, 1968, p. 14 and sources mentioned there; A. J. Rustum, *A Calendar of State Papers from the Royal Archives of Egypt relating to the affairs of Syria*, vol. 3, Beirut, 1942, p. 312 ff.; vol. 2, Beirut, 1941, pp. 457, 461–2, 464, 477–8, 485, 503, 510, 512, 514.
9. Smilianskaya, pp. 68–9, 77–8, 82; Ṭannūs al-Shidyāq, *Akhbār al-a'yān fī Jabal Lubnān*, Beirut, 1954, vol. 2, pp. 224–5; A. Ismail, *Histoire du Liban*, vol. 4, Beirut, 1958, p. 61.
10. Cf. Baer, *Studies*, pp. 98–9, and sources given there.
11. Ibid., pp. 99–101.
12. In addition to Smilianskaya (see note 1), the best analysis is Y. Porath, 'The Peasant Revolt of 1858–61 in Kisrawān', *Asian and African Studies*, vol. 2, 1966, pp. 77–157. See also D. Chevallier, 'Aux origines des troubles agraires libanais en 1858', *Annales-Economies, Sociétés, Civilisations*, vol. 14, no. 1, 1959; and T. Touma, *Paysans et institutions féodales chez les Druses et les Maronites du Liban du XVIIe siècle à 1914*, Beyrouth, 1971, vol. 1, pp. 266–78.
13. Cf. Ma'oz, p. 110.
14. See M. von Oppenheim, *Vom Mittelmeer zum persischen Golf*, Bd. 1, Berlin, 1899, p. 169 ff. See also A. Toynbee, *Survey of International Affairs*, 1925, vol. 1, London, 1927, p. 408; Hannā Abū Rāshid, *Jabal al-Durūz*, Cairo, 1926, pp. 56–7; N. Bouron, *Les Druzes*, Paris, 1930, pp. 214–15; Haytham al-'Awdāt, *Intifāḍat al-'āmmiyya al-fallāḥiyya fī Jabal al-'Arab*, Damascus, 1976; Shakeeb Salih, 'The British-Druze connection and the Druze rising of 1896 in the Hawran', *Middle Eastern Studies*, vol. 13, May 1977 (Cass, London), pp. 251–7.
15. Baer, *Studies*, pp. 101–2, and sources mentioned there.
16. For details and analysis of this revolt see Y. Porath, *The Palestine Arab National Movement 1929–1939: From riots to rebellion*, Frank Cass, London, 1977, ch. 9. Also Y. Arnon, *Fallāḥīm ba-mered ha-'aravī b'Eretz Yisrael 1936–1939*, Unpublished M.A. thesis, Hebrew University, Jerusalem, 1971.

16a. See *Oriente Moderno* (*OM*), 1937, p. 515; 1939, pp. 46–7, 212–13, 281. I am grateful to J. Vashitz for this information.

17. See H. H. Ayrout, *Fellahs*, Cairo, 1942, pp. 34–5.
18. Rony Gabbay, *Communism and Agrarian Reform in Iraq*, London, 1978, p. 101 (n. 56); Hanna Batatu, *The Old Social Classes and the Revolutionary Movements of Iraq*, Princeton, 1978, p. 467.
19. Baer, *Studies*, pp. 102–3.
20. *al-Ayyām* Aug. 14 and 15, 1951; *al-Inshā'*, Aug. 16 and Sept. 18, 1951; *al-Sha'b*, Sept. 12 and 19, 1951; *al-Ayyām*, Sept. 20, 1951; *Hamizrah Hehadash*, vol. 3, 1951/2, pp. 59, 171; *New York Times*, Aug. 16, 1951.
21. Gabbay, ibid., *Hamizrah Hehadash*, vol. 4, 1952/3, p. 117; vol. 5, 1953/4, p. 211; Batatu, pp. 467–8.
22. R. Mousnier, *Peasant Uprisings in seventeenth century France, Russia, and China*, New York & Evanston, 1970, p. 337.
23. E. R. Wolf, 'On Peasant Rebellions', in Teodor Shanin (ed.), *Peasants and peasant societies*, Penguin, 1971, pp. 264–5.
24. Baer, *Studies*, pp. 93–108, especially pp. 94 and 107–8.
25. From a report to Ibrāhīm Pasha dated 29 Dhū al-Qa'da 1253/24 Feb. 1838, explaining the defeat of the Egyptian army by the Druzes, Rustum, vol. 3, p. 339, no. 5312.
26. Bayle St. John, *Village life in Egypt*, London, 1852, vol. 1, pp. 294–5.
27. Cf. Baer, *Studies*, p. 100.
28. Cf. Mousnier, pp. 312–16.
29. Jabartī, vol. 4, p. 207, as quoted in G. Baer, *A history of landownership in modern Egypt*, London, 1962, pp. 3–4.
30. Cf. Porath, 'Kisrawān', pp. 81, 83, 90–1; Chevallier, p. 57.
31. Cf. Ma'oz, p. 110.
32. von Oppenheim, vol. 1, pp. 169–70.
33. Toynbee, pp. 415–16; quotation from French Government's *Provisional Report* for 1925, p. 14.
34. A. Raymond, *Artisans et commerçants au Caire au XVIIIe siècle*, vol. 2, Damascus, 1974, p. 791.
35. C. S. Sonnini, *Travels in Upper and Lower Egypt*, English translation, London, 1807, vol. 3, p. 273.
36. Jabartī, vol. 4, pp. 63, 142; J. A. St. John, *Egypt and Nubia*, London, 1845, p. 380; H. A. B. Rivlin, *The Agricultural policy of Muḥammad 'Alī in Egypt*, Cambridge, Mass., 1961, p. 201 (see also ch. VII for taxation); Report by Henry Salt, Alexandria, 12 August 1826, London, Public Record Office, F.0. 78/147.
37. Borg to Vivian, 24, 27, and 29 December 1877, F.O. 141/112; same to same, 3 March 1879, F.O. 141/128.
38. Shidyāq, pp. 62–3, 77 ff., Smilianskaya, p. 68.
39. Shidyāq, pp. 144–5, Smilianskaya, pp. 68–9.
40. Smilianskaya, pp. 53–4; Ismail, pp. 45–9.
41. Mikhā'īl Mashāqqa, *Mashhad al-'iyān bi-ḥawādith Sūryā wa-Lubnān*, Cairo, 1908, pp. 115–16.
42. von Oppenheim, vol. 1, p. 175.
43. Porath, 'Kisrawān', p. 85.
44. Barrington Moore, Jr., *Social Origins of dictatorship and democracy – Lord and peasant in the making of the modern world*, Boston, 1966, p. 472. See

also, for instance, R. Enders, 'Probleme des Bauernkrieges in Franken', in R. Wohlfeil (ed.), *Der Bauernkrieg 1524–26*, München, 1975, p. 95.

45. Mousnier, pp. 306–8.
46. R. P. Dore, *Land Reform in Japan*, London, 1959, pp. 11–12, 65.
47. N. G. Ranga, *Revolutionary peasants*, New Delhi, 1949, p. 40.
48. *Annals of Palestine, 1821–1841*, Manuscript by Monk Neophytos of Cyprus, edited by S. N. Spyridon, Jerusalem, 1938, (Neophytos in later references), pp. 73, 94.
49. Shidyāq, pp. 224–5; Ismail, pp. 51–5.
50. Cf. Rustum, vol. 3, p. 325, no. 5296; v. Oppenheim, vol. 1, p. 175; Salih, p. 254.
51. Cf. Rivlin, pp. 201 and 207; A. B. Clot-Bey, *Aperçu général sur l'Egypte*, Paris, 1840, vol. 2, p. 106–7.
52. Sir Valentine Chirol, *The Egyptian Problem*, London, 1920, pp. 134–41, 168.
53. Shidyāq, p. 227, Ismail, pp. 50–1.
54. Touma, pp. 509, 647; Ismail, p. 50. Cf. Mousnier, pp. 42–3, 80, 89, 308.
55. Borg to Malet, Cairo, 25 May 1880, F.O. 141/138; Hekekyan Papers, vol. 3, British Museum Add. 37450, ff. 152–3.
56. Toynbee, pp. 414–15.
57. H. Pirenne, *A history of Europe*, vol. 2, New York, 1958, p. 154; Mousnier, p. 120; F. Engels, *Der deutsche Bauernkrieg*, Berlin, 1930, p. 23; W. P. Fuchs, 'Der Bauernkrieg', in Wohlfeil, pp. 52–3.
58. Cf. Baer, *Studies*, ch. 4, pp. 62–78.
59. For detailed treatment of Lebanon's agrarian system in the 18th and 19th centuries see, in addition to Touma's work, D. Chevallier, *La société du Mont Liban à l'époque de la révolution industrielle en Europe*, Paris, 1971; I. F. Harik, *Politics and change in a traditional society, Lebanon 1711–1845*, Princeton, 1968.
60. The following is the summary of Porath, 'Kisrawān', pp. 84–5, who used primarily Chevallier, *Annales*, pp. 44, 52–8. Chevallier's analysis is based on documents from the archives of the Lebanese Department of Antiquities.
61. Anṭūn Ḍāhir al-'Aqīqī, *Thawra wa-fitna fī Lubnān*, Beirut, 1938, p. 72. Translation after M. Kerr, *Lebanon in the last years of feudalism, 1840–1868*, Beirut, 1959, p. 45, with small changes. For many details of abusive behaviour by the Khāzins towards their peasants see 'Aqīqī, pp. 72–7, including additions in footnotes.
62. Ismail, p. 322; Smilianskaya, p. 178.
63. Cf. E. R. J. Owen, *Cotton and the Egyptian Economy*, Oxford, 1969, p. 119.
64. D. Mackenzie Wallace, *Egypt and the Egyptian question*, London, 1883, pp. 227–8. For the acquisition of large estates by Ismā'īl see Baer, *Landownership*, pp. 39–40, and *passim*.
65. Hekekyan to Hale, Cairo, 29 March 1865, Hekekyan Papers, vol. 16, British Museum Add. 37463, ff. 300–2. In the same vein, Colquhoun to Russell, Cairo, 11 March 1865, No. 32, F.O. 78/1871.
66. Cf. Baer, *Landownership*, pp. 33–7, and sources quoted there.

67. A. Seal, *The emergence of Indian Nationalism*, Cambridge, 1968, pp. 79–80.
68. Ayrout, pp. 34–5.
69. Ch. Issawi, *Egypt at mid-century*, London, 1954, p. 130; *al-Ahrām*, June 24, 1951; Dec. 30, 1953; Jan. 18 and May 18, 1954; Rāshid al-Barāwī, *Ḥaqīqat al-inqilāb al-akhīr fī miṣr*, Cairo 1952, pp. 92, 189; G. Saab, *The Egyptian Agrarian Reform 1952–1962*, London, 1967, p. 13.
70. D. Warriner, *Land reform and development in the Middle East*, London, 1957, p. 93; *al-Ayyām*, Aug. 14, 1951.
70a. Batatu, p. 612.
71. For the 'Amāra laws see Ṣalāḥ al-Dīn al-Nāhī, *Muqaddima fī'l-iqṭā' wa-niẓām al-arāḍī fī'l-'Irāq*, Baghdad, 1955, pp. 48–55; Warriner, pp. 150–4. For fellah rebellions in the wake of the 'Amāra law see Gabbay, pp. 85, 100 (n. 41), 101 (n. 56); Batatu, p. 664.
71a. Batatu, p. 870.
72. Shidyāq, p. 145.
73. *al-Miṣrī*, Oct. 25, 1951.
74. Cf. sources mentioned in notes 18 and 21 above.
75. Neophytos, p. 91.
76. Fikrī Abāẓa, *al-Ḍāḥik al-bākī*, Cairo, 1933, pp. 74–6.
77. Shidyāq, pp. 227–8; Rustum, vol. 4, Beirut, 1943, pp. 395–6 (no. 6354); Ismail, pp. 57–8.
78. Cf. Touma, vol. 1, p. 199, note 46.
79. Cf. J. W. Redhouse, *A Turkish and English Lexikon*, Constantinople, 1921, p. 1669; *mubāya'ajī*.
80. The demands of the Kisrawān peasants are listed in two documents, one presented by the moderate north-western villagers ('Aqīqī, doc. no. 3, pp. 161–3) and one by the somewhat more extreme core of the rebellion ('Aqīqī, doc. no. 16, p. 178). Cf. Porath, 'Kisrawān', pp. 100–1, 107–8, where also scattered demands are mentioned according to the *Rapport*s of the Comte de Bentivoglio, French Consul in Beirut at the time.
81. V. Oppenheim, pp. 179–70. al-'Awdāt, p. 40, says that they demanded the abolition of the Shaykhs' privileges; land should belong to its tillers and houses to their occupants. No source for this is given, and these demands are not included in the declaration of April 1858 reprinted in full as an appendix (pp. 55–8).
82. Barrington Moore, p. 474.
83. G. Franz, *Der deutsche Bauernkrieg*, München und Berlin, 1933, pp. 7–72; Fuchs in Wohlfeil, p. 52.
84. Mousnier, pp. 341, 343. See also pp. 138, 186.
85. Franz, pp. 197–9.
86. Cf. Smilianskaya, p. 195 ff.; Porath, p. 100. A similar development had occurred in the German *Bauernkrieg* as well.
87. Cf. Porath, ibid. The same seems to have been true for the 1888–90 rebellion of the Druze Ḥawrān peasants, though in a poem composed by one of the Aṭrash notables he claims that the fellahs said the shaykhs had become superfluous (al-'Awdāt, pp. 37–41).
88. Cf. sources mentioned above, note 20, and G. Baer, *Population and Society*

in the Arab East, London, 1964, pp. 152–3; P. Seale, *The Struggle for Syria*, London, 1965, p. 120.

89. 'Aqīqī, p. 162 (art. 5).
90. Lady Duff Gordon, *Letters from Egypt (1862–1869)*, London, 1969, p. 209. On other *'mahdī'* leaders of Egyptian peasant revolts see below.
91. J. A. St. John, p. 379.
92. Smilianskaya, p. 84.
93. Quoted by Toynbee, p. 426.
94. 'Aqīqī, pp. 178, 180.
95. Ibid., p. 87; Porath, 'Kisrawān', p. 115.
96. Franz, pp. 75–6, 99–101.
97. *Mudhakkirāt Niqūlā Turk*, ed. by G. Wiet, Cairo, 1950, p. 22.
98. J. A. St. John, p. 379.
99. Neophytos, pp. 79–80.
100. Ibid., p. 89.
101. Menaḥem Mendel mi-Kamenets, *Qōrōth ha-'Itīm*, ed. by G. Kressel, Jerusalem, 1946, p. 36.
102. Salih, p. 254.
103. Toynbee, pp. 428, 432–3. For an account from the Nationalist point of view, with verbatim reproduction of Zayd al-Aṭrash's declarations, see Amīn Sa'īd, *al-Thawra al-'arabiyya al-kubrā*, vol. 3, Cairo, n.d., pp. 352–9.
104. Porath, *From riots to rebellion*, Frank Cass, pp. 269–70; Arnon, pp. 28, 60.
105. Porath, 'Kisrawān', p. 157, and details on pp. 119 ff.
106. Cf. Franz, p. 1; Engels, pp. 69, 95, 120, 123, 126, 129; N. Hampson, *A social history of the French Revolution*, London, 1963, p. 124 ff.
107. Ibrahim Aouad, *Le droit privé des Maronites*, Paris, 1933, p. 259; Harik, p. 112 (quoting Col. C. H. Churchill's *Mount Lebanon*).
108. Porath, 'Kisrawān', pp. 133–5; Smilianskaya, pp. 187–8; Chevallier, *Annales*, pp. 59–60.
109. Smilianskaya, p. 84; Ismail, p. 71.
110. Porath, 'Kisrawān', pp. 135–46.
111. Pirenne, p. 155; Mousnier, pp. 103, 133; Hampson, pp. 159–60.
112. Lady Duff Gordon, p. 209.
113. Mousnier, p. 324.
114. See above, pp. 72–4.
115. *Mudhakkirāt Niqūlā Turk*, p. 21.
116. See above, pp. 62–3.
117. Rustum, vol. 3, pp. 334–6, no. 3505.
118. Amīn Sa'īd, p. 288; E. P. MacCallum, *The nationalist crusade in Syria*, New York, 1928.
119. MacCallum, p. 129.
120. Ibid., pp. 144–6.
121. Amīn Sa'īd, pp. 327–8.
122. Toynbee, pp. 426, 428.
123. Cf. ibid., p. 451.
124. Iḥsān al-Nimr, *Tārīkh Jabal Nāblus wa'l-Balqā'*, vol. 1, Damascus, 1938, pp. 252–5; Ma'oz, p. 114.

125. Menaḥem Mendel mi-Kamenets, pp. 36, 48–9.
126. MacCallum, pp. 123, 163.
127. Neophytos, p. 86.
128. Jabartī, vol. 2, pp. 258–9, and see above, pp. 237–8.
129. Neophytos, pp. 74–82.
130. Ibid., p. 99.
131. Ibid., p. 97. Cf. also Rustum, vol. 2, p. 407, no. 3484.
132. Rustum, vol. 2, pp. 461–2, nos. 3733, 3736.
133. Col. Churchill, *The Druzes and Maronites under the Turkish rule*, London, 1862, pp. 104–5, 181. And see above, p. 86.
134. Porath, 'Kisrawān', p. 86.
135. Shidyāq, p. 225; Smilianskaya, p. 90, quoting de Testa.
136. Smilianskaya, p. 89.
137. Porath, 'Kisrawān', pp. 86, 92–3, 112; Smilianskaya, pp. 197–9.
138. 'Abd al-Raḥmān al-Rāfi'ī, *Thawrat 1919*, Cairo, 1946, vol. 1, pp. 141–2; Sir Valentine Chirol, *The Egyptian problem*, London, 1920, pp. 178–9. According to Aḥmad Shafīq, *Ḥawliyyāt Miṣr al-siyāsiyya*, vol. 1, Cairo, 1926, p. 256 – only on Thursday, 13 March.
139. Cf. Baer, *Studies*, pp. 101–2.
140. The following is based on Porath, *From riots to rebellion*, pp. 162–3, 168, 178–9, 181–2, 184, 264–6, 268.
141. 'Alī Mubārak, *al-Khiṭaṭ al-tawfīqiyya al-jadīda*, Cairo, Bulāq, 1304–6 A. H., vol. 12, p. 44. On the number 'forty' see, e.g., T. Canaan, *Mohammedan Saints and sanctuaries in Palestine*, London, 1927, pp. 289–91.
142. Shidyāq, vol. 2, p. 145; Ismail, p. 59, n. 2; Smilianskaya, pp. 88 and 218.
143. v. Oppenheim, p. 179, and cf. Salih, p. 257, n. 17; Porath, *From riots to rebellion*, pp. 247–8 (based on Ṣubḥī Yāsīn).
144. J. A. St. John, pp. 379–83.
145. Ismail, p. 82; Neophytos, pp. 80, 94.
146. Jabartī, vol. 2, p. 258; Report by Henry Salt, 12 August 1826, F.O. 78/147; Hekekyan Papers, vol. 7, Add. 37454, fol. 67b; Mubārak, vol. 11, p. 82; vol. 14, p. 53; Enclosure no. 3 in Malet to Granville, Cairo, 20 February 1882, Egypt No. 7 (1882), C. 3249, pp. 42–3; *al-Miṣrī*, 25 October 1951; and see sources quoted above, note 70.
147. Cf. Rustum, vol. 3, p. 404, no. 5444.
148. Cf. notes 8 and 16a above.
149. Smilianskaya, pp. 217–18 and note 125; Porath, 'Kisrawān', pp. 92, 105.
150. Cf. Smilianskaya, p. 224; Porath, 'Kisrawān', pp. 117–18.
151. See above, pp. 264–5 and note 55.
152. Sonnini, vol. 3, p. 273.
153. *Mudhakkirāt Niqūlā Turk*, p. 21.
154. Jabartī, vol. 4, p. 63.
155. J. A. St. John, pp. 378–83.
156. F.O. 141/112, 141/119, 141/128, *passim*.
157. Cf. Rāfi'ī, pp. 141 ff.
158. Shidyāq, p. 145. The four *aqālīm* were Iqlīm Jazzīn, Iqlīm al-Tuffāḥ, Iqlīm al-Kharrūb, and Iqlīm al-Ballān, all southern areas ruled by the Junbalāṭs

of the Shūf *muqāṭa'a*.

159. Ismail, pp. 60–1; Smilianskaya, pp. 78, 83.
160. Neophytos, pp. 75, 89, 97, 98; Rustum, vol. 2, pp. 398, 408, 419, 420 (nos. 3435, 3486, 3535).
161. Porath, *From riots to rebellion*, chs. 7–9, *passim*.
162. Toynbee, pp. 432, 435: Amīn Sa'īd, pp. 422–3, 459; McCallum, p. 168.
163. Cf. *New York Times*, Aug. 16, 1951.
164. Wolf, 'On peasant rebellions', pp. 268–70.
165. Franz, pp. 2–3; Fuchs, and F. Kopitzsch, 'Bemerkungen zur Sozialgeschichte der Reformation und des Bauernkrieges', in Wohlfeil, pp. 51, 52, 187; E. R. Wolf, *Peasant wars of the twentieth century*, New York 1969, p. 31 and ch. 1, *passim*.
166. I have dealt with these developments in great detail in Baer, *Studies*; Baer, *A history of landownership*; and G. Baer, *Introduction to the history of agrarian relations in the Middle East, 1800–1970*, Tel-Aviv, 1971 (in Hebrew).
167. Cf. Barrington Moore, p. 13, n. 23.
168. Mousnier, p. 42.
169. Barrington Moore, pp. 478–9.
170. Rustum, vol. 2, p. 397, no. 3433.
171. Neophytos, p. 91; Ma'oz, pp. 118–19. The name, spelt 'Amrū but pronounced 'Amr in Arabic, is variously misspelt in English transliterations as 'Amar or 'Āmir.
172. Neophytos, pp. 94–6; Rustum, vol. 2, p. 411, no. 3503; Nimr, pp. 249, 252–3.
173. Shidyāq, vol. 2, p. 145. Smilianskaya (p. 69) claims that he very soon deserted the rebel camp, but she gives no sources for this claim. On p. 86 she repeats the same claim with regard to the shaykhs and amīrs who headed the 1840 rebellion (see below) – again without recording any evidence. Since the factual parts of her book are well documented, such claims are suspicious.
174. Shidyāq, vol. 2, pp. 226–9; Smilianskaya, pp. 80, 86, 89.
175. Rustum, vol. 4, pp. 395–6, no. 6354; Ismail, p. 59; and see above, p.
176. Rustum, vol. 2, p. 462, no. 3736.
177. Ibid., vol. 3, p. 334, no. 5305.
178. v. Oppenheim, p. 170. Though many authors claim that this has been the case, it has recently been vigorously denied by al-'Awdāt (p. 58). In fact Shiblī al-Aṭrash does not figure among those who signed the April 1888 declaration (ibid, pp. 54–8). Moreover, he went into exile together with the other Ṭurshān (ibid., p. 41; Salih, p. 253). Apparently what had happened was that Shiblī had at first incited the rebellion, but later, under the leadership of the shaykhs of the smaller families, it turned against him. See Abū Rāshid, pp. 56–7; Bouron, p. 214.
179. Amīn Sa'īd, pp. 472–3.
180. *Mudhakkirāt Niqūlā Turk*, p. 21.
181. Hekekyan Papers, vol. 3, B.M. 37450, pp. 152–3.
182. Borg to Malet, Cairo, 25 May 1880, F.O. 141/138.
183. For details and sources see Y. Vashitz, 'The role of the *fallāḥūn* in the

Egyptian National Movement, 1881–1852', *Hamizrah Hehadash*, vol. 21, 1971, p. 6–7 (in Hebrew).

184. *Mudhakkirāt Niqūlā Turk*, pp. 32–3.
185. Jabartī, vol. 4, p. 63 (and pp. 64–5 for the long story of his exploits and end).
186. Mubārak, vol. 12, p. 44.
187. J. A. St. John, pp. 378–86; Mubārak, vol. 14, p. 76.
188. F. Mengin, *Histoire sommaire de l'Egypte sous le gouvernment de Mohammad-Aly*, Paris, 1839, pp. 5–6; Clot-Bey, vol. 2, p. 107; F.O. 78/126, *passim*; Rivlin, pp. 201–2.
189. Mubārak, vol. 11, p. 82; vol. 14, p. 95; Lady Duff Gordon, pp. 207–9.
190. Mubārak, vol. 14, p. 53. An exceptional case of religious leadership in the Fertile Crescent was the Naqshbandi Shaykh Khalīl Ibrāhīm who led the Kurdish peasants of northern Syria against their *agha*s (landlords) in the late 1930s. This may perhaps be explained by the upheavals in Syria at that time and the nearness of this area to the Turkish border and to Hatay which had just been annexed by Turkey. This subject, however, needs further study. For messianic leadership of the Indian Santhal peasant risings in 1855 see Ranga, pp. 37–8; Seal, p. 12. Cf. also Jean Nu-Pieds of Normandy in 1639 – Mousnier pp. 102, 106, or Hans Böheim, Pfeifer von Niklashausen in 1476 – Franz, pp. 78–92.
191. Cf. table in Baer, *Introduction to the history of agrarian relations*, p. 124. One dunum = 1,000 square metres or 0.247 acres. Cf. also Warriner, pp. 82–4.
192. *al-Ayyām*, and *al-Sha'b*, Aug. 14, 1951; *al-Sha'b*, Sept. 12, 1951; see also *Hamizrah Hehadash*, vol. 3, p. 59.
193. *al-Sha'b*, Aug. 14, 1951; *al-Inshā'*, Sept. 1951; *al-Sha'b*, Sept. 19, 1951; *al-Ayyām*, Sept. 20, 1951; *Hamizrah Hehadash*, vol. 3, pp. 170–1 (erroneously quoting *al-Sha'b* Sept. 17, instead of 19 – Sept. 17 was *'Īd al-Aḍḥā* and no newspapers were published on that day); Y. Oron, 'The History and the ideas of the Arab Socialist Renaissance Party', *Hamizrah Hehadash*, vol. 9, pp. 245–6; Seale, pp. 40, 120.
194. *Hamizrah Hehadash*, vol. 5, p. 211, quoting the Iraqi press of February and March 1954; Batatu, pp. 612–13, 664–5.
195. Chevallier, *Annales*, pp. 44, 46; Touma, vol. 2, p. 605.
196. H. Guys, *Beyrouth et Liban. Relations d'un séjour de plusieurs années dans ce pays*, Paris, 1850, vol. 2, p. 145 (quoted by Touma, vol. 2, p. 622, note 239).
197. Touma, vol. 2, p. 584; Aouad, p. 257.
198. A. Latron, *La vie rurale en Syrie et au Liban*, Beyrouth, 1936, pp. 207–8 (quoted by Chevallier, *Annales*, p. 55).
199. Cf. Smilianskaya, p. 209.
200. The following is a summary of Porath, 'Kisrawān', pp. 113–14.
201. For a discussion of the clergy's position in the Kisrawān revolt see above, p. 85.
202. For detailed discussion of this aspect of the 1936–8 rebellion in Palestine, see Porath, *From riots to rebellion*, chapters 7–9, especially pp. 264–5, and Arnon, p. 28 and *passim*.

203. Quoted by J. Migdal, *Peasants, politics, and revolution*, Princeton, 1974, p. 255, note 65.
204. Sonnini, vol. 3, pp. 273–4.
205. Chirol, p. 186.
206. *al-Miṣrī*, June 22 and 26, 1951, quoted by Vashitz, p. 13, note 79. In Palestine arson became a major feature of the revolt after its military and political defeat. See Porath, *From riots to rebellion*, p. 241.
207. Chirol, p. 187.
208. Hekekyan Papers, vol. 4, B.M. 37451, fol. 44a.
209. 'Azīz Khānkī, 'Ḥawādith al-ightiyāl fī'l-aryāf', *al-Ahrām*, Oct. 23, 1944. Cf. also Sir Thomas Russell, *Egyptian service 1902–1946*, London, 1949, p. 33.
210. Chirol, pp. 181, 186.
212. Amīn Sa'īd, vol. 3, p. 472.
212a. Gabbay, p. 121 n. 13, and p. 150 n. 121, and sources quoted there.
213. Mousnier, pp. 317–8.
214. Sonnini, vol. 3, p. 273.
215. Borg to Vivian, Cairo, Dec. 24 and 29, 1877, F.O. 141/112; Cherif to Vivian, Jan. 3, 1878, F.O. 141/119; Borg to Vivian, Cairo, March 3, 1879, F.O. 141/128.
216. *The Times*, Nov. 2, 1925, quoted by Toynbee, p. 438, n. 1.
217. Porath, *From riots to rebellion*, pp. 249, 266–7.
218. v. Oppenheim, vol. 1, p. 173. *al-kassār* was the term for gang fights in Iraqi towns – see 'Alī al-Wardī, *Dirāsa fī ṭabī'at al-mujtama' al-'irāqī*, Baghdad, 1965, pp. 297–8.
218a. *OM*, 1939, pp. 46–7.
219. Cf. Ranga, pp. 38, 74–5.
220. Jabartī, vol. 4, p. 142; Baer, *Studies*, p. 102, and sources mentioned there.
221. *Hamizrah Hehadash*, vol. 4, p. 211. Gabbay, p. 101 n. 56.
222. Egypt No. 7 (1882), C. 3249, *passim*.
223. *al-Miṣrī*, Oct. 25, 1951. For the description of a strike of agricultural labourers, without stating the time and place where it occurred, see Russell, p. 35.
224. Porath, 'Kisrawān', p. 99; *al-Ayyām*, Aug. 14, 1951; *New York Times*, Aug. 16, 1951; *Hamizrah Hehadash*, vol. 4, p. 117; Batatu, p. 664.
225. Porath, *From riots to rebellion*, p. 267.
226. Porath, 'Kisrawān', pp. 95–7.
227. v. Oppenheim, p. 170; Abū Rāshid, p. 57; Bouron, pp. 214–15; al-'Awdāt, p. 41; *OM*, 1939, pp. 46, 212.
228. *al-Ayyām*, Aug. 14, 1951; *al-Inshā'*, Aug. 16, 1951.
228a. Gabbay, p. 121 n. 13.
229. Porath, 'Kisrawān', pp. 98–9.
230. T. Shanin, 'Peasantry as a political factor', in Shanin (ed.), *Peasants and peasant societies*, p. 260.
231. V. Denon, *Voyage dans la Basse et la Haute Egypte*, London, 1819, p. 51.
232. Chirol, pp. 179, 181; Rāfi'ī, vol. 1, p. 142 ff.
233. Neophytos, pp. 81, 86, 87–8, 95.
234. Ismail, p. 61. Smilianskaya, p. 81; Shidyāq, vol. 2, p. 226.

235. Rustum, vol. 3, p. 377, no. 5378.
236. Toynbee, p. 425.
237. Ibid., p. 438.
238. E. Roih, 'The Druze Revolt: Communal Rising or War of Liberation', *Hamizrah Hehadash*, vol. 8, 1957, p. 113.
239. Arnon, p. 37; Porath, *From riots to rebellion*, pp. 237–8.
239a. *OM*, 1939, p. 212.
239b. Gabbay, p. 83.
240. Cf. A. Jaussen, *Coûtumes des Arabes au pays de Moab*, Paris, 1948, p. 377.
241. Jabartī, vol. 4, p. 63.
242. Arnon, p. 38.
243. Baer, *Studies*, pp. 97–8 and sources mentioned there; Rustum, vol. 2, p. 399, no. 3438.
244. Chirol, p. 181.
245. Neophytos, pp. 74 ff., 97–8; Rustum, vol. 2, p. 398, no. 3435; p. 407, no. 3484; p. 420, no. 3535; p. 461, no. 3733.
246. J. A. St. John, pp. 381, 383.
247. Porath, 'Kisrawān', p. 116. This is, of course, partly due to the fact that no serious battles were fought in this revolt.
248. Mubārak, vol. 14, p. 53.
249. See above, p. 289.
250. Ismail, pp. 60–1.
251. Cf. Vashitz, pp. 5–7, and sources mentioned there.
252. Neophytos, p. 84 ff., and *passim*.
253. Amīn Sa'īd, vol. 3, p. 451.
254. Porath, *From riots to rebellion*, pp. 186, 189, 191–2, 244–5, 247; Arnon, p. 69.
255. Dr. 'Abd al-'Azīz Rifā'ī, *Thawrat Miṣr sanat 1919*, Cairo, n.d. [1967], ch. 7, pp. 139–53.
256. Rāfi'ī, vol. 1, p. 142.
257. Cf. Seale, p. 177.
258. Migdal, pp. 208, 232.
259. Shidyāq, vol. 2, p. 145; Harik, pp. 212–13. In 1845, when Shakīb Effendi included the *wakīls* in his settlement, this was not any longer 'an entirely new institution', as Porath erroneously stated (Porath, 'Kisrawān', p. 83).
260. Harik, p. 247.
261. Ibid., pp. 247, 255.
262. Shidyāq, vol. 2, p. 328. Smilianskaya, p. 165, quotes a detailed description of the military structure of the *shuyūkh al-shabāb* organization by the Russian consul Bazili. For a picturesque description of their dresses and other details, as well as some of their political functions, see H., Y., and 'A, Abū Shaqrā, *al-Ḥarakāt fī Lubnān ilā 'ahd al-mutaṣarrifiyya*, Beirut, n.d., pp. 103–4.
263. Porath, 'Kisrawān', p. 83; Harik, pp. 272–4.
264. Porath, 'Kisrawān', pp. 88–9.
265. 'Aqīqī, p. 81.
266. Porath, 'Kisrawān', pp. 86–8, 93–4, 113–15, etc.
267. Mubārak, vol. 12, p. 44.

268. Chirol, p. 183, P. G. Elgood, *Egypt and the army*, London, 1924, p. 349.
269. See Porath, 'Kisrawān', pp. 112–15; Amīn Sa'īd, vol. 3, pp. 451–3, 472–3; and compare Porath, *From riots to rebellion*, p. 244 ff., and ch. 6–9 *passim*.
270. Porath, *From riots to rebellion*, pp. 190, 248. For judicial institutions in Kisrawān see Porath 'Kisrawān', pp. 112, 115. We have not come across information about similar institutions in Jabal Druze in 1925–7, but probably *ad hoc* arrangements were made there too.
271. Barrington Moore, pp. 479–80.
272. Jabartī, vol. 2, p. 259; and see above, pp. 237–8.
273. Mubārak, vol. 12, p. 44.
274. J. A. St. John, pp. 378–86; Mubārak, vol. 14, p. 76.
275. For references see Baer, *Studies*, p. 98, note 12.
276. For a short account of this development see Smilianskaya, p. 70.
277. Cf. Ma'oz, p. 14.
278. Abū Rāshid, p. 57; Bouron, p. 333; Toynbee, p. 408; al-'Awdāt, pp. 44–5.
279. Cf. Roih, p. 113.
280. Ma'oz, pp. 110–11. A similar topography, as well as special political conditions (see above, note 190) may have caused the partial success of the Kurdish peasant rebellion in Syria of the late 1930s, which consisted in a rather long exile of their *aghas*.
281. Borg to Malet, May 25, 1880, F.O. 141/138; Egypt No. 7 (1882), C. 3249, p. 42.
282. Cf. P. M. Holt, *Egypt and the Fertile Crescent, 1516–1922*, London, 1966, pp. 235–6.
283. For text see J. C. Hurewitz, *The Middle East and North Africa in World Politics, A Documentary Record*, Vol. 1, New Haven and London, 1975, p. 347.
284. For a detailed analysis of all these forces see Porath, 'Kisrawān', pp. 148–9, 153–7.
285. Porath, *From riots to rebellion*, pp. 301–2.
286. For full quotation see Baer, *Studies*, p. 103.
287. Nāhī, p. 52; Warriner, p. 154.
288. For this see Baer, *Population and Society*, pp. 153–4; *Introduction to the history of agrarian relations*, pp. 112–13.

INDEX

(The following names and terms which appear throughout the book are not included in the index: Arab, Egypt, fellah, Fertile Crescent, Middle East, Ottoman, shaykh, Turk, Turkey)